LIFE-SPAN COMMUNICATION
Normative Processes

COMMUNICATION TEXTBOOK SERIES

Jennings Bryant—Editor

Applied Communication

Teresa Thompson—Advisor

NUSSBAUM • Life-Span Communication:
Normative Processes

LIFE-SPAN
COMMUNICATION
Normative Processes

EDITED BY
JON F. NUSSBAUM
University of Oklahoma

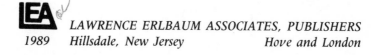

LAWRENCE ERLBAUM ASSOCIATES, PUBLISHERS
1989   Hillsdale, New Jersey   Hove and London

Lawrence Erlbaum Associates, Inc., Publishers
365 Broadway
Hillsdale, New Jersey 07642

Library of Congress Cataloging-in-Publication Data

Life-span communication: normative processes/Jon F. Nussbaum,
    editor.
    p. cm. —(Applied communications)
    Bibliography: p.
    Includes index.
    ISBN 0-8058-0195-2
    1. Interpersonal communication.   2. Communication—Psychological
aspects.   3. Developmental psychology.   I. Nussbaum, Jon F.
II. Series.
BF637.C45L53 1988
153.6—dc19   88-30047
                                                                        CIP

Printed in the United States of America
10   9   8   7   6   5   4   3   2   1

CONTENTS

CONTRIBUTORS

SHERYL PERLMUTTER BOWEN   Department of Communication Arts, Villanova University, Philadelphia, PA 19085

VICTOR G. CICIRELLI   Department of Psychological Sciences, Purdue University, West Lafayette, IN 47907

MARK E. COMADENA   Department of Communication, Illinois State University, Normal, IL 61761

VALERIE C. DOWNS   Department of Speech Communication, California State University, Long Beach, Long Beach, CA 90840

ROBERT L. DURAN   Department of Communication, University of Hartford, West Hartford, CT 06117

BETH HASLETT   Department of Communication, University of Delaware, Newark, DE 19716

JON F. NUSSBAUM   Department of Communication, University of Oklahoma, Norman, OK 73019

MARSHALL PRISBELL   Department of Communication, University of Nebraska, Omaha, Omaha, NB 68182

DIANE T. PRUSANK   Department of Communication, University of Oklahoma, Norman, OK 73019

SANDRA L. RAGAN Department of Communication, University of Oklahoma, Norman, OK 73019

WILLIAM K. RAWLINS Department of Communication, Purdue University, West Lafayette, IN 47907

JAMES D. ROBINSON Department of Communication, University of Dayton, 300 College Park, Dayton, OH 45469

ALAN L. SILLARS Department of Interpersonal Communication, University of Montana, Missoula, MT 59812

CYNTHIA STOHL Department of Communication, Purdue University, West Lafayette, IN 47907

TERESA L. THOMPSON Department of Communication, University of Dayton, 300 College Park, Dayton OH 45469

LAUREL KLINGER-VARTABEDIAN Department of Speech Communication, Wichita State University, Wichita, KS 67226

ANNE JOHNSTON WADSWORTH Department of Television, Radio, and Film, University of North Carolina, Chapel Hill, NC 27514

WILLIAM W. WILMOT Department of Interpersonal Communication, University of Montana, Missoula, MT 59812

LAUREN WISPE Department of Communication, University of Oklahoma, Norman, OK 73019

JOHN WOROBEY Department of Human Development, Rutgers, New Brunswick, NJ 08904

PREFACE

Life-Span Communication: Normative Processes is a unique collection of articles within the field of human communication. Twenty internationally recognized scholars have written original articles which stress communication as a developmental phenomenon. Each article is placed within a specific development phase. Each article is placed within the context of a normal life span. Each chapter does have meaning unto itself, yet, the purpose of this book is to emphasize that meaning inherent within any communicative act is bound by the point in one's life in which the act occurs.

The life-span approach toward human communication is inherently pragmatic. A close look at the title of each chapter emphasizes the very "real-world" issues that are addressed in this book. Beginning with infant/mother interaction to communication at the end of the life span, the book emphasizes "real humans" in "real interactions."

The book also emphasizes normative processes. I feel very strongly that the "first" book to address the life-span perspective within the field of communication should concentrate upon normal behavior. Whereas in other fields nonnormative issues are frequently discussed, the field of communication has yet to bank a knowledge base of fine literature addressing normal communication across the life span.

The book is divided into three major developmental phases across the life span: infancy/childhood; young adulthood/adulthood; and the elderly. The initial chapter introduces the theory and method of life-span development. The remaining chapters are placed within their respective developmental phases.

Communication scholars have recently begun to research the development of communication within childhood. The first part of this book includes articles on mother/infant interaction, children's strategies in initiating interaction with peers, the development of social networks in childhood, the development of communication apprehension in children, and the uses and effects of mass communication during childhood.

The second part of this book includes articles concentrating upon communication within young adulthood and adulthood. Chapters include content that address developmental issues in personal relationship for adults, dating competence among college students, communication between the sexes, communication competence in adulthood, adolescent friendships, and marriage across the life span.

The final part of this book is devoted to articles that discuss communication and the elderly. Within the last 10 years, several communication researchers have begun to systematically investigate communication and aging. This book includes chapters discussing the grandparent–grandchild relationship, the sibling relationship in later life, the influence of age difference in marriage longevity, the uses and effects of mass media and the elderly, and communication and dying.

The book is intended to be read as a whole. Although it may be tempting to read each chapter, or each collection of chapters within a developmental phase, and then separate the issues discussed into neat packages of information, each chapter must be viewed as an indicant of the life-long process of communication, or the point will be missed. Communication occurs throughout the life span. This book is an attempt to capture the richness and variety of human interaction throughout the entirety of one's life.

Jon F. Nussbaum

1 Life-Span Communication: An Introduction

Jon F. Nussbaum
University of Oklahoma

The life-span approach toward describing, explaining, and ultimately predicting human behavior has only recently become popular for researchers who investigate human development. The life-span approach emphasizes the lifelong nature of human development and asserts that our understanding of any human behavior at a particular point in one's life is enhanced by taking into account that individual's past history and, perhaps, his or her future expectations (Huyck & Hoyer, 1982). The disciplines of psychology, sociology, and human development have embraced the life-span approach which has manifested itself in a long series of life-span developmental books published by Academic Press (e.g., Baltes & Schaie, 1973; Datan & Ginsberg, 1975; Goulet & Baltes, 1970; Nesselroade & Reese, 1973). To this point, however, the field of communication has yet to utilize the life-span approach as a mechanism for understanding, describing, and explaining communicative phenomena.

THEORY

The major theme of any developmental approach toward the study of human behavior is change. Life-span developmentalists do not postulate any specific theory of change. Instead, they tend to be pluralistic, accepting several world views (the mechanistic paradigm, the organismic paradigm, and the dialectic paradigm are the most popular) as useful explanations of human development. A central concept within the life-span developmental perspective is process. Just discovering change is

1

not enough. One must strive to understand and explain the process of that change.

A popular misconception about the "process of change" revolves around the necessity of postulating stages of development. Piaget and Erickson have postulated stages in their theories of development, so stages must be a necessity! Actually, stages only serve as a tool to aid our understanding of human development. It would be very wrong to think that every behavior or cognition must pass through predetermined stages. Determining the existence of actual stages of development is a long and laborious task which often serves very little useful purpose.

Because life-span development is a relatively new field, many intriguing theoretical debates can be found in the recent literature. For a more exhaustive discussion of the theoretical underpinnings of life-span development please see Baltes, Reese, and Lipsett (1980), Baltes and Willis (1977), Goulet and Baltes (1970), and Overton and Reese (1973).

METHODOLOGY

The study of behavior across the life span has led to new methodologies consistent with an emphasis upon the process of change. In addition, several pragmatic "conventions" are currently utilized to aid the researcher interested in studying developmental processes. For instance, one convention with widespread acceptance is to divide the life span when possible into 10 life stages: preconception, prenatal, infancy, early childhood, late childhood, adolescence, early adulthood, middle adulthood, old age (young old, old, old-old), and death (Reese, 1978). Because of the newness of the life-span communication approach, this book divides the life span into three major life stages: infancy-childhood, young adulthood-adulthood, and the elderly.

The most common methodologies within life-span development are the cross-sectional method, the longitudinal method, and various sequential methods. Of these, the most utilized method is the cross-sectional method, which involves gathering information from individuals of different ages at one point in time. The major disadvantage of this approach is the confounding of cohort influences within the design.

The longitudinal method gathers information from the same individuals at different time intervals. This is the ideal method for individuals studying developmental change. However, the longitudinal method suffers from several severe problems which include repeated measurement, selective attrition, and tenure-related publication deadlines. For a complete description of the advantages and disadvantages of the longitudinal design with a summary of the major longitudinal studies from across the world see Schaie (1983).

The many problems associated with the previous methods led to the introduction of the various sequential data-collection strategies. The cohort, time, and cross-sequential strategies combine longitudinal and cross-sectional methods to eliminate many of the confounding problems. Baltes, Reese, and Nesselroade (1977) provided a very readable explanation of the sequential methods. In addition, those who are interested in a lengthier discussion of life-span methodologies for communication researchers should consult a recent article by Nussbaum (1988).

LIFE-SPAN COMMUNICATION

Life-span developmentalists would argue that one cannot understand any communicative phenomena without first discovering the developmental process of that communicative event. The communicative phenomena under investigation must be framed within the lifespan. If a life-span communication scholar is interested in investigating competent behaviors within a relationship, that scholar would be interested in explaining the process by which those behaviors developed not only within the relationship but also within the life-span that frames that relationship. In addition, how those competent behaviors are likely to change as the relationship progresses would be of interest.

Life-span communication is inherently pragmatic. The communication phenomena of interest to the life-span scholar is contextually bound by the life span. Thus, it does make a significant difference if the communication transpires between two college sophomores or if the communication transpires between two elderly residents of a nursing home. The life-span frame of the interaction gives meaning to the interaction. One cannot hope to understand human beings interacting or the communicative significance of that interaction without first coming to grip with the life-span context framing each interaction.

There are sound reasons why such a small amount of life-span research exists within the communication discipline. First, life-span paradigms and methodologies are not taught within communication at the graduate level in the majority of the doctoral granting institutions. Second, until recently very few outlets for this type of research existed. Finally, at the risk of insulting unnamed individuals, life-span research is a difficult, time-consuming endeavor. The researcher, at the very least, must leave the classroom to collect data, and at the very most, will devote a lifetime collecting data from a small segment of the population.

So, what is to be gained by studying communication from a life-span perspective? The first and most obvious gain for communication scholars who utilize the life-span approach when investigating the many constructs of interest to communication researchers would be an understanding of the complexity of such constructs. Communication behaviors not only change from one context to the next but also change from one age to the next within a context.

A second gain would be superior explanation. If one is able to capture communication as it develops, then one is able to present a much richer explanation of communication. This is especially true if a study is made of one individual over time. The tracking of the communication becomes the explanation.

Third, a life-span approach enhances predictive power. Any sophomore in high school can tell you that several points in space enhance predictability of future points. Trends can be analyzed and predictions based upon historical trends can be made.

Finally, intervention into the communication process can become a reality. Interventions can be designed and tested utilizing developmental data. Notions of when and how to intervene become clearer. In addition, this type of analysis does tend to personalize the communicative event to some extent so that everyone is not treated the same regardless of the communication difficulty.

REFERENCES

Baltes, P. B., Reese, H. W., & Lipsitt, L. P. (1980). Life-span developmental psychology. *Annual Review of Psychology, 31*, 65–110.

Baltes, P. B., Reese, H. W., & Nesselroade, J. R. (1977). *Life-span developmental psychology: Introduction to research methods.* Monterey, CA: Brooks/Cole.

Baltes, P. B., & Schaie, K. W. (1973). *Life-span developmental psychology: Personality and socialization.* New York: Academic Press.

Baltes, P. B., & Willis, S. L. (1977). Toward psychological theories of aging and development. In J. E. Birren & K. W. Schaie (Eds.), *Handbook of the psychology of aging* (pp. 128–154). New York: Van Nostrand Reinhold.

Datan, N., & Ginsberg, L. H. (1975). *Life-span developmental psychology: Normative life crises.* New York: Academic Press.

Goulet, L. R., & Baltes, P. B. (1970). *Life-span developmental psychology.* New York: Academic Press.

Huyck, M. H., & Hoyer, W. J. (1982). *Adult development and aging.* Belmont, CA: Wadsworth.

Nesselroade, J. R., & Reese, H. W. (1973). *Life-span developmental psychology: Research and theory.* New York: Academic Press.

Nussbaum, J. F. (1988). Methodological considerations in communication and aging research. In C. Carmichael, C. Botan, & R. Hawkins (Eds.), *Human communication and the aging process* (pp. 249–289). Prospect Heights, IL: Waveland.

Overton, W. F., & Reese, H. W. (1973). Models of development: Methodological implications. In J. R. Nesselroade & H. W. Reese *Life-span developmental psychology: Methodological issues* (pp. 65–86). New York: Academic Press.

Reese, H. W. (1978). Lecture given to graduate seminar in Advanced Developmental Psychology, West Virginia University.

Schaie, K. W. (1983). *Longitudinal studies of adult psychological development.* New York: Guilford Press.

PART I

INFANCY/CHILDHOOD

2 Mother–Infant Interaction: Protocommunication in the Developing Dyad

John Worobey
Rutgers University

There has been tremendous growth in the amount of research devoted to infant development in the last 20 years, with a concomitant increase in the number of studies that examine the behavior of mothers with their young. Early development, in particular early *social* development, may be the most rapidly expanding area of interest to those who study infancy (Hodapp & Mueller, 1982), with much of the research examining what infants and mothers bring to their communicative encounters. Whereas the current, extraordinary interest in human infants is due to a variety of independent factors and is guided by a number of theoretical approaches (Kagan, 1979), recent research and theory in mother–infant interaction has been influenced primarily by an ethological perspective (Bowlby, 1969). Such a viewpoint goes beyond the portrayal of maternal caregiving as a source of stimulation that simply promotes intellectual or personality development, to the premise that the evolutionary fitness of the organism is increased through social interaction (Campos, Barrett, Lamb, Goldsmith, & Stenberg, 1983). Not only are humans social animals (Lewis, 1987), they must engage in social interaction if they are to survive. But if one partner is without language, as is the infant, how is communication possible? When does true interaction begin? And how does it develop?

This chapter addresses these questions by outlining the growth of communication between infant and mother in the 1st year of life. The literature on early mother–infant interactions is surveyed, and the role of communicative effectiveness in establishing the first human relationship

7

is presented.[1] As an illustrative case, a theoretical approach to the dynamics inherent in the first interactions between newborns and their "new" mothers are detailed. Finally, a number of issues of relevance to research on the communication system in infancy are discussed.

THE BIDIRECTIONALITY OF EARLY INTERACTIONS

Historically speaking, the study of early parent–child relations has been primarily comprised of efforts to examine how the physical, social, and intellectual environment of the infant impacts on his or her development. Although the traditions of Freudian psychoanalysis and Watsonian behaviorism are markedly discrepant in regard to human functioning, Freud and Watson, nevertheless, converged in the importance they assigned to mothering. Thus, the degree to which parenting—and not "offspringing"—was of interest, meant that any investigation of early interaction would most likely focus on the effects of mothers on their infants.

In the past 20 years, however, we have witnessed a major reformulation of our perspective on the dynamics of mother–infant interaction. By the early 1970s, new information on infant competencies was assembled and synthesized (Stone, Smith, & Murphy, 1973), and in light of the recognition that both parents and children were capable of socializing each other (Bell, 1968; Rheingold, 1971), infants could now be viewed as affecting their caregivers (Lewis & Rosenblum, 1974). As a result, besides the increase in the number of investigations of infant development proper, research in "infant–other" interaction has grown exponentially, with data now available on premature (e.g., Landry, 1986), delayed (e.g., Mahoney, 1983), handicapped (e.g., Fraiberg, 1974), or at-risk infants (e.g., Field, 1983) in interaction with their mothers (e.g., Hock, 1980), fathers (e.g., Lamb, 1977), grandparents (e.g., Tinsley & Parke, 1984), or even infant peers (e.g., Fogel, 1979). By far and away, however, most of what we know regarding early social development derives from studies of mother–infant interaction.

The sampler of studies cited below do much to portray the infant as a communicating partner in an interactive system. Indeed, words such as *system, bidirectionality, synchrony, dialogue, reciprocity,* and *communication* themselves infer that two individuals are exchanging

---

[1]This survey is necessarily brief, with works selected that best showcase communicative interplay in the developing dyad. For comprehensive reviews of mother–infant interaction, the reader is encouraged to consult either Osofsky and Connors (1979), Parke and Tinsley (1987), or other recent volumes which appear in the references.

messages, in a verbal or nonverbal manner. That is, both partners participate, both partners contribute, both partners communicate. Inasmuch as
some authorities take the position that noncommunication is impossible
in a dyadic situation (Watzlawick, Beavin & Jackson, 1968), it has
become easier and easier to attribute a near-equal role to the infant,
regarding his or her contribution to the encounter. However, it must be
kept in mind that a mother–infant exchange is unlike most others between individuals. The infant is without language, is culturally naive, and
is physically dependent (Newson, 1979). The mother, in turn, is skilled in
language, is culturally sophisticated, and is in control (Tronick, Als, &
Adamson, 1979).

The issue of control, which is viewed by some as *the* issue of mother–
infant interaction (Hodapp & Mueller, 1982), means that no matter how
compelling the signals are that the infant emits, or how active and
responsive the infant appears, it is the mother, through her adjustments
and attributions, that makes the system work (Kaye, 1982; Tronick et
al., 1979). Researchers vary from those who recognize the young infant,
even the neonate, as a skilled communicator (Als, 1977; Brazelton, 1982)
to those who acknowledge the infant as responsive and effective, but not
yet capable of mutually shared intentions or meanings (Kaye, 1982;
Newson, 1977).[2] Regardless of their perspective, both sides would agree
that the mutuality in mother–infant interaction (Tronick, Als, &
Brazelton, 1977), if not yet true dyadic communication, is at the very
least protosocial (Newson, 1977), protoconversational (Bateson, 1979),
or as a precursor to what will soon emerge, protocommunication
(Fafouti-Milenkovic & Uzgiris, 1979).

STAGES OF MOTHER–INFANT INTERACTION

In part because the human infant is a developing organism, it is not
uncommon to describe its ontogeny by means of a stage framework. Such
approaches have been useful in portraying cognitive development
(Piaget, 1952), personality growth (Erikson, 1950), and most recently,
the differentiation of emotions (Sroufe, 1979). The study of mother–
infant interaction is no exception, and the models proposed by a number
of researchers will be loosely drawn upon in an effort to organize the
results from a wide array of studies. As with any such framework,

---

[2]A resolution to the debate on whether or not the young infant, without intersubjectivity, can truly be said to communicate lies beyond the scope of this chapter. The reader is
instead urged to consult Kaye (1982) for an excellent discussion of this issue, and Tronick
and Adamson (1980) for a compelling, alternate perspective.

beyond the beginning of the initial period, transitional ages and duration of stages are only approximate, with overlap more likely than not.[3]

Stage 1: Regulation

As is admittedly obvious, the human infant is utterly dependent on its caregiver in the first months postpartum. Nevertheless, the normal newborn is born equipped with a number of reflexes and abilities that help to ensure its survival. However, it is the signal behavior of crying (Bowlby, 1969), which most often draws mother near so that feeding and contact are even possible. The communicative function of the cry at this point is unintentional, but its effectiveness in bringing a caregiver to the scene is undeniable (Bell, 1974; Worobey, Laub & Schilmoeller, 1983).

Although much of the infant's first months are spent crying, sleeping, or feeding, it has been widely documented that states of true alertness are evident from the first days onward and that these alert periods reliably increase over the next 3 months (Brazelton, 1973; Wolff, 1966). Such progress notwithstanding, over 75% of the dyad's earliest interactions consist of soothing episodes (Robson & Moss, 1970) where bringing the infant down from an agitated, upset state to a calm, responsive state is the goal of at least the mother. Besides terminating the relatively noxious sound of the cry, holding the infant to shoulder serves to alert the infant (Korner, 1974). Once composed, even a newborn can fixate on the mother's moving face (Brazelton, 1982).

Although crying and alerting are incompatible, their temporal closeness during soothing is a useful example of the first stage of mother–infant interactions. Through cries, fusses, or squirms, the infant signals a difficulty with self-regulation of states (Als, 1977; Bowlby, 1969). Rather than "turning the mother off," however, the inability to self-soothe serves to draw the mother to her infant. As the mother improves in her ability to "read" her baby's cry (Wolff, 1969), she achieves greater success in helping with regulation. And as the newborn gradually integrates its own physiological, motoric and state systems, the ability to self-regulate evolves (Als, 1979; Greenspan & Greenspan, 1985). Through further observing rhythms in the infant's feeding and attention, the mother can begin to anticipate states of arousal (Kaye, 1982; Sander, 1976).

By 2 months, the infant is increasingly alert, more regular in smiling, and reliably able to make eye contact. This increase in regulatory abilities

---

[3]Although birth is the assumed starting point for mother–infant interactive possibilities, there are those (e.g., Brazelton, 1982) who hypothesize a period of intrauterine entrainment in the last trimester of pregnancy.

does much to promote the mother–infant bond, as visual fixation and frequent smiling, mirroring at times the identical behaviors exhibited by the mother, is taken by the mother as evidence that her infant can now recognize her (Robson & Moss, 1970).

Stage 2: Reciprocity

The second stage of dyadic development is marked by a greater equality between the communicating partners. By 3 months, the frequency of the infant's crying episodes are on the decline, with a concomitant increase in predictable alert periods. Coupled with sustained attention to faces and voices, in preference to toys or other objects (Brazelton, Kozlowski, & Main, 1974), the infant enters a stage of unmistakable sociability. Smiles are no longer ambiguous, as the infant responsively smiles to the mother's greetings and verbalizations. For her part, the mother begins to treat her infant as a person, that is, behaving as if her infant understands her overtures and has intentions to interact (Kaye, 1982; Newson, 1979).

The literature is rich with examples of mutuality in mother–infant interaction during these months. Stern (1974; 1977) has artfully described mutual gazing and mother–infant play as a vehicle for the regulation of stimulation. The mother alters her behavior, cuing on the infant's visual attention and state, whereas the infant gazes directly and averts when necessary, so as to optimize the level of arousal. Similarly, Brazelton and his colleagues have documented how in accelerating to a peak of excitement, the mother and infant bid for the other's attention, make widened-eye contact, smile, vocalize, and momentarily disengage by glancing away (Brazelton et al., 1974; Tronick et al., 1977, 1979). But for maternal touching or caressing, both partners contribute via similar modalities and seem to derive equivalent satisfaction.

Cooing develops in tandem with the infant's increased sociability and provides the infant with an additional channel for communication. Although babbling and lallation emerge later, the fact that the infant is making noncrying sounds serves to reinforce and elicit the mother's own use of words in interaction. Baby talk, that is, the higher-pitched, rhythmic-patterned, shortened form of speech that nearly all adults use with young infants was present in earlier weeks (Sachs, 1977). But with the advent of prelinguistic sounds, the infant's perceptual sensitivity to such input convinces the mother that a dialogue is now possible (Trevarthen, 1979).

Despite the reciprocal exchanges which clearly take place (Fogel, 1977; Sander, 1976), and the appearance that the infant initiates and terminates the interaction through visual fixation and gaze aversion

(Stern, 1974), it is still the mother who is in control (Tronick et al., 1979). She determines when and where the interactive bout may occur (Hodapp & Mueller, 1982) and modifies her facial, vocal, and other actions in order to maximize the infant's attention and participation (Brazelton et al., 1974).

Stage 3: Initiation

For the most part, mothers by now are tuned in to the level of their infants' interactive competence, reacting to vocalizations as communicative while identifying and encouraging sounds as communications (Harding, 1983). But by the second half of their 1st year together, the intensive face-to-face games that characterized their play at 3 or 4 months begin to decline (Fafouti-Milenkovic & Uzgiris, 1979). This is not a mark of disintegration, however, but an indication of higher organization.

The mother's tendency to be able to elicit social responses, which had given way to their reliable elicitation, are now unnecessary as the infant assumes increasing responsibility for the success of the interaction (Kaye, 1982; Kaye & Fogel, 1980). The infant can initiate the social exchange, and with advances in babbling, reaching, and affective expression at 7 or 8 months, can indicate a preference for certain activities (Sander, 1976). The mother's words elicit the infant's vocalizing, her smile begets a smile, and her mere appearance results in the infant's greeting the mother, indicating an expectation for an interactive episode (Greenspan & Greenspan, 1985).

Games like pat-a-cake or peek-a-boo, in which the infant was more like a spectator than participant at 5 months, are now mutually enjoyed as the infant can better flow with the rhythm of the procedures (Ratner & Bruner, 1978). In fact, besides the sheer pleasure they provide, games such as "How big? So big!" and "Where is . . . ?" demonstrate improvements in the infant's memory and understanding of conventional signs (Kaye, 1982). At the same time, the mother is understanding more of the infant's gestures. A glance away from the mother to an object results in the mother's following the gaze to that object, and then making commentary (Collis & Schaffer, 1975).

But interest in objects takes on importance in it's own right. The presentation of a rattle or toy elicits reaching, grasping, and exploration. And when the toy is a familiar one, it brings a familiar response, as the mother's memory of the infant's previous reaction to the inanimate object is at last shared by the infant (Kaye, 1982). Should the toy not respond as it did before, as predictably as the mother so often has, the infant's budding initiative has met with interference (Sander, 1976).

The role of imitation in these developing exchanges cannot be over-emphasized. In earlier stages instances of imitation were observable, whether mothers tried to duplicate the sounds that their infants made in babbling (Pawlby, 1977), or infants mimicked their mothers' exaggerated mouth opening (Meltzoff & Moore, 1977). But after 6 months, deliberate imitation becomes a striking feature of the mother–infant dialogue (Richards, 1974; Trevarthen, 1979). The mother, whose earlier, intuitive modelling was readily assimilated (Kaye, 1982; Stern, 1974), begins to assume a didactic role, actively providing her infant with problems and situations to facilitate learning (Papousek & Papousek, 1982). Yet with advances in the infant's imitative skill (Piaget, 1951), neither partner is overtaxed during these lessons.

Stage 4: Intention

As the infant nears 1 year of age, a new level of mother–infant interaction evolves, representing a marvelous blending of development in the physical, cognitive, and socioemotional domains. The infant's continued achievements in motoric control from grasping and manipulating through crawling and walking, mean that interaction and other contact with stimulation are no longer determined solely by the mother. Infants can now locomote after objects on their own if gesturing, pointing, or tugging on mother are ineffectual (Greenspan & Greenspan, 1985). Having already attained a sense of person permanence through repeated exchanges with the mother (Bell, 1970), the infant's appreciation for the permanency of objects makes their appeal irresistible (Piaget, 1952). Mothers are still interesting, but the exploration of the near environment with an endless number of new objects and individuals steers the infant into additional encounters. Such interactions further facilitate the infant's cognitive development, just as the infant's appreciation of permanence depended on the preceding sequence of responsive interactions (Ahmad & Worobey, 1983).

Continuing the didactic nature of the interactions that emerged during the initiative stage, the infant and mother now focus their play together on objects. Modelling by the mother is more obvious, with imitation by the infant an implicit goal (Kaye, 1982). The infant offers the mother an object, the mother accepts it thankfully, then returns it while naming it (Richards, 1974). The mother may direct the infant's attention to the object she is interested in, but the infant communicates readiness for sharing the task by first looking at her face (Hubley & Trevarthen, 1979). Thus, both partners are signalling their intentions.

By now the emotional attachment between infant and mother is evident to most any observer (Sroufe, 1979). A secure attachment represents more than an affectionate bond, however (Ainsworth, Bell, & Stayton, 1974). The executive behaviors of approaching and following while ensuring proximity (Bell, 1974; Bowlby, 1969) conversely allow for the infant's movement away from the caregiver when the situation merits exploration. As long as mother is within sight and smiling or nodding, a secure base for exploration exists (Ainsworth et al., 1974; Sander, 1976). Hence, mother–infant communication occurs even as the infant makes an effort to investigate the world beyond the caregiver.

Despite earlier instances of intentional behavior, intentional communication does not occur until the infant realizes that the mother's mind can be interfaced with his or her own (Bretherton & Bates, 1979). When both partners agree and understand that a word represents the same thing to each of them, their shared memory of the phenomenon in question gives way to shared language (Kaye, 1982). With the emergence of the first word, then, what objects and events are called becomes as important as the phenomenona themselves (Tronick & Adamson, 1980). Focalization on the mother thus makes room for a focus on language (Sander, 1976). As the study of language development has its own illustrious history (e.g., Lewis, 1936), suffice it to say that the shared meaning that mother and infant have now attained, should satisfy even the most rigorous criteria for intersubjectivity (Kaye, 1982; Ryan, 1974; Trevarthen, 1979).

FACILITATING COMMUNICATION IN THE MOTHER–NEWBORN DYAD

As has just been highlighted, interactive behavior in the mother–infant dyad evolves in a regular, yet increasingly complex manner, as the infant grows in social competency, and the mother acquires a greater sensitivity in interpreting her infant's communicative signals. Although no singular framework has guided the bulk of research in mother–infant interaction (Osofsky & Connors, 1979), a review of theoretical approaches to the study of early social development reveals a current emphasis on the ethological perspective (Campos et al., 1983). Such a perspective argues for the adaptive importance of social interaction, with the premise that the species-specific behaviors of mothers and infants have evolved to serve communicative functions. The first interactions between mother and newborn are in concordance with this approach, and to illustrate the usefulness of such a theory, the developmental criteria of Baltes, Reese, and Nesselroade (1977) are applied to the analysis of early interactions. Specifically, the description, explanation, and modification/optimization of early interactions are addressed in positing a theory of mother–newborn communication.

Description

At the risk of redundancy, the cursory description of newborn competencies presented earlier is here reiterated, in greater detail, to un-
derscore their significance for communication in the neonatal period.
Although comparatively helpless, the healthy newborn can reflexively
breathe, root, suck, and swallow on its own (Prechtl & Beintema, 1964).
If either breathing or swallowing is occluded, the newborn can right its
head, sneeze, cough, or spit up. Ventral sleep and shivering help to
maintain body temperature. Though vision and hearing are immature,
the newborn can see clearly at a short distance, localize sounds by
turning eyes and head, and make limited eye contact (Brazelton, 1973).
The newborn can fuss, fret, and cry, but also exhibits occasional smiling
and episodes of alertness, even within the first hour postpartum (Klaus &
Kennell, 1982; Wolff, 1969).

For her part, the mother acquaints herself with her newborn in an
orderly fashion, touching the neonate's extremites with her finger, then
moving to palm contact after a few minutes (Klaus, Kennell, Plumb, &
Zuehlke, 1970). Efforts to make eye contact while *en face* are apparent,
and speaking to the newborn in a high-pitched voice is not unusual
(Klaus & Kennell, 1982).

Despite the startles and cogwheel jerkiness that characterize the newborn's musculature, the ability to grasp and nestle is present, and when
directed at the caregiver, is extremely reinforcing (Brazelton, 1973).
Concerning their interaction, intriguing evidence exists that newborns
move in time with the structure of maternal speech (Condon & Sander,
1974). Such entrainment is further supported by the newborn's alerting
in response to soothing (Korner, 1974), and likelihood of closed eyes
when not in contact with the mother (Als, 1979).

Explanation

The preceding descriptive account suggests that the mother and newborn
are primed for interaction from their earliest moments together. Experimental studies document that newborns are most effectively calmed
by being held to the shoulder, as startling is inhibited and alerting usually
results (Korner, 1974). In turn, naturalistic studies show that holding as a
soothing strategy is employed over 80% of the time (Worobey et al.,
1983). Laboratory work indicates that newborns prefer their mother's
voice over other voices or inanimate sounds (DeCasper & Fifer, 1980),
and an "eyes and mouth" array is the most preferred visual configuration
just minutes after birth (Goren, Sarty, & Wu, 1975). Indeed, a moving
face and voice are arguably preferred over any inanimate stimulus

(Richards, 1974). Not coincidentally, the optimal focal distance of newborns (i.e., 9–10 inches) corresponds almost exactly to the distance that a mother's face is from her infant's while feeding, and the distance apart she will actively regulate their faces to be during interaction (Schoetzer, 1979).

Even the mother's anatomy is facilitative of communication, as her protruding breast allows the newborn's face to be somewhat removed from her body, and therefore free for visual exploration (Abercrombie, 1971; Als, 1977). From an anthropological perspective as well, the "baby" features of the newborn, that is, large head, flattened nose, and protruding cheeks (Bell, 1974; Tinbergen, 1951), may elicit more delicate treatment. In any case, an appearance of helplessness is likely adaptive, as mothers who report their own newborns as less motorically mature spend more time in responsively vocalizing to their infants at 1 month (Worobey & Schilmoeller, 1981).

Aside from this physical and perceptual synchrony, however, it is the social signalling and receptiveness characterizing these first encounters which may be the most critical aspect of early mother–infant interactions. After a flurry of investigations that examined the bonding between mothers and newborns as a function of early and extended contact (Klaus & Kennell, 1982), it has become increasingly clear that a process, beyond simple proximity, must account for sensitive interaction. Although an alert mother and newborn are an obvious prerequisite for communication (Als, 1979; Trause, 1977), it is the newborn's emitting of signals, and the mother's responding to the same, that initiates the system (Bowlby, 1969). Crying signals the mother to come to the infant or investigate what may be wrong if she is already in proximity. Following its normal course, crying should decline over the ensuing weeks. Likewise, the incidence of positive signals (i.e., smiling) should increase over the same period. Coupled with more frequent eye contact during their interactions, the mother will increasingly regard her newborn as a person. Indeed, Robson and Moss (1970) documented such a pattern as critical for the optimal growth of maternal attachment.

Modification/Optimization

The preceding analysis indicates that watching and smiling, behaviors that characterize adult forms of social communication, contribute greatly to the success of early mother–infant interactions. If such an assumption is correct, it suggests that mother–newborn encounters that showcase these social signals and provide the mother with an opportunity to recognize and respond to them should facilitate later interactions. The quality of mother–newborn interactions, and not simply the provision of early contact, may therefore by instrumental in the optimization of subsequent mother–infant interactions (Belsky & Benn, 1982; Worobey & Brazelton, 1987).

Interestingly enough, the pediatric setting, wherein the infant's welfare has traditionally been the focus of professional consultation, has in recent years served as a forum for examining communication between the physician, parent, and child as patient (Worobey, O'Hair, & O'Hair, 1987). The early postpartum period in particular, as suggested by the bonding theorists (Klaus & Kennell, 1982), lends itself well to the possibility of intervention, as in their first days together at least, the mother and newborn are away from most of the distractions of the outside world. The hospital setting, then, may serve as an appropriate place to test the prediction that interventions which showcase the newborn as a social being may facilitate early as well as subsequent maternal–infant communication.

Thanks in large measure to the availability of a neonatal assessment device (Brazelton, 1973), developed to assess neurological intactness and individual responsivity, a vehicle exists for sharing with mothers the unique strengths of their newborns through an interactive encounter. Over the course of a typical assessment, the newborn's behavior in moving from sleep through alertness up to a crying state is observed, with attention paid to how much assistance the neonate requires in maintaining homeostasis. What irritates the newborn is nevertheless of as much interest as which efforts are successful in consolation. If self-soothing via a hand-to-mouth maneuver results in quieting and alerting, one is struck with how the neonate appears to be programmed for interaction with the environment (Brazelton, 1979).

Once alert, the examiner moves a red ball and rattle across the newborn's line of vision, allowing the baby to orient to the visual and auditory display. Following this procedure, the examiner's face and voice are systematically presented, with the normal newborn preferring this animate diaplay over the previous stimuli. When held upright during the examination, the newborn can exhibit molding, head control, and further alerting. Should crying reoccur, the graded increase from talking, to touching, to rocking, or their combination comforts most newborns (Worobey et al., 1983). Talking a newborn "down" from an agitated state is extremely satisfying, as is the opportunity for eye-to-eye contact which results. Alert responsivity is carefully scored, but reflexes, motoric control, and smiles are credited as well. Although the examination was developed as a clinical tool for assessing neonatal competencies, it was perhaps inevitable that its utility as a device for highlighting caregiver–newborn communication would be recognized.

A growing number of studies have investigated the effectiveness of this technique in helping the new mother "get acquainted" with her newborn. They have varied in target population, directness of approach, and success in outcomes.[4] As a model for examining the merits of teaching about newborns versus interacting with newborns, an investigation by the present author is of relevance here.

While still hospitalized after delivery, mothers were informed of their newborn's capacities through either a verbal presentation, a visual demonstration, or a guided interaction, using the newborn assessment (Brazelton, 1973) as the foundation for intervention. At 2 weeks postpartum, mothers who were guided through the interactive encounter with their newborns rated their babies as highest in predictability and tolerance, and lowest in fussiness (Worobey, 1987). The mothers who only heard about the results of the assessment rated their newborns in the opposite fashion, with the mothers who watched the demonstration falling in between. The results at the 1-month observational follow-up were far more dramatic, as mothers who experienced the interactive encounter with their newborns exhibited more contingent interaction and embellished involvement than the mothers who witnessed the demonstration, who, in turn, outscored the mothers who had only received a verbal description of their newborn's capabilities (Worobey & Belsky, 1982). What is of meaningful significance is that these very maternal behaviors are those that appear to be the most consistently linked to secure attachment in later infancy (Sroufe, 1979).

It would thus appear that maternal sensitivity may be partially predicted through an intervention that provides the opportunity for communication between mother and newborn in the first days of life. However, although active interaction resulted in greater optimization, the value of passive strategies, wherein mothers are informed through watching or listening, are not to be dismissed. Indeed, positive effects from simple demonstrations of newborn competencies have been shown (Worobey, 1985). By the same token, it would be naive to presume that a single encounter, no matter how carefully choreographed, would result in long-term effects on mother-infant interaction (Belsky & Benn, 1982; Worobey & Brazelton, 1986). Success has been shown, for example, with repeated discussions of social capabilities in the course of routine well-baby visits (Whitt & Casey, 1982).

---

[4]See Worobey (1985) for a review. For a lively debate on the true effectiveness of using such approaches with mothers and newborns who are not deemed "at-risk," the reader is directed toward the commentaries by Worobey and Brazelton (1986) and Belsky (1986).

ISSUES IN THE STUDY
OF MOTHER–INFANT COMMUNICATION

In the interest of clarity, the preceding account of the developing mother–infant relationship is admittedly brief and all too general. Although generalizations do have their functional advantage, the study of mother–infant interactions is so strikingly complex that a few additional matters should be addressed. Specifically, the issues of individual differences, measurement, and context of observation require brief consideration.

Individual Differences

Although the stages of mother–infant interaction are described in a way that presumed applicability to all mother–infant pairs, the theme of this volume mandates that normative development by stressed. As noted in the introduction, the literature on mother–infant interaction has grown quite large, quite rapidly, with specialists increasingly examining the functioning of aberrant groups of infants, mothers, and families. Even so, limiting the present coverage to "normal" mothers and infants by no means implies that all dyads develop in quite the same manner.

Numerous researchers have found differences in responsivity, style, and sensitivity between mothers (Ainsworth et al., 1974; Brazelton et al., 1974), even when controlling for socioeconomic status (Kaye, 1982). Similarly, interest has recently surged in the study of individual differences in newborns (Brazelton, 1973; Worobey, 1986) and temperament throughout infancy (Bates, 1987). The readability of the infant, and the mother's ability to interpret her infant's signals (Goldberg, 1977; Tronick & Adamson, 1980) make recognition of the individualized contributions of both partners a prerequisite for fully understanding their interaction.

Measurement

The research designs employed in the studies discussed throughout this chapter are in many ways as different as the mothers and infants who were observed. Although some investigators, in a microanalytic fashion, coded and recoded infant and mother behaviors in 10th of a second units (Condon & Sander, 1974; Stern, 1974), others used global, yet well-defined rating scales to summarize behavior after an extended period of watching the flow of interaction (Ainsworth et al., 1974). Still others employed a middle ground, watching behaviors unfold for a few seconds, pausing to check off preselected behaviors, and resuming the observe-record sequence (Als, 1977; Worobey et al., 1983).

The advantages and disadvantages to each approach cannot be weighed here, but the choice of observational strategy (Bakeman & Gottman, 1987) and subsequent analysis of the data (Sackett, 1987) are issues that sould be addressed at the same time as the research problem is formulated. Observing, coding, and making sense of mother–infant interaction data are far more difficult tasks than merely asking "how much of what kind of behavior occurs" (Lewis & Lee-Painter, 1974).

Context

Similar to the unit of analysis issue, one must also consider the context within which mother–infant interaction is being observed (Belsky, 1977; Lewis & Rosenblum, 1974). The study of communication, in particular, may be best examined in the laboratory via the face-to-face interaction paradigm, wherein the constraints of caregiving do not interfere (Tronick et al., 1979). Indeed, face-to-face play has been invaluable in revealing the reciprocity that characterizes certain mother and infant exchanges (Brazelton et al., 1974; Stern, 1974). But something may be missed by zeroing in solely on a structured interaction in such a controlled setting.

In the Worobey and Belsky (1982) study discussed earlier, for example, an analysis of the entire hour's incidence of observed behaviors in the infants' homes revealed no significant differences in group performance. Yet, when the data were split into behaviors seen during play/ non-caregiving versus behaviors observed while bathing/dressing the newborn, the effects of the experimental treatment emerged, and favored the interactive mothers. Results from other work indicating that infant activity may be situationally determined, suggests that the context of observation may be an intervening variable itself (Worobey & Anderson-Goetz, 1985).

CONCLUSION

This chapter is an attempt to survey recent contributions to the study of mother–infant interaction. The argument is advanced that communication between mother and infant begins shortly after birth. Furthermore, as the foundation for later social interactions, the early communication process has implications for development in areas that go far beyond language acquisition. Inasmuch as an ever-increasing body of quality research exists, it would be nearly impossible to fully address all of the work that could have been included in the present effort. It is hoped, however, that the sampler of studies that this chapter touches on will stimulate the reader to refer to the original sources cited throughout, and if not to begin investigations into the realm of mother–infant interaction, to knowingly affirm the importance of early communication in later human development.

REFERENCES

Abercrombie, J. (1971). Face to face: Proximity and distance. *Journal of Psychosomatic Research, 15,* 395–402.

Ahmad, A., & Worobey, J. (1983). Attachment and cognition in a naturalistic context. *Child Study Journal, 14,* 185–203.

Ainsworth, M. D. S., Bell, S. M., & Stayton, D. J. (1974). Infant–mother attachment and social development: Socialization as a product of reciprocal responsiveness to signals. In M. P. M. Richards (Ed.), *The integration of a child into a social world* (pp. 99–135). London: Cambridge University Press.

Als, H. (1977). The newborn communicates. *Journal of Communication, 27,* 66–73.

Als, H. (1979). Social interaction: Dynamic matrix for developing behavioral organization. In I. C. Uzgiris (Ed.), *Social interaction and communication during infancy* (pp. 21–39). San Francisco: Jossey–Bass.

Bakeman, R., & Gottman, J. M. (1987). Applying observational methods: A systematic view. In J. D. Osofsky (Ed.), *Handbood of infant development* (2nd ed., pp. 818–854). New York: Wiley.

Baltes, P. B., Reese, H. W., & Nesselroade, J. R. (1977). *Life-span developmental psychology: Introduction to research methods.* Belmont: Wadsworth.

Bates, J. E. (1987). Temperament in infancy. In J. D. Osofsky (Ed.), *Handbood of infant development* (2nd ed., pp. 1101–1149). New York: Wiley.

Bateson, M. C. (1979). "The epigenesis of conversational interaction": A personal account of research development. In M. Bullowa (Ed.), *Before speech: The beginnings of human communication* (pp. 63–77). Cambridge: Cambridge University Press.

Bell, R. Q. (1968). A reinterpretation of the direction of effects in studies of socialization. *Psychological Review, 75,* 81–95.

Bell, R. Q. (1974). Contributions of human infants to caregiving and social interaction. In M. Lewis & L. A. Rosenblum (Eds.), *The effect of the infant on its caregiver* (pp. 1–19). New York: Wiley.

Bell, S. M. (1970). The development of the concept of object as related to infant–mother attachment. *Child Development, 41,* 291–311.

Belsky, J. (1977, April). *Mother–infant interaction at home and in the laboratory.* Paper presented at the biennial meeting of the Society for Research in Child Development, New Orleans.

Belsky, J. (1986). A tale of two variances: Between and within. *Child Development, 57,* 1301–1305.

Belsky, J., & Benn, J. (1982). Beyond bonding: A family centered approach to enhancing parent–infant relations in the newborn period. In L. Bond & J. Joffee (Eds.), *Facilitating infant and early childhood development* (pp. 281–308). Hanover, NH: University Press of New England.

Bowlby, J. (1969). *Attachment.* New York: Basic Books.

Brazelton, T. B. (1973). *Neonatal behavioral assessment scale.* Philadelphia: J.B. Lippincott.

Brazelton, T. B. (1979). Evidence of communication during neonatal behavioral assessment. In M. Bullowa (Ed.), *Before speech: The beginnings of human communication* (pp. 79–88). Cambridge: Cambridge University Press.

Brazelton, T. B. (1982). Joint regulation of neonate–parent behavior. In E. Tronick (Ed.), *Social interchange in infancy: Affect, cognition, and communication* (pp. 7–22). Baltimore, MD: University Park Press.

Brazelton, T. B., Kozlowski, B., & Main, M. (1974). The origins of reciprocity: The early mother–infant interaction. In M. Lewis & L. A. Rosenblum (Eds.), *The effect of the infant on its caregiver* (pp. 49–76). New York: Wiley.

Bretherton, I., & Bates, E. (1979). The emergence of intentional communication. In I. C. Uzgiris (Ed.), *Social interaction and communication during infancy* (pp. 81–100). San Francisco: Jossey–Bass.

Campos, J. J., Barrett, K. C., Lamb, M. E., Goldsmith, H. H., & Stenberg, C. (1983). Socioemotional development. In P. H. Mussen (Ed.), *Handbook of child psychology* (4th ed., Vol. 2, pp. 783–915). New York: Wiley.

Collis, G. M., & Schaffer, H. M. (1975). Synchronization of visual attention in mother–infant pairs. *Journal of Child Psychiatry and Psychology, 16,* 315–320.

Condon, W. S., & Sander, L. W. (1974). Synchrony demonstrated between movements of the neonate and adult speech. *Child Development, 45,* 456–462.

DeCasper, A. J., & Fifer, W. P. (1980). Of human bonding: Newborns prefer their mothers' voices. *Science, 208,* 1174–1176.

Erikson, E. H. (1950). *Childhood and society.* New York: Norton.

Fafouti-Milenkovic, M., & Uzgiris, I. C. (1979). The mother–infant communication system. In I. C. Uzgiris (Ed.), *Social interaction and communication during infancy* (pp. 41–56). San Francisco: Jossey–Bass.

Field, T. (1983). High-risk infants "have less fun" during early interactions. *Topics in Early Childhood Special Education, 3,* 77–87.

Fogel, A. (1977). Temporal organization in mother–infant face-to-face interaction. In H. R. Schaffer (Ed.), *Studies in mother–infant interaction* (pp. 119–151). London: Academic Press.

Fogel, A. (1979). Peer vs. mother directed behavior in 1- to 3-month-old infants. *Infant Behavior and Development, 2,* 215–226.

Fraiberg, S. (1974). Blind infants and their mothers: An examination of the sign system. In M. Lewis & L. A. Rosenblum (Eds.), *The effect of the infant on its caregiver* (pp. 215–232). New York: Wiley.

Goldberg, S. (1977). Social competence in infancy: A model of parent–infant interaction. *Merrill-Palmer Quarterly, 23,* 163–177.

Goren, C., Sarty, M., & Wu, P. (1975). Visual following and pattern discrimination of facelike stimuli by newborn infants. *Pediatrics, 56,* 544–549.

Greenspan, S. I. & Greenspan, N. T. (1985). *First feelings: Milestones in the emotional development of your baby and child.* New York: Viking.

Harding, C. G. (1983). Setting the stage for language acquisition: Communication development in the first year. In R. M. Golinkof (Ed.), *The transition from prelinguistic to linguistic communication* (pp. 93–113). Hillsdale, NJ: Lawrence Erlbaum Associates.

Hock, E. (1980). Working and non-working mothers and their infants: A comparative study of maternal caregiving characteristics and infant social behavior. *Merrill-Palmer Quarterly, 26,* 79–101.

Hodapp, R. M., & Mueller, E. (1982). Early social development. In B. B. Wolman (Ed.), *Handbook of developmental psychology* (pp. 284–300). Englewood Cliffs, NJ: Prentice-Hall.

Hubley, P., & Trevarthen, C. (1979). Sharing a task in infancy. In I. C. Uzgiris (Ed.), *Social interaction and communication during infancy* (pp. 57–80). San Francisco: Jossey–Bass.

Kagan, J. (1979). Overview: Perspectives on human infancy. In J. D. Osofsky (Ed.), *Handbook of infant development* (pp. 1–25). New York: Wiley.

Kaye, K. (1982). *The mental and social life of babies: How parents create persons.* Chicago: University of Chicago Press.

Kaye, K., & Fogel, A. (1980). The temporal structure of face-to-face communication between mothers and infants. *Developmental Psychology, 16,* 454–64.

Klaus, M. H., & Kennell, J. H. (1982). Labor, birth and bonding. In M. H. Klaus & J. H. Kennell (Eds.), *Parent–infant bonding* (pp. 22–109). St. Louis, MO: C.V. Mosby.

Klaus, M. H., & Kennell, J. H., Plumb, N., & Zuehlke, S. (1970). Human maternal behavior at first contact with her young. *Pediatrics, 46,* 187–192.

Korner, A. F. (1974). The effect of the infant's state, level of arousal, sex, and ontogenetic stage in the caregiver. In M. Lewis & L. A. Rosenblum (Eds.), *The effect of the infant on its caregiver* (pp. 105–121). New York: Wiley.

Lamb, M. E. (1977). Father–infant and mother–infant interaction in the first year of life. *Child Development, 48,* 167–181.

Landry, S. H. (1986). Preterm infants' responses in early joint attention interactions. *Infant Behavior and Development, 9,* 1–14.

Lewis, M. (1987). Social development in infancy and early childhood. In. J. D. Osofsky (Ed.), *Handbook of infant development* (2nd ed., pp. 419–493). New York: Wiley.

Lewis, M., & Lee-Painter, S. (1974). An interactional approach to the mother–infant dyad. In M. Lewis & L. A. Rosenblum (Eds.), *The effect of the infant on its caregiver* (pp. 21–48). New York: Wiley.

Lewis, M., & Rosenblum, L. A. (Eds.). (1974). *The effect of the infant on its caregiver.* New York: Wiley.

Lewis, M. M. (1936). *Infant speech: A study of the beginning of language.* London: Routledge & Kegan Paul.

Mahoney, G. (1983). A developmental analysis of communication between mothers and infants with Down's syndrome. *Topics in Early Childhood Special Education, 3,* 63–76.

Meltzoff, A., & Moore, M. K. (1977). Imitation of facial and manual gestures by human neonates. *Science, 198,* 75–78.

Newson, J. (1977). An intersubjective approach to the systematic description of mother–infant interaction. In H. R. Schaffer (Ed.), *Studies in mother–infant interaction* (pp. 47–61). London: Academic Press.

Newson, J. (1979). The growth of shared understandings between infant and caregiver. In M. Bullowa (Ed.), *Before speech: The beginnings of human communication* (pp. 207–222). Cambridge: Cambridge University Press.

Osofsky, J. D., & Connors, K. (1979). Mother–infant interaction: An integrative view of a complex system. In J. D. Osofsky (Ed.), *Handbook of infant development* (pp. 519–548). New York: Wiley.

Papousek, H., & Papousek, M. (1982). Infant–adult social interactions. In T. M. Field, A. Huston, H. C. Quay, L. Troll, & G. Finley (Eds.), *Review of human development* (pp. 148–163). New York: Wiley.

Parke, R. D., & Tinsley, B. J. (1987). Family interaction in infancy. In J. D. Osofsky (Ed.), *Handbook of infant development* (2nd ed, pp. 579–641). New York: Wiley.

Pawlby, S. (1977). Imitative interaction. In H. R. Schaffr (Ed.), *Studies in mother–infant interaction* (pp. 203–224). London: Academic Press.

Piaget, J. (1951). *Play, dreams, and imitation in childhood.* New York: Norton.

Piaget, J. (1952). *The origins of intelligence in children*. New York: International Universities Press.

Prechtl, H., & Beintema, D. (1964). *The neurological examination of the full term newborn infant*. London: Heinemann Medical Books.

Ratner, N., & Bruner, J. (1978). Games, social exchange, and the acquisition of language. *Journal of Child Language, 5*, 391–401.

Rheingold, H. (1971). The social and socializing infant. In D. A. Goslin (Ed.), *Handbook of socialization and research* (pp. 779–790). Chicago: Rand–Mcnally.

Richards, M. P. M. (1974). The development of psychological communication in the first year of life. In K. Connoly & J. Bruner (Eds.), *The growth of competence* (pp. 119–132). New York: Academic Press.

Robson, K. S., & Moss, H. A. (1970). Patterns and determinants of maternal attachment. *Journal of Pediatrics, 77*, 976–985.

Ryan, J. (1974). Early language development: Towards a communicatinal analysis. In M. P. M. Richards (Ed.), *The integration of a child into a social world* (pp. 185–213). London: Cambridge University Press.

Sachs, J. (1977). The adaptive significance of linguistic input to prelinguistic infants. In C. Snow & C. Ferguson (Eds.), *Talking to children: Language input and acquisition* (pp. 51–61). Cambridge: Cambridge University Press.

Sackett, G. P. (1987). Analysis of sequential social interaction data. In J. D. Osofsky (Ed.), *Handbook of infant development* (2nd ed, pp. 855–878). New York: Wiley.

Sander, L. W. (1976). Issues in early mother–child interaction. In E. N. Rexford, L. W. Sander, & T. Shapiro (Eds.), *Infant psychiatry: A new synthesis* (pp. 127–147). New Haven: Yale University Press.

Schoetzer, A. (1979). Effect of viewing distance on looking behavior in neonates. *International Journal of Behavioral Development, 2*, 121–123.

Sroufe, L. A. (1979). Socioemotional development. In J. D. Osofsky (Ed.), *Handbook of infant development* (pp. 462–516). New York: Wiley.

Stern, D. N. (1974). Mother and infant at play: The dyadic interaction involving facial, vocal, and gaze behaviors. In M. Lewis & L. A. Rosenblum (Eds.), *The effect of the infant on its caregiver* (pp. 187–213). New York: Wiley.

Stern, D. N. (1977). *The first relationship*. Cambridge, MA: Harvard University Press.

Stone, L. J., Smith, H. T., & Murphy, L. B. (Eds.). (1973). *The competent infant: Research and commentary*. New York: Basic Books.

Tinbergen, N. (1951). *The study of instinct*. London: Oxford University Press.

Tinsley, B. J., & Parke, R. D. (1984). The contemporary impact of the extended family on the nuclear family: Grandparents as support and socialization agents. In M. Lewis (Ed.), *Beyond the dyad* (pp. 161–194). New York: Plenum.

Trevarthen, C. (1979). Communication and cooperation in early infancy: A description of primary intersubjectivity. In M. Bullowa (Ed.), *Before speech: The beginnings of human communication* (pp. 321–347). Cambridge: Cambridge University Press.

Trause, M. A. (1977, March). *Defining the limits of the sensitive period*. Paper presented at the biennial meeting of the Society for Research in Child Development, New Orleans.

Tronick, E., & Adamson, L. (1980). *Babies as people: New findings on our social beginnings*. New York: Collier Books.

Tronick, E., Als, H., & Adamson, L. (1979). Structure of early face-to-face communicative interactions. In M. Bullowa (Ed.), *Before speech: The beginnings of human communication* (pp. 349–372). Cambridge: Cambridge University Press.

Tronick, E., Als, H., & Brazelton, T. B. (1977). Mutuality in mother–infant interaction. *Journal of Communication, 27*, 74–79.

Watzlawick, P., Beavin, J. H., & Jackson, D. D. (1968). *The pragmatics of human communication.* London: Faber.

Whitt, J. K., & Casey, P. H. (1982). The mother–infant relationship and infant development: The effect of pediatric intervention. *Child Development, 53,* 948–956.

Wolff, P. (1966). The causes, controls and organization of behavior in the neonate. *Psychological Issues, 5,* Monograph 17.

Wolff, P. (1969). The natural history of crying and other vocalizations in early infancy. In B. M. Foss (Ed.), *Determinants of infant behavior,* (Vol. IV, pp. 81–109). London: Methuen.

Worobey, J. (1985). A review of Brazelton-based interventions to enhance parent–infant interaction. *Journal of Reproductive and Infant Psychology, 3,* 64–73.

Worobey, J. (1986). Neonatal stability and one-month behavior. *Infant Behavior and Development, 9,* 119–124.

Worobey, J. (1987). Using the Brazelton Scale to influence mothering: A closer look. *Parenting Studies, 1,* 105–108.

Worobey, J., & Anderson-Goetz, D. (1985). Maternal ratings of newborn activity: Assessing convergence between instruments. *Infant Mental Health Journal, 6,* 68–75.

Worobey, J., & Belsky, J. (1982). Employing the Brazelton Scale to influence mothering: An experimental comparison of three strategies. *Developmental Psychology, 18,* 736–743.

Worobey, J., & Brazelton, T. B. (1986). Experimenting with the family in the newborn period: A commentary. *Child Development, 57,* 1298–1300.

Worobey, J., Laub, K. W., & Schilmoeller, G. L. (1983). Maternal and paternal responses to infant distress. *Merrill-Palmer Quarterly, 79,* 33–45.

Worobey, J., O'Hair, H. D., & O'Hair, M. J. C. (1987). Pediatrician–patient–parent communication. *Language and Communication, 7,* 293–301.

Worobey, J., & Schilmoeller, G. L. (1981, August). *Infant temperament, perceived infant temperament, and mother–infant interaction.* Paper presented at the annual meeting of the American Psychological Association, Los Angeles.

3 Children's Strategies in Initiating Interaction with Peers

Beth Haslett
University of Delaware

Sheryl Perlmutter Bowen
Villanova University

ON BECOMING COMPETENT COMMUNICATORS: CHILDREN'S STRATEGIES IN INITIATING INTERACTION

Effective communication skills help develop self-identity, establish social relationships with others, and provide the basis for collective social activity. Most scholars agree that basic language and communication skills are acquired in early childhood and subsequently refined by experience and maturity. In early childhood (the preschool years) both family and peers provide important contexts for acquiring communication skills. Within the family, authority relationships and socioemotional bonding between parent and child are important social accomplishments. From peers, young children learn about friendship and establish relationships outside their immediate family. Peer/peer interaction is interaction "among equals" because there is no adult accomodation to a child's desires.

In order to participate in peer/peer interactions, a child must learn to *initiate* and *sustain* dialogue with others. This study investigates how children initiate dialogue with other children. Although many studies have examined children's communication skills, relatively few have focused upon the communicative skills needed to *begin* a dialogue with another. We believe this first step is critical because if it is not successful, children lose an opportunity for sustained interaction with one another and, consequently, an opportunity for personal growth and development.

Initiating Dialogue

A series of investigations by Lubin and Forbes (1981) looked at how children attempted to enger playgroups. They videotaped four play-groups of six children (three males and three females); all the children were unfamiliar with one another. Each playgroup was videotaped for a 20-minute free-play session. Overall, 12 sessions were videotaped over a 3-week period.

Forbes and Lubin (1981, n.d.) analyzed the ways in which children gained entry into playgroups. Direct bids were attempts to enter the playgroup by announcing the children's intention to join (e.g., the child may ask to join the group, may directly enter the group activity, or may suggest a role he or she could play in the group). Indirect bids were behaviors that brought the child into contact with the group, but did not explicitly raise the issue of entering into the group's play. They found that 5-year-olds used more direct than indirect bids, and that they ignored negative responses as if they did not occur. Seven-year-olds tended to use more "face saving" techniques in order to mitigate rejection and were less likely to repeat a request or demand. Garvey (1977) found that preschoolers used some indirect requests, although they preferred to use direct requests.

Dodge, Pettit, McClaskey, and Brown (1986) also studied second-graders' entry behaviors. In an examination of children's cognitive processes and actual behaviors they found that entry behaviors considered competent and successful included: synchronous behavior, giving information, refraining from negative conflict, displaying connectedness (verbal strategies that make structural sense) and displaying positive reciprocity (pp. 22–23). In short, children rated as competent use behaviors that establish common ground, achieve positive reciprocity, and avoid conflict.

A study by Terlecka (1978), as reported by Shugar (1979), found significant age differences in the interactive patterns of preschool dyads. When initiating interactions, younger dyads drew their partner into their own activity whereas older dyads tended to start from a joint line of activity or from their partner's current activity. Over time, interactions changed from a focus on activity with objects to increased verbal activity. Older dyads differed from younger dyads in the topics and complexity of their talk. The majority of verbal activity reflected children's social interactions ith others, and the functions played by language varied as a result of who the child's partner was. Shugar concluded that children's social interaction with one another varies as a function of the purpose of the interaction, the age of the dyadic partners, and characteristics of the dyad.

Corsaro (1979) studied children's use of access rituals with peers. Two strategies were used about 80% of the time: nonverbal entry (which involved coming close to the play area) and producing a variant (which involved comment or acting out some action relevant to the ongoing play. Older children were less likely to be disruptive and usually negotiated claims about the ongoing play. No relationship was found between frequency of use of a given access ritual and its effectiveness. Sixty-five percent of the attempts to gain access involved only one attempt and a positive or negative response from the listener; however, one's changes to successfully access the ongoing play increased with repeated attempts at access.

General Communicative Skills

Other studies have explored preschoolers' communicative behavior in different contexts. Woods and Gardner (1980) found that dominant children were most successful in their requests, whereas submissive children were more polite. Haslett (1983) found that older preschoolers used more active strategies (initiating action or a request) than reactive strategies (responding to the action or talk of another). Mueller (1972), in his analysis of dyadic interaction, found that preschoolers responded to one another's untterances 62% of the time. Preschoolers were most effective when they had the listener's attention and used commands or questions. Garvey and Hogan (1973) found that dyads were effectively communicating with one another about 66% of the time. Garvey (1977) concluded that play provides an opportunity to develop and rehearse social interaction skills.

Gottman and Parkhurst (1980) found that preschoolers were able to have extended dialogues with one another. Older children talked more about activities, whereas younger children talked more about fantasy play. Acquaintanceship also influenced children's communication patterns, with younger friends engaging in more social comparison than older friends.

Strayer's (1980) ethological study of preschoolers' social organization examined social relationships among groups of children of varying sex, culture, and race. His analysis of social organization focused on dyadic exchanges, social relationships, and group structure. Generally, Strayer found that important organizational changes occur in the formation of social structures in preschool groups. By the end of the preschool years, at approximately 5 years of age, some children emerge as more competent members of the social group and play central roles in the dominance and affiliation structures in the group. In addition, these children appear to possess more advanced social skills.

Strayer found that the more dominant children in the groups initiated more control interactions. Those children occupying central positions in the group's afiliative network offered more proximity and contact exchanges. Dominant children also occupied high affiliation positions in the group. Dominant, highly affiliative children made significantly more aggressive, affiliative, and control exchanges than other children. Highly affiliative children also made significantly more altruistic gestures. For older children, high dominance and high affiliation were positively related to affiliative gestures. Dominant children also received significantly more social activity than other children and visual attention from other children. Dominant children also gave more visual attention to others. Finally, reciprocal control relations existed among highly dominant boys.

Although these studies focused on the general strategies children use in initiating and sustaining interaction, much more analysis is needed. In particular, a more detailed analysis is needed of the strategies preschoolers use in attempting to interact with others and to sustain these interactions because these processes are critical in developing relationships with others. The present investigation explores how children initiate interaction with other children in a free-play context. In addition, the differences between males and females in initiating interaction in different group situations was examined. Because important gender differences in communication exist, it seems likely they develop in early childhood.

Gender Differences in Communication

Significant differences as a function of gender have been found in a variety of human behaviors: in communication (Eakins & Eakins, 1978); language (Smith, 1985); patterns of friendship (La Gaipa 1981); children's play (Liss, 1983); and children's activity choices (Eisenberg, 1983). Although there is considerable debate over how to account for these gender differences, most scholars are also concerned about their implications for social growth and development. In particular, communicative patterns established in early childhood are believed to be significant influences on subsequent adult communication patterns; thus, early communicative development is of special concern because of its influence on interpersonal growth and developing social relationships.

It is well known that preschoolers prefer to play with same-sex peers and to participate in activities that are viewed as being sex-appropriate (i.e., boys engage in rough-and-tumble play; girls play with dolls). Early parental expectations undoubtedly play a major role in establishing and reinforcing sex role-behaviors (Maccoby & Jacklin, 1974).

As a consequence of differing adult expectations, boys and girls appear to have different patterns of interaction with their families.

Hinde, Easton, Meller, and Tamplin (1982), observing mother/child interactions in the home, found that males and females interact differently with their mothers. Shy girls asked more questions than shy boys; shy boys were active and hostile in their responses whereas shy girls were not; and shy boys had more activity changes than did shy girls. Moody, intense children, regardless of gender, tended to have negative (unfriendly) interactions with their mothers. In general, shy girls tended to have positive interactions with their mothers whereas shy boys tended to have negative interactions. Simpson and Stevenson-Hinde (1985) concluded that "sex of the child may influence the nature of interactions for a particular temperamental characteristic (shyness), and . . . that this infulence may be mediated through differing expectations of behavior for boys and girls (p. 51).

Most studies investigating gender differences in communicative behavior have focused on same-sex dyads. DiPietro (1981) found that male triadic preschool groups engaged in more rough-and-tumble play than did female triadic groups. Male play sessions were characterized by exuberant physical contact with each other and the stimulus toys; they were less likely to verbally structure play, whereas females often tried to structure play through self-generated rules and used toys in a novel fashion. Contact among the females tended to be verbal, whereas boys maintained physical contact. McGrew's longitudinal study of preschoolers (1972) found that females looked more, and looked more at peers than did boys. Boys used significantly more undirected vocalizations.

Smithers and Smithers (1984) found that 6- and 7-year-old children had well-developed concepts about sex role differentiation; boys and men viewed sex roles as being more differentiated than did girls and women. Reis and Wright (1982) found that even by age three, children have knowledge of sex-role stereotypes and that this knowledge increases with age. Connolly, Doyle, and Ceschin (1983), in their study of preschoolers' fantasy play, found that boys prefer fictitious or superhero roles, whereas girls prefer domestic/familial roles: these role preferences were exhibited at a very young age and remained stable through the preschool years. In general, young children prefer playmates of the same sex and activities that are considered sex-appropriate (Laosa & Brophy, 1972).

From the mounting evidence now available, it seems likely that gender differences in behavior may have their origins in early childhood. Gender differences in interaction appear to develop during this time and provide the basis for sex-role differentiation in later life. Gender differences also appear to vary as a result of group composition; that is, both men and women behave differently as a function of the gender composition of the group.

The Communicative Context:
The Composition of the Group

Children's interactions with one another vary as a function of a partner's gender and social characteristics. Gellert (1962) found that children's attempts to dominate their interactional partner varied as a function of who the partner was. More dominance was displayed when children were paired with the less assertive of two same-sex peers.

Bianchi and Bakeman (1983) also found that sex-typed behavior in preschoolers is influenced by different school environments. They also investigated whether or not the patterns of mixed-sex interaction among preschoolers continued in the early elementary years. Neither gender, age, or grade significantly influenced children's preferences for mixed-sex play. Children in first and second grade spent roughly 50% of their play time with a group that contained at least one member of the opposite sex. At the same time, however, there is a marked increase in the amount of same-sex play. Bianchi and Bakeman suggested that activities and behaviors previously considered sex typed (like sewing, etc., being a female task) are becoming less sex typed, and thus more flexibility in terms of acceptable behavior is beginning to emerge.

Because the composition of the group appears to influence the group's interaction, this study also varied the composition of the group. More specifically, we investigated whether interactional patterns would differ in same-sex groups (SS), mixed-sex groups (MS) and goups of one male and three females, or the reverse (termed the *isolate condition,* IS). Given past research, we anticipate finding differences in interaction as a function of gender and group composition.

RESEARCH QUESTIONS

We were interested in examining how children initiated play with their peers. Based on an analysis of previous research this study sought to integrate qualitative and quantitative methods in attempting to answer three research questions. 1) Do boys and girls use different strategies to initiate interaction? To answer this question, the authors identified initiating strategies and then coded the types of strategies. 2) Are boys and girls equally successful in their use of initiating strategies? Success of bids was measured by whether a strategy led to a verbal exchange longer than one interact, that is, two or more exchanges. c) How does group composition affect strategy use? It was hypothesized that children's use of initiating strategies would vary as a function of group composition.

METHOD

Subjects

One researcher had been observing children's play in the nursery for the previous 18 months, so the children knew her and were comfortable around her. During these observations, she took field notes, and audiotaped children's interactions; care was taken not to participate directly in the children's play, but only to observe. Because much of the nonverbal activity contextualized and defined the children's play, it was decided to videotape children at another site where equipment was readily accessible.

Using 5-year-olds from a northeastern preschool, groups of four children were videotaped for 20-minute free-play sessions. Two of the sessions consisted of same-sex groups (one male group; one female group), two were mixed-sex groups (two males and two females), or an isolate group (1 male and 3 females, or one female and three males). Although the situations were set up by the researchers, the children's play paralleled the play engaged in when in their normal preschool setting, and they appeared quite comfortable. The children knew one another and were asked to play in a defined area. The six videotaped episodes yielded approximately 120 minutes of videotaped interaction. Although only 12 children participated in the study, a substantial number of bids (177) were analyzed in this study.

Coding System

It was necessary to develop a coding system to look more specifically at the initiation of interaction and how it was subsequently sustained. Using prior research as heuristic guides, and careful, repeated observations of the six videotapes, the researchers developed a number of strategies used by the children to initiate play with their peers. Requests for explicit information from the adult present (who was just outside the play area) or from children which did not directly refer to their play (e.g., "Where's Jeffrey's mom?") were excluded. Gottman and Parkhurst (1980) used similar exclusions in their coding of children's talk.

Because children's interaction frequently shifts both topic and activity our first task was to segment their ongoing activity into episodes for subsequent analysis. After Haslett (1983), a communicative episode was defined as interaction that "maintained a common topic or focus of attention and which accomplished some interactional purpose" (p. 88). This operationalization of episodes is compatible with those used by other developmental scholars (Corsaro, 1979). The initial conversation of each communicative episode was analyzed for access bids in those episodes. The researchers excluded episodes in which the conversational topic changed during play, but did not represent any new access attempt. (For example, two children already talking, but talking about many different topics, are already accessible to one another and not negotiating access.)

Once the access episodes were defined, these episodes were viewed repeatedly and discussed by the researchers. Other studies' coding schemes were used as heuristic guidelines in developing grounded conceptual categories for our data.

The coding scheme, based upon repeated observations and discussions of the children's play, distinguished between directness or indirectness of bids. Direct bids specifically confronted the other interactants in some way, with questions, requests, commands, comments, or offers. Direct bids were also more explicit than indirect bids (i.e., requests like "Would you give me that toy?" were much more explicit than an indirect request such as, "That's a nice toy," said while looking where another child was playing and reaching out for the toy). Direct comments in which a child stated what he or she planned to do or what role he or she was going to take in relation to ongoing play were differentiated from indirect comments in which a child added supplemental details about his or her own play. (See Table 3.1.)

Often the classification of "comments" as direct or indirect was made on the basis of a judgment as to the rejection potential of the bid. Although all bids can be rejected, indirect comments can be easily "sloughed off" by other children and play will continue without interruption. If, on the other hand, when children are assigning roles for play and a child not previously engaged in the play makes a direct comment such as, "I'll be the grandpop" and is ignored by the children in the play setting, it is much more obvious. Overall, indirect bids were classified as either (a) comments or scene setters, (b) greetings to characters, (c) requests, or (d) questions.

A third global category also emerged from the data. Multipliers, or intensifiers, are verbal or nonverbal behaviors that are rarely used alone, but function with other utterances to get attention or to emphasize subsequent remarks (e.g., "Look," "John," "Wow," a pointing gesture, etc.). Children would often make a comment, preceded by "look," such as, "Look, I'm gonna go like this." Such statements would be coded as a direct comment with a multiplier. Corsaro (1979; 1981) considered some physical orientation changes as cues—we did not. Moving in close proximity to a playmate appears to be a necesary, but not *sufficient* condition

Table 3.1
Bids for Structuring Play

Direct Bids

Question	request for information ("Did you see this man?")
Request	request for goods/services ("Would you give me that toy?")
Command	order or demand ("Look at this (*object*).") ("Give me that toy.")
Comment	remark about play activities; sociable statement abut plans and roles ("I'm going to play with the cars.") ("I'll be the mommy.")
Offer	extension of goods/service to another ("Do you want this?") ("Do you want to play this?")
Other	e.g., challenge: ("I bet you can't do this.")

Indirect Bids

Set Scene	comment that set up the context of the play; ("That's my car and there's our garage.")
Request	indirect request for goods/service ("There was a man over here in this pile near you.")
Question	request for information not directly tied to play; usually an attempt to change focus. ("Who made this picture over here?")
Other	e.g., greeting to character ("Hi mommy.")

Multipliers/Intensifiers of Bids: Serve as attention-getters. These were coded as either used alone or tacked onto another verbal strategy.

Look
Name of child.
Exclamation.
Action/Nonverbal.

---

for gaining entry to ongoing play. Thus, in our study, nonverbal correlates of verbal behavior were noted when viewing the videotapes and used to help contextualize the children's talk. Only overt, intensifying nonverbal behaviors were coded separately as bids.

After coding the bids, the bids were analyzed along the dimensions of success of the bids, types of bids, and whether these bids varied as a function of group composition.

Reliability

Each of the researchers scored one-half of the episodes. Then each researcher scored one-half of the other *E*'s data. Overall, 25% of the data was dual coded as a reliability check. Agreement between coders was 91%.

RESULTS:
GENDER AND INITIATION STRATEGIES

Although boys used more verbal bids than girls, gender itself does not seem to account for differential strategy use, at least in sheer numbers (101 vs. 70, X^2 n.s.). Nor was gender significant in predicting the success of the bid ($X^2 = 3.05$, $df = 1$, $p < .08$). The most frequently used strategy, overall, was indirect scene setting. Over one-third of all play bids fell into this category and of them, almost three-quarters was successful in initiating a sequence of play-related action.

Boys. In terms of individual types of strategies, boys used more direct questions and direct comments than girls. Boys never used indirect requests as initiating bids and were more likely to accompany a verbal bid with an intensifier such as "look" or a child's name. Overall, boys used 62% direct strategies and 38% indirect bids. Initiating bids for boys were successful approximately half the time across all conditions.

There was some variation in the success rates for particular strategies; commands, for instance, were accepted only 17% of the time, whereas other strategies such as offers and comments, were more often the start of further interaction. Table 3.2 contains comparisons of bid types and success rates for boys, girls, and all children combined.

Girls. Only two types of bids were chosen more frequently by girls than by boys: direct offers and indirect questions. Girls never used indirect greetings or nonverbal or solo intensifiers, whereas boys did, albeit infrequently. Girls expressed only a slight preference, overall, for direct bids: 53% were direct compared with 47% indirect bids. However, girls were more successful in their attempts to initiate play: 64% of their bids were picked up by at least one other child; 36% were rejected. Girls' commands were accepted 60% of the time, whereas, indirect comments were successful only 22% of the time. Unlike boys, when girls used multipliers with verbal strategies they were always successful.

Group Composition

The composition of the play group made a significant difference in the number of bids used to initiate interaction ($X^2 = 21.89$, $df = 2$, $p < .001$). Group composition was also significantly related to the success of the bids ($X^2 - 9.34$, $df = 2$, $p < .009$). In the isolate condition, more bids were unsuccessful (57% unsuccessful vs. 43% successful). In the other

Table 3.2
Bid Type and Success Rate as a Fuanction of Gender*

Type of Bid	Males		Females	
Direct Bids	% of Use	Success Rate (%)	% of Use	Success Rate (%)
QUESTION	11	27	3	0
REQUEST	4	50	1	100
COMMAND	12	17	14	50
COMMENT	20	50	9	33
OFFER	3	100	10	86
OTHER	1	100	4	67
MULTI W/dir	17	35	14	100
MULTI ACTION	6	67	7	—
MULTI ALONE	6	33	1	100
Indirect Bids				
SCENE/COMMENT	30	47	40	22
GREETING	2	50	—	—
REQUEST	—	—	4	33
QUESTION	2	100	6	100
MULTI W/dir	14	57	3	100
MULTI ACTION	1	100	—	—
MULTI ALONE	1	0	—	—

*Several of the strategies were not used frequently (6 or fewer times), and were dropped from further analyses of individual strategy use. These were: Direct "other," indirect greeting, indirect request, and indirect multiplier, both alone and action.
*For Table 2 all childrens' bids, the % of each strategy is out of 100%. The % success is for each type of bid individually; if there were 10 questions and 5 of them were successful, questions would have a 50% success rate.

conditions, about twice as many bids were successful compared to the unsuccessful bids (mixed sex: 66% successful vs. 34% unsuccessful; same sex: 67% successful vs. 33% unsuccessful).

Direct bids were more often rejected and indirect bids more often accepted in the structuring of children's play ($X^2 = 7.83$, $df = 2$, $p < .001$). More direct bids were used in the mixed-sex and isolate groups, and more indirect bids in the same-sex groups. Table 3.3 shows children's strategy use in the three groups (MS = mixed sex, SS = same sex, I = isolate). In this table, each group condition is considered as 100% of all strategies, showing how girls and boys used strategies relative to one another. This analysis shows that females were significantly more successful in the mixed-sex groups than the males ($X^2 = 5.99$, $df = 1$, $p = 0.1$).

Table 3.3
Type of Bid Used as a Function of Gender and Group Condition*

	Group Condition					
	Mixed Sex		Same Sex		Isolate	
Bid Type						
Direct	F	M	F	M	F	M
QUESTION	0	1.5	0	10.3	2.6	9.1
REQUEST	1.5	4.6	0	0	0	1.3
COMMAND	13.8	1.5	0	6.9	1.3	11.7
COMMENT	1.5	20.0	0	3.4	6.5	7.8
OFFER	9.2	3.1	0	0	1.3	1.3
MULTI W/dir	13.8	12.3	0	3.4	1.3	10.3
MULTI ACTION	0	0	0	6.9	0	5.2
Indirect						
SCENE/COMMENT	15.3	12.3	34.5	27.6	10.3	18.2
QUESTION	4.6	3.1	0	0	1.3	0
MULTI W/dir	0	7.7	0	20.6	2.6	3.9
Total						
SUCCESS	41.5	24.6	31.0	31.0	11.7	31.2
NOT SUCCESS	9.2	24.6	6.9	24.1	22.1	35.1
DIRECT	29.2	32.3	3.7	29.6	19.5	44.2
INDIRECT	21.5	16.9	37.0	29.6	14.3	44.2

*=Raw frequencies converted to percentages.

Boys in Groups. Boys use twice as many direct strategies when in mixed-sex and isolate conditions. They use equal numbers of direct and indirect bids when they are with other boys. In the isolate and same-sex groups, boys attempt to initiate more often than do girls; in the mixed groups, the bids attempts are relatively equal. In all of their attempts to initiate play, boys are successful roughly half of the time.

When specific strategies are examined, it is apparent that children use different strategies in different situations. For example, boys use commands more often in the isolate condition, and use indirect questions only in mixed groups. In the mixed-sex groups, boys select direct comments most frequently; this strategy is not chosen frequently in other groups. Multipliers with direct strategies are used by boys fairly often in the mixed-sex and isolate conditions. In the same-sex group, however, males use intensifiers with their indirect scene-setting comments, the most often chosen strategy, Intensifiers used alone were chosen only in the same-sex and isolate groups.

Table 3.4
Successfulness and Directness of Bids as a Function of Gender and Group Composition*

| | Group Condition | | | | | | |
| | Mixed Sex | | Same Sex | | Isolate | | |
	F	M	F	M	F	M	Means
Successful	82	50	82	56	35	47	59
Not Successful	18	50	18	44	65	53	41
Direct	58	66	9	50	58	67	51
Indirect	42	34	91	50	42	33	49

*Expressed as percentages

Girls in Groups. Girls use significantly fewer direct bids with other girls; in the other two groups girls express only a slight preference for direct bids. Girls' success in initiating bids also differs across conditions. In the mixed-sex and same-sex groups, girls' bids are much more often accepted, whereas in the isolate condition, the bids are more often rejected. Table 3.4 presents success and directness information for girls and boys separately.

Commands, offers, and indirect questions are used by girls more often in the mixed-sex condition, and rarely chosen in other groups. Girls rarely select direct questions as a strategy for initiating play. Multipliers accompanying direct verbal strategies are chosen fairly often in the mixed group, but rarely in the other groups. Interestingly, when with other girls, girls choose only indirect scene-setting comments.

Talk Time. The difference in number of bids across groups was not a reflection of the amount of talk children produced. On the contrary, in the isolate groups, which incurred the most bid attempts, children talked only 29% of the total play time (on average). In the same-sex groups, the boys talked 79% of the time, and the girls talked 28% of the play time. The mixed-sex groups yielded about 45% talk time.[1]

---

[1]The bulk of the talking in the boy's group was due to one dominant male, J, who is discussed later. He contributed 59% of the total talk to the boys' play session, and contributed 71% of the talk in the mixed group, and 39% of the talk as the isolate male with three females.

DISCUSSION

As Cherry (1978) noted, an adequate understanding of the complexity of children's communication behavior appears to require microlevel analyses which reflect how children actually communicate in everday settings. This study found significant differences in children's interaction style as a function of the child's gender and the gender composition of the playgroup. Marked individual differences were also found in children's level of interaction skills. The type of access bids made varied as a function of the group composition with significantly more bids being made in the isolate condition than in the other group conditions. Fewest bids were made in the same-sex groups. Because children prefer same-sex playmates, they may have been most comfortable with and knowledgeable about interacting in same-sex groups and thus felt little need to make deliberate play bids. In contrast, the isolate condition, being a fairly atypical play situation, may have required more bids as children attempted to interact in that setting. This interpretation seems supported by the significantly higher proportion of unsuccessful bids in the isolate condition—children may have perceived more need to deliberately structure their play, yet were more unsuccessful in doing this in the isolate condition.

As found in other studies, children demonstrated a preference for direct play bids. However, indirect play bids were significantly more successful (i.e., they secured uptake from the listener) than direct bids. Indirect bids appear to put less social pressure on both speaker and respondent because one can ignore an indirect bid, without directly rejecting the speaker. However, the most socially adept children appear to ignore rejection and try other bids—often over fairly long periods of time.

Gender differences in specific bids used indicate that girls most often used indirect strategies, especially those setting the scene, regardless of group condition. Boys also use indirect scene-setting bids, although in the isolate and mixed-sex condition, they also use a substantial number of direct commands and comments. Scene-setting bids appear to be important for initiating interpersonal interaction; it serves to establish a common ground for the children, a social process that Gottman (1983) suggested is very important in establishing friendships.

If direct and indirect bids are indicative of the explicitness of attempts to structure play, it would seem that gender roles are operative in the play of 5-year-olds. Girls seem to use only an indirect approach with other girls. This holds true with adult communication literature, which suggests women are much more cooperative in their talk and build on one another's utterances (Maltz & Borker, 1982), whereas men tend to compete for floor time.

The sex-typed play activities are also an interesting footnote to this study. The girls played house and prepared a meal in their same-sex group, whereas the boys acted out a variety of action-related scenes involving airplanes, cars, and farms. The mixed-sex groups seemed to break into same-sex pairs and engage in sex-typed play.

Several interesting patterns of interaction were also revealed in the data and are discussed in more detail. These patterns suggest a hierarchy of developing interactional skills, which reflects children's growing awareness of creating and responding to interactional opportunities.

Hierarchy of Social Interaction Skills

Prior studies (Bianchi & Bakeman, 1983; Dodge et al., 1986; Dorval & Eckerman, 1984; Strayer, 1980) note that children vary in their social interaction skills. The results of the present study confirm the presence of strong differences in interactional skills among same-aged children, all of whom were judged to be functioning adequately in their preschool environment.

Three different levels of interactional skill are suggested by the current study. The highest level of interactional skill, the *agenda setters,* characterized children who initiated and dominated play in their dyad or group. These children tended to dominate in terms of overall amount of talk; they both gave more and received more bids, tended to be more physically active, played over a greater area, and were very persistent (i.e., they repeated play bids despite initial negative responses).

Two children in this study (A, a female, and J, a male) were clearly agenda setters, as measured by their verbal and physical activity, and used communication as a major strategy in their play. Preschool teachers independently rated these two children as the most socially and cognitively developed of their age group and as well liked by their peers. This also tends to confirm other studies that have found relationships between children's dominance and affiliation ratings (Strayer, 1980).

The second level of interactional skill, the *responders,* were children who responded appropriately to play bids and could successfully maintain the interaction. However, they did not establish the play agenda or initiate change. Responders exhibited considerable communicative skill in their ability to recognize an opportunity for interaction and to respond appropriately.

The lowest level of interactional skill, the *isolates*, were children who either did not recognize an opportunity to interact with others, or were unable to respond appropriately. Children on this level frequently appeared to be engaged in parallel play—playing in close proximity to others, but oblivious to others' play or activity. If awareness of others' activities was demonstrated, they did not appear to know how to respond appropriately, or their responses were so weak (i.e., not persistent) that they were overlooked or ignored. These children appear to be similar to Garnica's omega children (1981). In her analysis of kindergarten children, Garnica found that lower-status children (omega children) are generally left alone in a group and ignored by their peers (and appear to be unnoticed by their teachers). Little conversation is directed toward omega children, and they rarely initiate contact with others. Comments directed toward others are often ineffectual, and Garnica suggested that this raises questions about their ability to interact effectively because they have little, if any, opportunity for interaction.

Three children in the present study could be classified as omega children; in over 60 minutes of recorded interaction, only two play bids were made, both by the same child, and both were unsuccessful. As Lubin and Forbes (1981) noted "it appears that whatever the age level, children matched with their peer group on the ability to control the messages sent and interpret the messages received are more likely to have a positive experience in that peer group. Adaptation to the peer culture may rest on this match. . . . In our formal discussion of children who were relatively low in psychological inference, we generally agreed that these children seemed to be somewhat 'out of touch' with the play-group action, often the butt of deceptive or sarcastic behavior . . ." (p. 22).

Rubin (1982) found that isolate children display less dramatic play; are viewed as less cognitively and socially competent by their teachers; and typically ask adults to intervene on their behalf. Such children are not often approached by other children and often engage in solitary play. When Rubin and Borwick (1984) paired isolate children with more sociable peers, isolate children produced significantly fewer requests. Putallaz and Gottman (1981) also noted the differing behavior of more and less popular children. One indication is the hovering behavior, with verbal bids, that newcomers and less popular children engage in. Such findings are complemented by the results of the current investigation.

Two examples will help illustrate these different skill levels. The first example reflects the communicative behavior characteristic of agenda setters. A's communication is active, persistent, and allows her to participate in the play of her three male peers.

Tape 627 Subjects: A female;
J, T, and M (males) (line 22048)

1. M: We got these things, right?
2. T: (unintelligible)
3. J: Look I can sit up there.
4. M: Hey, me too!
5. The top comes off.
> 6. A: I wuv ya. [picks up a play teddy bear, which has "I wuv
        you" written on it, and extends it to the three boys]
7. J: I know.
8. Look, we got these neat things to see, this opens.
> 9. A: I wuv ya. I wuv ya.
10. J: What does that mean? I wuv ya?
11. A: Wuv ya.
12. J: What does that mean? I don't know.
13. A: I luv you.
14. M: I . . . I . . . this is our cover. He needs a cover/
15. A: /I wuv you.
16. J: Get her out of here.
17. A: I wuv you.
18. M: I said get outta here.
19. A: I said I wuv ya. (unintelligible).

[*about 1 minute later*]
20. J: My own jacket. My own jacket.
21. This is a jacket?
>22. A: Uh, . . . it's a ballet suit.
23. J: Alright . . . a ballet suit.
24. J: Look, he's so big that its breaking!
25. Cradle break. My cradle broke.
26. A: I wuv you.
27. M: Look, he's got a camping bag.
28. J: You lost your feet.
29. M: I'm camping.
30. A: I lost my feet!
31. J: Hey, let me show ya something really neat. Take his feet off.
31. A: (laughs loudly)

32. J: Let me put another one on—I need another one. He's going to
         do something!
33. A: I know what I can do!
33. J: Let go! What's he gonna do?
35.   I know what he's going to do.

[continued play with A, J, and M]
[> indicates a bid]

This excerpt illustrates several important skills. First, A is very persistent, even though she is told explicitly (in lines 16 and 18) to go away.
Secondly, she is able to engage J's attention at a number of different
points (lines 6, 9, and 22) and, eventually, this leads to inclusion in the
boys' play. Since J and M are best friends, and A is a single female in the
group, such inclusion is quite remarkable in view of preschoolers' preferences for same-sex playmates. Less skilled children in this isolate condition made no bids for play or were ignored. Third, not only did A succeed
in entering the group's activity, but she was also instrumental in establishing the play agenda for a prolonged time.

In contrast to A, an agenda setter even under difficult circumstances, is
S's performance in a mixed-sex group. S is trying to get the attention of
his male playmate in the group, J.

Tape 87: S and J (Males); H and C (Females)
(line 126)

S: Hey, hey J! I'll fix it. I'll fix it. Right there. Right here. The truck.
J: Oooh! Look at my little airplane.
S: Hot racers. Two hot racers. [car sounds]
[S initially looks at J, but when J makes a return bid inviting S's response,
S continues on with his cars and fails to incorporate J's response. S then
moves away.]

Several similar instances occur in the videotape, when S makes a comment that is typically ignored. However, if the comment is picked up, S
does not continue the interaction. It appears as if S does not recognize an
opportunity to continue the interaction, nor does he realize that persistent efforts need to be made. S has only fleeting interactions with J, and
none with the two females. He seems unable to sustain collaborative play
with his peers, even in view of the "privileged" status he has by being the
only other male for J to interact with. Like Rubin's isolates, S appears to
be inept at responding and initiating interaction with peers. In contrast, J,

an agenda setter, interacts numerous times with the two females and is able to establish different play activities with them.

As Duck (1983) noted, for relationships to develop, communication must be appropriate to the situation and appropriately timed as well: Isolates appear unskilled at recognizing and responding to interactional opportunities. In the 2 hours of videotape data on children examined in the present study, only two play bids by isolates were made, and they appear to be accidental, rather than intentional, bids.

Responsiveness

This study confirms the interactive, collaborative nature of play. Participants cooperate with one another in order to initiate and sustain their activity. In adult/child conversation, the adult is often credited with keeping the interaction going. However, in peer/peer interaction, both partners need to keep the interaction going because both have limited cognitive and social experience. This can easily be seen in the two excerpts just cited.

Children who are playing with one another generally appear to follow the cooperative maxim. That is, they are following the conversational maxims of manner, quality, relevance, and clarity. Of these maxims, the most important appears to be manner, which reflects the timing of the communicative behavior, and relevance, which ties the communicative behaviors to the ongoing play activity. Violating either manner or relevance results in unsuccessful play bids or unsuccessful responses.

As opposed to the competent behaviors discussed earlier, Dodge, et al. (1986) found that entry behaviors rated as incompetent (and usually unsuccessful as well) included disruptive behaviors, nagging, incoherent behaviors, disagreeing with the host child without citing a rule or reason, and many changes in physical orientation.

Responsiveness on the part of children in this study also refelcts the importance of repeated messages: Children are persistent in giving their play bids. Generally, the more socially skilled the child, the more messages they send in an attempt to attract another's attendion and engate them in activity. Haslett (1983), in her study of children's arguments, found that older children used more active communicative strategies, whereas younger preschoolers tended to use more reactive strategies. Use of active strategies indicated children were attempting to influence the play around them, rather than just passively reacting to it. Corsaro (1979) found that repeated access attempts were more successful than just single attempts. Eisenberg and Garvey (1981) found that insistence was one of the main communicative strategies used among children in their arguments. Typically insistence refers to the repeated sending of messages conveying the same or similar points.

Monitoring

In order to initiate or respond effectively, children need to be aware of the play activity around them. This awareness depends upon accurate monitoring of the surrounding activity. Generally, the more socially skilled the child, the more monitoring the child does. The most interesting evidence of monitoring appears in the behaviors of both A and J, the most socially skilled children. Both A and J were very active during their play and moved around more than their peers. A, a female agenda setter, was typically located in a position which allowed her to visually scan the entire play area. Strayer (1980) found that girls gaze more and gaze more at peers than do males. Both made responses to the play of children around them, even though they were not directly involved in the play themselves. For example, while playing with another child, J followed the conversation of two girls engaged in playing with dolls and he fixed a broken wheel on a small doll carriage for them. He immediately returned to his own activity of playing with racers afterward.

The continuous and changing nature of play also requires participants to monitor play activity so that relevant responses can be made at appropriate times. For the least socially skilled children, the *isolates*, problems appear to occur with their general responsiveness: Children sometimes failed to properly identify a bid to play; at other times, they failed to respond appropriately; or failed to time their responses or bids appropriately. Being responsive appears to be a very complex task, requiring children to make accurate judgements concerning their behaviors and the right moment to respond.

Directness of Bids

Haslett (1983) found that preschoolers relied on very direct communicative strategies—commands, demands, and denials. Other studies, like those of Lubin and Forbes, have also found a general preference for using direct communicative strategies.

Although there is a preference for direct bids, even direct bids must be negotiated between speakers and listeners so that all partners agree on the play activity. As can be seen in the following example, negotiations often are prolonged and difficult. This excerpt is taken from a 10-minute segment in which most of the girls' time is taken up by negotiating what should be done and who should do it.

Tape 627: Four females, A. H. J and C
(line 1500)

1. A: Here.
2. H: Or pretend this is the table [*gestures to the wall*]
3. J: No, I didn't want this.
4. J: Or pretend this is a table!!!

[*20 seconds*]
  5. A: No [*to H*]
  6. J: Put the plate right here and—chomp, chomp.

[*30 seconds*]
  7. A: No, we're—we're eating right here.

[*20 seconds*]
  8. H: I'm making dinner.
  9. A: We're eating right here. [*walks away*]
  10. H: Mom, I made some stew. Let me make it cook.

[*5 minutes*]
  11. H: Mom, I cooked dinner. Let me cook dinner.
  12. J: What is that? Stew?
  14. A: Nuh uh [*whining tone*]
  15. H: What do you want it to be?
  16. J: Chicken noodle soup.

Although the three girls are all playing around a play stove, there is clearly no agreement on who is doing what. Finally, in line 15, H asks specifically what is needed in order to come to some agreement about the play context. Subsequent discussion continues to elaborate the cooking theme, but now the girls are complementing and cooperating with one another in the elaboration of their play. This activity dominates the play for that period, although more than half their time was consumed in their negotiations. Considerable communicative skill and flexibility was needed to successfully set up an agreed-upon play activity.

Adapting to Rejected Bids

From this evidence, it does not appear that maintaining face is something that 5-years-olds do frequently or with much skill. They are often rejected, yet this does not deter the more communicatively competent children. They are likely to try other ways of integrating themselves into ongoing play, or to try other ways of initiating play activity. In connecting competence, popularity, and success, Putallaz and Gottman (1981) found that in groups of popular and unpopular children, popular children's bids were rejected 30% of the time. Clearly, however, the less communicatively skilled children take their rejections in a different way. In the episodes analyzed here, the children with the poorest skills tend not to try other attempts if their bids are rejected by others. It could be that they simply do not know alternative strategies to try, and so they do not participate in the interactive arena, as suggested by Rubin (1982).

An example of a less skilled girl involves P, who tries to get involved in interaction by asking direct questions of her playmates. This in itself does not seem inappropriate, but her questions are either ignored, or answered with an abrupt statement and the play moves on to something else. As the following excerpt shows, P seems unable to integrate herself into the ongoing activities of the others. She often reverts to individual and isolated play.

Tape 622; J (male); A, E, P (Females)
(line 24444)

P: You want to play this?
E: What?
P: You want to play this?

[*10 seconds*]
E: No, I'm playing this.

Communicative Skill

Like Strayer's study, this study found that the most dominant children (e.g., A and J) were the most active; they made more successful bids than their peers and, surprisingly, had more unsuccessful bids. The important point seems to be their generally high level of communicative activity; they monitor ongoing activity, attempt to establish a play activity, and generally persist in those bids until finally successful. Agenda setters, in brief, appear to *create* opportunities for interaction to a significantly greater degree than do their peers. And most of the strategies they use to establish play are communicative in nature: Talk is an important tool in establishing social relationships with others, as the following excerpt shows. According to our ranking, J is an agenda setter, M is a responder, and T is an isolate.

Tape 624; Males, J, M, T, and O
(line 31668)

1. M: That's our little cars
2. J: Aw let him have these two since . . .
3.   you can have these. See, he's got a hole
4.   and this pushes him.
5. M: [7 seconds] Hey!
6. J: Here, T.
7.   We got a lot of purple and he wants some . . .
8.   and you can have him.
9. M: Yeah, cause that's the baby . . .
10.   **that's the baby/**
11. J: /you don't have to if you don't want
10.   . . . If you don't want to have the baby.

[*continued play with J, M, and O*]

This exchange makes several points. First, it shows how sensitive J is to the lesser skills of his playmate. T watches what is going on, but rarely contributes. In the two groups where T was observed in this study, he spoke 1% or less of the total talk time. By standing up for T, J gives him the opportunity to defend himself, but T does not. J's statement could be seen as serving two functions, then: He keeps the boys from arguing and shows T how he could have responded on his own behalf.

CONCLUSIONS AND IMPLICATIONS

This research demonstrates that children use different communicative strategies in their bids for play with other children. Although this analysis is based on a small sample, these initiation strategies did vary according to the group's composition, children's gender, and ther communicative skill. Children's skill levels appear to vary from setting agendas, in which children create opportunities for play, to isolates, who appear unable to recognize and respond to play opportunities. Playing with peers provides important interactional opportunities for children: Through play, they develop relationships with one another and much of their play appears to be structured verbally.

Play thus appears to be an opportunity to experiment with developing and maintaining relationships: Children's playing with one another requires many of the same skills adults need in order to develop interpersonal relationships with others. Both situations require participants to create opportunities for getting to know one another, whether as playmates or as potential friends. Such opportunities must be recognized and responded to, and one's response must be coordinated with another.

Undoubtedly, many of the communicative skills learned in early childhood have direct implications for adult communication. If children are not able to gain access to others, they miss the give-and-take of cooperation and conflict with others and the learning from others. Rubin (1982) concluded that the frequency of certain types of nonsocial play (like solitary-dramatic play) is negatively correlated with measures of social and social cognitive competence. He also found, similar to our findings, that isolate children receive fewer social overtures than their peers. In a further study, Rubin and Borwick (1984) found a direct link between sociability, competence, and communication. As they observed:

> With increasing sociability, the amount of socially directed speech increased, the success rates of requests increased, and the "costliness" of the directives produced increased. In short, with increased sociability, communicative overtures that reflected assertiveness and self-assurance likewise increased.

Although their data, like ours, is limited by small sample size, the importance of good communication skills for adequate social development nevertheless seems clear.

Although there has been increasing attention paid to social skills training, much of this has been focused on adults. Earlier intervention, especially with young children, in improving their communicative skills (and thus facilitating their general social development) would appear to be very useful. The implications for life-span development stemming from such intervention programs are substantial. New social skills and experiences may occur as a result of improving a child's communication abilities, and some negative consequences (e.g., relative isolation, social rejection from peers, and benevolent neglect by adults) might be avoided.

Finally, the range and diversity of communicative skills—from early childhood to late adolescence—again reminds us that development does not occur in a simple, linear fashion. Each developmental phase may well require different sets of communicative skills, applied in diverse contexts; and mature, old skills may become reconstructed into new skills. The understanding of life-span communicative development may depend, in part, on more fully understanding the richness and complexity of communication at different stages of life.

REFERENCES

Bianchi, B., & Bakeman, R. (1983). Patterns of sex typing in an open school. In M. Liss (Ed.), *Social and cognitive skills* (pp. 219–232). New York: Academic Press.

Connolly, J. Doyle, A., & Ceschin, F. (1983). Forms and functions of social fantasy play in preschoolers. In M. Liss (Ed.), *Social and cognitive play* (pp. 71–90). New York: Academic Press.

Corsaro, W. A. (1979) 'We're friends, right?': Children's use of access rituals in a nursery school. *Language in Society, 8,* 315–336.

Corsaro, W. A. (1981). Friendship in the nursery school: Social organization in a peer environment. In S. Asher & J. Gottman (Eds.), *The development of children's friendships* . Cambridge, MA: Cambridge University Press.

DiPietro, J. (1981). Rough and tumbel play: A function of gender. *Developmental Psychology, 17,* 50–58.

Dodge, K. A., Pettit, G. S., McClaskey, C. L., & Brown, M. MN. (1986). Social competence in children. *Monographs of the Society for Research in Child Development, 49*(2, Serial No. 206).

Dorval, B., & Eckerman, C. O. (1984). Developmental trends in the quality of conversation achived by small groups of acquainted peers. *Mongraphs of the Society for Research in Child Development, 49* (2, Serial No. 206).

Duck, S. (1983). *Friends for life.* Brighton, Sussex: The Harvester Press.

Eakins, B., & Eakins, G. (1978). *Sex differences in human communication.* Boston: Houghton Mifflin.

Eisenberg, N. (1983). Sex-typed toy preferences: What do they signify? In M. Liss (Ed.), *Social and cognitive skills'.* New York: Academic Press.

Easenberg, A. & Garvey, C. (1981). Children's use of verbal strategies in resolving conflict. *Discourse Processes, 4,* 149–170.

Forbes, D., & Lubin, D. (1981). *The impact of interpretive procedures on peer interaction.* Paper presented at the International Conference on Culture and Communication, Philadelphia, PA.

Forbes, D., & Lubin, D. (with M. Schmidt & P. Van der Laan). Verbal social reasoning and observed persuasion strategies in children's peer interactions. Unpublished paper, Peer Interaction Project, Harvard Graduate School of Education.

Garnica, O. (1981). Social dominance and conversational interation—the Omega child in the classroom. In J. Green & C. wallat (Eds.), *Ethnography and language in educational settings.* Norwood, N.J: Ablex.

Garvey, C. (1977). Play with language and speech. In s. Ervin-Tripp & E. Mitchell-Kernan (Eds.), *Child discourse.* New York: Academic Press.

Garvey, C., & Hogan, R. (1973). Social speech and social interaction: Egocentrism revisited. *Child Development, 44,* 562–568.

Gellert, E. (1962). The effect of changes in group composition on the dominant behavior of young children. *British Journal of Social and Clinical Psychology, 1,* 168–81.

Gottman, J. M. (1983). *How children become friends. SRCD Monograph, 48,* 3.

Gottman, J., & Parkhurst, J. (1980). A developmental theory of friendship and acquaintanceship processes. In A. Collins (Ed.), *Minnesota Symposium on Child Development,* Volume 13. Hillsdale, NJ: Lawrence Erlbaum Associates.

Haslett, B. (1983). Preschoolers' communicative strategies in gaining compliance from peers: A developmental study. *Quarterly Journal of Speech, 69,* 84–99.

Hinde, R. A., Easton, D. F., Meller, R. W., & Tamplin, A. M. (1982). Temperamental characteristics of 3–4-year-olds and mother–child interaction. *Temperamental Differ-*

ences in infants and young children. CIBA Foundation Symposium No. 89, 66–80. London: Pitman.

La Gaipa. J. (1981). Children's friendships. In S. Duck & R. Gilmour (Eds.), *Personal relationships,* Vol. 2. New York: Academic Press.

Laosa, L. M., & Brophy, J. (1972). Effects of sex and birth order on sex-role development and intelligence among kindergarten children. *Developmental Psychology, 6,* 409–415.

Liss, M. (1983). *Social and cognitive skills: Sex roles and children's play.* New York: Academic Press.

Lubin, D., & Forbes, D. (1981). *Understanding sequential aspects of children's social behavior: Conceptual issues in the development of coding schemes.* Paper presented at the Biennial Meeting of the Society for Research in Child Development, Boston.

Maccoby, E., & Jacklin, C. (1974). *The psychology of sex differences.* Stanford: Stanford University Press.

Maltz, D., & Borker, R. (1982). A cultural approach to male–female miscommunication. In J. Gumperz (Ed.), *Language and social identity.* Cambridge: Cambridge University Press.

McGrew, W. C. (1972). The maintenance of verbal exchanges between young children. *Child Development, 43,* 930–938.

Putallaz, M., & Gottman, J. M. (1981). Social skills and group acceptance. In S. Asher & J. Gottman (Eds.), *The development of children's friendships.* Cambridge, MA: Cambridge University Press.

Reis, H. T., & Wright, S. (1982). Knowledge of sex-role stereotypes in children aged 3 to 5. *Sex Roles,* No. 10, 1049–1056.

Rubin, K. (1982). Social and social-cognitive developmental characteristics of young isolate, normal and sociable children. In K. Rubin & H. Ross (Eds.), *Per relationships and social skills in childhood.* New York: Springer-Verlag.

Rubin, K., & Borwick, D. (1984). Communicative skills and sociability. In H. Sypher & J. Applegate (Eds.), *Communication by children and adults* (pp. 152–170). Beverly Hills: Sage.

Shugar, G. (1979). Per face-to-face interactions at ages three to five. *International Journal of Psycholinguistic Research, 5,* 17–38.

Simpson, A. E., & Stevenson-Hinde, J. (1985). Temperamental characteristics of three-to four-year-old boys and girls and child–family interactions. *Journal of Child Psychology, and Psychiatry, 26,* 43–53.

Smith, P. (1985). *Language, the sexes and society.* Oxford: Blackwell.

Smithers, A., & Smithers, A. G. (1984). An exploratory study of sex role differentiation among young children. *Educational Review, 36,* 87–98.

Strayer, F. (1980). Social ecology of the preschool peer group. In A. Collins (Ed.), *Development of cognition, affect and social relations.* Minnesota Symposia on Child Psychology, Vol. 13. Hillsdale, NJ: Lawrence Erlbaum Associates.

Terlecka, T. (1978). *Descriptive analysis of dyadic interaction of preschool children and speech role in the process.* Unpublished master's thesis, Polish Institute of Psychology, University of Warsaw.

Woods, B., & Gardner, R. (1980). How children get their way: A naturalistic study of directives. *Communication Education, 29,* 264–272.

4 Children's Social Networks and the Development of Communicative Competence

Cynthia Stohl
Purdue University

Communicative competence entails the acquisition of knowledge about social processes, knowledge that can be only attained through diverse, supportive social interactions. From a finite set of experiences within their social networks, children come to recognize and perform acceptable and unacceptable communicative behaviors.

The dominant traditions of developmental research propose an impressive patchwork of processes that affect the development of communicative competence, but all fail to consider adequately the full impact of the complex, interwoven fabric of children's social affiliations on the development of communicative skills. Although social structure has long been recognized as an important component in children's development (Hartup, 1979), there is an absence of research and information concerning the interactive structure of children's environments.

The purpose of this study is to examine the social matrix within which communicative development takes place and examine the relationship between attributes of children's social networks and the development of perceived communicative competence. Although most network research has been done with adult populations (e.g., Rogers & Kincaid, 1981) this chapter demonstrates the benefits of utilizing a social network perspective for viewing development across the life span (see also Bryant, 1985; Cochran & Brassard, 1979; Tietjen, 1982).

A child's social network consists of all people in and outside the household who regularly interact with the child. The formal and substantive features of social networks are believed to impact directly upon specific processes and abilities that are constituents and/or determinants of children's communicative competence. For the purposes of this study communicative competence is conceptualized as the ability to attain relevant interactive goals in specified social contexts using socially appropriate means and ways of speaking which result in positive outcomes with significant others.

The chapter is in five parts. First, a brief explication of the relationship between social networks and communicative competence is presented. Second, relevant network attributes are discussed and their potential relationship with competence is hypothesized. Third, the procedures of the study are explicated and fourth, the results are presented. The final section deals with the implications of the study.

SOCIAL NETWORKS AND THE DEVELOPMENT OF COMMUNICATIVE COMPETENCE

Five relatively distinct traditions have informed most empirical work focused on the development of communicative competence: Chomskian linguistics, social learning theory, cognitive/developmental theory, sociolinguistics, and pragmatics. A review of these dominant traditions suggests several determinants of increasing communicative ability in children. These include: observing others (e.g., Chomsky, 1965; Dickson, 1981), imitating others (Bandura & Walters, 1963), taking the role of the other (Flavell, 1977; Piaget, 1954) problem solving (Ammon, 1981), ordering and classifying relevant information (Wang, Rose, & Maxwell, 1973) and abstracting regularities from social interactions, including the formulation of a perspective about what is expected and appropriate (Hymes, 1971; Shantz, 1981).

In general, social networks influence these determinants by providing motivational incentives, opportunities for social interaction, and cognitive and social stimulation (Cochran & Brassard, 1979). Other people within children's networks play a critical role in the development of communication skills by providing role models (Bandura & Walters, 1963) and directly teaching and reinforcing proper communicative behavior (Ammon, 1981; Shantz, 1981). Network members may provide the impetus for social perspective taking (Boissevaine, 1974) and give feedback (Wang et al., 1973).

Network attributes influence the quality and quantity of these behaviors by mediating the degree to which the network provides diverse role models (Milroy & Margraine, 1980) and emotional support (Cochran & Brassard, 1979). The structural configuration of network members may comprise a norm-enforcing mechanism (Bott, 1957). Interconnected networks are more likely to generate consistent messages regarding the expectations, evaluations, and world view of the community (Hirsch, 1979). In brief, there are many attributes of social networks that may affect the content and form of children's social experience. The following section identifies the attributes that are expected to exert the greatest developmental influence.

RELEVANT ATTRIBUTES
OF SOCIAL NETWORKS

Personal networks vary along three dimensions: structural, interactional, and spatio/temporal. The structural dimension transcends specific relationships and applies directly to the network itself. The interactional dimension incorporates the characteristics of each dyadic relationship including the types of activities and sentiments that are carried out within each relationship. The spatio/temporal dimension includes those properties of the network that frame and regulate social experiences.

Seven salient network attributes associated with these three dimensions are expected to be relevant for the study of children's development. Although most network literature deals exclusively with adults, it is believed that the network attributes that have been identified as important for adults when "exchanging information in order to reduce their uncertainty; when they are in a new job or organization; when they are learning about a new idea" (Rogers & Kincaid, 1981, p. 89) are also salient for children in their attempts to understand and be understood in the social world.

Structural Dimension

The structural dimension includes size, degree of interconnectedness, and diversity within the network. These attributes relate to the theoretical possibility of persons interacting with one another.

Size

Although Cochran and Brassard (1979) characterized size as little more than a starting point for an analysis of social network effects, results suggest it is an extremely important network attribute. Directly, size is of importance in that it determines the number of possibilities a child has for interaction. Size affects the availability of role models and all supportive functions the network can provide. Adults with larger networks report more positive perceptions of themselves (Weiss, Henderson, Campbell, & Cochran, 1980) and are more satisfied (Roberts & O'Reilly, 1978). Indirectly, size is a limiting factor for a network's diversity and is inversely related to the degree of interconnectedness.

The greater the number of people within a network the more likelihood there is to be cognitive and social stimulation. In the only study linking network size to children's ability, Feiring and Lewis (1981) found size was positively related to children's IQ scores. Thus, size is expected to be positively related to the perceived levels of children's communicative competence (H1).

Interconnectedness

Interconnectedness or density is the degree to which members of the network communicate with one another independent of a context involving the child. It is an index of the potential communication between members of the network in which the child is not present (Boissevaine, 1974). The "degree of interconnectedness" is the average number of relations each person in the network has with others in the network.

There is general consensus that highly interconnected networks put more normative pressure on individuals than networks with low interconnectedness (Bott, 1957; Milroy and Margraine, 1980). In studies across the life span, there is evidence to suggest that the greater the degree of interconnectedness within the network, the greater pressure there is for a person to adopt the norms and values (including linguistic and nonverbal behavioral norms) of the local group.

The perspective taken in this study views competency as the child's performance of language in socially appropriate ways, that is, perceived according to norms of the group. In a highly interconnected network we can expect that (a) the norms and expectations of the group are made very apparent; (b) there are consistent models of behavior; (c) rewards are given for "appropriate" communicative behavior; and (d) there is consistency in both positive and negative reinforcements. Thus, to the degree that the interconnected group has norms that are shared by the evaluating group, network interconnectedness and perceived communicative competence should be positively related.

However, the compelling developmental arguments of sociolinguist Basil Bernstein raises questions about such an hypothesis. Bernstein (1971) argued that when the intent of another person can be taken for granted and communication is carried out against a backdrop of common assumptions and interests (as there are in highly interconnected networks) there is high predictability, alternatives are reduced, and a lexicon is drawn from a narrow range. Significantly there is less need to raise meanings to the level of explicitness or elaboration. Within these networks, it is likely that individuals will not provide rich linguistic models for the child, nor will they provide functional feedback when a child does not explicitly state what he or she wants.

Theoretically, these conditions should have serious developmental consequences. It is essential that children learn that meanings are not always obvious to the listener (Flavell, 1968; Piaget, 1954; Shantz, 1981). Second, children must learn there is a need to adapt speech to the listener's frame of reference (Flavell, 1968) and apply this knowledge to their own communication. Researchers suggest that children benefit by being given explicit information about the inadequacies of their messages (Ammon, 1981) and observing the negative functional effect of poor referential skills (Bruner, 1978). Thus, interconnectedness is expected to be negatively related to communicative competence (H2).

Diversity

The diversity or range (Burt, 1980) of a social network is measured by the amount of variability on such characteristics as age, sex, educational level, and occupational status. Although few network researchers have investigated the direct influence of diversity on individuals' behavior, developmentalists strongly argue for the importance of a diverse environment. Allen and Brown (1976) posited that the pragmatic implications of their comprehensive research review on the nature of communicative competence include:

> Children should be exposed to a variety of communication opportunities—opportunities for interaction with a wide variety of participants, opportunities for talking about topics of interest, opportunities for engaging in a wide range of communication acts, and opportunities for communication in diverse environments. (p. 254)

Bronfenbrenner (1979) strongly contended that diversity is the key to positive developmental outcomes. He argued that involvement in joint activity in a range of structurally different settings, in varying subcultural contexts, requires the individual to adapt to a variety of people, tasks, and situations, thus "increasing the scope and flexibility of his cognitive competence and social skills" (p. 76).

Certain types of network homogeneity have been posited to affect adversely communicative development. Bates (1975) found that children who receive most of their linguistic input from peers are at a relative disadvantage when compared with children who learn primarily from adults. Burleson (1985) suggested that frequent interaction with children, per se, is not the causal factor in retardation of communicative development. Rather, he posited that children who interact frequently with peers spend less time interacting with adults; it is lack of interaction with adults that slows children's communicative development. Although both peer and adult interactions are significant for children's development, adapted speech for younger children by other children does not facilitate language in the same way adult linguistic adaptations do (Berko-Gleason & Weintraub, 1978). Overall, diverse environments provide the impetus for social perspective taking. The existence of different viewpoints and the need to adapt communicative behavior (Flavell, 1977) is emphasized. Furthermore, the greater likelihood of misunderstanding encourages the child to adapt his or her speech to the listener's characteristics (Robinson, 1981). Role-taking skills develop more rapidly with an increased amount and breadth of experience (Rubin, 1982) possibly because diverse systems provide greater variety of role models from which to expand the repertoire of communication strategies. Thus, diversity is expected to be positively related to communicative competence (H3).

Interactional Dimension

The interactional attributes—multiplexity and satisfaction—function to regulate the overall strength and influence of each relationship in the network.

Multiplexity

Multiplexity has been viewed in two ways: (a) it refers to the number of contents, activities, and/or functions in the relationship (Fischer, 1977) and (b) as the number of role relationships (kin, neighbor, coworker) any two people have with each other (Mitchell & Trickett, 1980). In this study role multiplexity encompasses five possible role relationships and content multiplexity is derived from 10 domains of activities that adults may share with children.

Researchers investigating adults' social networks find both types of multiplex relationships are more enduring, intense, supportive, and intimate (Craven & Wellman, 1973; Hirsch, 1979; Mitchell, 1974). Researchers suggest that the variation in the number and kinds of activities individuals share may explain the relative amount of influence of each network member. Individuals with multiplex relationships are expected to care more for the child, have a greater investment in the child's well being, and thereby enhance the developmental potential of the interactions (Cochran & Brassard, 1979).

Adults involved in intense relationships with children will pick up, interpret, comment upon, extend, and repeat what the child has said (Dore, 1977). The more involved the adults are with the child the more likely they will suspend interpretation procedures and deal overtly with the vagueness and ambiguity in the child's message, although these processes take more time (Corsaro, 1977). Because these types of behaviors are associated with increasing communication abilities, multiplexity is expected to be positively related to levels of perceived communicative competence (H4).

Satisfaction

Satisfaction refers to the degree to which an individual is satisfied with the dyadic relationships that make up the network. Although satisfaction has not been empirically linked to network effects, attraction research suggests that an individual's behavior is modified by the degree of attraction that is felt for the other. People will spend more time with, pay closer attention to, and be more responsive (Bates, 1976; Levinger, 1974) to people to whom they are attracted.

Recent works on "child effects" suggest that these behaviors on the part of the child will influence adults' behaviors which in turn will influence children's behaviors. High levels of positivity to adults has been associated with use of more reasoning about consequences (Keller & Bell, 1979) shorter, simpler sentences (Bohannon & Marquis, 1977), higher levels of nonverbal positivity (Bates, 1976), and greater disclosures (Teyber, Messe, & Stollack, 1977). The degree of satisfaction, therefore, is expected to be positively related to the occurrence of behaviors that enhance the developmental potential of interaction (H5).

Spatio/temporal Dimension

The spatio/temporal attributes—frequency and continuity function as constraints on the possible effects of other network attributes.

Frequency of Contact

Frequency of interaction refers to how often network members interact with the child. Studies with adult populations suggest that infrequent social interaction and high isolation are associated with lower satisfaction, lower performance, and less motivation (Roberts & O'Reilly, 1978). Studies with children suggest that frequent opportunity to interact is associated with more rapid development in role-taking skills

(Nahir & Yussen, 1977; West, 1974) and contact with friends and nonrelated adults is positively related to the cognitive development of young children (Feiring & Lewis, 1981). Furthermore, the greater the amount of interaction, the more likely it is that the child will be able to experiment with, observe, and develop socially appropriate interaction strategies, role-taking abilities, role behaviors, and so on. Thus, frequency of interaction is expected to be positively related to levels of perceived competence (H6).

Continuity

The continuity of the network refers to the average length of time network members have known the child. Although no direct relationship between continuity and competence is expected, relationships that have existed over a long period of time have increased likelihood to be multiplex (Wellman, 1979), more stable (Hirsch, 1979), more intense (Perrucci & Targ, 1982), and more predictable (Berger & Calabrese, 1975). Therefore, continuity within networks will be examined but no direct effect on competence is posited.

The following section describes the study designed to explore the relationship between these network attributes and the development of communicative competence.

THE STUDY

Subjects

A total of 55 children and their mothers took part in the study. The 32 males and 23 females had a mean age of 52.1 months (SD = 7.5 months). All children attended locally funded day-care centers and were of lower socioeconomic status. Eleven day-care center teachers participated in the competence assessment of the children.

General Procedures

After obtaining the permission of the day-care centers' director, parents of all children in two centers were contacted by letter informing them of the study and asking permission for the child to participate. Once permission was received, both parts of the research project were undertaken simultaneously. Each child received competence evaluations from three day-care teachers and parent interviews were conducted to collect the social network data.

Assessment of Competence

The assessment of children's communicative competence was based upon teachers' perceptions of children's performance of four functional competencies: controlling, heuristic, informative, and expressive, as well as sociolinguistic and interactive competencies. A 35-item scale was developed specifically for this study (Stohl, 1983). Teachers were asked to rate on a 7-point Likert-type scale how often a child communicated in a specific manner. The higher the rating the more often a child was perceived to communicate in the specified way. After a 2-hour introduction to the way in which the scale should be used, each teacher was given competence measures for 27 randomly assigned children. To insure uniformity of interpretation teachers were told to use the day-care center as the social environment in which to evaluate the children's communicative behavior.

The decision to use day-care center teachers as evaluators of the children's competence rather than employing ethnographic methods (e.g., Watson-Gegeo & Boggs, 1979), hypothetical scenarios (Asher & Hymel, 1981), social judgment tasks (Edlesky, 1977), listener-adapted tasks (Delia, Kline, & Burleson, 1979), or persuasive, comforting or referential tasks (e.g., Burleson, 1985) is detailed in Stohl (1983). In brief, the other methods were not chosen because they did not best serve the research interest. The research question does not focus upon any particular skill or type of response under a defined set of conditions and so listener-adapted communication, social judgment, or persuasive strategy tasks were inappropriate. The conceptualization of competence as a multidimensional construct that includes the ability to perform many communicative functions and serves many social purposes, calls for a global assessment, and no suitable measure of any sort is available. Furthermore, the successful utilization of scales in exploratory research conducted for similar purposes (Rodnick & Wood, 1973; Slobin, 1967) provided evidence that the procedure can be useful and acceptable although not ideal.

Day-care center teachers were chosen as the informants for many reasons. First, next to the parents, teachers have the largest responsibility for, spend the most time with, and evaluate children more than any other group. Second, day-care center teachers are trained to work with children of this young age; hence, they have a baseline of acceptable and appropriate behavior. Day-care teachers spend at least 35 hours a week with the children, and thus, are well-situated to make observations and assessments of competence over time and in a variety of contexts. Third, day-care teachers' evaluations are believed to have significant and long-term consequences for the children. Finally, because there are many teachers who deal regularly with the same children, multiple assessments are available for the same children. These multiple ratings provide a more stable and representative measure of the children's ability.

The Measurement of Children's Social Networks

A social network inventory was developed specifically for this study. On the inventory a social network is described as: . . . all people in and outside the household who interact regularly in activities of some sort with the child.

Four basic techniques have been used for collecting network data: self-report, other report, direct observation, and unobtrusive observation. Self-report methods can be based on individual recall of links, completion of a network roster, in which all potential links are identified apriori by the researcher (Albrecht, 1984), or the completion of a communication log or diary (Burt & Minor, 1983). Direct observation of communication activity includes observations by an independent observer over a prolonged period of time (Brass, 1981). Other report measures include a significant other reporting the links of the focal individual and unobtrusive methods include utilizing archival data such as datebooks, newspaper articles, and so forth (Burt & Minor, 1983). In this study network data was collected from the mother of the child. The rationale for this decision is presented following.

First, the young age of the children precludes the use of any self-report measures of network activity. Second, because there was an interest in all regular monthly contacts, an observation period of 2 months, 24 hours a day would be needed to get a minimally representative sample of the children's communication activity. Clearly the amount of time and resources needed to conduct this sort of investigation, as well as the overwhelming invasion of privacy such an endeavor mandates, made this choice unrealistic. Third, archival data was not available for these children. They are too young to keep diaries, and there was no formal method of record keeping used by any agency that dealt with communication contacts. Thus, the choice was made to use parent reports of children's communication links. Mothers were the chosen parent because of the high percentage of children who lived in single-parent (mother) homes.

Furthermore, although Bernard and Killworth (1977) and Bernard, Killworth & Sailer (1982) cast grave doubt on an individual's ability to recall specific communication incidents, the type of informational recall required in this study is not of the same sort. Mothers are not expected to remember any specific interactions but rather are asked simply to describe who repeatedly interacts with their children. The relatively high control parents have of very young children's social life minimizes the possibility that the children may have communication links of which parents are unaware. Individual network interactions and interpretive or evaluative judgments that require attributions that may be highly unreliable were not required in the collection of data. Nonetheless, it must be recognized that parents may be an unreliable data source. Parents own levels of competence may influence the composition and structure of the network that is reported. Every attempt was made to elicit the same degree of quality of information from each parent. The task required a minimal level of competence. The criteria for network membership were clearly articulated, and two samples of the social-network inventory were prepared and presented to the mother as examples.

RESULTS

Communicative Competence Scale

The communicative competence scale was highly reliable (Chronbach's alpha = .94) (Chronbach, 1951) and the correlation among teachers' individual standardized ratings ranged from .65 through .97 (X = .89, SD = .93). Principal components factor analysis with oblique rotation identified two factors on which teacher's perceive children's communicative abilities: effectiveness and politeness. Both factors were strongly associated with global assessments of competence (r = .72, r = .89). The correlation between the two factors was .59. The items on each factor were summed and the summations were averaged across teachers to get a composite score for the factor. A global assessment score was calculated by summing and averaging the scores for the two overall items. Further details regarding the development of the scale, its psychometric properties and item analysis can be found in Stohl (1983).

The results indicate that girls were perceived as significantly more effective (F = 3.92, p < .05, female X = 4.6, male X = -3.7), more polite (F = 11.96, p < .001, female X = 3.3, male X = -1.5), and had significantly higher global assessment scores than boys (F = 5.45, p < .02, female X = .09, male X = -.05). Older children were also perceived as significantly more competent on all three measures: general effectiveness (F = 9.63, p < .001, X = 9.1, 4.0, -11.2), politeness (F = 3.92, p < .05, X = 1.5, 1.1, -2.2), and global assessment (F = 7.57, p < .001, X = .9, .5, -1.1). Post hoc Neumann Keuls tests found 4- and 5-year-olds to be significantly more competent than 3-year-olds on all perceived competence scores. Furthermore, 5-year-olds were significantly more competent in perceived effectiveness and global assessment than were 4-year-olds.

Social Network Attributes

A total of 965 network links, including 90 natural parents, 25 step parents, 10 parental intimates, 55 siblings, 83 aunts, 53 uncles, 94 cousins, 125 grandparents, 185 friends of the family, 57 neighbors, 18 teachers, 19 babysitters, 145 friends, 5 doctors and nurses, and 1 minister were identified as significant people within 55 children's networks.

There is great diversity among the social networks. For example, some children had only one relative in their network whereas others had as many as 23. The average age of network members varied from 12 to 43 years. Some children saw network members on an average of 5 times per week, some as little as 1.7 times per week. These large variations suggest that children grow up in structurally and substantively different social environments.

Network attributes are not independent. Table 4.1 presents the Pearson correlation coefficients for each network attribute, sex, age, and competence score.

Not surprisingly, age was positively related to the mean length of network relationships ($r = .34$) and length of time in the day-care center ($r = .46$). Three interactional attributes were positively related to children's age: the number of members who participate in educational activities ($r = .37$), go on special outings ($r = .35$), and the degree of content multiplexity ($r = .34$).

Except for musical activities ($r = .30$), sex was not related to network attributes. However, this may have been a function of the children's age. As they develop and have more control over their own social environments significant sex differences in network attributes may emerge.

Relationship Between Social Network
Attributes and Communicative Competence:
Tests of Hypotheses

Two regression equations were developed for each competence measure. A hierarchical regression model was designed so that the explained variance could be decomposed into orthogonal components. The hierarchical procedure requires the stepwise entry of predictor variables according to their logical or causal priority. Age and sex are significant predictors of communication abilities. Thus, in the first equation sex and age were entered on the first step and then all network attributes including the specific diversity and activity domains were entered. In this manner the contribution of network attributes to explained variance could be assessed independent of sex or age effects.

Because size had such a high correlation with other variables and can be viewed as causally prior to the other environmental factors within the network, a second regression equation was developed. In this equation, age and sex were entered first, then size of the network and then all other attributes. Table 4.2 presents the results of the regression analyses. For all three competence evaluations a large proportion of variance is explained. Sex, age, and network attributes accounted for 78% of the variance in global assessment of competence ($F[19,35] = 6.69$, $p < .001$), 69% in perceived effectiveness ($F[19,35] = 4.18$, $p < .001$) and 58% for politeness ($F[19.35] = 2.08$, $p < .029$).

Sex explained 19% of the variance for perceived effectiveness and 9% for global assessment. A large proportion of the variance (17%) was explained by sex for the politeness score. Age explained 18% more variance for general effectiveness, 7% for politeness, and 22% for global assessment. Thus, between 24% and 31% of the variance in the sample was explained by a child's sex and age.

Perceived Effectiveness.   In the first regression equation perceived effectiveness had two network attributes that substantially contributed to explaining variance—content multiplexity, and homogeneity of role relationships. The activity domains communication, creative activities, and special outings also contributed significantly to the explained variance. These five network variables contributed 33% explained variance. Communication alone accounted for 20%.

Entering size into the regression equation prior to any other network variables altered the results. Multiplexity and homogeneity of role relationships were no longer significant predictors. Only the specific network activities of communication and special outings contributed significantly to the regression equation.

Perceived Politeness.   Two domains of network activities, special outings and television, and satisfaction contributed significantly to explaining variance in perceived politeness (25%). When size was entered as the first network attribute, satisfaction dropped out of the equation.

Global Assessment.   Five variables were strong predictors of global assessments of competence. Communication activities, content multiplexity, special outings, size, and homogeneity of role relationships accounted for 40% of the variance. Communication alone accounted for 26% of the variance explained beyond the age and sex of the child. When entering size directly after children's age and sex, multiplexity was no longer a significant contributor to the regression equation. These results

Table 4.1
Pearson Correlation Coefficients, Network Attributes,
Demographics and Perceived Competence Scores

	Size	Interconnectedness	Age	Relational	Racial	Sexual	Educational	Occupational	Content Multiplexity
						Diversity			
Size									
Interconnectedness	−.26								
Diversity									
Age	−.13	.11							
Relational	.17	−.40	.18						
Racial	.02	.06	.01	.05					
Sexual	.13	.06	.12	.08	.07				
Educational	.07	.10	.03	.14	.10	.08			
Occupational	.10	.03	.07	.12	.08	.10	.03		
Content Multiplexity	.16	.19	−.13	−.28	−.03	.17	.06	.12	
Role Multiplexity	.26	.01	−.24	.23	.06	.07	.19	−.04	.20
Activities									
Creative	.72	.11	−.05	.45	.05	−.03	.18	.06	.25
Music	.22	−.19	.17	.14	.05	.03	.36	−.21	.29
Physical	.72	−.14	−.27	.43	.13	.07	−.01	.13	.23
Educational	.68	−.27	.02	.49	−.06	−.06	.31	.16	.16
Caretaking	.60	−.04	.08	.17	.18	.06	−.02	.01	.01
Communication	.84	−.24	.06	.51	−.02	.01	.08	−.09	.04
Special Outings	.71	−.17	−.16	.51	.05	−.09	.17	.06	.15
Play	.83	−.21	−.41	.64	−.06	−.01	.03	.03	.05
Housework	.26	−.11	.14	.15	.03	.15	.15	.01	.01
Television	.39	−.19	.08	.27	.01	−.13	.01	#.04	.21
Satisfaction	.23	−.24	.08	.13	.00	.08	.20	.14	.14
Frequency	.69	.01	−.19	−.48	.09	−.07	−.07	.22	.22
Continuity	.11	.14	.38	.28	.13	.02	−.22	.13	.13
Demographics									
Sex	.14	−.10	.10	.15	.03	−.04	.16	.26	.07
Age	.21	−.28	−.14	−.11	.09	.05	−.06	−.06	.24
Perceived Competence									
Effectiveness	.38	−.26	.06	.24	.04	.10	.19	.08	.32
Politeness	.36	−.06	−.04	.24	.06	.09	.10	.18	.16
Global Assessment	.44	−.25	.07	.27	.03	.07	.24	.27	.34

Role Multiplexity	Activities										Satisfaction	Frequency	Continuity
	Creative	Music	Physical	Educational	Caretaking	Communication	Special Outings	Play	Housework	Television			
.14													
.10	.39												
.23	.77	.52											
.20	.64	.32	.43										
.19	.42	.08	.40	.51									
.17	.73	.24	.69	.69	.56								
.23	.61	.24	.56	.61	.51	.69							
.24	.66	.32	.60	.58	.49	.71	.67						
.01	.16	.05	.20	.24	.08	.24	.17	.26					
.03	.02	−.08	.28	.10	.22	.26	.16	.08	.06				
.22	.16	.19	.24	.23	.02	.32	.33	.17	.07	.29			
.26	.64	.16	.59	.37	.33	.58	.53	.67	.00	.15	.22		
.06	.08	.09	.16	.38	.27	.27	.27	.05	.19	.18	.12	.21	
−.06	.14	.30	.11	.04	.00	.23	.04	.20	.11	−.18	.19	.19	.05
.29	.18	−.01	.29	.18	.27	.27	.35	.27	.11	.15	−.30	.15	.35
.14	.41	.24	.40	.49	.31	.63	.51	.38	.10	.02	.31	.27	.25
.19	.34	.17	.33	.36	.28	.50	.56	.42	.10	−.09	.34	.29	.31
.14	.49	.27	.49	.48	38	.70	.62	.44	.12	.01	.34	.32	.27

strongly indicate that network attributes are associated with levels of perceived competence.

Hypothesis 1 states that network size would be positively related to competence. Although size has significant positive zero-order correlations with perceived competence ($r = .38, .36, .48, p < .005$), it is important to note that the beta weight is negative for size when it enters the regression equation after network activities. This is because the high correlations between size and communicatiaon activities ($r = .84$) establishes a pattern of correlation, which Cohen and Cohen (1975) call "net suppression" (p. 89). This pattern, consisting of all positive correlations, may be understood as demonstrating that, in spite of its positive zero-order correlation with competence, the function of size in the multiple correlation and regression is primarily in suppressing a portion of the variance of communication activities. The absolute partial correlation for communication activities with perceived competence is higher than the partial correlation for size. In other words, by removing the variability in size due to communication activities, the variance left in size is negatively associated with perceived competence.

Thus, although the results of the correlational analysis support Hypothesis 1, the regression suggests that it is not size per se that is associated with competence, but rather that size provides the opportunity for networks to provide developmentally enhancing activities. In large networks, where these activities are not shared, the child is dealing with a social world that is not dealing with him or her. In those circumstances, network size is negatively associated with communicative development.

Degree of interconnectedness was expected to be negatively related to perceived levels of competence (H2). Although interconnectedness did not enter the regression equations, the zero-order correlations show a negative association with perceived levels of effectiveness ($r = .25, p < .01$) and politeness ($r = .24, p < .01$). Interconnectedness is also negatively related to network size ($r = .27, p < .01$) and has a strong negative association with relational diversity ($r = -.40, p < .001$). Thus, interconnectedness does not independently contribute to explaining competence variation, but it is associated with those conditions that are detrimental to the development of perceived competence.

Hypothesis 3 posited that diversity would be positively related to competence. The evidence suggests that diversity in the domains of sex, occupational status, age, and educational level are not associated with levels of perceived competence. However, homogeneity of role relationships did enter the regression equation and was negatively associated with perceived levels of politeness ($r = -.24, p < .03$), effectiveness ($r = -.24, p < .03$), and global assessment ($r = -.27, p < .02$). The results indicate that children who interact with a combination of relatives, friends, neighbors, and so on, are perceived as more competent than those who interact predominantly with individuals comprising one relational domain. In this sample, 90% of the homogeneous networks were composed almost entirely of relatives.

Although Hypothesis 4 stated that content and role multiplexity would be positively related to perceived competence, the evidence suggests that only content multiplexity is associated with levels of effectiveness ($r = .32, p < .01$) and global assessment ($r = .34, p < .005$).

The developmental benefits of interacting with many people in many domains are clearly demonstrated in the correlational analysis and especially by the large percentage of variance explained by communication activities and special outings. Television watching is the only network activity that is negatively correlated with perceptions of politeness and global assessments of communicative competence ($r = -.33, -.25, p < .03$).

Satisfaction is positively related to all three perceptions of competence ($r = .35, .29, .36, p < .01$) providing some support for hypothesis 5. However, satisfaction does not make a significant contribution to the prediction of perceived effectiveness or global assessment.

The data partially support Hypothesis 6. Although there are significant zero-order correlations between frequency of interaction and all three competence scores ($r = .27, .29, .32, p < .01$), the high correlations with network size ($r = .62$) and network activities (r's range from .26 through .68) explain why it does not make an independent contribution to the explained variance in the regression equation.

DISCUSSION

The results of this study illustrate that children's social networks are qualitatively and quantitatively different from one another. These differences go beyond the typically studied demographic characteristics of network members and can be measured, compared, and contrasted. The data provide strong evidence for the importance of network attributes across the life span. Diversity in both structural and interactional attributes is related to enhanced development. However, before discussing the implications of the results a note of caution must be attached to the following discussion. That is, the directionality or causality of the relationships covered is unclear.

Specifically the data show that children who have more network members participating in communication activities and special outings are perceived to be more competent than those children whose networks

Table 4.2
Summary of Multiple Regression Analyses for Three Competence Scores

Perceived Effectiveness

	(size not forced into the equation)					(size entered on step 2)			
Step	Variable	Beta at Stop Entered	R^2	F	Step	Variable	Beta at Stop Entered	R^2	F
1	Sex	.30	.11	10.36	1	Sex	.30	.11	10.36
	Age	.42	.28			Age	.42	.28	
2	Communication	.49	.48	15.92	2	Size	.27	.35	9.28
3	Content Multiplexity	.27	.55	15.42	3	Communication	.86	.53	14.07
4	Creative Activities	-.24	.57	13.22	4	Special Outings	.32	.57	13.27
5	Special Outings	.18	.59	11.51					
6	Relational Diversity	-.21	.61	10.48					

Politeness

Step	Variable	Beta at Stop Entered	R^2	F	Step	Variable	Beta at Stop Entered	R^2	F
1	Sex	.44	.17	8.38	1	Sex	.44	.17	8.38
	Age	.19	.24			Age	.19	.24	
2	Special Outings	.46	.43	12.82	2	Size	.24	.30	7.33
3	Television	-.20	.47	10.96	3	Special Outings	.55	.44	9.72
4	Satisfaction	.15	.49	9.28	4	Television	-.20	.47	8.59

Global Assessment

Step	Variable	Beta at Stop Entered	R^2	F	Step	Variable	Beta at Stop Entered	R^2	F
1	Sex	.28	.09	11.49	1	Sex	.28	.09	11.49
	Age	.46	.31			Age	.46	.31	
2	Communication	.57	.57	22.56	2	Size	.32	.41	11.43
3	Multiplexity	.29	.64	22.42	3	Communication	.97	.62	20.78
4	Special Outings	.24	.67	19.91	4	Special Outings	.46	.72	24.74
5	Size	-.56	.72	20.90	5	Relational Homogeneity	-.22	.74	22.21
6	Relational Homogeneity	-.20	.74	18.89					

do not supply these experiences. At least three interpretations of these data are possible. First, is the "network effects" interpretation. It is appealing and somewhat seductive to argue that children are more competent *because* people talk to them more and take them more places. Second, a "child effects" interpretation suggests that children may be spoken to more often or taken more places precisely because they are more competent. The child who is impolite, hard to understand, or uses inappropriate speech patterns is less appealing to converse with, and perhaps, more likely to be left at home.

A third alternative, an "interaction effects" explanation is used in the interpretation of these data. That is, there is a cyclical relationship between perceived communicative competence and relevant network attributes. Joint activities between network members and the child are simultaneously the *source,* the *process,* and the *outcome* of communicative development. These activities are the *source,* insofar as they provide discrepancies, variability rules, expectations, and reinforcement for developing competence; the *process,* in terms of how actual participation in the activities requires the child to use communication in new and varied ways; and the *outcome,* insofar as the more competent child will be involved in more of these activities than the child who is perceived as less competent.

There is one other caveat to the discussion. The results of this study are based upon *teachers' perceptions* of children's communicative competence. Although competence is assumed to be reflected in performance and perceptions of competence are based on actual behavior, judgments of competence are conceptually the most distant from actual determinants of competence. Thus, the empirical relationship found between network attributes and the social judgment of significant others is interpreted as a strong indication of the important relationship between the complex interwoven fabric of children's social affiliations and the development of children's communicative competence. Nevertheless, it does not indicate a direct relationship with performance.

The Importance of Network Diversity

It is significant to note the similarity between the findings of this study and the work of Feiring and Lewis (1981) regarding the importance of diverse social experiences. Just as these data suggest that the least competent children are enmeshed in significantly smaller networks than the most competent children, Feiring and Lewis reported size was positively related to 3-year-olds' cognitive abilities. Specifically they found upper middle-class children had significantly larger networks ($X = 28$) than middle-class children ($X = 23.8$) and scored significantly higher on the Stanford Binet Intelligence test.

However, it is hard to imagine, as Feiring and Lewis (1981) implied, that a 4.2 person difference in size is directly related to cognitive development. Rather, the analysis here suggests differences in size act upon the social environment in ways that are salient for cognitive and communicative development. The importance of size as a network attribute is influenced by the degree to which size produces diverse and developmentally enhancing activity; although the zero-order correlation between size and perceived competence is positive, when all variance associated with other network attributes is removed from size, the partial correlation is negatively associated with perceptions of competence.

Two other more speculative conclusions about diversity are suggested by the multivariate analysis. In this study the percentage of relatives is negatively related to perceptions of communicative competence and to specific network activities such as communication and special activities. Feiring and Lewis (1981) also reported that less competent middle-class children not only have smaller networks but have more contact with relatives than upper-class children. Possibly relatives do not tend to engage children in positive developmental experiences to the extent that other people do. Furthermore, there may be a monotonic relationship between social-class and social-network attributes. The attributes which distinguish among social strata seem to also distinguish between the social networks of more and less competent children within the same stratum.

However, size, degree of homogeneity, and interconnectedness may be of importance for perceived competence only at the lower end of the socioeconomic scale. The high degree of interconnectedness within a network was rooted in large clusters of relatives. These strong ties serve as norm-enforcing mechanisms and communicate the expectations and values of a close-knit group quite effectively (Milroy & Margraine, 1980). To the degree that middle-class families have similar communicative expectations as the school and other contexts in which the child functions, the less detrimental high degrees of interconnectedness and homogeneity may be. Middle-class children may require fewer role models and less communicative experience to master the competencies required outside their homes.

Parents in this study seemed to be aware of the negative developmental effects of network homogeneity. Mothers of children in both large and small highly dense networks expressed their early fears of sending their children to day-care centers where "nobody would understand" the child. The entrance into a new setting that had no links with the child's own network provided the first impetus for some to teach their children socially appropriate terms for "going to the potty," making nice, nice," and so forth. It seems that to the degree children only interact with relatives or other people with common assumptions and shared identifications there is less need to raise meanings to the level of explicitness (Bernstein, 1971).

Interactional as well as structural diversity is also an essential aspect of social network experiences. Content multiplexity was related to levels of competence. Perhaps as children get older, participate in more extracurricular activities, and increase the likelihood of role multiplex relationships, the association between diversity and competence may evolve even more strongly.

Communication activities and special outings emerged as the most predictive attributes of perceived competence. In contrast to most other network activities, communication (e.g. talk over problems, tell stories, play word games, pretend roles, etc.) and special outings (e.g. nature walks, movies, shopping) introduce children to new modes of interaction, new rules and expectations, create discrepancies and unpredictability and increase role-taking experiences and role observation. Experiences beyond the most familiar contexts help children to realize that another person's point of view cannot be taken for granted and that other people do not have access to the context that originally generated the speech (Bernstein, 1971; Dickson, 1981).

The only activity that was negatively associated with perceived competence was television watching. Controlling for size of network, the number of people who watched television with the child was negatively correlated with the amount of people involved in educational activities, creative activities, communication activities, special outings, and play. Hence, watching television with network members may be generally related to lower perceptions of competence not because anything is inherently wrong with watching television (in fact we do not know if less competent children actually watch more television) but rather if people are watching television with the child they are not doing other developmentally stimulating activities. This interpretation is supported in the mass communication literature. A persistent theme by Comstock, Chafee, Katzman, McCombs, and Roberts (1978) is that most children watch television when there is nothing better or necessary to do. Furthermore their research suggests that the amount of television watching reduces the amount of time devoted to social gatherings away from the home, in conversations, and in travel related to leisure and movies (p. 154).

The spatio/temporal attributes of a child's social network were not strong predictors of perceived competence. However, there was a strong negative correlation between frequency and relational diversity. Once again, the data indicate that interactions with relatives may not be as developmentally enhancing as interactions with friends and nonrelated adults.

Statistical analysis, however, cannot fully explain the importance of social networks nor capture their dynamic force. During the collection of the social network data the environmental impact of statistically significant network attributes was continually demonstrated.

For example, the statistical analyses indicate that children who see a larger, diverse set of people are perceived as more competent than those who interact with fewer people who are more similar to one another. My experiences in many of these children's homes were indicative of the pragmatic and emergent effects of these structural network attributes. For example, during the 2 hours spent in one child's home (size = 11, interconnectedness = .61) there were no visitors or telephone calls. Two uncles were watching television. Occasional interruptions by the child were met with the response "Go watch TV." The mother told me it was "so nice to have me there" she "never had a chance to talk with anyone except my mother." The afternoon was "typical" of her life.

A second child's home (size = 20, interconnectedness = .45) provided a startling contrast. Six people stopped by during the two hours I was there. An aunt stayed and played with the child, a friend of the mother had a long conversation with the child (in the doorway) regarding who I was, a neighbor invited the child to take a walk. The environment was rich and stimulating. Clearly, motivational incentives and cognitive and social stimulation for increasing communicative abilities found in the second home were not available in the first home.

The positive developmental effects of network linkages and interconnectedness emerged from a conversation with a third mother. At the end of the interview she told of her sudden realization of luck. In the past year she and her child had undergone a crisis. Although at the time she couldn't bring herself to talk to the day-care teachers about her attempted suicide, they had become increasingly supportive to both her and the child. Now, 8 months later, completing the interconnectedness matrix, she realized that the psychiatric nurse she regularly dealt with was friends with one of the day-care teachers. She now assumes the nurse told the teacher something about the crisis (I checked and she had) which thereby modified the teachers' behavior in ways that were developmentally supportive.

Overall, the results of this study suggest there are structural and interactional attributes of children's social networks that enhance the development of communication skills. Future research, however, must be cognizant of, and take into account the limitations of the study and network analysis in general. The incorporation of multiple methods and multiple measures are needed to deal with issues of reliability. Furthermore, structurally equivalent networks are not necessarily equal. The saliency of specific network attributes may vary as a function of when or who or what is assessing individual's competence. Obviously, the causal relationship between networks and competence needs to be explored utilizing a longitudinal study. Specific network structures critical for development at age 4 may not be as important at age 8, 12, 20, and so on. As greater focus is put on the interactional fabric of social relations across the life span, the greater understanding we can have of development. This chapter suggests that the origins of competence lie within the tapestry of interpersonal relationships whose effects can be further unraveled through social network analysis.

REFERENCES

Albrecht, T. (1984). An overtime analysis of communication patterns and work perceptions among managers. In R. Bostrom (Ed.), *Communication Yearbook 8* (pp. 538–557). Beverly Hills, CA: Sage.

Allen, R. R., & Brown, K. L. (1976). *Developing communicative competence in children.* Skokie, IL: National Textbook.

Ammon, P. (1981). Communication skills and communicative competence: A neo-Piagetian process-structural view. In W. P. Dickson (Ed.), *Children's oral communication skills* (pp. 13–34) New York: Academic Press.

Asher, S., & Hymel, S. (1981). Children's social competence in peer relations: Sociometric and behavioral assessment. In G. J. Whitehurst & B. J. Zimmberman (Eds.), *The functions of language and cognition* (pp. 125–127) New York: Academic Press.

Bandura, A., & Walters, R. H. (1963). *Social learning and personality development.* New York: Holt, Rinehart & Winston.

Bates, E. (1975). Peer relations and the acquisition of language. In M. Lewis & L. Rosenblum, (Eds.), *Friendship and peer relations* (pp. 259–292) New York: Wiley.

Bates, E. (1976). *Language and context: The acquisition of pragmatics.* New York: Academic Press.

Berger, C. R. & Calabrese, R. J. (1975). Some explorations in initial interactions and beyond: Toward a developmental theory of interpersonal communication. *Human Communication Research, 1,* 99–112.

Berko-Gleason, J. & Weintraub, S. (1978). Input language and the acquisition of communicative competence. In K. E. Nelson (Ed.), *Children's language* (Vol. 1). New York: Gardner Press.

Bernard, H., & Killworth, P. (1977). Informant accuracy on social network data II. *Human Communication Research, 4,* 3–18.

Bernard, H., Killworth, P., & Sailer, L. (1982). Informant accuracy in social network data V. *Social Science Research, 11,* 30–66.

Bernstein, B. (1971). *Class, codes and control: Theoretical studies towards a sociology of language* (Vol. II). London: Routledge & Kegan Paul.

Bohannon, J. N., & Marquis, A. L. (1977). Children's control of adult speech. *Child Development, 48,* 1008–1014.

Boissevain, J. (1974). *Friends of friends: Networks, manipulators and coalitions.* New York: St. Martins Press.

Bott, E. (1957). *Family and social network*. London: Tavistock.

Brass, D. J. (1981). Structural relationships, job characteristics, and worker satisfaction and performance. *Administrative Science Quarterly, 26*, 331–348.

Bronfenbrenner, U. (1979). *The ecology of human development: Experiments by nature and design*. Cambridge: Harvard University Press.

Bruner, J. S. (1978). From communication to language: A psychological perspective. In I. Markova (Ed.), *The social context of language* (pp. 17–48) London: Wiley.

Bryant, B. (1985). The neighborhood walk: Sources of support in middle childhood. *Monographs of the Society for Research in Child Development*, Serial no. 210, Vol. 50.

Burleson, B. (1985). Communication skills and peer relationships in childhood: An overview. In M. McLaughlin (Ed.), *Communication Yearbook 9*, Beverly Hills, CA: Sage.

Burt, R., & Minor, M. (1983). *Applied network analysis*. Beverly Hills, CA: Sage.

Burt, R. S. (1980). Models of network structure. *Annual Review of Sociology, 6*, 79–141.

Chomsky, N. (1965). *Aspects of linguistic theory*. Cambridge, MA: MIT.

Cochran, M. M., & Brassard, J. A. (1979). Child development and personal social networks. *Child Development, 50*, 601–616.

Cohen, J. & Cohen, P. (1975). *Applied multiple regression/correlational analysis for the behavioral sciences*. NJ: Lawrence Erlbaum Associates.

Comstock, B., Chaffee, S., Katzman, N., McCombs, M., & Roberts, D. (1978). *Television and human behavior*. New York: Columbia University Press.

Corsaro, W. (1977). Adult interactive styles with children. *Language in Society, 5*, 183–207.

Corsaro, W. (1979). We're friends, right? Children's use of access rituals in nursery school. *Language in Society, 8*, 315–336.

Craven, P., & Wellman, B. (1973). The network city. *Sociological Inquiry, 43*, 57–88.

Cronbach, L. J. (1951). Coefficient alpha and the internal structure of tests. *Psychometrika, 16*, 297–334.

Delia, J. G., Kline, S.J., & Burleson, B. R. (1979). The development of persuasive communication strategies in kindergarteners through twelfth graders. *Communication Monographs, 46*, 241–256.

Dickson, W. P. (Ed.). (1981). *Children's oral communication skills*. New York: Academic Press.

Dore, J. (1977). O them sheriff: A pragmatic analysis of children's responses to questions. In S. Ervin-Tripp & C. Mitchell-Kernan (Eds.), *Child discourse* (pp. 139–164). New York: Academic Press.

Edlesky, C. (1977). Acquisition of an aspect of communicative competence: Learning what it means to talk like a lady. In S. Ervin-Tripp & C. Mitchell-Kernan (Eds.), *Child discourse* (pp. 225–243). New York: Academic Press.

Feiring, C., & Lewis, M. (1981). *The social networks of three-year-old children*. Paper presented at the Society for Research in Child Development Convention, Boston.

Fischer, C. S. (Ed.). (1977). *Networks and places: Social relations in the urban setting*. New York: The Free Press.

Flavell, J. (1968). *The development of role taking and communication skills in children*. New York: Wiley.

Flavell, J. H. (1977). *Cognitive development*. Englewood Cliffs, NJ: Prentice-Hall.

Hartup, W. W. (1979). The social worlds of childhood. *American Psychologist, 34*, 944–950.

Hirsch, B. J. (1979). Psychological dimensions of social networks: A multi-method analysis. *American Journal of Community Psychology, 7*, 263–277.

Hymes, D. (1971). *Foundation in sociolinguistics*. Philadelphia, PA: University of Pennsylvania.

Keller, B., & Bell, R. Q. (1979). Child effects on adults' method of eliciting altruistic behavior. *Child Development, 50*, 1004–1009.

Milroy, L., & Margrain, S. (1980). Vernacular language loyalty and social network. *Language in Society, 9,* 43–70.

Mitchell, R. E., & Trickett, E. J. (1980). Task force report: Social networks as mediators of social support: An analysis of the effects and determinants of social networks. *Community Mental Health Journal, 16,* 27–40.

Nahir, H. T., & Yussen, S. R. (1977). The performance of kibbutz- and city-reared Israeli children on two role-taking tasks. *Developmental Psychology, 13,* 450–455.

Perrucci, R., & Targ, D. (1982). *Mental patients and social networks.* Boston: Auburn House.

Piaget, J. (1954). *The language and thought of the child.* New York: New American Library.

Roberts, K. H., & O'Reilly, C. A. (1978). Organizations as communication structures: An empirical approach. *Human Communication Research, 4,* 283–293.

Robinson, E. J. (1981). The child's understanding of inadequate messages and communication failure: A problem of ignorance or egocentrism? In W. P. Dickson (Ed.), *Children's oral communication skills* (pp. 167–204) New York: Academic Press.

Rodnick, R., & Wood, B. (1973). The communication strategies of children. *The Speech Teacher, 22,* 114–122.

Rogers, E., & Kincaid, D. (1981). *Communication Networks: Toward a new paradigm for research.* New York: The Free Press.

Rubin, R. (1982). Assessing speaking and listening competence at the college level: The communication competency assessment instrument. *Communication Education, 31,* 19–32.

Shantz, C. (1981). The role of role-taking in children's referential communication. In W. P. Dickson (Ed.), *Children's oral communication skills* (pp. 181–211) New York: Academic Press.

Shulman, N. (1976). Network analysis: A new addition to an old bag of tricks. *Acta Sociologia, 19,* 307–322.

Slobin, D. (Ed.). (1967). *A field manual for cross-cultural study of the acquisition of communicative competence.* CA: University of California Press.

Stohl, C. (1983). Developing a communicative competence scale. In R. N. Bostrom (Ed.). *Communication Yearbook 7* (pp. 685–716). Beverly Hills, CA: Sage.

Teyber, E., Messe, L., & Stollack, G. (1977). Adult responses to child communications. *Child Development, 48,* 1577–1582.

Tietjen, A. M. (1982). The social networks of preadolescent children in Sweden. *International Journal of Behavioral Development, 5,* 111–130.

Wang, M., Rose, S., & Maxwell, J. (1973). *The development of the language communication skills task.* Learning Research and Development Center, University of Pittsburgh.

Watson-Gegeo, K., & Boggs, S., (1977). From verbal play to talk story: The role of routines in speech events among Hawaiian children. In S. Ervin-Tripp & C. Mitchell-Kernan (Eds.), *Child discourse* (pp. 67–90). New York: Academic Press.

Weiss, H., Henderson, C., Campbell, M., & Cochran, M. (1980). *The effects of informal social networks on mothers' perceptions of themselves as parents: A preliminary report.* Paper presented at the biennial meeting of the Society for Research in Child Development, Boston.

Wellman, B. (1979). The community question: The intimate network of East Yorkers. *American Journal of Sociology, 84,* 1201–1231.

West, H. (1974). Early peer group interaction and role-taking skills: An investigation of Israeli children. *Child Development, 45,* 1118–1121.

5 Communication Apprehension in Children

Mark E. Comadena
Illinois State University

Diane T. Prusank
University of Oklahoma

Communication apprehension refers to a broadly based affective response to communication. Since 1970, when the term *communication apprehension* (CA) first appeared in the literature (McCroskey, 1970), a relatively small, but meaningful body of literature has addressed the causes and consequences of CA in children. This research, unfortunately, depicts a rather negative picture of the high communication-apprehensive child. It appears that CA may develop early in life, prior to the child's arrival at the elementary school, and interfere significantly with the social and educational development of the child.

This chapter examines the nature of CA, factors that contribute to its development in children, the social and educational consequences of CA in children, and methods for measuring and treating CA in children. We conclude the chapter with a discussion of some issues in need of additional research.

THE NATURE OF CA

CA is defined as an individual's level of fear or anxiety associated with real or anticipated communication with another (McCroskey, 1984). It is important to note that CA refers to a subjective, emotional response to communication. CA is, therefore, conceptually distinct from shyness (Zimbardo, 1977), reticence (Phillips, 1968), and unwillingness to communicate (Burgoon, 1976), in that these constructs refer to behavioral withdrawal or disaffiliation resulting from numerous factors, not necessarily fear or anxiety about communication. Not all individuals who choose to disaffiliate from others suffer from high CA. Furthermore, high CA may not necessarily cause one to disaffiliate (McCroskey, 1984). This conceptual distinction has important implications for both the measurement and treatment of social inhibition and disaffiliation (Leary, 1983a, 1983b).[1]

McCroskey (1982, 1984) maintained that personality and situational constraints placed on one in a social situation may interact to produce four different types of CA: traitlike CA, generalized-context CA, person-group CA, and situational CA. Traitlike CA refers to fear or anxiety associated with communication across a wide variety of contexts. Here CA is viewed as a relatively enduring disposition of the personality. Studies of CA in children (and most studies of adults) have utilized a traitlike orientation in the measurement of CA.

Generalized-context CA refers to fear or anxiety associated with communication in a given context (e.g., dyadic interactions, groups, and public speaking). Here, the individual experiences CA in only specific contexts. Perhaps the most common type of generalized-context CA is stage fright, a fear of speaking before an audience. Generalized-context CA is also viewed as a relatively enduring disposition of the personality.

Person-group CA refers to fear or anxiety associated with communication with specific individuals or groups across time. According to McCroskey (1984), this form of CA is less a function of the personality of the individual than the specific situational constraints placed on him or her by the individual or group with whom he or she is interacting. The nature of the relationship one has with another or with a group, specifically the level of familiarity one has with that individual or group, influences one's level of person-group CA. As interpersonal familiarity with another increases, anxiety resulting from communication with that other decreases.

Finally, situational CA refers to fear or anxiety associated with communication with a specific individual or specific group at a specific time. Situational CA may fluctuate widely as a function of changes in the specific constraints produced by different individuals or different groups. For example, a student who is generally not at all anxious to interact with a teacher about homework assignments may experience extreme CA if he or she were requested to stay after class to talk to the teacher

---

[1]Since communication apprehension is both conceptually and empirically distinct from shyness, and since shyness in children has been reviewed in detail in several recent publications (Asendorpf, 1986; Buss, 1986; Cheek, Carpentieri, Smith, Rierdan, & Koff, 1986), we have limited our review and discussion to research on communication apprehension.

(McCroskey, 1984). The unusual request by the teacher and the uncertainty associated with the interaction is likely to cause high CA.

In summary, CA is a broadly based affective response toward real or imagined communication with another individual or group. According to McCroskey and Beatty (1986), CA may exist "as a trait-like predisposition toward communication and as a state-like response to a given communication situation" (p. 280). Having provided a conceptual definition of the nature of CA, we next examine theory and research on the causes of CA in children.

CAUSES OF CA IN CHILDREN

What causes a child to experience fear or anxiety when communicating with another? Surprisingly little research has addressed this very important question. Theoretically, a number of factors may contribute to the development of CA in children.

Research by Kagan and Reznick (1986) suggests that some children may be given a biological push toward developing CA. Kagan and Reznick (1986) noted that individual differences in inhibition to the unfamiliar, a tempermental disposition that appears to have a genetic origin, remains relatively stable from infancy to young adulthood. Compared to their uninhibited counterparts, inhibited individuals are more likely to report feelings of anxiety in social situations (Kagan & Reznick, 1986). Plomin and Daniels' (1986) review of the behavioral-genetic studies of shyness prompted them to conclude that "heredity influences individual differences in shyness more than in any other personality trait, beginning as early as infancy" (p. 78). Although the term *shyness* is never consistently defined in the research literature (Leary, 1983b), it generally refers to the tendency to experience both anxiety and inhibition in social situations (Leary, 1983b). Research has revealed moderate correlations ($r = .57$, $r = .63$) between shyness (behavioral inhibition) and CA (McCroskey & Beatty, 1986). Although this is not direct evidence indicating that CA has a genetic basis, it appears that some children, especially those who for genetic reasons are wary of others, may be predisposed to experience high levels of CA in some social situations, especially those involving unfamiliar others. In short, we probably should not overlook genetic factors in the development of CA.

Although heredity may contribute to the development of CA in some individuals, most theorists contend that factors in the home and school environments play a more meaningful role in its development. McCroskey and Beatty (1986) maintained that reinforcement patterns for communication may be the single most important factor in the development of CA in children. Specifically, children who are rewarded for their communications with others develop positive attitudes toward communication and positive expectations for their communication behavior. These positive expectations lead to feelings of confidence as a communicator; neither anxiety nor fear is associated with these positive expectations (McCroskey, 1984). Children who are consistently or inconsistently punished for their communication attempts, on the otherhand, develop negative attitudes toward communication and negative expectations concerning their communication behavior. When forced to communicate, these negative expectations will cause the child to experience fear and anxiety (McCroskey, 1984).

Research by Daly and Friedrich (1981) identified reinforcement patterns as a significant factor in the development of CA. In that study (Daly & Friedrich, 1981), 241 undergraduate students were asked to complete a measure of CA (McCroskey, 1970) and two questionnaires designed to record retrospective perceptions of various communication patterns encountered at home and in elementary and secondary school. Regression analyses indicated that encouragement and reward for communication in the home and a communication permissive atmosphere in the elementary school significantly predicted CA scores. The manner in which parents and teachers respond to the communication attempts of children appears to be a significant factor in the development of CA.

Modeling may also account for the development of CA in some children. The parent who openly expresses fear and anxiety about a social engagement (e.g., the presentation to the board of directors, or the presentation at the PTA) may cause his or her child to expect negative outcomes for similar communication situations. Thus, negative expectations for communication behavior may not only be acquired through trial and error but through vicarious observations of significant others, such as parents, siblings, or teachers.

Although modeling processes appear to be a plausible theoretical explanation for the development of CA, there is little empirical support for this developmental factor. One study (Beatty, Plax, & Kearney, 1984) that compared the effects of reinforcement patterns and modeling on the development of CA revealed no support for modeling. In that study (Beatty et al., 1984), 310 undergraduate students completed a measure of CA, the encouragement-reward scales used in the Daly and Friedrich (1981) study just described, as well as a questionnaire designed to assess communication modeling effects. The modeling scales asked respondents to retrospectively describe their parents' CA and the extent to which parents were rewarded or punished because of their CA. Results revealed that reinforcement patterns were better predictors of CA than modeling. However, the authors (Beatty et al., 1984) cautioned that their results do not rule out modeling as a factor in the development of CA. Rather, the authors suggested that perhaps individuals other than parents (e.g., teachers, siblings, and peers) may serve as behavioral models for children.

Finally, poor social-communicative skills have been suggested as factors in the development CA (Leary, 1983b; McCroskey & Beatty, 1986). The skills deficit position maintains that feelings of fear and anxiety result from poor social-communicative skills or the perception that one's skills are poor (McCroskey & Beatty, 1986). CA may result, then, when one feels his or her social skill will cause others to perceive him or her negatively. We could find no research on the extent to which poor social-communicative skills contribute to the development of CA in children.

In summary, empirical work on the causes of CA has been slow to develop. At this time, heredity, reinforcement for communication, modeling, and poor social skills are seen as factors that may contribute to the development of CA in children.

CONSEQUENCES OF CA

Numerous negative consequences are associated with CA in adults (see Daly & Stafford, 1984). The growing literature on the consequences of CA in children indicates that CA may have very negative effects in children as well, effects that may have long-term implications for children.

One negative effect associated with childhood CA is low student learning. The negative relationship between CA and student learning is based on the notion that students high in CA avoid or withdraw from classroom communications with teacher and peers—to avoid experiencing the anxiety they have associated with communication. Comadena and Prusank (1988) examined the relationship between CA and academic achievement in 1053 elementary and middle-school students in Grades 2–8 in a midwestern community. CA was operationally defined as scores on the Measure of Elementary Communication Apprehension (MECA; Garrison & Garrison, 1979). Academic achievement was operationally defined as scores on the Stanford Achievement Test; national percentile rank scores in language, mathematics, and reading were examined. Results indicate that students with high CA (with MECA scores greater than one standard deviation above the mean for the sample) had the lowest levels of achievement on all three measures of achievement. In mathematics, students low in CA had achievement scores that were 23% higher than students high in CA. A study of 144 students enrolled in grades 2–5 in the laboratory school of a large midwestern university revealed similar results (Prusank & Comadena, 1987). Correlations between CA (as measured by the MECA) and six achievement variables from the Iowa Tests of Basic Skills were negative and significant (Prusank & Comadena, 1987). The correlations ranged from $r = -.18$ (reading) to $r = -.25$ (work skills). These studies indicate that CA and student learning are meaningfully and negatively related. High CA is associated with low levels of student learning.

The pattern of behavior that may result from high CA may cause teachers to develop negative achievement expectations of the high communication-apprehensive child. These expectations may explain the negative relationship between CA and academic achievement. McCroskey and Daly (1976) asked 460 elementary school teachers to rate the probable academic success of two fictional elementary school students. Teachers were given a written description of a student who was described as either high or low in communication apprehension and asked to estimate the likelihood the student would experience success in nine areas: reading, arithmetic, social studies, science, art, deportment, relationships with other students, overall achievement, and success in future education. The high communication-apprehensive child (Jimmy) was described as a very quiet individual who sat at the back of the classroom and who liked to work alone. The low communication-apprehensive child (Billy), on the otherhand, was described as a very outgoing individual who sat in the front of the class and who frequently participated in class discussions. Results indicate that teachers possessed significantly lower expectations on all success variables, except deportment, for the high CA student. The results of a recent study by Schaller and Comadena (1988) confirm McCroskey and Daly's (1976) findings. These are important findings given the profound effect teacher expectations may have on student learning (Rosenthal & Jacobson, 1968).

Students may develop more negative attitudes toward school as a result of their CA. Hurt and Preiss (1978) correlated CA scores of 118 middle-school students with their final grades and a measure of their attitudes toward school. In addition to finding a negative correlation between CA and student learning, the researchers observed that high CA was associated with less positive attitudes toward school. CA accounted for approximately 20% of the variance in students' attitudes toward school. The significant negative correlation observed between CA and attitude toward school, coupled with a nonsignificant partial correlation between attitudes toward school and final grades, lead the authors to conclude that "a positive attitude toward communication is a necessary condition to be met in order to insure that maximal learning for every student is facilitated" (p. 326).

There is some research that suggests that high CA may have a negative effect on the quantity and quality of childhood interpersonal relationships. Hurt and Preiss (1978) found that high communication-apprehensive individuals were not considered to be highly desirable targets of communications from teachers and peers. Teachers expect high communication-apprehensive students, compared to low communication-apprehensive students, to experience less success in their interpersonal relationships with other students (McCroskey & Daly, 1976). Shy subjects in Ishiyama's (1983) study reported more incidences of loneliness and felt that their shyness interfered with their ability to develop friendships with peers.

The low level of social approach associated with high CA may influence children's perceptions of their communication-apprehensive peers. These perceptions may explain why high communication-apprehensive children experience difficulty in forming quality relationships with other students. Richmond, Beatty and Dyba (1985) provided 1520 students in Grades 3–12 with a written description of either a "talkative" or "quiet" peer. Results indicate that the talkative peer was rated more approachable and more intelligent.

In summary, research indicates that CA may have numerous negative consequences for the child. High CA is associated with low levels of student learning, negative teacher expectations, negative attitudes toward school, and low likelihood of experiencing positive interpersonal relationships with teachers and peers.

TREATING CA IN CHILDREN

Three techniques have been employed to treat CA: systematic desensitization, cognitive restructuring, and social-skills training. In systematic desensitization (Wolpe, 1958), an individual high in CA is trained (counterconditioned) to reduce the arousal associated with real or imagined communication (stimulus) by learning to pair the arousing stimulus with a learned relaxation response. Because systematic desensitization primarily addresses the physiological arousal associated with communication, this technique is the recommended treatment for individuals who experience unusually high levels of arousal from communication exchanges (McCroskey & Beatty, 1986). Friedrich and Goss (1984) provided a comprehensive review of research on the effectiveness of systematic desensitization as a method for treating various types of CA.

In cognitive restructuring, individuals are trained to identify and replace anxiety arousing self-statements (e.g., "I know I'm going to appear funny."), which are often irrational in nature, with more adaptive, logical, and nonarousing coping statements (Fremouw & Scott, 1979). Fremouw (1984) and Fremouw and Scott (1979) discussed the cognitive restructuring technique as a method for treating CA.

In social-skills training, one seeks to alleviate the anxiety associated with communication by providing the high communication-apprehensive individual with specific social skills that will allow him or her to develop greater confidence as a communicator. Kelly (1984) provided a thorough review of the skills-training approach as a method for treating CA and other social-communicative dysfunctions.

McCroskey and Beatty (1986) maintained that systematic desensitization and cognitive restructuring are both highly and equally effective methods for treating CA in adults (See Fremouw, 1984; Fremouw & Zitter, 1978, McCroskey, 1972; McCroskey, Ralph, & Barrick, 1970). Social-skills training has not been used extensively to treat CA. However, research indicates that in some situations, social skills training may effectively reduce CA (Fremouw & Zitter, 1978).

Although systematic desensitization, cognitive restructuring, and social-communication skills training have been found to be effective in reducing CA in adults, little research has compared the relative effectiveness of these three techniques for treating CA in children. All three approaches can be used successfully with children. Johnson, Tyler, Thompson, and Jones (1971) were able to significantly reduce speech anxiety in a group of eighth-grade students using systematic desensitization and skills training. Zimbardo (1981) maintained that systematic desensitization is an effective method for treating shyness in children. Although we could find no study that utilized cognitive restructuring to treat CA in children, this technique has been used to successfully modify other personality dispositions in children (Meichenbaum, 1979).

MEASURING CA IN CHILDREN

McCroskey (1984) maintained that because CA is an affective response to communication, it is best measured by self-report instruments. There are three self-report instruments to measure CA in children available in the published literature.

McCroskey (1970) developed the Personal Report of Communication Apprehension-7 (PRCA-7) and PRCA-10 to measure CA in the 7th and 10th grades, respectively. Both scales represent adaptations of a reliable and valid instrument designed to measure CA in adults—the PRCA-College. To construct the PRCA-7 and PRCA-10, PRCA-College items were either reworded or replaced with new items to reflect situations that are appropriate to individuals in the early grade levels. Both instruments contain 20 Likert-type statements with five response options. Items address communication in dyadic, group, and public contexts. Both scales are designed to provide a single index of traitlike CA. McCroskey (1970) reported an internal reliability estimate of .87 for the PRCA-7 ($n = 72$) and .88 for the PRCA-10 ($n = 123$). Data concerning the validity of the instruments were not reported.

The Measure of Elementary Communication Apprehension (MECA) contains 20 questions that address a child's feelings toward communication in a variety of social situations found in the school environment (Garrison & Garrison, 1979). The MECA uses language that is appropriate for children and incorporates a progression of smiling and frowning faces for response options. Garrison and Garrison (1979) reported internal reliability estimates of .76 and .80 for two samples of children in Nebraska ($n = 595$) and West Virginia ($n = 2, 375$). Test–retest reliability (over a 2-week period) conducted on the Nebraska sample was .80. Garrison and Garrison (1979) maintained that a highly stable factor structure obtained for the MECA and the positive, but moderate, correlations observed between the MECA and other measures of CA are evidence of the validity of the instrument. As further evidence of its validity, recent research has found the MECA to significantly predict academic achievement scores in samples of elementary (Comadena & Prusank, 1988; Prusank & Comadena, 1987) and middle-school students (Comadena & Prusank, 1988). Because the MECA uses smiling and frowning faces as response options, this instrument would be most appropriate in studies of young children; older students may feel belittled by this format. The MECA should be orally administered to young children.

Whereas the MECA was designed to be used with elementary school children, the Personal Report of Communication Fear (PRCF; McCroskey, Andersen, Richmond, & Wheeless, 1981) was designed to measure CA in the elementary- and secondary-grade levels. The PRCF consists of 20 Likert-type statements with five-step response options designed for easy comprehension by students at the elementary and secondary grade levels. The reliability and validity of the scale was investigated in a study of 2,228 students in grades k through 12, and 875 college students (McCroskey et al., 1981). Reliability estimates ranged from .70 (grades K–3) to .90 (grades 10–12). The PRCF was highly correlated with the MECA (in grades 4–6) and a short form of the PRCA, indicating that the instrument has concurrent validity (McCroskey et al., 1981). McCroskey (1984) noted that PRCF should be orally administered to young (preliterate) children because they may experience difficulty responding to the negatively worded items contained on the instrument (e.g., disagreeing with a negatively worded item). Administrators should work slowly with young children, making sure that they understand each statement and that they accurately record their responses to each statement.

DIRECTIONS FOR FUTURE RESEARCH

Although a significant amount of research has accumulated on CA since McCroskey (1970) first introduced the construct, a relatively small amount of that research has involved children. Most of that research has examined the consequences of childhood CA. Many questions remain to be answered in this area. The following are some issues we feel are in need of research.

A number of questions remain concerning the development of CA. This is, perhaps, the most significant issue in the study of CA and the one we know least about. In theory, a number of factors, such as heredity, reinforcement patterns, modeling, and social-communicative skills, may contribute to the development of CA in children. Some research points to reinforcement patterns in the home and elementary school (Daly & Friedrich, 1981; Beatty et al., 1984) as a significant contributor to the development of CA. We know little, however, about the specific socialization patterns of parents and teachers that may cause a child to develop high CA. Furthermore, we have no empirical data concerning the extent to which reinforcement patterns, modeling, and social-skill development interact to produce CA in children. It is reasonable to assume that by grades 3 and 4, when traitlike CA appears to stabilize (McCroskey et al., 1981), different combinations of these factors interact to produce CA in children. The results of Daly and Friedrich's (1981) study indicate that we should critically examine social processes in the elementary classroom as they contribute to the development of CA.

A number of important questions remain concerning the treatment of CA in children. Though much research has compared the relative effectiveness of systematic desensitization, cognitive restructuring, and social-skills training for treating CA in adults, relatively little literature is available on the effectiveness of these approaches for treating CA in children. Since CA may have many causes, we should explore the effectiveness of treating children for different sources of their CA. At what age can we begin to effectively treat children for their CA? What is the long-term effectiveness of treatment? Is there a technique that can be utililzed by teachers in the elementary school classroom to effectively reduce CA in children?

Research is needed which explores the classroom consequences of CA in children. Research indicates that there is a significant and negative relationship between CA and student learning among elementary- and middle-school students. However, the studies in this area are correlational in nature. We know little about the causal relationship between CA and student learning. Although it is highly likely that high CA causes low levels of learning in many children, it is possible that low levels of learning result in lower self-esteem and subsequently higher CA. Studies that utilize true experimental designs will clarify the causal nature of the relationship between CA and academic achievement.

Finally, we believe that systematic observational studies of the classroom behaviors of low and high communication-apprehensive students would be very informative. If high CA indeed causes lower levels of student learning, then one would expect to find qualitative and/or quantitative differences in the classroom behaviors of low and high communication-apprehensive students. Observational studies would enhance our understanding of the relationship between CA and student learning. In addition, such research may explain why high communication-apprehensive children are perceived as less desirable targets of communication from teachers and peers and why teachers form negative achievement expectations of the high communication-apprehensive child. Such research would help explain the negative consequences associated with high CA and provide specific suggestions for treatment.

REFERENCES

Asendorpf, J. (1986). Shyness in middle and late childhood. In W. H. Jones, J. M. Cheek, & S. R. Briggs (Eds.), *Shyness: Perspectives on research and treatment* (pp. 91–103). New York: Plenum Press.

Beatty, M. J., Plax, T. G., & Kearney, P. (1984, November). *Reinforcement vs. modeling theory in the development of communication apprehension: A retrospective analysis.* Paper presented at the annual convention of the Speech Communication Association, Chicago.

Burgoon, J. K. (1976). The unwillingness to communicate scale: Development and validation. *Communication Monographs, 43,* 60–69.

Buss, A. H. (1986). A theory of shyness. In W. H. Jones, J. M. Cheek, & S. R. Briggs (Eds.), *Shyness: Perspectives on research and treatment* (pp. 279–294). New York: Plenum Press.

Cheek, J. M., Carpentieri, A. M., Smith, T. G., Rierdan, J., & Koff, E. (1986). Adolescent shyness. In W. H. Jones, J. M. Cheek, & S. R. Briggs (Eds.), *Shyness: Perspectives on research and treatment* (pp. 105–115). New York: Plenum Press.

Comadena, M. E., & Prusank, D. T. (1988). Communication apprehension and academic achievement among elementary and middle school students. *Communication Education, 37,* 270–277.

Daly, J. A., & Friedrich, G. (1981). The development of communication apprehension: A retrospective analysis of contributory correlates. *Communication Quarterly, 29,* 243–255.

Daly, J. A., & Stafford, L. (1984). Correlates and consequences of social-communicative anxiety. In J. A. Daly & J. C. McCroskey (Eds.), *Avoiding communication: Shyness, reticence, and communication apprehension* (pp. 125–143). Beverly Hills, CA: Sage Publications.

Fremouw, W. J. (1984). Cognitive-behavioral therapies for modification of communication apprehension. In J. A. Daly & J. C. McCroskey (Eds.), *Avoiding communication: Shyness, reticence, and communication apprehension* (pp. 209–215). Beverly Hills, CA: Sage Publications.

Fremouw, W. J., & Scott, M. D. (1979). Cognitive restructuring: An alternative method for the treatment of communication apprehension. *Communication Education, 28,* 129–133.

Fremouw, W. J., & Zitter, R. E. (1978). A comparison of skills training and cognitive restructuring-relaxation for the treatment of speech anxiety. *Behavior Therapy, 9,* 248–259.

Friedrich, G., & Goss, B. (1984). Systematic desensitization. In J. A. Daly & J. C. McCroskey (Eds.), *Avoiding communication: Shyness, reticence, and communication apprehension* (pp. 173–187). Beverly Hills, CA: Sage Publications.

Garrison, J. P., & Garrison, K. R. (1979). Measurement of oral communication apprehension among children: A factor in the development of basic speech skills. *Communication Education, 28,* 119–128.

Hurt, H. T., & Preiss, R. (1978). Silence isn't necessarily golden: Communication apprehension, desired social choice, and academic success among middle-school students. *Human Communication Research, 4,* 315–328.

Ishiyama, I. F. (1983). Shyness: Anxious social sensitivity and self-isolating tendency. *Adolescence, 14,* 903–911.

Johnson, T., Tyler, V., Jr., Thompson, R., & Jones, E. (1971). Systematic desensitization and assertive training in the treatment of speech anxiety in middle-school students. *Psychology in the Schools, 8,* 263–267.

Kagan, J., & Reznick, J. S. (1986). Shyness and temperment. In W. H. Jones, J. M. Cheek, & S. R. Briggs (Eds.), *Shyness: Perspectives on research and treatment* (pp. 81–90). New York: Plenum Press.

Kelly, L. (1984). Social skills training as a mode of treatment for social communication problems. In J. A. Daly & J. C. McCroskey (Eds.), *Avoiding communication: Shyness, reticence, and communication apprehension* (pp. 189–207). Beverly Hills, CA: Sage Publications.

Leary, M. R. (1983a). The conceptual distinctions are important: Another look at communication apprehension and related constructs. *Human Communication Research, 10,* 305–312.

Leary, M. R. (1983b). *Understanding social anxiety: Social, personality, and clinical perspectives.* Beverly Hills, CA: Sage Publications.

McCroskey, J. C. (1970). Measures of communication bound anxiety. *Speech Monographs, 37,* 269–277.

McCroskey, J. C. (1972). The implementation of a large-scale program of the systematic desensitization for communication apprehension. *Speech Teacher, 21,* 255–264.

McCroskey, J. C. (1982). Oral communication apprehension: A reconceptualization. In M. Burgoon (Ed.), *Communication Yearbook 6* (pp. 136–170). Beverly Hills, CA: Sage Publications.

McCroskey, J. C. (1984). The communication apprehension perspective. In J. A. Daly & J. C. McCroskey (Eds.), *Avoiding communication: Shyness, reticence, and communication apprehension* (pp. 13–38). Beverly Hills, CA: Sage Publications.

McCroskey, J. C., Andersen, J. F., Richmond, V. P., & Wheeless, L. R. (1981). Communication apprehension of elementary and secondary students and teachers. *Communication Education, 30,* 122–132.

McCroskey, J. C., & Beatty, M. J. (1986). Oral communication apprehension. In W. H. Jones, J. M. Cheek, & S. R. Briggs (Eds.), *Shyness: Perspectives on research and treatment* (pp. 279–294). New York: Plenum Press.

McCroskey, J. C., & Daly, J. A. (1976). Teachers' expectations of the communication apprehensive child in the elementary school. *Human Communication Research, 3,* 67–72.

McCroskey, J. C., Ralph, D. C., & Barrick, J. F. (1970). The effect of systematic desensitization on speech anxiety. *Speech Teacher, 19,* 32–36.

Meichenbaum, D. (1979). Cognitive-behavioral modification: Future directions. In P. Sjoden, S. Bates, & W. S. Dockens, III, (Eds.), *Trends in behavior therapy* (pp. 55–65). New York: Academic Press.

Phillips, G. M. (1968). Reticence: Pathology of the normal speaker. *Speech Monographs, 35,* 38–49.

Plomin, R., & Daniels, D. (1986). Genetics and shyness. In W. H. Jones, J. M. Cheek, & S. R. Briggs, (Eds.), *Shyness: Perspectives on research and treatment* (pp. 63–80). New York: Plenum Press.

Prusank, D. T., & Comadena, M. E. (1987, May). *Communication apprehension and academic achievement among elementary school students.* Paper presented at the annual convention of the International Communication Association, Montreal, Canada.

Richmond, V. P., Beatty, M. J., & Dyba, P. (1985). Shyness and popularity: Children's views. *The Western Journal of Speech Communication, 49,* 116–125.

Rosenthal, R., & Jacobson, L. (1968). *Pygmalion in the classroom: Teacher expectation and pupils' intellectual development.* New York: Holt, Rinehart & Winston.

Schaller, K. A., & Comadena, M. E. (1988, April). *Teacher expectations of the communication apprehensive student.* Paper presented at the annual meeting of the Central States Speech Association, Schaumburg, IL.

Wolpe, J. (1958). *Psychotherapy by reciprocal inhibition.* Stanford, CA: Stanford University Press.

Zimbardo, P. G. (1977). *Shyness: What it is, what to do about it.* Reading, MA: Addison–Wesley.

Zimbardo, P. G. (1981). *The shy child: A parent's guide to preventing and overcoming shyness from infancy to adulthood.* New York: McGraw–Hill.

6 *The Uses and Effects of Mass Communication During Childhood*

Anne Johnston Wadsworth
University of North Carolina at Chapel Hill

INTRODUCTION

Of all the communication contexts that children encounter, their interaction with mass media is perhaps the one that most concerns several publics, including parents and policy makers. Television, in particular, is so much a part of American family life that it sometimes provides the setting for family interaction and communication. For children, mass communication allows them to experience worlds beyond their own lives and circumstances. Television, in particular, can show children things they cannot experience in any other way. Although there is research on all areas of mass media and children, the area of television and children dominates the studies. Perhaps a reason for this dominance may be the perceived power that television has traditionally been seen as having with children. Because of the preoccupation with television in the research, this chapter is also focused on television and children, although other areas of mass communication are discussed. There are many excellent reviews on media and children, and these are not rereviewed here. Instead, emphasis is on current research and the trends that appear in the research.

The chapter is organized into three main sections. The first section covers the research on the uses, needs, and functions that media serve for children. In the second section, the "effects" of media on children are reviewed with emphasis on the areas of advertising, sex-role socialization, achievement, and violence. The final section addressed is that of children's own communication/response to television: how they negotiate television and come to understand media. Emphasis here is on studies approaching television interaction from a developmental perspective and on research that has looked at how children process media communication. In addition, the research on the development of critical viewing skills and "media literacy" in children is addressed in this section.

MEDIA USE AND THEORIES

In order to understand the interaction between children and media, it is probably first important to understand the unique aspects of children as an audience for media. Several scholars have suggested that children are a unique audience because of their limited knowledge of aspects of the world, their eagerness to learn, their different approaches to learning, and their vulnerability to all socialization influences (Barcus, 1983; Dorr, 1986). In addition there are several explanations of how and why children use the media they do. One way of viewing media use by children is to see it as a modeling of parents' and friends' media use habits. Past research has found evidence that children may model their television viewing patterns after the patterns of families or friends (Comstock, Chaffee, Katzman, McCombs, & Roberts, 1978; McDonald, 1986). However, recent research suggests the relationship is not a simple one; other factors may influence how and why children use certain media. (McDonald, 1986; Wartella, Alexander, & Lemish, 1979). One approach to understanding the factors that influence children's media use is suggested by the uses and gratifications approach. As with the modeling theory of children's media use, research within the uses and gratifications theory has found that children have different needs for media consumption than do adults (Wartella et al., 1979).

A theory that attempts to integrate modeling, and uses and gratifications theory is the "reorganization theory" (Brown, 1976; Wartella et al., 1979). Brown (1976) argued that functions of television for children are best looked at in terms of a continuum ranging from needs that are always present to needs that occur at various times. In addition to needs, other factors determine media consumption, including type of media content, the child's control over selecting specific content in different media, and the child's ability to "read" or understand a particular medium's content (Brown, 1976). In terms of their consumption of media, based on this theory, children simply "reorganize" their media use in different situations and at different ages (Wartella et al., 1979).

Functions, Roles, and Needs of Media

Subsumed under all of these theories is the notion that children are "active" users of media with their own patterns and motives for consumption. One of the areas that supports this notion is the area that has found definite functions, roles, and needs of media for children. One of the primary roles that television has been found to play for children is as a time-consuming activity (Dorr, 1986). In some cases, television functions as an activity of habit for children (Rubin, 1977), perhaps as a result of the pervasiveness of television. In some households, televisions are constantly on and are used as a background to virtually any family activity (Feilitzen, 1976; Lee & Browne, 1981; Medrich, 1979; Palmer, 1986). For example, Lee and Browne (1981) found that the use of media as a way to pass time and as a background to other things was one of the most important reasons for watching television for a sample of Black teenagers.

Some researchers have argued that television viewing and family routine are inseparable in most families (Palmer, 1986) and that research must first understand the pervasiveness of television before investigating its content and influence (Medrich, 1979). In some families, television is used quite extensively as a babysitter for children while parents attend to other duties (Gantz & Masland, 1986). An interesting aspect about these "background" and time-passing functions of media is that they are functions that remain persistent throughout childhood whereas other functions and uses of media change (Lometti, Reeves, & Bybee, 1977; Rubin, 1985).

A second group of functions that media serve for children are "social" functions, and researchers have found that children's media use is frequently tied to other social activities in childhood (Feilitzen, 1976; Frazer, 1981; James & McCain, 1982; Reid & Frazer, 1980). Media are sometimes used by children to draw others into interaction with them (Frazer, 1981; Reid & Frazer, 1980). Children frequently use television to create a specific social situation and use media content to involve others in social interaction (Frazer, 1981; Reid & Frazer, 1980). James and McCain (1982) found that television program themes and characters were used as content for play among preschool children. In addition, children used this type of play to not only embellish their play with others but to reinforce friendships and to establish social status within their friendships.

Lull (1980b) suggested that the social uses of television generally fall into two broad categories. One group of social uses can be best described as "structural uses" that involve much of the functions already discussed, including such things as use of television as a background to other activities, as a device to punctuate time, and as a way to regulate talk patterns. Another group of social uses is called "relational uses", which include use of television to facilitate communication, to initiate or avoid interpersonal contact, and to provide social learning. Lull (1980b) argued that the investigation of some of the relational uses of television is revealing: "Television and other mass media, rarely mentioned as vital forces in the construction or maintenance of interpersonal relations, can now be seen to play central roles in the methods which families and other social units employ to interact normatively" (p. 198).

In addition to social and background/time-consuming functions, media also serve entertainment, informational, social identity, escapist, companionship, arousal, and excitement functions for children (Dembo & McCron, 1976; Feilitzen, 1976; Rubin, 1977) although not always consistently for all ages of children. There are several factors that may influence the effectiveness of media in serving certain functions for children, including the nature of the particular medium, the age of the child, the type of media fare or programming, and the family use of media.

Nature of Specific Media

Although the same function may be served by various media, the inherent characteristics of certain media may make them more effective in serving that function than other media. A Swedish study by Feilitzen (1976) revealed that other media served some but not all of the same functions as television (such as entertaining, informative, social, escapist, and background functions) but did not serve these functions as well as did television. For example, radio served many of the same functions that television did, but children preferred television to radio in satisfying these needs.

As general television viewing drops off as adolescence approaches, teenagers tend to turn to specific television content and to alternative media to satisfy emerging needs. Avery (1979) in a review of research on media use by adolescents finds that adolescents tend to turn away from indescriminate television viewing and become increasingly interested in news programming and newspapers. Magazine reading tends to increase at this age, mainly as a source of entertainment. Along with the decline in television viewing is an increase in record playing and radio playing which, according to Avery (1979), may correspond for the need to be alone or with peers and away from family.

Use of Specific Media Programming

In addition to using different media for different reasons, children also have unique responses to specific media programming. Some evidence exists that children may actually prefer adult programs to children's programs (Webster & Coscarelli, 1979), and there is some evidence that children are drawn both to children and adult programming for specific media content. (Drew & Reeves, 1980).

Reasons for using specific media content or the functions of that content for children are as diverse as the types of media content available.

As mentioned previously, heavy use of music by teenagers may correspond to emerging privacy and independence needs in that group. Although general television viewing decreases in adolescence, attention to certain types of programming tends to increase. For example, teenagers are the largest audience for music videos on television, and the advent of music videos may be a contributing factor to the increase of television viewing among adolescents (Lull, 1985). In a recent study, reasons for watching music television by adolescents included to see and hear favorite music, for entertainment and enjoyment and to see the way the music was "acted out" for them (Sun & Lull, 1986).

News content also becomes important as a child matures, and need for information as well as other reasons tend to move adolescents toward news programming (Drew & Reeves, 1980). Prisuta (1979) found that the best predictor of adolescents' viewing of television news was the adolescent's perception of how important others (peers) might see news viewing. Although there is some attraction to newspapers for informational needs, in general, teenagers do not read newspapers. In one study of newspaper readership among teenagers, reasons given for not reading the newspaper included lack of time, lack of newspaper availability in the home, and lack of relevant articles (Cobb, 1986).

Changes in Media Use
from Childhood to Adulthood

Many researchers argue that for children, a prime determinant in use and motive for using media is age (Rubin, 1985; Wartella et al., 1979). As with use of news and attention to news programming, other media use factors are influenced as children move through adolescence and adulthood. One of the reasons that age may be a good determinant of media use is that it is a good indicator of the person's social envirionment (Rubin, 1985).

Rubin (1985) in a review of media use, found that motives for using media change throughout the life span and that certain motives for using television become less important with increasing age. Several motives for using media, such as time-passing uses and habitual uses, remain persistent for children and adolescents. Lometti et al. (1977) found that television use for entertainment and surveillance motives decreases with age, whereas television use for behavioral guidance increases in childhood.

As mentioned previously, as children move through adolescence, attention to news programming tends to grow (Avery, 1979) because of growing informational needs (Dimmick, McCain, & Bolton, 1979; Lee & Browne, 1981). In addition, teenagers tend to turn away from general television viewing and increasingly spend time with popular music and radio (Avery, 1979; Lull, 1985).

Use of Media Within Families

Other factors that may influence media use are family interaction patterns and communication styles. Gantz and Masland (1986) found that mothers who emphasized familial harmony and agreement in interpersonal relationships (high socio-oriented mothers) reported greater use of television as a babysitter. Mothers who encouraged their children to challenge ideas of others and express their own (high concept-oriented) reported less use of television as a babysitter.

According to Lull (1980a), socio-oriented individuals tend to watch more television and find it useful for things such as companionship, communication facilitation, and social learning. However, for concept-oriented families, television is not seen as a useful social resource and is rejected as a means of facilitating family communication.

SOCIALIZATION AND EFFECTS

Media use by children is typically seen as a way of understanding how children respond to and incorporate the images of media. As indicated, factors such as age and individual motives can influence how children use and respond to media forms and content. Media use is an important topic not so much in understanding the patterns of use for their own sake, but that by understanding the patterns of exposure and use, researchers can understand how children are influenced and socialized by media.

General Factors Influencing "Media" Socialization

The socialization of children through mass communication and particularly through television is a process that is not yet fully understood. The socialization of children by media is of particular concern because of the widely held beliefs that what children learn in early years will stay with them throughout their lives. All of the things that influence use of media may also influence the socialization of children through the media. For example, if media use patterns indicate that adolescents and teenagers are most likely to be drawn away from general television viewing and drawn to radio listening and popular music playing, this may help researchers in understanding how influential these types of media content might be.

Other variables, some specific to the individual child, some specific to the media used, and some specific to the family environment, may influence the socialization of children by media.

Child-Centered Mediators

Age has already been discussed as one child-centered factor that may affect media consumption and comprehension and subsequent response to media. Related to this is a child's communication development (Wartella et al., 1979), including such things as a child's linguistic growth, his or her ability to understand social behavior and, finally, his or her development of logical abilities. Other aspects of a child's development that may affect how a child responds to media, and particularly to television, include perceptual propensities, store of real-world knowledge, affective components, imagination, and a knowledge of generic symbols (language) (Rice & Wartella, 1981). In addition, experience with some situation or circumstance may also act as a modifier of the child's perception of the realism of television portrayals (Elliot & Slater, 1980).

Attention to television is also an important component in regard to what is understood and processed (Pingree, 1986). Husson (1982), in a review of children's attention to television, found three factors that appear to impact the way children attend to the television screen and influence their overall pattern of attention: the attributes of what is on television at the time; the child's level of cognitive development; and, the nature of the viewing environment. Another factor that may determine a child's attention and comprehension of televison is channel capacity (Cohen & Salomon, 1979). That is, whether the child is engaging in shallow, superficial processing of the material or in deeper, complex processing may determine what influence the content of the medium (in this case, television) will have (Cohen & Salomon, 1979).

Media-Centered Mediators

In addition to things that are child-centered, factors inherent in the medium may influence a child's consumption of and response to media. Complexity of programs, visual attention, and certain production techniques may influence a child's response to television (Acker & Tiemens, 1981; Collins, 1981; Krull & Husson, 1980; Rice & Wartella, 1981; Welch & Watt, 1982). Acker and Tiemens (1981) found that certain production characteristics were misinterpreted by young children; for example, children sometimes believed close-up shots of something actually indicated an increase in the size of the item. Several studies have shown that certain production characteristics may have a marker function for children and signal the type of content to follow (Collins, 1981; Wright & Huston, 1981).

Family-Centered Mediators

A final component that mediates, in general, the socialization influence of media is the interaction among family members about media. Although some researchers say that simple parental coviewing of television can mediate the influence, other researchers argue that it is the type of interaction that mediates the influence (Corder-Bolz, 1980). According to Corder-Bolz, mass media are "secondary social agents" in the socialization of children and are most "persuasive" when they provide information about things for which children will have no other sources of information. Desmond, Singer, Singer, Calam, and Colimore (1985) found that comprehension of television by kindergarteners and first-graders and their beliefs about reality of television are linked with parental mediation styles about television and more general patterns of discipline. Generally, the more specific the comments about television content, the more children tend to gain from the mediation. Also, parents can be very influential in determining the amount of viewing and children's general attitude toward and perceptions of the importance of television (Singer, Zuckerman, & Singer, 1980).

Messaris and Sarett (1981) suggested that parental comments about television programming had four distinct consequences for children: learning of interpretational skills both through parents contributing additional information needed to interpret material and through parental comment about the truth of the television message; articulation of cognitive categories through parental translation of images into verbal concepts or parental comparison between television characters and real-life people; overt behavioral consequences as affected by parental advice concerning some television character's actions or parental reward/ punishment of child's imitation of some televised behavior; and development of social relationships through parental responses to children's identification with some characters.

Specific Areas of Socialization and Effects

Overall, the ability of media images and messages to socialize and influence children is mediated by numerous factors within the child, the media, and the family or social environment. In addition, the ability of media to be powerful socializing and influencing agents may also vary depending upon the area of social life being studied.

In a review of studies on television's effect on social reality, Hawkins and Pingree (1981) found that "most studies show evidence for a link between the amount of viewing and beliefs, regardless of the kind of social reality studied" (p. 349). Several areas have been studied in terms of what aspects of children's lives are influenced by media, including topics such as violence, aggression, prosocial behavior, advertising and consumer behavior, political behavior, school achievement, and sex-role orientation. All of these topics have been extensively researched and reviewed; only advertising, sex-role socialization, achievement, and violence are covered here. Several general influences on media's ability to socialize and affect have already been mentioned; in this section, the focus is on a review of the ways in which children are affected within each of these content areas and which general mediation factors are influential within each of these areas.

Advertising

The influence of advertising on children has been of concern in part because of the fear that advertising influences children's demands on parents to buy certain products. Research seems to indicate that advertisers are aware of the child in the audience when the ads are created; in a review of types of advertising to children, Barcus (1980) noted that several presentation and attention-getting devices are used in selling to children including the use of musical jingles, authority figures, repetition, unusual sound or video techniques, animation techniques, magic, and fantasy.

Children use advertising for various reasons. As mentioned before, it is used to initiate discussion with parents about the purchase of a product. In addition to that, however, research has also found that children use commercials to draw family members into social interaction. Reid and Frazer (1980) found evidence that children are "capable of knowingly interpreting and using commercials to change the character of viewing situations by involving others in planned social interaction" (p. 156). In their study commercials were used by children to draw others into conversations and activities, to gain information from parents and siblings about the commercial messages, and to avoid the demands or requests of others, especially those made by parents.

Despite arguments of product companies that advertising has no great influence on children, Atkin (1980), in a summary of the effects of television advertising on children, found evidence showing that television advertising plays a dominant role in shaping product preferences and increases children's awareness about certain toys and foods. Other effects, according to Atkin (1980), are that advertising may actually contribute to conflicts between parents and children, because of the tension created when children request the purchase of some product, and don't receive it. Children may also become unhappy as a result of advertising because of their inability to obtain the product, because of the inability of the product featured in the advertising to live up to the performance expectations portrayed in the commercial, and because of the dissatisfaction children may have of their own social situation in comparison with the lifestyles depicted in the commercials (Atkin, 1980). Several things have been found to mediate these effects of advertising. Individual differences in the child and age differences appear to mediate the influence of advertising on children, with children becoming more adept at understanding the selling intent behind advertising as they get older (cf. Murray, 1980; Wartella, 1980). In reviews of much of this literature, Murray (1980) and Wartella (1980) suggested that research indicates that attention to the ad, comprehension of the ad, and use of the advertising information in consumer activities may differ among individual children.

According to Wartella (1980) some research suggests that attention to ads may vary depending upon different techniques and characteristics used in the ads as well as their placement in a program. Although networks have argued they already use program/commercial separators, Palmer and McDowell (1979) argued that young children are still not able to discriminate between programs and commercials. Faber, Perloff, and Hawkins (1982) found that children at the role-taking stage in development and who are able to understand social relations are better able to understand the purpose of commercials.

Several other factors have been found to mediate the influence of advertising on children. One is parental mediation and discussion of advertising (Robertson, 1979), and the other is the use of instructional sequences to help children be critical and skeptical of product advertising. Use of educational strategies and instructional units has been shown to be an effective way to increase children's awareness about the intent and motives of commercials and to decrease their beliefs in the truthfulness of the ads and their vulnerability to the selling appeals of the ads (Christenson, 1982; Donohue, Henke, & Meyer, 1983; Roberts, Christenson, Gibson, Mooser, & Goldberg, 1980). Roberts et al. (1980) found that their instructional units were more effective on those children who initially were most susceptible (younger and view more television) to commercial appeals.

Sex-role Socialization

Another area of socialization for children is that of sex-role socialization. Past research in media has shown that depictions of women, Blacks, and other minorities are typically shallow and stereotyped (Barcus, 1983;

Williams, LaRose, & Frost, 1981). In a review of this literature, studies of television shows designed for children indicate that traditional sex-roles permeate, sex-biased images are common, males dominate in numbers, and women are shown more in family roles, whereas men are shown in high-status jobs. Also, male characters are shown as being knowledgable, independent, and aggressive, whereas female characters are shown as romantic, submissive, and emotional (Barcus, 1983).

These portrayals are important because it is believed that children may believe these portrayals to be accurate and true. This may be particularly true for children who have no other source of information about these persons portrayed—children who through family situations are only exposed to traditional role models. In some cases, children may have very definite notions about appropriate male/female behavior and interpret television portrayals based on their preconceived notions (Durkin, 1984). Pingree (1983) found that children who watched a lot of television had stereotyped views of women and in particular believed that women did not work outside the home. However, in contrast with past research, which tends to show that children identify and "learn more" from same-sex characters, Siverman-Watkins, Levi, and Klein (1986) showed that children of both sexes recalled equal amounts of information from both a male and a female television newscaster.

As previously mentioned, exposure to other role models may mediate a child's stereotyping of men and women as portrayed on television. Exposure to "counter-stereotyping" on television may influence children to view sex-roles in less traditional ways (Williams et al., 1981). In particular, Williams et al. (1981) found there was some receptiveness to counter-stereotyping, particularly among girls, and suggested that modeling of a behavior seen on media will increase if the character is attractive to the child, if the character is positive toward the behavior and the behavior is specific and definite, and if the child can relate to the others in the portrayal as being like their significant others.

Achievement

A third area of great concern has been about media's influence on school achievement and on other language and verbal skills in children. Most of the research on achievement and television viewing indicates there is a negative relationship between amount of television exposure and academic achievement, reading skills, language skills, and IQ (Burton, Calonico, & McSeveney, 1979; Morgan & Gross, 1980; Potter, 1987). However past research suggests that it may be important to consider the effects of individual types of media on the various kinds of achievement (Potter, 1987; Roberts, Bachen, Hornby, & Hernandez-Ramos, 1984). For example, the viewing of news programs tends to be

positively correlated with achievement, whereas entertainment programming is negatively related to language and other skills achievement
(Potter, 1987). Several researchers have suggested the time-displacement
hypothesis may help explain the relationship between television viewing
and achievement, IQ, language, and reading skills (Morgan & Gross,
1980; Potter, 1987; Roberts et al., 1984; Selnow & Bettinghaus, 1981).
In addition to television viewing "displacing" time that could be spent on
school work and on practicing other skills, Morgan and Gross (1980)
argued that in terms of reading skills, television viewing may make
children more impatient with reading.

As a communication form, television has also been found to influence
other types of communication. For example, Peirce (1983) found that
writing ability and creative writing were negatively correlated with the
amount of television viewing hours among fifth-, seventh-, eighth-, and
ninth-graders. Selnow and Bettinghaus (1981), based on past research,
suggested that children who are exposed to long hours of television
language models might be influenced in terms of their language development. In their study on preschool children, children who watched more
television had less sophisticated language.

Other forms of communication that appear to be influenced by television viewing are film making and verbal style (Greenfield, 1984; Griffin,
1985). Griffin (1985) discovered that television forms were very influential in determining how children made films. In making the films,
children used the visual forms and styles they had been exposed to in
their television viewing. In a study by Greenfield (1984), when retelling a
story, children who had seen the story on television made more vague
references to the story's characters than did those who had only heard the
story on the radio.

Several factors may mediate the influence of media, and, specifically,
of television viewing on achievement. Television-related variables, such
as the existence of television-watching rules and the child's orientations
to and involvement with television, in addition to amount of viewing
may play an important role in achievement (Fetler, 1984; Roberts et al.,
1984). Television viewing, for example, has been found to have detrimental effects on various types of achievement once it goes over a certain
"threshold" of hours spent watching each week (Fetler, 1984; Roberts et
al., 1984).

Violence and Aggression

Of all the areas that have been researched, none has been more
extensively looked at and investigated than that of media's influence on
violence and aggression in children. Many of the "cultural indicators

studies" have found that children's programming contains large amounts of television violence and that heavy viewing of television contributes to an exaggerated view of a violent world (Gerbner & Gross, 1980; Gerbner, Gross, Signorielli, Morgan, & Jackson-Beeck, 1979). More recently, television viewing was shown to be related to a "distorted television reality" about the nature and amount of violence in the world (Pingree, 1983).

In the early 1970s, reports from the Surgeon General argued that television violence could be harmful to children. In a review of the early literature, Liebert (1972) found that the bulk of studies showed that children were being exposed to heavy doses of violence on television and that they "can and do retain some of the aggressive behaviors" (p. 27) and are able to reproduce them. More recent reviews (Murray, 1980; Rubinstein, 1980) also suggest that the evidence indicates that televised violence can be harmful to viewers and that there is an association between television viewing of aggression and measures of aggression. In general, early studies of violence show that "at least under some circumstances, exposure to televised aggression can lead children to accept what they have seen as a partial guide for their own actions. As a result, the present entertainment offerings of the television medium may be contributing, in some measure, to the aggressive behavior of many normal children" (Liebert, 1972, p. 29). In addition to the effects of television violence on aggressive behavior, other effects of television violence, according to Liebert, Sprafkin, and Davidson (1982) include arousal, copying of behavior, and value shaping (viewers may see violence as way of life and normal).

In recent years, researchers have attempted to explain what factors influence the detrimental effects of viewing television violence. Comstock et al. (1978) argued that television violence could be influential only in providing children with models of appropriate and inappropriate behavior and in providing information about the likely consequences of behavior. Comstock et al. (1978) found that performance of violent behavior increased if violence viewed on television was seen as justified and if it was performed by certain (favorite) characters. In some research, amount of time spent viewing television violence was related to increased aggression (Gerbner & Gross, 1980; Gerbner et al., 1979; Singer, Singer, Singer, & Rapaczynski, 1984).

Another group of factors that influence how children will react to televised violence is the individual characteristics of the child (Comstock et al., 1978). Huesmann and Eron (1984) argued that fantasizing about specific aggressive acts observed on television increased the probability that aggressive acts would be performed. In a review by Dorr and Kovaric (1980) of the various individual differences that can mediate the effects of television violence, the majority of studies show no differences due to age, cognitive ability, sex, ethnicity, social class, and most personality characteristics. However, they found that the propensity for aggression did account for differences with more aggressive persons being more affected by viewing television violence. Other research shows that it is not necessarily just aggressively predisposed children who are affected by viewing violent television (Huesmann & Eron, 1986a).

Other factors that influence the effects of televised violence include parental mediation, perception of the acceptability of the aggressive acts, if the behavior is seen as being rewarded or justified, and if it is seen as an appropriate way to solve problems, (Comstock, 1980; Huesmann & Eron, 1986a). Comstock (1980) suggested that the behavioral influence of televised violence is contingent on social approval (seems to be approved); efficacy (likely to result in a reward); relevance (appropriate to a given circumstance and realistic); and arousal (levels of excitation). Huesmann and Eron (1984) found that taking part in a discussion of how unrealistic and nonconstructive violent behavior helped in reducing the harm of viewing the violence.

Much of the research on television's influence on violent behavior has been conducted in the United States. Several researchers have become interested in what might account for different levels of influence from televised and film violence. Groebel (1986) suggested that research must be careful when defining aggression because of cultural differences. Studies done in other countries have not shown the same relationships among watching televised violence and aggression in children (Bachrach, 1986; Fraczek, 1986; Lagerspetz & Viemero, 1986; Sheehan, 1986). Several researchers suggest that perhaps the reason might be because television violence has a realistic component and counterpart in real-life U.S. culture, whereas in other countries, such as Australia and Finland, where there is relatively little violence in the culture, the violence on television seems unreal, with no real-life counterpart (Groebel, 1986; Lagerspetz & Viemero, 1986; Sheehan, 1986). Huesmann and Eron (1986b) suggested that for many of these other cultures "because violence appears on television to a much larger extent than in real life, the television provides even more opportunities to experience violence than real life does" (p. 5).

NEGOTIATION OF TELEVISION

Research on the effects and use of television and other media by children has provided information about the ways in which children are exposed to media and how that exposure influences them. However, television is not only used by children; it is a "dominant activity" (Watkins, 1985) for children and adolescents and needs to be understood as a major activity in children's lives. In the last decade, researchers have attempted to understand how children learn to understand television, or how they negotiate the conventions and language of television. Within this area, researchers have explored the ways in which television, in particular, and television's characters are viewed as real; the ways in which children come to understand the schedule, format, programming, and language codes of television; and, finally, the ways in which children "interact" with television and with others in the presence of television.

Understanding Television

Attention to television begins at a very early age. According to Lemish (1987), attention to television begins with an infant's attention to sound and images as opposed to specific content. By the time the child is 2 years old, he or she has developed a definite interest in specific content (Lemish, 1987). Children also begin to talk to television at a very early age and, in some cases, television "adjusts" its language to the child with several studies finding that the language in children's programming on television may be altered to fit a child's style and ability, making it more meaningful for children. Rice (1984) found in a study of the language used in children's television that there was an adjustment in the programs to correspond to what would be understood by children. Other studies showed that the linguistic features of educational programs were very similar to the adjustments and dialogue that mothers use in their story telling and interactions with young children (Rice, 1984) and that the verbal interaction between children and television resembles the book-reading routine of parents and children (Lemish, 1987).

Children are assisted in their understanding of television by older siblings who are sometimes called upon to provide more information and explain how something was done or what will happen next (Alexander, Ryan, & Munoz, 1984). Alexander et al. (1984) suggested this reveals the strong interpretive nature of sibling interaction with the older sibling interpreting for the younger. Learning about television and making sense of television takes place, according to Alexander et al. through this communication and interaction with siblings.

Jaglom and Gardner (1981) in a developmental look at how children come to understand television—characterize children as anthropologists confronting a new land.

> Like the anthropologist, the child beholds a novel, confusing world that she must attempt to unravel—in this case, the televised world of flickering

images and sounds. With relatively little help from informants, he or she must examine these messages, classify them, and establish a meaningful organization. . . . In the course of these "ethnographic" explorations, they must learn to make distinctions as well as to draw connections among various programs and characters. Children also must discover the rules that govern the world of television. . . . But, unlike the anthropologist, the child has not had special training; thus her achievement in coming to understand the worlds transmitted by television is remarkable indeed. (p. 10)

Television Reality

As explorers who must uncover the conventions of television, children must first understand what is real and not real on television. Most of the research indicates that young children do not discriminate well between what is real and not real on television.

Singer and Singer (1981) found "evidence that preschoolers and early elementary school aged children are confused by television, and that their failures of comprehension are reflected not only in response to specific plots but in more general misrepresentations of the nature of reality and fantasy or in distortions of facts about the 'outside world'" (p. 383). Further research also indicates that young children do not discriminate among different types of characters on television, such as human, puppet, and cartoon (Quarfoth, 1979). Although there is some fear that children do not understand what is real and not real on television, in an observational study, Wolf (1987) found that, in general, children from 4 to 12 knew well what was real and not real on television.

According to a study by Fernie (1981), children see unrealistic characters on television as being very different from real people; however, several realistic characters on television were thought to be very similar to real people the children knew, and, in some cases, these realistic television characters were seen in a more well-rounded way than were the real people. In addition, traits of certain television characters may be influential in "priming" children to use these traits in describing real-life people (Reeves & Garramone, 1982; Reeves & Garramone, 1983).

Several researchers have posited a developmental model of how children come to understand the reality of characters (Kelly, 1981; Morison, Kelly, & Gardner, 1981). Kelly (1981) showed that younger children tended to use real-life comparisons in their judgment of reality—does this exist in the real world? Is it possible or impossible? As the children grew older, they viewed television as a representation of life and understood it was created by someone else. Older children tended to use plausibility instead of possibility in their judgment of if something was real. In addition to these criteria, research shows that familiarity with television rules, programs, and conventions may also assist in children's judgment of reality (Morison et al., 1981). Other research suggests that the degree of familiarity with television programs may not play a significant role in helping a child discriminate between reality and fantasy on television; rather, it may be more important for children to understand the conventions of television (Morison, McCarthy, & Gardner, 1979).

What is real and what is not real is generally a large component of what parents, and more specifically, what mothers talk about with children when the topic is television. Messaris and Kerr (1983) found that mothers make comments about behavior that a child has seen, give additional information about a television topic, and make comments about the relationship between television and reality. In addition, there is evidence that the mother's specific comments about the reality of television characters do influence the child's perception of the realism of the character (Messaris & Kerr, 1984)

In a more specific study by Messaris (1987) on the types of comments made about the realism of television, there were three types of issues that mothers had to deal with: telling a child that some things on television are make-believe and cannot happen in real life; telling them that some realistic things on television are too good to be true and are improbable; and telling children that some disturbing pictures on television (immorality, poverty) are very often pictures of reality. In general, Messaris (1987) found that mothers are often encouraging children to believe that the images on television are real.

Critical Viewing of Television

Because of the influence of television and media on children, several researchers have explored the types of things that would be useful in educating children to have better television viewing skills. Lloyd-Kolkin, Wheeler, and Strand (1980) suggested that for high school students, four critical television viewing abilities would need to be developed: evaluating and managing television-viewing behavior, questioning the reality of television programs, recognizing the persuasive arguments and messages on television, and recognizing the effects of television on their daily life. Several researchers say that children, not just teenagers, need to be taught critical viewing skills (Dorr, Graves, & Phelps, 1980; Singer & Singer, 1981; Singer, Zuckerman, & Singer, 1980). These researchers have found several strategies that have improved even young children's ability to critically view television. Several lessons include learning about different types of programs and how they are made, learning about the differences between reality and fantasy on television, learning about special effects and about the purpose and intent of commercials, and learning how to use other information sources for comparison to television information.

SUMMARY AND CONCLUSION

It is evident from the research on children and media that media occupy important roles for and offer unique functions to children. Contrary to very early beliefs about children and media, children are far from being passive respondents to media. Research clearly shows that children actively select media for particular purposes. As children's environment and social situation change and they move into young adulthood, they "reorganize" (Wartella et al., 1979) their use of media to suit the new needs and lifestyles they are experiencing.

As children consume media, they are, in turn, influenced by its depictions of culture and conventions. Media serve as socializers of children, showing them images and representations of real life, many of which are not always accurate. But, as with all socializing agents where the information presented is not always accurate, media present their own version of reality in their depiction of the world.

Not only do media serve as socializing agents for children, but their content permeates other aspects of children's communication and social interaction. News events and newspaper "mini-pages" are used in schools as instructional material, media themes and dramas are used as content for play and as material to draw others into conversation and interaction, and, in some cases, media information and portrayals serve as the only source of information by which children judge what exists in society.

This use of media by children does not imply that children absorb this material and readily understand the codes of media. Particularly for television, children must learn to negotiate or understand the structure and form of the medium. Like other skills, children's understanding of television is something that develops gradually throughout childhood and that can be assisted through parental interaction and educational strategies.

Based on the studies reviewed here and elsewhere, there appear to be several findings and trends offered by research about children and media, and more specifically, about children and television.

It has been shown that media occupy important roles as socializers of children and cannot be discounted simply because they cannot directly punish, reward, discuss, or argue with children. Recent research has indicated the importance of understanding the nature of the mediating influences on media socialization processes. In particular, several groups of mediators seem important. One group include children's individual age and developmental differences, their various needs and orientations, their literacy in reading television, and their exposure to other sources or examples of the life depicted on television. A second group of mediators are those that exist in the child's environment and include such things as parental involvement with and monitoring of media use (specifically, television), and parental interaction with children about the portrayals and images in media.

A second trend in the research is to view television and other media as offering a communication environment to children. As such, the interaction between children and television is viewed as a communication phenomenon. Numerous researchers have argued for looking at children's television viewing as a social activity; one that offers communication and interaction opportunities for children and families. According to this argument, children cannot be viewed as reacting to television but rather as interacting with television. The research on learning of critical viewing skills and the development of media literacy seems to support the notion that children actively participate in their understanding of television and can develop critical consumption behaviors with regard to media. As a result of these studies, research should study children's use and viewing of television from a child's point of view. In some cases, as other researchers have argued, adult researchers may make inferences about media content and what is shown to children without first understanding how these younger "researchers" are approaching and coming to understand the content and messages.

Another area that has provided useful information in understanding children and media are those studies that have looked at the negotiation of media from a developmental perspective, describing children's developing interaction and attention to media's various languages. This documentation of age differences has offered important information about the interaction between media and children, but it seems important to move beyond documenting age differences and work toward an integration (as some researchers have attempted to do) of these differences and toward the development of some model of life-span use and influence.

Because of television's dominance in this area, it is particularly important to continue our understanding of the relationship between television and children. To do this, it seems most useful to regard television viewing as a social activity that involves children in communication with others, with themselves, and with the television messages.

REFERENCES

Acker, S. R., & Tiemens, R. K. (1981). Children's perceptions of changes in size of televised images. *Human Communication Research, 7,* 340–346.

Alexander, A., Ryan, M. S., & Munoz, P. (1984). Creating a learning context: Investigations on the interaction of siblings during television viewing. *Critical Studies in Mass Communication, 1,* 345–365

Atkin, C. K. (1980). Effects of television advertising on children. In E. L. Palmer & A. Dorr (Eds.), *Children and the faces of television* (pp. 287–305). New York: Academic Press.

Avery, R. K. (1979). Adolescents' use of the mass media. *American Behavioral Scientist, 23,* 53–70.

Bachrach, R. S. (1986). The differential effect of observation of violence on kibbutz and city children in Israel. In L. R. Huesmann & L. D. Eron (Eds.), *Television and the aggressive child: A cross-national comparison* (pp. 201–238). Hillsdale, NJ: Lawrence Erlbaum Associates.

Barcus, F. E. (1980). The nature of television advertising to children. In E. L. Palmer & A. Dorr (Eds.), *Children and the faces of television* (pp. 273–285). New York: Academic Press.

Barcus, F. E. (1983). *Images of life on children's television.* New York: Praeger.

Brown, J. R. (1976). Children's uses of television. In R. Brown (Ed.), *Children and television* (pp. 116–136). London: Collier Macmillan.

Burton, S. G., Calonico, J. M., & McSeveney, D. R. (1979). Effects of preschool television watching on first-grade children. *Journal of Communication, 29,* 164–170.

Christenson, P G. (1982). Children's perceptions of TV commercials and products: The effects of PSAs. *Communication Research, 9,* 491–524.

Cobb, C. J. (1986). Patterns of newspaper readership among teenagers. *Communication Research, 13,* 299–326.

Cohen, A. A., & Salomon, G. (1979). Children's literate television viewing: Surprises and possible explanations. *Journal of Communication, 29,* 156–163.

Collins, W. A. (1981). Schemata for understanding television. In H. Kelly & H. Gardner (Eds.), *Viewing children through television* (pp. 31–45). San Francisco: Jossey-Bass.

Comstock, G. (1980). New emphases in research on the effects of television and film violence. In E. L. Palmer & A. Dorr (Eds.), *Children and the faces of television* (pp. 129–148). New York: Academic Press.

Comstock, G., Chaffee, S., Katzman, N., McCombs, M., & Roberts, D. (1978). *Television and human behavior.* New York: Columbia University Press.

Corder-Bolz, C. R. (1980). Mediation: The role of significant others. *Journal of Communication, 30,* 106–118.

Dembo, R., & McCron, R. (1976). Social factors in media use. In R. Brown (Ed.), *Children and television* (pp. 137–166). London: Collier Macmillan.

Desmond, R. J., Singer, J. L., Singer, D. G., Calam, R., & Colimore, K. (1985). Family mediation patterns and television viewing: Young children's use and grasp of the medium. *Human Communication Research, 11,* 461–480.

Dimmick, J. W., McCain, T. A., Bolton, W. T. (1979). Media use and the life span. *American Behavioral Scientist, 23,* 7–31.

Donohue, T. R., Henke, L. L., & Meyer, T. P. (1983). Learning about television commercials: The impact of instructional units on children's perceptions of motive and intent. *Journal of Broadcasting, 27,* 251–261.

Dorr, A. (1986). *Television and children: A special medium for a special audience.* Beverly Hills, CA: Sage.

Dorr, A., Graves, S. B., Phelps, E. (1980). Television literacy for young children. *Journal of Communication, 30,* 71–83.

Dorr, A., & Kovaric, P. (1980). Some of the people some of the time—But which people? Televised violence and its effect. In E. L. Palmer & A. Dorr (Eds.), *Children and the faces of television* (pp. 183–199). New York: Academic Press.

Drew, D. G., & Reeves, B. B. (1980). Children and television news. *Journalism Quarterly, 57,* 45–54, 114.

Durkin, K. (1984). Children's accounts of sex-role stereotypes in television. *Communication Research, 11,* 341–362.

Elliott, W. R., & Slater, D. (1980). Exposure, experience and perceived TV reality for adolescents. *Journalism Quarterly, 57,* 409–414, 431.

Faber, R. J., Perloff, R. M., & Hawkins, R. P. (1982). Antecedents of children's comprehension of television advertising. *Journal of Broadcasting, 26,* 575–584.

Feilitzen, C. (1976). The functions served by media: Report on a Swedish study. In R. Brown (Ed.), *Children and television* (pp. 90–115). London: Collier Macmillan.

Fernie, D. E. (1981). Ordinary and extraordinary people: Children's understanding of television and real life models. In H. Kelly & H. Gardner (Eds.), *Viewing children through television* (pp. 47–58). San Francisco: Jossey–Bass.

Fetler, M. (1984). Television viewing and school achievement. *Journal of Communication, 34,* 104–118.

Fraczek, A. (1986). Socio-cultural environment, television viewing, and the development of aggression among children in Poland. In L. R. Huesmann & L. D. Eron (Eds.), *Television and the aggressive child: A cross-national comparison* (pp. 119–159). Hillsdale, NJ: Lawrence Erlbaum Associates.

Frazer, C. F. (1981). The social character of children's television viewing. *Communication Research, 8,* 307–322.

Gantz, W., & Masland, J. (1986). Television as babysitter. *Journalism Quarterly, 63,* 530–536.

Gerbner, G., & Gross, L. (1980) The violent face of television and its lessons. In E. L. Palmer & A. Dorr (Eds.), *Children and the faces of television* (pp. 149–162). New York: Academic Press

Gerbner, G., Gross, L., Signorielli, N., Morgan, M., & Jackson-Beeck, M. (1979). The demonstration of power: Violence profile no. 10. *Journal of Communication, 29,* 177–196.

Greenfield, P. M. (1984). *Mind and media: The effects of television, videogames, and computers.* Cambridge, MA: Harvard University Press.

Griffin, M. (1985). What young filmmakers learn from television: A study of structure in films made by children. *Journal of Broadcasting and Electronic Media, 29,* 79–92.

Groebel, J. (1986). International research on television violence: Synopsis and critique. In L. R. Huesmann & L. D. Eron (Eds.), *Television and the aggressive child: A cross-national comparison* (pp. 259–281). Hillsdale, NJ: Lawrence Erlbaum Associates.

Hawkins, R. P., & Pingree, S. (1981). Using television to construct social reality. *Journal of Broadcasting, 25,* 347–364.

Huesmann, L. R., & Eron, L. D. (1984). Cognitive processes and the persistence of aggressive behavior. *Aggressive Behavior, 10,* 243–251.

Huesmann, L. R., & Eron, L. D. (1986a). The development of aggression in American children as a consequence of television violence viewing. In L. R. Huesmann & L. D. Eron (Eds.), *Television and the aggressive child: A cross-national comparison* (pp. 45–80). Hillsdale, NJ: Lawrence Erlbaum Associates.

Huesmann, L. R., & Eron, L. D. (1986b). The development of aggression in children of different cultures: Psychological processes and exposure to violence. In L. R. Huesmann & l. D. Eron (Eds.), *Television and the aggressive child: A cross-national comparison* (pp. 1–27). Hillsdale, NJ: Lawrence Erlbaum Associates.

Husson, W. (1982). Theoretical issues in the study of children's attention to television. *Communication Research, 9,* 323–351.

Jaglom, L. M., & Gardner, H. (1981). The preschool television viewer as anthropologist. In H. Kelly & H. Gardner (Eds.), *Viewing children through television* (pp. 9–30). San Francisco: Jossey–Bass.

James, N. C., & McCain, T. A. (1982). Television games preschool children play: Patterns, themes and uses. *Journal of Broadcasting, 26,* 783–800.

Kelly, H. (1981). Reasoning about realities: Children's evaluations of television and books. In H. Kelly & H. Gardner, (Eds.), *Viewing children through television* (pp. 59–71). San Francisco: Jossey–Bass.

Krull, R., & Husson, W. (1980). Children's anticipatory attention to the TV screen. *Journal of Broadcasting, 24,* 35–48.

Lagerspetz, K., & Viemero, V. (1986). Television and aggressive behavior among Finnish children. In L. R. Huesmann & L. D. Eron (Eds.), *Television and the aggressive child: A cross-national* comparison (pp. 81–117). Hillsdale, NJ: Lawrence Erlbaum Associates.

Lee, E. B., & Browne, L. A. (1981). Television uses and gratifications among black children, teenagers, and adults. *Journal of Broadcasting, 25,* 203–208.

Lemish, D. (1987). Viewers in diapers: The early development of television viewing. In T. R. Lindlof (Ed.), *Natural audiences: Qualitative research of media uses and effects* (pp. 33–57). Norwood, NJ: Ablex.

Liebert, R. M. (1972). Television and social learning: Some relationships between viewing violence and behaving aggressively (overview). In J. P. Murray, E. A. Rubinstein, & G. A. Comstock (Eds.), *Television and social behavior* Vol. 2, pp. 1–42). Washington, DC: Government Printing Office.

Liebert, R. M., Sprafkin, J. N., & Davidson, E. S. (1982). *The early window: Effects of television on children and youth* 2nd ed. New York: Pergamon.

Lloyd-Kolkin, D., Wheeler, P., & Strand, T. (1980). Developing a curriculum for teenagers. *Journal of Communication, 30,* 119–125.

Lometti, G. E., Reeves, B., & Bybee, C. R. (1977). Investigating the assumptions of uses and gratifications research. *Communication Research, 4,* 321–338.

Lull, J. (1980a). Family communication patterns and the social uses of television. *Communication Research, 7,* 319–334.

Lull, J. (1980b). The social uses of television. *Human Communication Research, 6,* 197–209.

Lull, J. (1985). The naturalistic study of media use and youth culture. In K. E. Rosengren, L. A. Wenner, & P. Palmgreen (Eds.), *Media gratifications research: Current perspectives* (pp. 209–224). Beverly Hills: Sage Publications.

McDonald, D. G. (1986). Generational aspects of television coviewing. *Journal of Broadcasting and Electronic Media, 30,* 75–85.

Medrich, E. A. (1979). Constant television: A background to daily life. *Journal of Communication, 29,* 171–176.

Messaris, P. (1987). Mother's comments to their children about the relationship between television and reality. In T. R. Lindlof (Ed.), *Natural audiences: Qualitative research of media uses and effects* (pp. 95–108). Norwood, NJ: Ablex.

Messaris, P., & Kerr, D. (1983). Mothers' comments about TV: Relation to family communication patterns. *Communication Research, 10,* 175–194.

Messaris, P., & Kerr, D. (1984). TV-related mother–child interaction and children's perceptions of TV characters. *Journalism Quarterly, 61,* 662–666.

Messaris, P., & Sarett, C. (1981). On the consequences of television-related parent–child interaction. *Human Communication Research, 7,* 226–244.

Morgan, M., & Gross, L. (1980). Television viewing, IQ and academic achievement. *Journal of Broadcasting, 24,* 117–133.

Morison, P., Kelly, H., & Gardner, H. (1981). Reasoning about the realities on television: A developmental study. *Journal of Broadcasting, 25,* 229–241.

Morison, P., McCarthy, M., & Gardner, H. (1979). Exploring the realities of television with children. *Journal of Broadcasting, 23*, 453–463.

Murray, J. P. (1980). *Television and youth: 25 years of research and controversy*. Boys Town, NB: The Boys Town Center for the Study of Youth Development.

Palmer, P. (1986). *The lively audience: A study of children around the TV set*. Sydney, Australia: Allen & Unwin.

Palmer, E. L., & McDowell, C. N. (1979). Program/commercial separators in children's television programming. *Journal of Communication, 29*, 197–201.

Peirce, K. (1983). Relation between time spent viewing television and children's writing skills. *Journalism Quarterly, 60*, 445–448.

Pingree, S. (1983). Children's congnitive processes in constructing social reality. *Journalism Quarterly, 60*, 415–422.

Pingree, S. (1986). Children's activity and television comprehensibility. *Communication Research, 13*, 239–256.

Potter, W. J. (1987). Does television viewing hinder academic achievement among adolescents? *Human Communication Research, 14*, 27–46.

Prisuta, R. H. (1979). The adolescent and television news: A viewer profile. *Journalism Quarterly, 56*, 277–282.

Quarfoth, J. M. (1979). Children's understanding of the nature of television characters. *Journal of Communication, 29*, 210–218.

Reeves, B., & Garramone, G. M. (1982). Children's person perception: The generalization from television people to real people. *Human Communication Research, 8*, 317–326.

Reeves, B., & Garramone, G. M. (1983). Television's influence on children's encoding of person information. *Human Communication Research, 10*, 257–268.

Reid, L. N., & Frazer, C. F. (1980). Children's use of television commercials to initiate social interaction in family viewing situations. *Journal of Broadcasting, 24*, 149–158.

Rice, M. L. (1984). The words of children's television. *Journal of Broadcasting, 28*, 445–461.

Rice, M., & Wartella, E. (1981). Television as a medium of communication: Implications for how to regard the child viewer. *Journal of Broadcasting, 25*, 365–372.

Roberts, D. F., Bachen, C. M., Hornby, M. C., & Hernandez-Ramos, P. (1984). Reading and television: Predictors of reading achievement at different age levels. *Communication Research, 11*, 9–49.

Roberts, D. F., Christenson, P., Gibson, W. A., Mooser, L., & Goldberg, M. E. (1980). Developing discriminating consumers. *Journal of Communication, 30*, 94–105.

Robertson, T. S. (1979). Parental mediation of television advertising effects. *Journal of Communication, 29*, 2–25.

Rubin, A. (1977). Television usage, attitudes and viewing behaviors of children and adolescents. *Journal of Broadcasting, 21*, 355–369.

Rubin, A. M. (1985). Media gratifications through the life cycle. In K. E. Rosengren, L. A. Wenner, & P. Palmgreen (Eds.), *Media gratifications research: Current perspectives* (pp. 195–208). Beverly Hills, CA: Sage.

Rubinstein, E. A. (1980). Television violence: A historical perspective. In E. L. Palmer & A. Dorr (Eds.), *Children and the faces of television* (pp. 113–127). New York: Academic Press.

Selnow, G. W., & Bettinghaus, E. P. (1982). Television exposure and language development. *Journal of Broadcasting, 26*, 469–479.

Sheehan, P. W. (1986). Television viewing and its relation to aggression among children in Australia. In L. R. Huesmann & L. D. Eron (Eds.), *Television and the aggressive child: A cross-national comparison* (pp. 161–199). Hillsdale, NJ: Lawrence Erlbaum Associates.

Singer, D. G., & Singer, J. L. (1981). Television and the developing imagination of the child. *Journal of Broadcasting, 25*, 373–387.

Singer, D. G., Zuckerman, D. M., & Singer, J. L. (1980). Helping elementary school children learn about TV. *Journal of Communication, 30*, 84–93.

Singer, J. L., & singer, D. G., & Rapaczynski, W. S. (1984). Family patterns and television viewing as predictors of children's beliefs and aggression. *Journal of Communication, 34*, 73–89.

Siverman-Watkins, L. T., Levi, S. C., & Klein, M. A. (1986). Sex-stereotyping as factor in children's comprehension of television news. *Journalism Quarterly, 63*, 3–11.

Sun, S., & Lull, J. (1986). The adolescent audience for music videos and why they watch. *Journal of Communication, 36*, 115–125.

Wartella, E. (1980). Individual differences in children's responses to television advertising. In E. L. Palmer & A. Dorr (Eds.), *Children and the faces of television* (pp. 307–322). New York: Academic Press.

Wartella, E., Alexander, A., Lemish, D. (1979). The mass media environment of children. American Behavioral Scientist, 23, 33–52.

Watkins, B. (1985). Television viewing as a dominant activity of childhood: A developmental theory of television effects. *Critical Studies in Mass Communications, 2*, 323–337.

Webster, J. G., & Coscarelli, W. C. (1979). The relative appeal to children of adult versus children's television programming. *Journal of Broadcasting, 23*, 437–451.

Welch, A. J., & Watt, J. H., Jr., (1982). Visual complexity and young children's learning from television. *Human Communication Research, 8*, 133–145.

Williams, F. LaRose, R., & Frost, F. (1981). *Children, television, and sex-role stereotyping.* New York: Praeger.

Wolf, M. A. (1987). How children negotiate television. In T. R. Lindlof (Ed.), *Natural audiences: Qualitative research of media uses and effects* (58–94). Norwood, NJ: Ablex.

Wright, J. C., & Huston, A. C. (1981). Children's understanding of the forms of television. In H. Kelly & H. Gardner (Eds.), *Viewing children through television*, (pp. 73–88). San Francisco, CA: Jossey–Bass.

PART II

YOUNG ADULTHOOD/ ADULTHOOD

7 Developmental Issues in Personal Relationships

William W. Wilmot

Alan L. Sillars
University of Montana

Our personal relationships, composed of communicative interchanges with family members, work associates, friends, romantic partners, and acquaintances are of paramount importance to our lives. The patterning and evolution of our relationships over the life course are the "stuff our lives are made of" (Levinson, 1986). It is through our personal relationships that we develop, mature, and work through our own individual developmental issues across the life span. The immense importance of our personal relationships has, however, not been matched by an appropriate research focus in the available literature. In most research on adult development, for example, relationships are often not placed in their proper central role. Further, recent research on relationships has been limited to the initiation, maintenance, and dissolution of relationships. As a result, both the adult development and relational development literatures ignore salient issues pertaining to life-span concerns about relationships.

The study of individual adult development is in its infancy, having arrived on the scene in the last 30 years or so (Levinson, 1986). But, this booming baby does not make for a complete family. In order to provide a comprehensive picture of life-span development, a central component must be knowledge about relationships per se, not just as an interesting adjunct to individual adult development issues. This chapter overviews current approaches to relationship development, suggests extensions into innovative perspectives for both individual and systemic views, notes the shortcomings of the life-span perspective, and concludes with a call for a central focus on change processes in relationships. Such a shift will

119

necessitate new directions in both the content of research and the methodology of choice for the researcher.

CURRENT PERSPECTIVES ON RELATIONSHIP DEVELOPMENT

There is increasing recognition of the importance of personal relationships by both the mass media and the social sciences. One only has to pick up the latest issue of a magazine to find articles on "how to survive the loss of your lover" or "ten easy steps to marriage happiness." In the academic world, there has been a concomitant focus on relationships and communication. In the available research, there have been theoretical notions advanced to help us understand how relationships develop and decay. The most notable theoretical perspectives range from equity theory in social psychology to a variety of developmental perspectives linking communication and relationship development. All the perspectives focus on the "development" of the relationship over time. For instance, Berger and his colleagues have speculated that "uncertainty" is central to the process of relationship development (Berger & Calabrese, 1975; Berger & Bradac, 1982; Berger et al., 1976; Clatterbuck, 1979). They postulated that as a relationship develops over time, the central distinguishing feature of uncertainty affects other variables such as self-disclosure. Their notions, however, seem most relevant to the initial phases of interaction (VanLear & Trujillo, 1986).

A more comprehensive view of the development of relationships appears in the classic work of Altman and Taylor (1973). They considered eight dimensions of communication and proposed that relationships go through four stages of phases of development: (a) orientation, (b) exploratory affective exchange, (c) full affective exchange, and (d) stable exchange. Using slightly different terminology, Knapp (1984) specified more finely tuned stages for relationship development and dissolution. He suggested that communication in relationships varies between narrow–broad, stylized–unique, difficult–efficient, rigid–flexible, awkward–smooth, public–personal, hesitant–spontaneous and overt judgment suspended–judgment given. Relationships, in turn, go through growth and decay phases produced and reflected by these communication patterns. Knapp also expanded the perspective of Altman and Taylor by specifying that relationships move through these stages: initiating, experimenting, intensifying, integrating, bonding, differentiating, circumscribing, stagnating, avoiding, and terminating.

Others have focused on select parts of the developmental process. VanLear and Trujillo (1986) for instance, followed five weeks of interaction between acquaintances. Their data suggests these stages: (a) uncertainty, (b) exploratory affect, (c) interpersonal growth, and (d) interpersonal stability. Wilmot (1987), though overviewing literature on the development-dissolution continuum, took a dialectical perspective and emphasized the fluctuation inherent in "stabilized" relationships. The notion of communication spirals, for instance, highlights natural fluctuations within existing relationships. In addition, the work also specifies postdissolution processes of relationships by examining how relationships are redefined.

Prior to Altman and Taylor (1973), data on relationships did not consider the developmental aspects of relationships. As a result of their work and subsequent perspectives, however, more data and theorizing has "come of age" and focused on some part of the initiation-maintenance-dissolution continuum. This much needed expansion into the beginning-to-end developmental perspective does not, however, address all the important issues regarding relationships across the life span. First, most research clusters on the two ends of the process, either examining initiation or dissolution. The sometimes lengthy "stable" phases of relationships are often given only cursory treatment. Since over half of all marriages still do not lead to divorce, studies should examine the ongoing fluctuations in "stable" relationships, not just the initiation and dissolution phases. Second, a host of interesting and potentially fruitful questions regarding relationships have not been asked. The following section suggests an orientation that expands our view of the "development" of personal relationships over the life span.

BROADENING THE PERSPECTIVE

Cognitive Changes in Adulthood

The vast bulk of perspectives on our cognitive developments underrepresent the changes in cognitive structure for adults. The expression, "I wonder what I will be when I grow up," illustrates a cultural belief that developmental alterations occur prior to adulthood. Yet, in terms of our cognitive views of relationships, it is doubtful whether all changes cease upon physical maturity. The opportunities for understanding individual changes over time are legion. For instance, as we mature, we develop relationship schemata; sets of categories about our personal relationships. Relationship schemata in adulthood have been the subject of investigations by Planalp (1985) and Wilmot and Baxter (1984, 1989). One of the central findings is that individuals have (a) relational labels ("friends"; "romantic partners") connected to (b) criterial attributes ("friends are trustworthy") that are judged based on (c) communicative indicators ("you know a friend can be trusted when he helps you when you are broke").

As adults, relationship schemata continue to change. Some categories may change as a consequence of acquiring new roles (e.g., supervisor, step-parent), which leads to a richer and more differentiated view of certain relationship types. Relationship schemata may also change as a function of changing needs and priorities throughout the life span. For example, friendship schemata typically undergo redefinition during major life changes, such as marriage, parenthood, divorce, and retirement. For instance, marriage may force redefinition of the friendship network that each person had prior to marriage. Unless the spouses maintain rigidly segregated friendship networks, as in the case of blue collar couples studied by Komarovsky (1962), friendship circles will tend to be narrowed and accommodated to the new identity of the individuals as a "couple." A likely consequence is that friendship may become more specialized following marriage. That is, people will have golfing buddies, other couples that they have over for dinner, or families that they go camping with, rather than general friendships that satisfy a broad set of companionate functions. Parenthood probably exaggerates this trend, because maintenance of the basic family unit absorbs increasingly more attention with the addition of each new member. Divorce reverses this process, as friendships that were previously based on interactions "as a couple" must be renegotiated or discarded (Weiss, 1975). Retirement may also promote monumental changes in friendship if a person's social interactions prior to retirement are centered around work activities and coworkers. The loosening or severing of ties with work may increase companionship needs and lead to a softening of sex-typed (e.g., dominant and instrumental) traits among males in favor of more companionate and expressive traits (Lieberman, 1978; Treas, 1975; Zube, 1982). Such changes are more than a matter of exchanging one friend for another; they entail evolving forms of friendship.

A myriad of questions might be raised about relational schemata. The points just discussed are merely illustrative. A more comprehensive view of relational schemata would include a response to such questions as the following:

1. How are our categories for relationships developed? How do we learn to distinguish between relational categories such as friendship and romantic relations?
2. Under what conditions do our expectations for relationships change? When do we transform our relational schemas to correspond with a changing reality?
3. Do relationship schemata operate cross-culturally in a similar fash-

ion? If the processes are identical, are the content dimensions disparate (the expectations for friendships, for example)?

4. How do individuals adjust their schemas based on life experiences? If
   one has a prototype for a relational type, how is that modified by
   experience?

5. What role does communication play in shaping and altering our
   cognitive schemas for relationships?

A second way to trace cognitive changes in adulthood is to study the
metaphors that people use to describe relationships. Metaphor is presumed to reflect thought, in fact, Lakoff and Johnson (1980) suggested
that all thought is essentially metaphorical (i.e., we always understand
one thing in terms of something else). The role of metaphor in personal
relationships has produced interested speculation (e.g., Bochner, 1976;
Weick, 1979), but uncertainty about how to study metaphor seems to
have stunted research in the area. Interpretation of metaphor is only
slightly easier than dream analysis and should be viewed just as cautiously. Still, metaphor appears to be a fertile if elusive subject, particularly
with respect to the level of interdependency experienced within relationships. Metaphors are highly personal, content-dependent forms of
expression. From this standpoint, the very existence of shared metaphors
is a sign of increased interdependence. Cohen (1979) suggested that
metaphors achieve intimacy because they signal a commonality of purpose that excludes others. Similarly, Baxter (1987) investigated the "symbols of relationship identity" for individuals. She found that individuals
use symbols as "metacommunicative 'statements' about the abstract
qualities of intimacy, caring, solidarity, etc. which parties equate with
their relationships" (Baxter, 1987, pp. 262–263).

Not only does the development of personal metaphors indicate increased interdependence, the type of metaphor may also indicate the
direction that this interdependence takes. Stephen and Enholm (1987)
found that couples could be classified based on their use of simile (which
suggests likeness, equality, or interchangeability among partners), analogy (which suggests separate but functionally interdependent identities),
or paradox (suggesting mutual exclusion, contradiction, or opposition).
The latter type of metaphor implies an antagonistic form of interdependence; thus, couples who compared their relationship to paradoxical items (e.g., "odd/even," "advance/retreat") expressed less
commitment, adjustment, and agreement than couples who found simile
("glue/paste") or analogy ("horse/buggy," "shoes/socks") relations more
characteristic of marriage. In a study of cross cultural differences, Deetz
(1981) concluded that Malaysian students used more holistic metaphors
to describe personal relationships (e.g., a perfectly round fruit

in which the halves cannot be distinguished) than American students. American students expressed metaphors in which the relationship is viewed as a separate entity (e.g., as a building, woven fabric, or journey) formed by individual actions. Both sets of metaphors stress interdependence, yet interdependence in the American sense is based on interaction between separate identities, not on an indivisible whole. As yet, we do not know if changes in a couples' view of their interdependence fluctuates over the life span. It may be that successful couples undergo change from the individualistic to holistic patterns. Or, there may be other sweeping alterations that correspond to either increases or decreases in marital quality. Finally, the therapeutic implications of changes in metaphors have not been explored. It could be that substitution of more holistic metaphors would bring concomitant changes in one's relational satisfaction.

Clearly, research on our metaphoric understandings of relationships from childhood to old age would give us useful information about the cognitive processing of relationships. When an individual characterizes a relationship as "solid as a rock" that is a very different picture than saying one's marriage is like a "rocky boat at sea, with continual storms almost swamping it." We need to launch full-scale studies of the symbolic and metaphoric processes by which individuals make sense of their relationships.

Of course, there are numerous other questions to be raised regarding the cognitive development of individuals within relationships. One can look at the motives for friendship (McAdams & Losoff, 1984), how we process "negative relationships" (Neimeyer & Neimeyer, 1985), or the complexity of impressions and how complexity interrelates with communication in relationships (O'Keefe & Delia, 1982). One recent developmental view examines complexity with respect to relationship constructs (Schofield & Kafer, 1985). The SOLO taxonomy ("The Structure of the Observed Learned Outcome") takes observable outcomes such as responses to "Why do you need a good friend?" and sorts them hierarchically based on complexity of responses. Schoefield and Kafer (1985) would classify children's responses to "Why do you need a good friend?" as follows:

Prestructural: So they have a good friend.

Unistructural: So they have someone to play with.

Multistructural: For someone to play with, to walk to school with, and to let her new friends show her around, to talk to and go swimming with her. To help her and to go places with.

Relational: With a good friend you can share things and have things in common. Otherwise, you get tired of each other. (p. 157)

The SOLO taxonomy moves us past stages based on age and toward stages based on qualities of responses. As such, it provides a grounded, yet theoretical perspective based on relationship understanding per se. Such a relationship-based focus will be more heuristic and realistic than overall schemes based on nonrelational criterion, such as age.

The Individual and Transindividual Focus

Most work on relationships still takes an individual unit of analysis, either highlighting a select feature of communication, examining changes in an individual's communication over time, or aggregating individual scores into a composite score. For instance, Knapp, Wiemann, and Daly (1978) highlighted the differences in communication associated with different relationship terms by surveying a multitude of persons and their relationships. Similarly, the Baxter and Wilmot (1984, 1985) studies looked at secret tests and taboo topics in personal relationships. Other research also uses individual responses to construct notions about relationships. The Dickson-Markman (1984) study on self-disclosure to close friends as a function of age assesses different individual's reported self-disclosure. She then compared the disclosure rates across the individuals surveyed and found that relationships may not be that different across the life span. Some studies of marital satisfaction also limit their view to the expressions of only one of the partners, for example, tracing marital satisfaction over time. Even the classic studies on the development of children's friendships, derive their conclusions based on the accumulation of individual children's responses (Selman & Selman, 1979).

An alternative perspective for studying relationships is to incorporate relational units of analysis composed of either (a) nonsummative combinations of each person's perspective and communication or (b) systemic variables that transcend the individual's involved. Illustrative of the first approach is work by Stephen (1985). He followed couples over a 5-week time period, assessing both partner's views throughout the period. He found that couples had an "emergent couple reality" shaped by mutual influences from both persons and that other important variables were similarity, joint commitment, and agreement between partners.

Married couples have been studied from the "transindividual" perspective, especially regarding transition phases such as child birth. Lips and Morrison (1986) found that in response to the first pregnancy both spouses developed a positive shift to themselves as a couple unit with a stronger orientation toward family relationships. Anderson, Russell, and Schumm (1983) noted that the presence of children directly decreased the overall touch, talk, and smiling of married spouses. And, summarizing a rather vast body of research, Belsky, Lang, and Rovine (1985) noted that during and after pregnancy, both partners experienced a lessening of satisfaction and love. One interesting side note to their research is that husbands and wives begin with divergent views of the marriage but end up with similar appraisals. Further, wives converge more toward husbands than vice versa (Belsky et al., 1985). Both persons see a decrease in romance and friendship and a move toward a "partnership" over time. Most researchers see child rearing as an added stress that tends to reduce marital satisfaction initially (see Sillars & Wilmot, this volume). Ade-Ridder and Brubaker, (1983) suggested that those with a high quality marriage usually experience a decline in satisfaction during child rearing and then bounce back, whereas low quality marriages stay low.

All personal relationships are probably characterized by some asymmetry—divergent perspectives of the two partners (Duck & Miell, 1984; Neimeyer & Neimeyer, 1985). These divergent perspectives, rather than providing troubling "nonfitting" data become the prime variables of interest in transindividual research. The ebb and flow of mutual understanding and perception become the essence of the relationship itself, constructed by the actions and views of both participants (Wilmot, 1987).

Understanding remains problematic even in long-term intimate relationships. Misunderstanding stems not so much from ignorance about the other in these contexts as it does from bias. Intimate partners may have a wealth of information about one another; however, with the wealth of information there is greater temptation to view the sources of information selectively and to engage in less self-conscious testing and revision of inferences about the partner. Thus, spouses who may have held conversations numbering in the tens of thousands have shown little understanding of one another on some sensitive issues (Sillars, Pike, Jones, & Murphy, 1984). Further, couples who demonstrated a direct style of communication had no greater understanding of one another than nondisclosive and evasive couples (Sillars et al., 1984; Zietlow, 1986). Relationship partners selectively process messages based on their preconceptions, mood state and other factors. For example, dissatisfied married couples remember negative messages more accurately than satisfied couples (Sillars, Weisberg, Burggraf, & Zietlow, 1988). Of course, relationship partners may also know one another well on the matters of importance to them and usually we would expect communication to help rather than hinder understanding. Still, understanding is not a constant. For example, misunderstanding may suddenly become an acute issue during periods of stress and personal change. During stable periods partners are apt to press for understanding only up to the point that a comfortable interdependence is achieved.

As a final note, the paradigm suggested years ago by Laing, Philipson, and Lee (1966) could serve as an organizing scheme for transindividual research. Their notions of agreement–disagreement, understanding–misunderstanding, feeling understood–feeling misunderstood, and realizing and failing to realize that one is understood or misunderstood remain sound. All of the concepts are constructed based on combinations of participants' perspectives and are solidly transpersonal. The scheme deserves much more research attention than it has received.

The second main approach to personal relationships advances the transindividual focus to the next level—systemic variables. Systemic notions move beyond recognition of the individual players and chart overall progress of the system across time. Basically, such systemic approaches focus on stages or phases of relationships. Works tend to cluster into (a) those taking a life-span or age perspective and (b) those that are addressed specifically to relationships. The typical life-span perspective tends to look at the more macro issues—stages in life (and, we presume) relationships over time. The basic presupposition is that each "season" or stage in life has its purpose, and there are appropriate developmental tasks to be accomplished at each stage. Illustrative of such macro notions of life-span development is Levinson's work (1986). He proposed the stages and the appropriate tasks as follows:

EARLY ADULT TRANSITION (17 to 22) developmental bridge between preadulthood and early adulthood.

ENTRY LIFE STRUCTURE FOR EARLY ADULTHOOD (22 to 28) is the time for building and maintaining an initial mode of adult living.

AGE 30 TRANSITION (28 to 33) is an opportunity to reappraise and modify the entry structure and create the basis for the next life structure.

CULMINATING LIFE STRUCTURE FOR EARLY ADULTHOOD (33 to 40) is the vehicle for completing this era and realizing our youthful aspirations.

MIDLIFE TRANSITION (40 to 45) is another of the great cross-era shifts, serving both to terminate early adulthood and to initiate middle adulthood.

LIFE STRUCURE FOR MIDDLE ADULTHOOD (45 to 50) like its counterpart above, provides an initial basis for life in a new era.

AGE 50 TRANSITION (50 to 55) offers a mid-era opportunity for modifying and perhaps improving the entry life structure.

CULMINATING LIFE STRUCTURE FOR MIDDLE ADULTHOOD (55 to 60) is the framework in which we conclude this era.

LATE ADULT TRANSITION (60 to 65) is a boundary period between middle and late adulthood, separating and linking the two eras. (p. 7)

Basically, this developmental perspective suggests that the life cycle evolves through definable forms. It is an extension of the early developmental work that tended to examine stages culminating in adulthood. For example, as children grow older their concepts of friendship grow more complex, as illustrated in the notions of Selman (McAdams & Losoff, 1984; Scholfield & Kafer, 1985). All of these "developmental" views, though pinpointing individual development, have a transindividual perspective by specifying stages of development for all individuals across some designated time span. As just noted, one of the more robust findings regarding the overall marriage patterns in our culture are that over time marriage satisfaction shows an initial decline. The only argument in the literature is whether the decline is linear or whether it is curvilinear with an "upswing" after the children leave home.

The second major cluster of work consists of classificatory schemes specifically keyed to relationships. The Knapp (1984) notions of stages of relationships discussed earlier continue to offer a useful perspective for understanding relationships per se. More specialized works also exist. Baxter (1984) set forth a data-based model of trajectories for disengagement in relationships. Her work highlights the actions inherent in disengagement, such as direct or indirect disengagement actions, single or multiple "passes", attempted or unattempted repair actions, and either termination or continuation of the relationships. One of the key features of her scheme is that it is targeted specifically to limited phases of relationships, and it illuminates some of the complexity the participants face during the dissolution. Undoubtedly, more sophisticated and data-based models of relational development will emerge in the near future because of the intense interest in the development of relationships (Duck, Lock, McCall, Fitzpatrick, & Coyne, 1984).

Relationship Constellations

Just as individual responses fail to reveal everything of interest about interpersonal relationships, dyadic relationships fail to reveal everything of interest about a person's network of relationships. Basically, we need to broaden our view beyond individuals and dyads. As Levinson (1986) said, "it requires us to examine the life course in its complexity, to take into account the external world as well as the self, to study the engagement of the self in the world, and to move beyond an encapsulated view of the self" (p. 11). Each of us is, above all, interconnected to a variety of relationships throughout our life course.

Our relationship constellations fluctuate as we mature. As we grow, the sphere of relationships also grows, yet we remain firmly rooted in the family (Shulman, 1975). Much has been said in recent years about the "pulling up roots" stages of early adulthood where we move farther away from our families. And, once people marry and have children, movement back toward the family is the norm (Shulman, 1975). However, because studies of the entire constellations are lacking, it is easy to overgeneralize about the movement away from the family. In one unpublished survey, college students were asked to list their "five most important relationships." What emerged was that the bulk of the closest relationships were from the family of origin even though these students were at the "pulling up roots phase" (Wilmot, 1980). Shulman found a similar pattern, with the closest relationships being overrepresented by kin. Some potential questions for research on the "constellation" of relationships are:

1. What are some varieties in relationship constellations for individuals?
2. What variables are associated with diversity in relational constellations?
3. How do close relationships of one type (closeness to kin for example) impact on other close relationships (romantic relationships)?
4. What is the impact of life satisfaction when relational constellations constrict or expand over the life span?
5. What "network" variables can be used to describe personal relationships? For example, does the "density" and "multiplexity" of relationships in organization have application to personal relationships?
6. Are there stable individual patterns across relationships? For example, what proportion of people construct communication systems in a second marriage that mirror the patterns in the first? What patterns of friendship are repeated across disparate individuals?
7. Do individuals learn new patterns of initiating, maintaining, and dissolving important relationships?
8. Do the same relationships serve vastly different functions across the life span? For example, do friendships serve markedly different functions before and after the exit of children from the home?
9. With half the population going through divorce, how does the "blended family" differentially impact all other relationships?

If studies successfully incorporate information about entire networks of relationships and take a longitudinal perspective, new insights about the comparison of individual patterns and relationships can be opened. Table 7.1 illustrates a comprehensive perspective on both (a) individual

Table 7.1
Relational Constellations

Age	Birth	10	20	30	Individual 40	50	60	70	Death

Relationship Type
A. Kin
   1. Father —————————————/
   2. Mother ——————————————————/
   3. Sibling 1 ——————————————————/
   4. Sibling 2 ——————————————————
   5. Child 1 ———————————————
   6. Child 2 ————————————————
B. Friends
   1. —
   2. —
   3. ——————————————————
   4. ————
   5. ——
   6. ————
   7. ——————
   .
   .
   .
C. Romantic Partners
   1. —
   2. -
   3. ——
   4. -
   5. —
   6. Spouse ———————————————
   7. Affair ——
D. Others
   1. Business Partner ——————
   2. ————
   3. ——
   4. ——————
   5. ———
   .
   .
   .

/ = death of person

development and (b) relationships across the life span. For purposes of illustration, only three types of close relationships are included, (a) kin, (b) friends, and (c) romantic partners, with all other relationships indicated by "others." A hypothetical person's life-span relational patterns are included. Note that at any one age, the relational constellations are considerably different than any other. This hypothetical individual lives to 70 years of age, and during that time experiences considerable fluctuation in kin, friend, and romantic relationships.

Although entirely hypothetical, it does demonstrate the lack of comprehensiveness in most studies of relationships and communication. If we study one's current relationship with a romantic partner, for example, we may be ignoring crucial kin and friendship relations that have a direct impact on the romantic relationship (Parks & Adelman, 1983). For example, Kalmuss and Seltzer (1986) found that spouse abuse was more likely in a remarriage and reconstituted families than first marriages. Likewise, if we assess the quality of a marriage during or after the brief one-time affair of our hypothetical person, we will probably attain different results. Any full understanding of an individual's relational development across time will incorporate the constellation of fluctuating relationships (Wilmot, 1987). One of the by-products of such an expansion of viewpoint will be the inclusion of other relationships into research domains. For example, communication researchers rarely study sibling and other kin relationships, dealing almost exclusively with friend and romantic relations. Geotting (1980) found, for example, that siblings assist one another with support in child rearing, then face the task of dealing with the care and support of their own parents in their declining years, then can help one another with their own problems associated with aging. And, as people grow older they tend to express more compatibility and closeness to their siblings than they previously did (Geotting, 1986). Such processes, interwoven with friend and romantic connections have not been fully explored for the rich insights they can offer.

CAUTIONS AND CAVEATS

A life-span perspective on relationships can nudge us to broaden our perspective and begin to see relationships from birth to death as important. However, the life-span perspective is not sufficient by itself. For example, most studies using the life-span perspective look at marital discord, satisfaction, or adjustment and their relation to a stage of the family life cycle. But, because the stage of life cycle correlates with the age and number of years married to a current spouse, all of the measures are related. In the sociologist jargon, we need to partial out the cohort effects from these findings and not simply generalize by saying that marriages change due to the stage of life (Hudson & Murphy, 1980). In addition, the life-cycle model accounts only for a trivial amount of variance in the selected dependent variables (Hudson & Murphy, 1980; Anderson, Russell, Schumm, 1983).

The life-span perspective is also limited because it tends to concentrate analysis around major life transitions such as marriage, child rearing, or death of spouse (Norton, 1983). Yet, we all know that even during times of relative "stability" considerable change is occurring. Stable relationships are, in fact, only stable by comparison to times of greater flux. Relationships oscillate back and forth, and can contain considerable fluctuation even in "stable" times (Baxter & Wilmot, 1983; Wilmot, 1987). One useful perspective for studying relationships across the life-span would be to assess their fluctuations between dialectical extremes across time (Altman, Vinsel, & Brown, 1981; Baxter, 1982; Wilmot, 1987). At a minimum, relationships need to be seen as "in process" at all times, allowing us to highlight some of the fascinating and complex movements within them.

Basically, if we want to fully understand relationships we have to insist on two things: (a) studying change in relationships and (b) using longitudinal research to give us the necessary data. Cross-sectional snapshots of relationships across time, though providing interesting insights, bypass some of the most provocative types of information. A variety of strategies are possible ranging from repeated measures to, at a minumum, forms of retrospective recall. Work by Stephen (1985) and Baxter and Wilmot (1986) demonstrates the utility of such processural approaches.

The life-span perspective gives us an opportunity to refocus on the critical issues of relationship development. Undoubtedly, major life-turning points will shed interesting light on relationships, but the central issues for studying relationships are lodged in the realm of change processes. Whether our chosen focus is on changes in the individual's processing of relationships, systemic variables, or alteration in relational constellations across time, the most critical issues regarding relationship development are located in the nature of change, both within and across relationships.

REFERENCES

Ade-Ridder, L. A., & Brubaker, T. H. (1983). The quality of long-term marriages. In T. H. Brubaker (Ed.), *Family relationships in later life* (pp. 21–30). Beverly Hills: Sage Publications.

Altman, I., & Taylor, D. A. (1973). *Social penetration: The development of interpersonal relationships.* New York: Holt, Rinehart & Winston.

Altman, I., Vinsel, A., & Brown, B. B. (1981). Dialectic conceptions in social psychology: An application to social penetration and privacy regulation. In L. Berkowitz (Ed.), *Advances in experimental social psychology,* (Vol. 14, pp. 107–160). New York: Academic Press.

Anderson, S. A., Russell, C. S., & Schumm, W. R. (1983). Perceived marital quality and family life-cycle categories: A further analysis. *Journal of Marriage and the Family, 45*(1), 127–139.

Baxter, L. A. (1984). Trajectories of relationship disengagement. *Journal of Social and Personal Relationships* (Vol. 1, 29–48).

Baxter, L. A. (1987). Symbols of relationship identity in relationship cultures. *Journal of Social and Personal Relationships, 4,* 261–280.

Baxter, L. A., & Wilmot, W. W. (1985). Taboo topics in close relationships. *Journal of Social and Personal Relationships, 2,* 253–269.

Baxter, L. A., & Wilmot, W. W. (1983). Communication characteristics of relationships with differential growth rates. *Communication Monographs 50,* 264–272.

Baxter, L. A., & Wilmot, W. W. (1984). Secret tests: Social strategies for acquiring information about the state of the relationship. *Human Communication Research, 11*(2), 171–201.

Baxter, L. A., & Wilmot, W. W. (1986). Interaction characteristics of disengaging, stable and growing relationships. In R. Gilmour & Duck S. (Eds.), *The emerging field of personal relationships* (pp. 145–159). Hillsdale, NJ: Lawrence Erlbaum Associates.

Belsky, J., Lang, M. E., & Rovine, M. (1985). Stability and change in marriage across the transition to parenthood: A second study. *Journal of Marriage and the Family, 47*(4), 855–865.

Berger, C. A., & Bradac, J. J. (1982). *Language and social knowledge: Uncertainty in interpersonal relations.* London: Edward Arnold.

Berger, C. A., & Calabrese, R. J. (1975). Some explorations in initial interaction and beyond: Toward a developmental theory of interpersonal communication. *Human Communication Research, 1,* 99–112.

Berger, C. A., Gardner, R. R., Clatterbuck, G. W., & Schulman, L. S. (1976). Perceptions of information sequencing in relationship development. *Human Communication Research, 3,* 29–46.

Bochner, A. (1976). Conceptual frontiers in the study of communication in families, *Human Communication Research, 2,* 381–396.

Clatterbuck, G. W. (1979). Attributional confidence and uncertainty in initial interaction. *Human Communication Research, 5,* 147–157.

Cohen, T. (1979). Metaphor and the cultivation of intimacy. In S. Sacks (Ed.), *On metaphor* (pp. 1–10). Chicago: University of Chicago Press.

Deetz, S. (1981). Interpretive research in intercultural communication: Metaphor analysis as an example. Paper presented to the Speech Communication Association Convention, Anaheim, CA.

Dickson-Markman, F. (1984). *Communication with friends across the life cycles: Some preliminary findings.* Paper presented at the Western Speech Communication Association Convention, Seattle, Washington.

Dickson-Markman, F. (1986). Self-disclosure with friends across the life cycles. *Journal of Social and Personal Relationships, 3,* 259–264.

Duck, S., Lock, A., McCall, G., Fitzpatrick, M. A., & Coyne, J. C. (1984). Social and personal relationships: A joint editorial. *Journal of Social and Personal Relationships, 1,* 1–10.

Duck, S. W., & Miell, D. (1984). Towards a comprehension of friendship development and breakdown. In H. Tajfel, C. Fraser, & J. Japars (Eds.), *The Social dimension: European developments in social psychology.* CUP: Cambridge.

Goetting, A. (1986). The developmental tasks of siblingship over the life cycle. *Journal of Marriage and the Family 48*(4), 703–714.

Hudson, W. W., & Murphy, G. J. (1980). The non-linear relationship between marital satisfaction and stages of the family life cycle: An artifact of type I errors? *Journal of Marriage and the Family 42*(2), 263–267.

Kalmuss, D. & Seltzer, J. A. (1986, February). Continuity of marital behavior an remarriage: The case of spouse abuse. *Journal of Marriage and the Family, 48,* 113–120.

Knapp, M. L. (1984). *Interpersonal communication and human relationships.* Boston: Allyn & Bacon.

Knapp, M. L., Wiemann, J. M., & Daly, J. A. (1978). Nonverbal communication: Issues and appraisal. *Human Communication Research, 4*(3), 271–280.

Komarovsky, J. (1962). *Blue-collar marriage.* New York: Random House.

Laing, R. D., Phillipson, H., & Lee, A. R. (1966). *Interpersonal Perception.* Baltimore: Perennial Library.

Lakoff, G., & Johnson, D. *Metaphors we live by.* (1980). New York: McGraw–Hill.

Levinson, D. J. (1986). A conception of adult development. *American Psychologist, 41*(1), 3–13,

Lieberman, M. A. (1978). Social and psychology determinants of adaptation. *International Journal of Aging and Human Development, 9,* 115–126.

Lips, H. M., & Morrison, A. (1986). Changes in the sense of family among couples having their first child. *Journal of Social and Personal Relationships, 3,* 393–400.

McAdams, D. P., & Losoff, M. (1984). Friendship motivation in fourth and sixth graders: A thematic analysis. *Journal of Social and Personal Relationships, 1,* 11–27.

Neimeyer, G. J., & Neimeyer, R. A. (1985). Relationship trajectories: A personal construct contribution. *Journal of Social and Personal Relationships, 2,* 325–349.

Norton, A. J. (1983). Family life cycle: 1980. *Journal of Marriage and the Family, 45*(2), 267–275.

O'Keefe, B. J., & Delia, J. G. (1982). Impression formation and message production. In M. E. Roloff & C. R. Berger (Eds.), *Social cognition and communication* (pp. 33–72) Beverly Hills: Sage Publications.

Planalp, S. (1985). Relational schemata: A test of alternative forms of relational knowledge as guides to communication. *Human Communication Research, 12* (1), 3–29.

Parks, M. R., & Adelman, M. B. (1983). Communication networks and the development of romantic relationships: An expansion of uncertainty reduction theory. *Human Communication Research 10*(1), 55–79.

Schofield, M. J., & Kafer, N. F. (1985). Children's understanding of friendship issues: Development by stage or sequence? *Journal of Social and Personal Relationships 2,* 151–165.

Selman, R. C., & Selman, A. P. (1979). Children's ideas about friendship: A new theory. *Psychology Today, 114,* 71–80.

Shulman, N. (1975). Life-cycle variations in patterns of close relationships. *Journal of Marriage and the Family, 37*(4), 813–821.

Sillars, A. L. (in press) Communication, uncertainty and understanding in marriage. In B. Dervin, L. Grossberg, B. O'Keefe, & E. Wartella (Eds.), *Rethinking communication, Vol. 2: Paradigm exemplars.* Newbury Park, CA: Sage.

Sillars, A. L., Pike, G. R., Jones, T. J., & Murphy, M. A. (1984). Communication and understanding in marriage. *Human Communication Research, 10,* 317–350.

Sillars, A. L., Weisberg, J., Burggraf, C. S., & Zietlow, P. H. (1988). *Communication and understanding revisited: Married couples' understanding and recall of conversation.* Unpublished Manuscript, University of Montana.

Stephen, T., & Enholm, D. K. (1987). On linguistic and social forms: Correspondences between metaphoric and intimate relationships. *Western Journal of Speech Communication, 51,* 329–244.

Stephen, T. D. (1985). Fixed-sequence and circular-causal models of relationship development: Divergent views on the role of communication in intimacy. *Journal of Marriage and the Family, 47*(4), 955–963.

Treas, J. (1975). Aging and the family. In D. Woodruff & J. Birren (Eds.), *Aging: Scientific perspectives and social issues.* New York: D. Van Nostrand.

VanLear, C. A. Jr., & Tujillo, N. (1986). On becoming acquainted: A longitudinal study of social judgement processes. *Journal of Social and Personal Relationships, 3,* 375–392.

Weick, K. R. (1979). *The social psychology of organizing.* Reading, MA: Addison-Wesley.

Weiss, R. S. (1975). *Marital separation.* New York: Basic Books.

Wilmot, W. W. (1980). *Relationship Constellations,* Unpublished Study, University of Montana: Missoula, MT.

Wilmot, W. W. (1987). *Dyadic Communication* (3rd ed.) (1987) New York: Random House.

Wilmot, W. W., & Baxter, L. A. (1989). *The relationship schemata model: On Linking relationships with communication.* Paper presented to Western Speech Communication Association Convention, Spokane, WA Feb. 1989.

Wilmot, W. W., & Baxter, L. A. (1983, Summer). Reciprocal framing of relationship definitions and episodic interaction. *Western Journal of Speech Communication, 47,* 205–217.

Wilmot, W. W., & Baxter, L. A. (1984). *Defining relationships: The interplay of cognitive schemata and communication.* Paper presented to the Communication Theory and Research Interest Group, Western Speech Communication Association Convention, Seattle, WA.

Zietlow, P. H. (1986). *An analysis of the communication behaviors, understanding, self-disclosure, sex roles, and marital satisfaction of elderly couples and couples in earlier life stages.* Unpublished doctoral dissertation, Ohio State University.

Zube, M. (1982). Changing behavior and outlook of aging men and women: Implications for marriage in the middle and later years. *Family Relations, 31,* 147–156.

8 Rehearsing the Margins of Adulthood: The Communicative Management of Adolescent Friendships

William K. Rawlins
Purdue University

The pivotal role of friendship during adolescence is recognized by writers on both subjects (Coleman, 1980; Douvan & Adelson, 1966; Dubois, 1974). This period comprises a watershed for friendship for various reasons. Developmental changes in cognitive abilities and personal and social expectations interactively engender and complicate the adolescent's aptitude and inclinations for friendship. Moreover, the pursuit of identity, intimacy, and appropriate public comportment coalesce in adolescent friendships, which can be functionally significant over the life course. This chapter explores some of the developmental tasks, problematics, and socially constituted exigencies involved in the communicative management of friendships during mid to late adolescence.

I begin by surveying critical, emerging features of the situated endeavors of adolescents to achieve communicatively their self-definitions in conjunction with their social nexus. Friendships figure significantly in this process. Then I describe the continuously enacted premises and the nature of adolescents' ongoing communication with their parents and/or friends. Next, I detail the complex of issues involved in communicating with friends within peer culture. The chapter concludes with implications of managing friendships within multiple social systems for adolescent being-in-the-world, development of communicative competence and evaluative standards for appraising self's and others' behaviors.

ADOLESCENCE AND FRIENDSHIP:
AN OVERVIEW

One can demarcate the lower limits of adolescence physiologically with the onset of puberty and the upper limits sociologically with the assumption of the responsibilities of marriage and full-time work (Campbell, 1969). A central problem in analyzing and accomplishing friendships during this period derives from its status as essentially preparatory for adult life. The activities of adolescents are typically evaluated not as ends in themselves but primarily as opportunities to learn and practice behavioral skills or cognitions that foster well-adjusted adulthood. Campbell (1969) observed, "What is now will not be then, and the really important things come not now but later" (p. 843). The temporal perspective of adolescence is skewed toward the future.

Meanwhile, developmental tasks of adolescence, like articulating one's identity, sense of values, and communicative practices for managing intimacy, might be preempted or robbed of their potential for developing internal resources if conducted according to narrow, adult models for appropriate interaction in a conventionalized, competitive workaday world. Several authors argue after Douvan and Adelson (1966) that "learning friendship" is one of the primary challenges of adolescence and that this process can provide significant emotional cultivation, moral grounding, and communicative skills if pursued for its own inherent value instead of solely as a proto-adult practice (Erikson, 1968; Mitchell, 1976; Youniss & Smollar, 1985). Certain changes in social cognition reaching fruition during adolescence make such interpersonal relationships possible.

The development of formal operations in adolescence comprises a radical change in one's mental capabilities, which Elkind (1984) termed "thinking in a new key." Formal operations entail a shift from thinking in the present to envisioning a world of possibilities. Thinking about the future, hypothetical reasoning, and testing of conjectures become characteristic modes of thought (Adams & Gullotta, 1983). Increasingly, the adolescent thinks about thoughts and begins to formulate and critically evaluate his or her ideals. Such self-examination in conjunction with developing skills in social perspective taking is necessary for discovering the mutual expectations of an interpersonal relationship like friendship (Selman, 1981). Attempts to test these conceptions and ideals in relations with other peers occur (La Gaipa, 1979).

Research reveals the implications of these cognitive abilities for conceiving of friendship. Peevers and Secord (1973) found that by 11th grade, subjects used more differentiated statements to describe friends and nonfriends, demonstrated greater interpersonal involvement with friends, and recognized situational and temporal changes in friends and nonfriends. Kon and Losenkov (1978) also discovered that older adolescents could more precisely distinguish degrees of friendship and differentiate between friends and companions. In short, by mid to late adolescence, sophisticated thinking about friendship is in evidence. Epstein (1983) observed, "Older children can consider simultaneously all available information about the self, the friend, the friendship, the implications of friendship for the future, and the demands of the environment in which the friendship will occur" (p. 44).

The aptitude for and openness to friendship play crucial roles in the adolescent pursuits of identity and intimacy. The critical task of adolescence is to develop an identity (Douvan & Adelson, 1966; Elkind, 1984; Erikson, 1968; Marcia, 1980). According to Douvan and Adelson (1966), "In our society the adolescent period sees the most intense development of friendship. . . . He is about to crystallize an identity, and for this needs others of his generation to act as models, mirrors, helpers, testers, foils" (pp. 178–179). Young people at this stage begin to separate themselves from their families and to develop friendship bonds in a world of peers (Epstein, 1983). Leading to adult autonomy, these friendships provide a crucible for forging "a workable, acceptable identity" (Douvan, 1983, p. 63).

Adolescents need close companions to confide in and talk with about their day-to-day concerns (Johnson & Aries, 1983; Mitchell, 1976; Naegele, 1958). Conflict with parents, fears of rejection by the peer group, anxiety regarding emerging sexuality, and various pressures at school are often significant issues for discussion. Intimacy is a necessity. Conger (1979) maintained that:

> People need, in adolescence perhaps more than at any other time in their lives, to be able to share strong and often confusing emotions, doubts and dreams with others. . . . This means that acceptance by peers generally, and especially having one or more close friends, may be of crucial importance in a young person's life. (p. 66)

Indeed, the need for acceptance and validation of self and the need for intimacy are closely associated in adolescence (Horrocks & Benimoff, 1966; Kon & Losenkov, 1978; Smollar & Youniss, 1982). The young person trying out different self-conceptions wants to feel the validity of both the process and the products. This highly individualized pursuit requires personal validation by someone who views self independently of historical precedents, as might occur in the family, or societal role requirements, as might occur in school or work (Kelvin, 1977). In the process of explaining themselves to each other over a period of time, adolescent friends help articulate each other's identities. Thus, developing a personalized identity and experiencing intimacy appear to be counterparts that interpenetrate during adolescent friendship (Kon, 1981).

The functional significance of adolescent friendship is closely aligned with its role in the search for selfhood and intimacy. Because peer friendships provide an arena for communication independent of the family and historical precedents of interaction, for the first time, choice exists in establishing enduring personal bonds with others (Kon & Losenkov, 1978). Friendships are achieved, not ascribed. The adolescent is compelled to develop the communication skills requisite for a voluntaristic relationship characterized by much give and take and interpersonal negotiation (Naegele, 1958; Rawlins, 1983; Suttles, 1970). As Piaget (1932) and Sullivan (1953) noted, this type of relationship involves cooperating with peers regarding crucial personal concerns rather than pleasing authority figures.

However, in adolescence one's identity also derives from participating in a negotiated, public order of peer relations. For example, study friends and sports friends might confirm or challenge one's abilities in these "objective" domains with limited exposure to one's feelings about such evaluation. Likewise, one may "hang around" with activity and school friends with varying success in sociability. These "everyday" interactions communicate a multifaceted social appraisal of the presented self to the extent that a person elects to participate in them (Berger & Luckman, 1966).

Simultaneously, a person developing more personal, subjective ties in the dyadic realm of closer friendship can discuss and interpret experiences occurring in the public arena with peers and their implications for personal worth. At risk are core conceptions of the self and feelings that may contrast with public views. A trusted, intimate other like a best or close friend is necessary for such dialogue. Developing or sustaining these private views of self may devalue or threaten the validity of evaluative standards held outside of the friendship. Though such discussions may brace a person for further interaction with peers and/or parents and possibly result in altered behavior toward others, their content should remain confidential. Consequently, adolescent friendships occupy an experiential continuum ranging from peer-oriented, public comportment and appraisal to friend-oriented, private communication and evaluation.

The adolescent's self-conscious efforts at self-definition, friendship formation, and social integration interpenetrate and are permeated with rhetorical and dramatistic qualities. Indeed, Elkind (1967, 1980) maintained that adolescents in particular are prone to feel constantly "on stage" for two reasons. First, developing formal operations makes adolescents self-conscious; they are "preoccupied with themselves and assume that other people share that preoccupation" (Elkind, 1980, p. 435). Accordingly, they construct an "imaginary audience" that is always closely observing their actions in given situations. Second, adolescents are self-centered and develop "personal fables" or narratives celebrating their uniqueness and importance and their destinies (Elkind, 1967, 1980). These two tendencies lead to adolescent concern that other people are discussing them and reviewing their self-presentations.

Such concern appears justified. Consider the multiple and interconnected social systems potentially enveloping the family during adolescence—"best" and various close friendships; friendship cliques and peer pecking orders; sexual relationships and dating networks; voluntary, elected, or selected clubs, religious organizations, student councils, newspapers, and honor societies; athletic, musical, cheerleading, artistic, and academic competitions; part-time jobs; not to mention "Kings" and "Queens" of proms and homecoming dances, and so on. Others appraise the adolescent in each of these areas according to various evaluative criteria, some specific to a given enterprise and others involving complex combinations of rankings in diverse domains. *All are socially constructed and communicated: many contradict each other.*

One's family's criteria for evaluating self mostly reflect particularistic and subjective concerns; basically, they are developed to foster emotional security in a child (Eisenstadt, 1956). As the adolescent's encompassing social nexus unfolds, however, the knowledge and appraisal of intimate friends and romantic partners may outstrip the family's in private matters. Simultaneously, the objective rankings of the young person's public pursuits according to universalistic achievement criteria eclipse the family's judgments of behavior in those endeavors as well (Eisenstadt, 1956). The normative composition of the adolescent's worlds rapidly becomes much less clear-cut. Irreducible to simple, predetermined moral codes with attendant "sanctioning agents" (Campbell, 1969, p. 843), standards of behavior emerge through interaction across a variety of circumstances according to objective, subjective, and intersubjective criteria.

The acute self-consciousness and theatrical sensibilities of adolescents seem understandable and functional in this ecology of manifold audiences and appraisals. The attempt to define one's identity involves consciously stylizing oneself in various ways and trying out different versions and images of who one is and/or could become (Campbell, 1969). In this process one is also choosing the particular audiences whose opinions will matter. Because one's activities and associates are subject to multiple interpretations and judgments, the adolescent must begin to decide who he or she is "playing to." In short, adolescents are engaged in the reflexive process of consolidating their self-conceptions and identities as well as the social systems within which they can be developed and sustained.

Within this field of possibilities, friendships occupy a peculiar niche. Though crucial for adolescent development, they essentially comprise a marginal category of social relationships when viewed through the lens of adult socialization. The significance of friendships is difficult to identify precisely and, consequently, pales in comparison with (a) athletic endeavors, which "teach life," that is institutionalized teamwork, coupled with a competitive ethic; (b) academic endeavors, which teach appropriate skills and attitudes for occupational achievement; (c) cross-sex romantic endeavors, which teach ways of expressing fulfilling sexual urges and anticipate the reproductive functions and the religious and legal bonds of marriage; and (d) family endeavors, which teach intergenerational continuity and duty to one's blood relatives. Friendships have no clear normative status within this publicly constituted hierarchy of role relationships; yet they may compete with, complement, substitute for, or fuse with these other types of social bonds (Hess, 1972).

Despite its marginal status, friendship functions intriguingly as a "double agent," weaving in and out of the adolescent's various social worlds, concurrently fulfilling goals of personal growth and social integration (Rawlins, in press). Ironically, even though friendships offer adolescents the opportunity to transcend public and parental appraisals and to negotiate private standards for behavior, statistically the demographic profiles of such friends closely resemble each other as well as their families of origin (Campbell, 1969). Adolescent friends are typically the same age, gender, race, grade in school, and social status (Campbell, 1969; Kandel, 1978b). Moreover, they tend to share fundamental values (Douvan & Adelson, 1966) and similar attitudes toward academic pursuits (Ball, 1981; Epstein, 1983; Kandel, 1978b), peer culture (Berndt, 1982, Kandel, 1978b), and illicit activities like drinking and drug use (Kandel, 1978b). Clearly, however, these conclusions are based on research that cannot definitively distinguish between similarities in outlooks preceding friendships and those developing through interaction within them (Kandel, 1978a).

Even so, some important ironies accompany the double agency of adolescent friendships. One involves the idea that adolescent friendships comprise a fundamental nexus for developing an autonomous identity and beginning to separate from one's parents. In this process, persons who are similar to the adolescent confirm already held attitudes and values and individuals who are different urge change (Epstein, 1983). However, adolescents typically befriend persons who are similar to them in many ways. Thus, the relationships conceivably offering the adolescent a forum for personalized questioning, critique, and value formation frequently reflect similar moral horizons as one's family of origin. The double agency of friendship thereby constitutes an arrangement wherein the limits of one's inherited world views can be tested in a privately negotiated realm whose evaluative contours, though permissive, are typically not drastically different from one's family. To the extent they diverge, they facilitate and encourage idiosyncratic options for defining self yet heighten the potential for conflict with other social formations. To the extent they mirror conventional social practices, they limit self or mutually conceived choices and minimize the friction and challenges of contesting standards.

COMMUNICATING WITH PARENTS AND/OR FRIENDS

This chapter views adolescents as active participants in their own social–emotional development as opposed to merely passive respondents to adult socialization practices. The persons they converse with, listen to, and ignore have important implications for developing their self-conceptions, conceptions of social relationships, and criteria for assessing both. Whom they select, and why and how adolescents choose to interact with others are therefore seminal concerns. Accordingly, Melissa Holl and I recently presented an intelligible frame for understanding 11th-graders' verbal descriptions of managing communication with their parents and friends that reflects the active view advanced previously and challenges the traditional dyadic conception of adolescent friendships as developing in opposition to relationships with parents (Rawlins & Holl, 1988).

These adolescents' descriptions of their interactions with parents and friends suggested dialectical interplay between the two groups' reactions that shaped the ongoing achievement of the young persons' activities and self-perceptions. As a result, they reported choosing different conversational partners according to the nature of the topic, the anticipated type of response, and the degree of caring manifested in the relationship.

Two dialectical principles appeared to inform their decisions about potential interactants. These were termed the dialectic of historical perspective and contemporary experience, and the dialectic of judgment and acceptance. Overall, parents were conceived as viewing adolescent concerns from the remove of a historial perspective. The fact that they had already "been through" most of the events and predicaments that might worry these young people recommended their input. Moreover, parents' knowledge of the potential impact of certain courses of action on later life choices was considered "wisdom."

Even so, our participants did not always want the existential distance and measured perspective of their parents. For matters involving seemingly current sensibilities and knowledge of the present stakes of action, they elected to talk with friends. They felt that persons who were currently living through similar quandaries would better understand and resonate their significance. The dialectic of historical perspective and contemporary experience formulates these adolescents' association of the former with parents and the latter with friends in choosing interlocutors.

Another dialectical principle, which we call the dialectic of judgment and acceptance, informed their choices as well. I mentioned earlier the significant desire and need in adolescence for acceptance by others. Our participants were no exception; they greatly valued people who understood and accepted them and resented and avoided people who judged and criticized or otherwise "put them down."

They viewed parents as much more likely than their friends to criticize them. Parents had certain expectations for their behavior, and violations of them resulted in various unfavorable reactions by parents communicating a low evaluation of the adolescent, for example, yelling, badgering with questions, and criticizing.

In contrast, our respondents perceived their friends as typically accepting them for who they were and not criticizing them. The dialectical juxtaposition identified in our participants' overall association of judgment and criticism with parents and acceptance with friends corresponds with similar findings by Larson (1983) and Youniss and Smollar (1985) even though these investigations utilized quite different research methods.

However, the matter of anticipating judgment from parents and acceptance from friends did not necessarily dictate these adolescents' decisions about conversational partners even if accompanied by a desire for historical perspective from parents or contemporary input from friends. A further consideration mediating our participants' perceptions of their parents' judgmental tendency and their friends' acceptance was the degree of perceived caring. Overall, they felt that their parents cared for them more than their friends did and that their criticisms derived from a genuine concern for the adolescent's well-being. In contrast, friends were often more inclined to accept, even encourage actions not in the young person's best interests because they did not care as deeply for the individual as his or her parents. Thus, parental caring might impel the adolescent to risk a critical reaction, despite an otherwise apparent credo for achieving and protecting independence from parental scrutiny, "Don't tell parents things you did wrong."

Other research also reveals that maintaining a caring and supportive relationship with one's parents is a crucial part of developing as an autonomous person during adolescence (Youniss & Smollar, 1985). For example, O'Donnell (1976) reported that adolescents' self-esteem more closely correlates with feelings toward parents than toward friends. And Greenburg, Siegel, and Leitch (1983) endorsed a conception wherein "the development of ego autonomy and optimal adjustment are promoted by the development of independence in the context of warm relatedness to one's parents" (p. 383).

Even so, none of our participants seemed categorically inclined to speak only to parents or friends about everything. They reflected on the types of responses they might receive from parents and friends, their temporal perspectives, evaluative stances, and the degree of their caring. Their conversational options, however, were not mutually exclusive, nor did they necessarily pit parents and friends against each other. Functioning as counterparts, as alternative voices in the ongoing conversation comprising the adolescent's social construction of self, these people complement, correct, and mediate each other's views and standards.

COMMUNICATING WITH FRIENDS WITHIN PEER CULTURE

As mentioned earlier, the peer culture of adolescence potentially transcends the purview of the family. The multiple social systems of the teen years utilize interlaced evaluative criteria ranging from those more subjective and intimate than one's family to those more objective and public. Desiring acceptance by close associates and/or peers in general, adolescents continually face the challenge of developing communicative skills appropriate for managing differing social relationships and exigencies that may be at odds with each other.

Adolescents we interviewed noted a tension between popularity and friendship (Rawlins & Holl, 1987). Popularity involves recognition and respect by others, a high profile. Further, it requires numbers of people and is a public achievement based on demonstrable qualities and accomplishments or appearances. Students remarked that popularity could accompany success in sports or school, for example, but it frequently involves a fairweather or opportunistic quality to the companionship, not necessarily trust or confidence. Popular people are "fun" and impressive to be seen with.

In contrast, friendship involves acknowledgment, acceptance, and selection by a particular individual. Based on personal qualities and another's understanding of one's feelings and thoughts, it is a more private, dyadic achievement. Friends have fun together but also take each other seriously.

Talk with close friends performs critical functions in structuring a sense of self and relationships with others (Rawlins & Holl, 1987). Trusting a friend implies mutually negotiated responsibilities and expectations regarding interaction within and outside of the friendship. Conversation between friends should be accepting and uncritical. Honest feedback describing how the friend and other peers perceive self is desired if rendered sensitively. A friend must talk prudently with others about self, preserving confidences and refraining from criticism. Violating trust is a poignant act that can subvert an individual's self-image and/or perceptions of how others see him or her; such breaches strongly and negatively affect and frequently end particular friendships, and rearrange friendship networks.

The two realms of private communication and public comportment appear to require different styles of relating to others. Strategies fostering popularity may inhibit a particular friendship and vice versa. Popular people are frequently too busy with activities or juggling acquaintances to have the time or commitment for intimate friendships (Horrocks & Benimoff, 1966). Further, popular persons may be selected as friends for the wrong reasons. One male we interviewed advised, "Being popular is when people know you, they're not really, you can consider them sometimes your friends but really they just hang around you because you're known and maybe they'll get known." Having what it takes to be respected by peers in general may not always result in affection by particular individuals. In contrast, peers might reject an overly exclusive pair of friends because of their conspicuous self-sufficiency. When friends are not available to others or appear too close, peers can express resentment in numerous ways.

Adolescents must learn to position themselves in communication systems involving overlapping and contradictory demands. Recently, Buhrmester and Furman (1986) observed, "Social competencies develop through experiences in interactions that require these competencies" (p. 44). Clearly, one's communicative abilities are challenged in attempting to maintain close and/or superficial friendships during adolescence, with their inevitable internal conflicts, problems arising from responsibilities to different friends, romantic partners and family, and the unclear and shifting boundaries marking the larger social system of peers (Rawlins & Holl, 1987). However, individuals limiting their range of social experiences, for example, to highly conventionalized or sequestered intimate relationships, will similarly constrain their scope of practiced communicative competencies.

Two genres of communicative competencies become necessary in early adolescence for managing the broad variety of possible relationships. Social competence describes the cognitions and performances requisite for handling everyday public interactions with groups of peers. "Intimacy competence" refers to the cognitions and performances necessary for negotiating close dyadic relationships (La Gaipa, 1979). Consequently, the communicative management of popularity versus close friendships theoretically involves different structural properties, conceptions, and performance skills. Following Sullivan, Buhrmester and Furman (1986) argued that preadolescent peer-group interactions foster adeptness at cooperation, compromise, and competition, suggesting, "Children who master these modes of interaction are likely to be accepted and popular in the peer group" (p. 56). By comparison, the "collaborative structure" of their developing friendships encourages "high level perspective-taking skills, modes of empathic support, and altruistic concern for friends' needs" (p. 56). Buhrmester and Furman (1986) clearly acknowledged that people can learn and utilize both sets of skills in either social domain. However, the characteristic exigencies of remaining popular or preserving a friendship would magnify the salience of their associated skills in their respective interactions.

The interlaced peer networks and ongoing personal relationships of adolescence constitute a complex and intimidating social environment within which to embrace or avoid the problematics and satisfactions of developing these contradictory yet complementary competencies. Adolescents' enactments of the communicative possibilities of this social environment range from public to private excesses, and include various individually pursued and contextually negotiated combinations.

Polar Public Comportment

Certain modes of communicative behavior reflect publicly constituted extremes. The characteristic stance involves excessive other-directedness (Riesman, 1961), stifling adherence to social conventions, and surface engagements with people. Young people exhibiting these modes may differ, however, in their principal audience. One pattern of behavior is designed for positive appraisal by peers. The individual gauges his or her actions, opinions, and morals primarily in terms of their appeal to peers. Such an orientation, "the tyranny of the peer group" (La Gaipa, 1979), is typically associated with early adolescence and tends to dissipate with the approach of young adulthood (Douvan & Adelson, 1966).

A variation of the preceding pattern includes communicative behavior primarily targeted for adult audiences and approval. Button (1979) stated:

> Many people who lack close friends seem to act with other people at a functional or organizational level. They often make all their contacts

through interests or activities and play a valuable part in organizing the activity, club, or association. They may assume—and be trapped in— leadership roles. Many young people of this kind have great social poise, and are seen by teachers or youth workers as having considerable social accomplishment and may be very valuable to the adult as helpers. The person concerned is so often able to relate easily and readily with older and younger people, but is in difficulty in relating warmly to peers. (pp. 194–195)

Though both modes may prove functional in peer-group contexts and for public interactions later in life, several authors worry about exclusive reliance on or cultivation of such communicative practices (Button, 1979; Erikson, 1968; Mitchell, 1976). Douvan and Adelson (1966) argued that this facility may be only "manner-deep," comprising a retreat into extroversion and a "social persona" (p. 208). The deeper questions, anxieties, and problems of adolescent identity development remain unresolved, and the adolescent forms the habit of social presentation as a dubious salve for personal quandaries.

Polar Private Conduct

Specific modes of communicative behavior suggest privately constituted excesses as well. Such patterns involve extremes of innerdirectedness (Riesman, 1961), highly idiosyncratic notions of appropriate actions, and overweening expectations of intimate bonds. Naegele (1958) described "isolates" who seem to develop a deviation-amplifying retreat into their private selves in light of overly idealized conceptions of friendship. He presented a penetrating analysis of this disturbing predicament:

> Higher ideals restrict opportunities and enhance the chance of disappointment. Fewer can come up to one's expectations and these, in not being met, are thought about rather than acted. Thought, in turn, generates a degree of self-consciousness which makes easy encounters with others difficult and leads to a sense of isolation. (pp. 247–248)

Different but also restrictive patterns involve orienting oneself almost exclusively to the confines of one's family, or adopting or cleaving to a sole intimate friend or romantic partner to avoid the potential stresses or challenges to self-conceptions arising from sustained or episodic interchange with others (Douvan & Adelson, 1966).

Clearly, between such public and private extremes runs a gamut of relational alternatives. For many adolescents different types of friendships are negotiated along an experiential continuum ranging from peer-oriented, public domains to specific other-oriented private interaction. Elsewhere, we have detailed a gradient of friendship types distinguished by adolescents according to their potential for private knowledge and evaluation of self- and public exposure (Rawlins & Holl, 1987). These include best, close, average, and specialized friends, as well as "friends you say hi to in the halls." Within the diverse friendships, different levels of trust allow for various degrees of talk, and the nature and amount of shared activities fluctuate as well.

Such friendships exist within the social system of peers and continually respond to external as well as internal demands and evaluations. To a degree, these contravening pressures are realized and handled by "hanging around" with a variety of people and participating in the gradient of friendships just described. "Hanging around" provides the fluidity between friends and other peers that makes possible the fulfillment and/or subversion of both status systems' expectations at once. One can be with friends while visible and active with peers. However, a strategic consideration is that who one "hangs out" with constitutes an expression of self open to others' scrutiny and comment. Elkind (1967) emphasized that adolescents are "more concerned with being the observed than with being the observer" (p. 1030). Thus, one may deploy one's friends in light of peer appraisal, for example, studying with someone but avoiding being seen hanging around with him or her. Conversely, who a person hangs out with may affect whether one is chosen as a friend.

Actively managing such an array of relationships in interpenetrating contexts fosters comprehensive competencies in communicating, including social and intimate adeptness. Stressing the potential of the adolescent milieu for developing social competence, Campbell (1969) argued, "Skill in the casual cordiality that marks the business world and the country club is acquired with relative ease when one's life-space is flooded with age-mates toward each of whom one invests a modest but only modest, degree of positive affect" (p. 842). Even so, the complementary necessity for intimacy competence was strongly endorsed by Erikson (1968):

Where a youth does not accomplish such intimate relationships with others—and, I would add, with his own inner resources—in late adolescence or early adulthood, he may settle for highly stereotyped interpersonal relations and come to retain a deep *sense of isolation*. If the times favor an impersonal kind of interpersonal pattern, a man can go far, very far, in life and yet harbor a severe character problem doubly painful because he will never feel really himself, although everyone says he is "somebody." (135–136)

Thus, the challenge is to develop skills in both sociability and intimacy. One needs to master conventional social practices and appropriate public demeanor. However, one must also learn how to manage close, personalized relationships, and to cultivate inner assets. Such differential competencies—like expressing casual cordiality without being too glib and sincere affection without being too cloying—require a spectrum of involvements for their practice and development. Multiple types of social engagements enable the adolescent to acquire a diversified sense of audiences and to participate in their construction with attendant expectations of self and others and standards of appraisal.

The gender-linked tendencies in handling this process are both clear and complex. Overall, adolescent female friendships are characterized as "involved" (Fischer, 1981), more exclusive and intimate than males' (Kon & Losenkov, 1978), closer emotionally (Douvan & Adelson, 1966; Youniss & Smollar, 1985), and more inclined to disclose and discuss personally involving topics (Johnson & Aries, 1983; Youniss & Smollar, 1985). In contrast, adolescent male friendships are described as "uninvolved" (Fischer, 1981), more inclusive and group-related than females' (Kon & Losenkov, 1978), disclosing less, and talking mostly about activity-oriented issues (Johnson & Aries, 1983; Youniss & Smollar, 1985). By and large, then, young women appear to evidence intimacy competence earlier than young men during adolescence (Fischer, 1981).

However, some of these authors argue that males' and females' conceptions of close friendship may be more similar than the preceding data suggest, but a significantly larger percentage of young women are describing close friendships (Youniss & Smollar, 1984). Across a variety of studies and samples, Youniss and Smollar (1985) reported a large minority of male respondents indicating a pattern of responses "clearly different from those given by the majority of all the subjects" (p. 127). The superficiality of this sizable minority's depictions skews their male samples. Thus, both female and male adolescents who do manage close friendships within the domains we have considered are likely to confront and address similar socially constituted exigencies with corresponding potential for developing intimacy competence. Johnson and Aries (1983) noted, "For all participants, frequent conversations with close, same-sex friends revolve around concerns about self, relationships, and the web of daily activities" (p. 225). Moreover, despite gender differences in content issues reportedly discussed with parents, our male and female participants reported equivalent conversational topics with friends as well as a common overall pattern characterizing their interactional rationales for talking with friends and/or parents within their multifaceted social milieux (Rawlins & Holl, 1988). Perhaps, the extensive documentation of adolescent females' greater intimacy competence derives from the fact that more females embrace the challenge and consequently learn how to communicate with close friends sooner.

CONCLUSIONS AND IMPLICATIONS

This chapter reflects a view of adolescent development as praxis (Rawlins, in press). Adolescents do not simply and passively respond to the socialization practices of an already determined social structure. Nor are they precluded from any influence on their own moral and cognitive development formulated as a self-contained and invariant sequence of stages. Rather, I argue that young people participate in an interactive process wherein their capacity for self-consciousness and reflexivity emerges partly as a function of cognitive developments and partly as a function of the various social systems continuously produced and reproduced in their everyday interactions. As adolescents' social horizons broaden and their experiences diversify, the normative composition of social domains becomes less uniform and explicit. Within these various interconnected social orders amidst multiple audiences and evaluative criteria, the marginality and double agency of friendships comprise problematic domains and fundamental resources for articulating one's identity, communicative competencies, and values. Thus, the ability to conceive of one's self and one's relationships shapes and reflects one's communicative choices in enacting, negotiating and, thereby, constituting one's self and one's relationships.

As a double agent adolescent friendship simultaneously engenders social integration and personal growth for its participants. Friendship is symbolic for adolescents. To peers and parents it indicates choosing and/or being chosen by another person, thus symbolizing social acceptance. At the same time having a close friend represents autonomy from peers and parents. Friends can negotiate their own standards within the friendship and become less influenced by the opinions of others (Suttles, 1970). Nevertheless, most adolescents want to be accepted by their parents and peers as well as their friends, producing several interrelated social domains for developing and appraising one's interactional adeptness. As a result, striving for intimacy with friends, preserving caring relationships with parents, and achieving recognition by peers constitute regenerative communicative exigencies.

In the interpenetrated negotiation of adolescent intimacy, public action and identity, the social construction of self as a responsible being and the nature and significance of one's relationships are at issue. Accordingly, viewing friendship activities as marginal practices that potentially distract from or interfere with preparation for more objective adult pursuits comprises a limited and limiting conception. Rather, managing friendships might be conceived as the opportunity to develop moral and interpersonal sensibilities shaped by and answering to particular intersubjective standards, ones that endorse conventional behavior in certain instances and alternative courses of action in others. Importantly, they require an investment of self in their own production and articulation; an enactment of reasoned and concerned social interaction is inherent in their composition. Thus, Youniss and Smollar (1985) observed that within their possibilities for enhancing each individual's sense of personal identity, adolescent close friendships embody prosocial values and social responsibility. Berndt (1982) added that communication with friends "can serve as a foundation for egalitarian relationships with colleagues, neighbors, or spouses in adulthood" (p. 1448).

Several research questions await answers. What communicative habits are formed in managing the variety of friendships during adolescence? How, precisely, do young people reconcile cross-cutting evaluative standards? Do concepts like intimacy competence and social competence delineate certain types of communicative strategies that are domain specific or do they represent more general skills merely applied to more or less public and private circumstances? How consistent are the gender associated differences and similarities in friendships and what do they demonstrate about the development of communicative competence? Are certain adult agendas established by adolescents who primarily constitute themselves in peer group settings as opposed to close friendships and vice versa? Are particular communicative capacities preempted in either case? How important are the quantity and scope of relationships versus their quality and depth? What are the possibilities for training young people to diversify their repertoires in managing relationships? Can we identify distinctive generic predicaments that characterize the various types of friendships during adolescence and suggest particular communicative skills?

Indeed, the boundaries between adolescence and young adulthood cannot be clearly drawn. How do friendships function to forestall or facilitate the transition? If one of the adolescent's chief tasks is "learning friendship" (Douvan & Adelson, 1966), how is one to know that he or she is pursuing a functional curriculum?

REFERENCES

Adams, G. R., & Gullotta, T. (1983). *Adolescent life experiences*. Monterey, CA: Brooks/Cole.
Ball, S. J. (1981). *Beachside comprehensive*. Cambridge, MA: Cambridge University Press.
Berger, P., & Luckman, T. (1966). *The social construction of reality*. Garden City, NY: Doubleday.

Berndt, T. J. (1982). The features and effects of friendship in early adolescence. *Child Development, 53,* 1447–1460.

Buhrmester, D., & Furman, W. (1986). The changing functions of friends in childhood: A neo-Sullivanian perspective. In V. J. Derlega & B. A. Winstead (Eds.), *Friendship and social interaction* (pp. 41–62). New York: Springer–Verlag.

Button, L. (1979). Friendship patterns. *Journal of Adolescence, 2,* 187–199.

Campbell, E. Q. (1969). Adolescent socialization. In D. A. Goslin (Ed.), *Handbook of socialization theory and research* (pp. 821–859). Chicago: Rand McNally.

Coleman, J. C. (1980). Friendship and the peer group in adolescence. In J. Adelson (Ed.), *Handbook of adolescent psychology* (pp. 408–431). New York: Wiley.

Conger, J. (1979). *Adolescence: Generation under pressure.* New York: Harper & Row.

Douvan, E. (1983). Commentary: Theoretical perspectives on peer association. In J. L. Epstein & N. Karweit (Eds.), *Friends in school: Patterns of selection and influence in secondary schools* (pp. 63–69). New York: Academic Press.

Douvan, E., & Adelson, J. (1966). *The adolescent experience.* New York: Wiley.

Dubois, C. (1974). The gratuitous act: An introduction to the comparative study of friendship patterns. In E. Leyton (Ed.), *The Compact: Selected dimensions of friendship* (pp. 15–32). St. Johns: Institute of Social & Economic Research.

Eisenstadt, S. N. (1956). *From generation to generation.* Glencoe, IL: Free Press.

Elkind, D. (1967). Egocentrism in adolescence. *Child Development, 38,* 1025–1034.

Elkind, D. (1980). Strategic interactions in early adolescence. In J. Adelson (Ed.), *Handbook of adolescent psychology* (pp. 432–444). New York: Wiley.

Elkind, D. (1984). *All grown up and no place to go.* Reading, MA: Addison–Wesley.

Epstein, J. L. (1983). Examining theories of adolescent friendships. In J. L. Epstein & N. Karweit (Eds.), *Friends in school: Patterns of selection and influence in secondary schools* (pp. 39–61). New York: Academic Press.

Erikson, E. (1968). *Identity, youth and crisis.* New York: W. W. Norton.

Fischer, J. L. (1981). Transitions in relationship style from adolescence to young adulthood. *Journal of Youth and Adolescence, 10,* 11–23.

Greenberg, M. T., Siegel, J. M., & Leitch, C. J. (1983). The nature and importance of attachment relationships to parents and peers during adolescence. *Journal of Youth and Adolescence, 12,* 373–386.

Hess, B. (1972). Friendship. In M. W. Riley, M. Johnson, & A. Foner (Eds.), *Aging and Society* (pp. 357–393). New York: Russell Sage Foundation.

Horrocks, J. E., & Benimoff, M. (1966). Stability of adolescents' nominee status, over a one-year period, as a friend by their peers. *Adolescence, I,* 224–229.

Johnson, F. L., & Aries, E. J. (1983). Conversational patterns among same-sex pairs of late-adolescent close friends. *The Journal of Genetic Psychology, 142,* 225–238.

Kandel, D. B. (1978a). Homophily, selection, and socialization in adolescent friendships. *American Journal of Sociology, 84,* 427–436.

Kandel, D. B. (1978b). Similarity in real-life adolescent friendship pairs. *Journal of Personality and Social Psychology, 36,* 306–312.

Kelvin, P. (1977). Predictability, power and vulerability in interpersonal attraction. In S. Duck (Ed.), *Theory and practice in interpersonal attraction* (pp. 339–354). London: Academic Press.

Kon, I. (1981). Adolescent friendship: Some unanswered questions for future research. In S. Duck & R. Gilmour (Eds.), *Personal relationships 2: Developing personal relationships* (pp. 187–204). New York: Academic Press.

Kon, I. S., & Losenkov, V. A. (1978). Friendship in adolescence: Values and behavior. *Journal of Marriage and the Family, 40,* 143–155.

La Gaipa, J. J. (1979). A developmental study of the meaning of friendship in adolescence. *Journal of Adolescence, 2,* 201–213.

Larson, R. W. (1983). Adolescents' daily experience with family and friends: Contrasting opportunity systems. *Journal of Marriage and the Family, 44,* 739–750.

Marcia, J. E. (1980). Identity in adolescence. In J. Adelson (Ed.), *Handbook of adolescent psychology* (pp. 159–187). New York: Wiley.

Mitchell, J. J. (1976). Adolescent intimacy. *Adolescence, II,* 275–280.

Naegele, K. D. (1958). Friendship and acquaintances: An exploration of some social distinctions. *Harvard Educational Review, 28,* 232–252.

O'Donnell, W. J. (1976). Adolescent self-esteem related to feelings toward parents and friends. *Journal of Youth and Adolescence, 5,* 179–185.

Peevers, B. H., & Secord, P. F. (1973). Developmental changes in attribution of descriptive concepts to persons. *Journal of Personality and Social Psychology, 27,* 120–128.

Piaget, J. (1932). *The moral judgement of the child.* New York: Harcourt Press.

Rawlins, W. K. (1983). Negotiating close friendship: The dialectic of conjunctive freedoms. *Human Communication Research, 9,* 255–266.

Rawlins, W. K. (in press). A dialectical analysis of the tensions, functions and strategic challenges of communication in young adult friendships. In J. A. Anderson (Ed.), *Communication Yearbook, 12,* Newbury, CA: Sage.

Rawlins, W. K., & Holl, M. (1987). The communicative achievement of friendship during adolescence: Predicaments of trust and violation. *The Western Journal of Speech Communication, 51,* 345–363.

Rawlins, W. K., & Holl, M. (1988). Adolescents' interaction with parents and friends: Dialectics of temporal perspective and evaluation. *Journal of Social and Personal Relationships, 5,* 27–46.

Riesman, D. (1961). *The lonely crowd.* New Haven & London: Yale University Press.

Selman, R. L. (1981). The child as a friendship philosopher. In S. R. Asher & J. M. Gottman (Eds.), *The development of children's friendships* (pp. 242–272). Cambridge: Cambridge University Press.

Smollar, J., & Youniss, J. (1982). Social development through friendship. In K. H. Rubin & H. S. Ross (Eds.), *Peer relationships and social skills in childhood* (pp. 279–298). New York: Springer–Verlag.

Sullivan, H. S. (1953). *Interpersonal theory of psychiatry.* New York: Norton.

Suttles, G. D. (1970). Friendship as a social institution. In G. J. McCall (Ed.), *Social relationships* (pp. 95–135). Chicago: Aldine.

Youniss, J., & Smollar, J. (1985). *Adolescent relations with mothers, fathers, and friends.* Chicago: University of Chicago Press.

9 Dating Competence Among College Students

Marshall Prisbell
University of Nebraska at Omaha

Concerns about dating and heterosocial relationships are frequent and often serious ones among college students (Bath, 1961; Galassi & Galassi, 1979; Martinson & Zerface, 1970). Martinson and Zerface (1970) concluded that college students are more concerned and interested in learning to get along with the opposite sex than with help in learning about their abilities, interests, and personalities. Borkovec, Stone, O'Brien, and Kaloupek (1974) surveyed undergraduate students and found that 15.5% of the males and 11.5% of the females reported some degree of anxiety related to being with a member of the opposite sex. Additionally, 32% of the males and 38.5% of the females reported anxiety about meeting someone for the first time. Arkowitz, Hinton, Perl, and Himadi (1978) found that nearly one-third of college students reported anxiety about dating. Shmurak (1973) reported that of various social situations, 54% of the male sample and 42% of the female sample had difficulty in dating. Moreover, Klaus, Hersen, and Bellack (1977) concluded that "finding possible dates" was one of the most difficult tasks for undergraduate college students. Because of the problems related to dating, Arkowitz et al. (1978) concluded that heterosocial avoidance may interfere with the development of intimate relationships and may be related to problems of depression, alcoholism, sexual dysfunction, academic failure, and loneliness (Arkowitz, 1977; Galassi & Galassi, 1979; Pilkonis & Zimbardo, 1979; Shaver, Furman, & Buhrmester, 1985).

It is relevant to note that the physical and social environment of college life may provide opportunities for the development and refinement of one's dating and relationship skills. Nonetheless, minimal dating

155

remains a significant life problem for large numbers of young, college students (Martinson & Zerface, 1970). The purpose of this chapter is to examine the conceptual nature of dating and to identify factors affecting one's dating practices. The chapter concludes with a discussion of future directions that research needs to explore.

THE NATURE OF DATING

Dating Practices and Functions

Before discussing the conceptual nature of dating, it is necesary to elaborate on the general practices of functions of dating. For instance, Klaus, Hersen, and Bellack (1977) reported that male and female students had similar number of dates per month ($M = 5.49$ for males and $M = 5.65$ for females). The authors also indicated that the most difficult stages of dating for both sezes were finding dating partners, initiating contact with prospective dates, initiating sexual activity, avoiding or curtailing sex, and ending a date. Specifically, females reported more difficulty finding prospective dates and ending a date, whereas males reported more difficulty initiating telephone contact in obtaining dates. In another study on dating skills, Muehlenhard, Koralewski, Andrews, and Burdick (1986) found that males were more eager to be asked out then females were to ask.

Research has also focused on the functions of dating. First, dating is seen as a pleasurable activity for the couple (Bowman, 1948; Burgess & Locke, 1945; Waller, 1937; Winch, 1968). Winch (1968) concluded:

> Dating provides an opportunity to explore the personality and values of another human being in a situation of erotically-tinged fun-oriented recreation. (p. 507)

Dating also provides a status-grading function for college students. Burgess and Locke (1945) suggested that dating is a competitive game whereby one's prestige is determined by the number of high-ranking persons of the opposite sex one dates. Another function of dating is the influence that dating has on one's self-image. Bowman (1948) and Winch (1968) noted that by not obtaining "the best date," one may develop feelings of inferiority. A fourth function suggests that dating activities enhance one's knowledge of social skills (Bowman, 1948). In other words, by engaging in dating activities, individuals practice and learn the necessary skills for effective dating. Finally, dating is seen as playing a major role in mate selection whereby one learns what type of person(s) provides the most satisfying relationship (Winch, 1968).

Conceptualization of Dating

Dating has been defined in terms of heterosocial competence. Heterosocial competence is seen as a subset of social and communication competence (Conger & Conger, 1982) and can be defined as "the degree to which a person is successful in heterosexual interactions that have as their immediate goal the recurrence of similar interactions" (p. 316). This definition is consequence-oriented (e.g., maintaining conversation and/or increasing the frequency of future dates with the same person) and suggests a behavioral outcome for assessing competence. This definition, however, fails to identify specific behaviors required for successful performance and does not isolate those factors contributing to heterosocial competence or incompetence.

Another way to conceptualize dating and heterosocial competence is to identify variables that contribute to approach/avoidance behaviors in terms of satisfaction in and frequency of dating. According to Arkowitz (1977), Galassi and Galassi (1979), Perri (1977), and Prisbell (1987a, 1982), eight factors have been identified as contributing to approach/avoidance behaviors in dating.

Conditioned Anxiety.   If individuals have one or more unpleasant, rewarding dating encounters, they will become clasically conditioned to various cues in those situations. Galassi and Galassi (1979) contended that, "anxiety is then aroused when anticipating or responding to related situations and results in impaired performance, avoidance, or escape" (p. 134). Such unpleasant experiences may include a date not showing for the encounter, a date complaining about the evening, a date being strictly self-centered, and the like. Thus, if an individual experiences unpleasant outcomes before or during a date, then the performance expectation for the overall date is negative. This reinforces, for individuals, the belief that they are not competent dates. Therefore, individuals avoid future dating encounters.

Skills in Dating.   Such skills as initiating a conversation, knowing how to plan a date, conversational appropriateness and timing, and nonverbal communicative behaviors are important to successful dating. Many individuals, however, lack such skills (Galassi & Galassi, 1979). Such skills deficits may lead individuals to avoid dating encounters.

Apprehension About Dating.   For some individuals, the dating situation can elicit feelings of nervousness, tenseness, and anxiousness, causing the individual to behave in a manner representative of those internal states.

To reduce such unpleasant states, individuals will not approach the dating situation.

Dating Expectations.   In this instance, the individual has the necessary skills to perform but given negative self-evaluations and "excessively high performance standards, unrealistic expectations, irrational beliefs, faulty perceptions, or misinterpretations of feedback" (Galassi & Galassi, 1979, p. 135), the individual does not perform. The nature of such faulty perceptions may explain why certain individuals avoid dating encounters.

Physical Attractiveness.   Galassi and Galassi (1979) contended that individuals who are perceived as physically attractive have greater chances for obtaining dates. Also, one's own perceptions of attraction may be just as important in determining dating activities (Morrison & Bellack, 1981). In explaining the role of physical attraction in dating, researchers must expand the conceptualization of physical attraction to include an individual's feelings and attitudes toward their own physical attractiveness.

Importance of Dating.   This variable is best conceptualized by one's attitude toward dating in terms of importance, interest, or desire. In this sense, the individual can make a conscious choice not to date.

Activity.   Individuals may not approach dating due to their involvement in activities. For example, an individual may not have time to date because of school assignments, a part-time job, or involvement in organizations.

Proximity.   Proximity is defined as the physical closeness or distance between individuals. Several studies have indicated that students tend to develop stronger friendships with those students who share their classes, live in the same dormitory or apartment building, or who sit near them, than with those who are separated (Byrne, 1961). Proximity has also been noted as an important factor in mate selection (Clarke, 1952). Consequently, proximity may also determine dating patterns.

Research examining the relationship between the heterosocial competence variables and satisfaction in and frequency of dating shows only a moderate relationship between the two sets of variables (Prisbell, 1987a). Nonetheless, for research purposes, this conceptualization provides various explanations of minimal or nondating. This eight-factor model would be useful in assessing heterosocial difficulties and aid in the treatment of dating problems.

CORRELATES OF HETEROSOCIAL COMPETENCE

Social-Communicative Anxiety

Social-communicative anxiety has been conceptualized and measured in many different ways. Regardless, studies have consistently found that anxiety affects individuals' dating patterns such that nonanxious individuals approached the dating situation significantly more than anxious individuals. For instance, in studying communication apprehension and dating behavior, McCroskey and Sheahan (1978) found that high apprehensive college students had fewer dates, were more likely to date one person to the exclusion of others and less likely to accept a blind date. Parks, Dindia, Adams, Berlin, and Larson (1980) concluded that high apprehensive individuals were more likely to date exclusively. Moreover, individuals with higher levels of communication apprehension reported greater degrees of conditioned anxiety and apprehension about dating and indicated less degrees of physical attractiveness and skills in dating (Prisbell, 1982).

Other studies have indicated that heterosocial anxiety was positively related with a desire to avoid social situations and inversely related to dating frequency (Heimberg, Harrison, Montgomery, Madsen, & Sherfey, 1980). Dodge, Heimberg, Nyman, and O'Brien (1987) used a behavioral diary method to examine the daily heterosocial interactions of high and low socially anxious college students in the natural environment. The authors found that high-anxious students engaged in fewer interactions over a 2-week period and reported greater anxiety, poorer performance, and less satisfaction with their performance than low-anxious students. Socially anxious students reported having fewer interactions on campus than socially nonanxious students. It was concluded that socially anxious students are less likely to place themselves in available areas for interactions and generally lack established circles of casual friends and acquaintances.

In related areas of social anxiety, McCroskey and Richmond (1987) found that individuals with low levels of willingness to communicate are likely to have fewer dates, engage in exclusive dating, and to date less people than individuals with higher levels of willingness to communicate. Social avoidance and distress (Watson & Friend, 1969) has also been explored in relation to dating behavior. Social avoidance and distress refers to the discomfort, fear, and social anxiety in same and opposite-sex interactions. Wallanger, Conger, Mariotto, Curran, and Farrell (1980) found that SAD scores correlated −.54 with skills in dating. Additionally, scores on the SAD have been shown to adequately discriminte between high- and low-frequency daters (Arkowitz, Lichtenstein, McGovern, & Hines, 1975). In addition, Prisbell (1983b) found that individuals with high levels of SAD reported lower degrees of skills in dating and physical attractiveness, and higher degrees of conditioned anxiety and apprehension about dating.

Furthermore, Himadi, Arkowitz, Hinton, and Perl (1980) found that infrequent male daters were less adjusted than frequent male daters based on scores of the Eysenck Personality Inventory. These findings did not hold true for females. However, a study by Greenwald (1978) indicates that infrequent female daters had lower levels of self-esteem than frequent female daters. Finally, fear of negative evaluation scores discriminated between high- and low-frequency male and female daters (Watson & Friend, 1969) as well as for a study only using a male sample (Glasgow & Arkowitz, 1975).

It can be concluded from the preceding studies that individuals may avoid dating due to the social-communicative anxiety that they experience about dating. Specifically, individuals experiencing anxiety generally feel they lack the necessary skills to date (e.g., initiating and maintaining conversations prior to and during dates). Furthermore, anxious persons fail to approach dating due to a lack of confidence, negative self-perceptions of physical attractiveness, and a belief that they will be negatively evaluated by their prospective dating partners.

Loneliness and Shyness

Research had demonstrated consistent relationships among heterosocial competence, loneliness, and shyness (c.f., Jones, Cheek, & Briggs, 1986; Peplau & Perlman, 1982). Although some studies have concentrated on loneliness and dating activities, an abundance of the literature has focused on social contacts and the reasons lonely people give for their feelings of loneliness. For instance, Rubenstein and Shaver (1982) found that lonely people atttribute their lonely feelings to: having nothing to do, being alone, and having no spouse or lover. In addition, it was found that lonely individuals spent more weekend evening alone more so than nonlonely individuals (Jones, Hansson, & Smith, 1980; McCormack & Kahn, 1980; Russell, Peplau, & Cutrona, 1980). A lack of dating is seen as a contributing factor in explaining these results.

Other research supports the contention that lonely individuals have limited and dissatisfying social relations. Loneliness was related to degree of romantic involvement and number of close friends (Russell et al., 1980). In fact, even when involved in dating, satisfaction with one's dating activities was a better predictor of loneliness than number of dates (Cutrona, 1982; Cutrona & Peplau, 1979). Moreover, it has been described that lonely males often times desperately search and cling to their opposite-sex partner (Teicher, 1972). These relationships are largely based on dependence and fear of isolation and loneliness. This may also contribute to one's realational and dating dissatisfaction.

In research directly examining dating and loneliness, Russell (1982) concluded that loneliness was negatively related to frequency of social activities with friends and dating partners. Russell (1982) noted that students who were not dating at all were much lonelier than students dating casually or regularly. In addition, Brennan and Auslander (1979) reported that lonely students date less frequently than nonlonely students. In fact, students who never had a steady dating partner reported that they were more lonely than students who had steady dating partners (Jones et al., 1980).

The importance of dating during college has been stressed by Cutrona (1982). Cutrona (1982) investigated loneliness and the process of social adjustment of new college students and found that students who remained lonely throughout the school year most often stated that "finding a boyfriend/girlfriend" was the only way they would overcome their loneliness.

Finally, Prisbell (1983a; 1987b) explored the relationships between loneliness and heterosocial competence. It was found that college students with low levels of loneliness reported greater degrees of skills in dating, positive self-perceptions of physical atractiveness, greater proximity to members of the opposite sex, more satisfaction with dating, and a greater frequency of dates than college students with high levels of loneliness. In addition, low levels of loneliness was related to lower degrees of conditioned anxiety, dating expectations, and apprehension about dating. It appears that lonely individuals lack the necessary skills to initiate dates, perceive dating to be tricky and deceptive, have limited contact with opposite-sex members, and experience nervousness about dating (Prisbell, 1983a; 1987b).

In addition to the research on dating and loneliness, there have been attempts to have nondaters overcome their lonely feelings. Young (1981) suggested to lonely, nondaters ways to meet members of the opposite sex. Suggestions focused on overcoming problems of proximity and included:

1. contacting old acquaintances;
2. asking friends to arrange a date with someone who seems compatible;
3. becoming involved in a club of one's interest;
4. joining groups that are geared to the single person (e.g., single dances or bars); and
5. meeting one's college classmates.

Finally, Young (1981) maintained that lonely, nondaters should not anticipate rejection prior to initiating dates, and realistically weigh the rewards/costs of unsatisfying partners or relationships.

In addition to the literature on loneliness and dating, research has also explored the relationship between heterosocial competence and shyness. When college students confront dating situations, which requires them to initiate new relationships, shyness may be a barrier. Moreover, it was found that shy people lack self-confidence and become tense when seeking out new dating partners, therefore, avoiding the dating situation (Prisbell, 1983a). Studies have indicated that shy subjects tend to maintain greater interpersonal distance in encounters with the opposite sex (Carducci & Webber, 1979). Jones and Carpenter (1986) summarized previous research and concluded that shy persons have fewer social opportunities than others. Finally, shy persons reported lower frequency of dating, less satisfaction with the relationships they did have, and fewer intimate friends of the opposite sex (Cheek & Busch, 1981; Jones & Carpenter, 1986; Jones, Freeman, & Goswick, 1981; Jones & Russell, 1982).

Jones and Carpenter (1986) concluded that shy students who go away to college were most in need of social skill development and confidence to make friends. In addition, Richmond (1984) concluded that the loneliness of shy students is consistent with their reluctance to form dating relationships. Taken together, then, shy and lonely individuals seem to avoid dating due to both cognitive and behavioral problems.

Heterosocial Skills

Heterosocial skills are seen as being part of the more global system of social skills but are considered different from those needed in other social situations (Galassi & Galassi, 1979; Richardson & Tasto, 1976). Nonetheless, skills in dating enable one to initiate, maintain, and terminate a social and/or sexual relationship with a member of the opposite sex (Barlow, Abel, Blanchard, Bristow, & Young, 1977). Malatesta and Adams (1986) discuss heterosocial skills in more general terms, which include:

1. sensitivity to and discrimination of relevant heterosocial cues;
2. evaluation and process of relevant data to arrive at hypotheses about a given individual partner and social context;
3. the selection and effective execution of an appropriate response from an adequate skills repertoire; and
4. processing and responding to feedback from the other person in order to determine behavior effectiveness and hypothesis validity (p. 511).

Research focusing on skills in dating for combined samples of males and females revealed that nondaters avoid social interactions, rate themselves as having minimal skills including difficulties initiating dates and have less knowledge about responding verbally to approach cues (Curran, Little, & Gilbert, 1978; Twentyman, Boland, & McFall, 1981). Lipton and Nelson (1980) indicated that having the ability to initiate dates discriminated between high- and low-frequency daters. In addition, studies have indicated that conversational skills (i.e., talk time) discriminated more frequently than other behaviors between high- and low-frequency daters (Greenwald, 1977; Martinez-Diaz & Edelstein, 1979; Twentyman & McFall, 1975). Even though talk time was seen as a good discriminator between the contrasting groups, it was reasoned that talk time was only one behavior of the more general category of conversational skill. Other behaviors that differed between daters and nondaters included voice and conversational form (Barlow et al., 1977), and sense of timing in terms of vocal and gesture use (Fischetti, Curran, & Wessberg, 1977).

Finally, Young (1981) asserted that many individuals who want to date may be engaging in socially unacceptable behaviors. These behavioral areas focused on trying too hard to make impressions, self-disclosing too much information too soon, being passive, and self-effacing. Young (1981) stated that individuals avoid social contacts because they believe they are unattractive, unlikable, dull and boring, and stupid. These perceptions were seen as a result of the individual lacking skills in dating.

In a study examining assertiveness and heterosocial competence, Prisbell (1986) found that dating expectations, apprehension about dating, skills in dating, physical attractiveness, and proximity differed between high- and low-assertive college students. It was concluded that assertive individuals were more likely to approach and initiate conversations with members of the opposite sex in order to obtain a date more so than nonassertive individuals. In addition, assertive individuals were seen as being realistic about the dating situation, having the necessary skills to date, feelings comfortable about dating, having positive images of their physical make-up, and coming in contact with members of the opposite sex more so than nonassertive individuals. It seems that learning assertive behaviors may benefit the nondater.

Many investigators have explored skills in dating using male and female samples independently. A study of female subjects by Williams and Ciminero (1978) indicated that heterosocial skills were related to the number of different males dated, perceived attractiveness, assertiveness, and trait anxiety. Moreover, females rating themselves as heterosocially skillful were judged to be skillful, as showing interest, and as having the ability to initiate conversations more so than females rating themselves as heterosocially unskillful. Greenwald (1977, 1978) reported that high-frequency female daters perceived themselves to be more assertive, and were judged to be more physically attractive, socially skillful, and interpersonally attractive than low-frequency female daters. In terms of conversational skills, Glasgow and Arkowitz (1975) found that high-frequency female daters spoke longer than low-frequency female daters.

Research has also explored effective ways females could initiate dates with males (Muehlenhard & McFall, 1981). Results indicated that when the male likes the female, he is likely to be pleased if she takes the dating initiative. This result was consistent with a previous study by Walster, Walster, Piliavin, and Schmidt (1973), which found that males tend to prefer females who are friendly to them rather than those who play hard-to-get. Finally, Muehlenhard, et al., (1986) found a number of behaviors females can use to convey their interest in dating a male. These behaviors include: giving a phone number, being responsive, being able to end 3-second or 10-second pauses, engaging in backchanneling, using eye contact, smiling, touching, and so forth. The authors concluded that these cues will increase the females chances of being asked out by males and having males accept their dating invitation.

Physical Attractiveness

Numerous studies have examined the role of physical attractiveness and dating (Berscheid & Walster, 1974; Brislin & Lewis, 1968; Curran & Lippold, 1975; Huston, 1973; Murstein, 1972, 1976; Shepherd & Ellis, 1972). For instance, it has been documented that more physically attractive persons date more often (Berscheid, Dion, Walster, & Walster, 1971; Spreadbury & Reeves, 1979). Berscheid et al., (1971) found that judges ratings of physical attractiveness significantly correlated (.61) to the number of dates one had in the past year for a sample of college females, whereas the correlation was .25 for male subjects. In addition, physical attractiveness was related to the desire to go on first dates (Crouse & Mehrabian, 1977; Stroebe, Insko, Thompson, & Layton, 1971) and the desire to see each other again on second dates (Brislin & Lewis, 1968; Glasgow & Arkowitz, 1975; Tesser & Brodie, 1971; Walster, Aronson, Abrahams, & Rottman, 1966). Finally, Chess, Thomas, and Cameron (1976) found that individuals lower in physical attractiveness were less likely to have a steady dating partner than their counterparts of higher physical attractiveness.

Research has also focused on general satisfaction with dating and physical attractiveness. Reis, Nezlak, and Wheeler (1980) and Reis et al., (1982) concluded that individuals higher in physical attractiveness had more favorable social interactions as compared to those lower in physical attractiveness. Moreover a strong relationship existed between physical attractiveness and liking on first dates (Curran, 1973; Curran & Lippold, 1975; Tesser & Brodie, 1971; Walster et al., 1966). Similarly, Byrne, Ervin, and Lamberth (1970) and Coombs and Kenkel (1966) have shown that similarity is related to the attraction partners feel toward one another after first dates.

Studies examining sex differences, physical attractiveness, and dating reveal that women of higher physical attractiveness date more, have more friends, are in love more, and have more sexual experiences than women of average or lesser physical attractiveness (Kaats & Davis, 1970). In a study by Black (1974), male subjects' desire to be both friends and/or to date was substantially greater for the female higher in physical attractiveness as compared to her counterpart. Similar findings were also found by Pellegrini, Hicks, and Meyers-Winton (1979). Finally, physical attractiveness of the dating partner was more relevant to males liking their dates than to females liking their dates (Coombs & Kenkel, 1966; Curran, 1973). However, female choices were modified by race, religion, intelligence, campus status, and concerns about dancing ability and dress (Coombs & Kenkel, 1966).

In other studies exploring the desire to date and physical attractiveness, likelihood of acceptance as a dating partner was considered. Huston (1973) found that males selected the more physically attractive female when assured of acceptance, but not otherwise. However, when asked about the likelihood of female acceptance, the males estimated that females of higher physical attractiveness would be less likely to accept them as a date. Furthermore, the males' self-ratings of their physical attractiveness related to their estimates of their chances of acceptance for a date. In examining female subjects, Hagiwara (1975) found that their self-ratings of physical attractiveness were negatively related to perceived desirability of a male date.

In researching the importance of physical attractiveness in the desirability of dating partners, Allen (1976) analyzed the variable of race. Findings reveal that subjects were not willing to accept a date with someone of another race, however, females gave race more weight than physical attractiveness, whereas males gave physical attractiveness more weight than race.

Spreadbury and Reeves (1979) concluded that physical attractiveness was significantly more predictive of dating behavior than personality. Walster et al. (1966) suggested that social desirability contributes to a person's appeal when being evaluated as a dating partner. Social desirability was defined as the sum of physical attractiveness, popularity, personality, status, and other resources. Rubin (1973) and Woll,

McMeen, and Bray (1982) found age similarity to be an important social desirability factor when looking for a dating partner. However, Harrison and Saeed (1977) found that males were more likely to seek someone younger, whereas females were more likely to seek someone older. Furthermore, Harrison and Saeed (1977) found that status is a social desirable characteristic in choosing a dating partner for females but not for males. Green, Buchanan, and Heurer (1984) found that higher status and physical attractiveness were significant predictors of males being chosen by females, whereas the only predictor of females being chosen by males was physical attractiveness. Also, the authors found that males who were older than females and had more status and attractiveness than other males increased their chances of dating, and females who were younger than males and more attractive than other females increased their chances for dating.

Research has also used samples of ongoing dating couples. Critelli and Waid (1980) measured physical attractiveness, romantic love, and dominance from 123 dating couples. Results indicated that the person who considered the other to be more physically attractive tended to have greater love for that partner and indicated greater submission in their relationship. The authors concluded by stating:

> while attractiveness plays an important role in partner selection and initial attraction, once a dating relationship is established, one's overall level of physical attractiveness appears to decrease in importance as a determinant of the variability in attraction between partners. (p. 627)

Research also indicates dating problems associated with physical attractiveness, which range from jealously to relational disengagement. White (1980) found that for couples who were casually and seriously dating, the partner with relatively higher physical attractiveness tended to have more friends of the opposite sex and worried less about their partner's potential involvement with another person. This may lead the partner to experience jealousy. In studies examining commitment during ongoing dating relationships, (Kramer, 1978) concluded that the most important factor in determining commitment was amount of time spent together followed by physical attractiveness.

CONCLUSIONS AND FUTURE RESEARCH DIRECTIONS

This chapter has reviewed several factors affecting college students' dating practices. Although the studies reviewed conceptualize and measure dating in a variety of ways, it is clear and consistent that low-frequency daters differ on a number of important variables from high-frequency daters. This final section suggests directions for future dating-related research.

Conceptual Issues

Despite the considerable amount of research on dating, limited advances have occurred in the area of conceptualization. Previous research exploring dating has used a number of different terms to define dating (i.e., social skills, social competence, heterosexual social skills, heterosocial skills, and heterosocial competence). Few researchers have bothered to specify the meaning of these terms. Because of the inability to define these terms, problems arise when comparing results from previous research (c.f., Arkowitz, 1977; Conger & Conger, 1982; Wessberg, Mariotto, Conger, Farrell, & Conger, 1978). It is suggested that dating be conceptualized as heterosocial competence. Heterosocial competence, then, focuses on those factors affecting one's satisfaction in and frequency of dating (Prisbell, 1987a) and is considered a subset of the more global area of communiction competence. Thus, heterosocial competence is comprised of both cognitive and behavioral factors that reflect the individuals apprehension about dating, dating expectations, conditioned anxiety about dating, proximity of the opposite sex, importance of dating, perceptions of physical attractiveness, skills in dating, and activity. These factors can be considered as affecting one's approach or avoidance behavior toward dating as well as one's satisfaction in and frequency of dating.

Physical Attractiveness

An area of heterosocial competence that warrants further attention is physical attractiveness. Physical attractiveness needs to be investigated in terms of the differences in physical attractiveness between high- and low-frequency daters (Glasgow & Arkowitz, 1975) as well as for males and females (Arkowitz, 1977). Glasgow and Arkowitz (1975) pointed to the powerful effects of physical attractiveness in determining how others respond to us, particularly in first impressions. Researchers need to determine the characteristics of physically attractive and unattractive individuals in relation to satisfaction in and frequency of dating. A person's appearance, in terms of dress, grooming, hairstyle, and so on, may in fact modify his or her physical attractiveness. One can pay more attention to "appearance training" (Curran & Gilbert, 1975) in developing treatment programs for minimal daters and even "attractive" peers, for this purpose, might be a useful addition to these programs.

Skills in Dating

Another area that needs further conceptualization relates to the construct of social skills. To date, social skills have either emphasized global ratings or the frequency of verbal and nonverbal behaviors. Simple frequency counts of behavior do not adequately measure timing and reciprocity of interpersonal behavior. In addition, Lewinsohn (1975) defined socially skilled behavior entirely in terms of the consequences of the behavior. It seems that researchers need to include an evaluation of the response consequences of interpersonal behavior as part of a definition of socially skilled behaviors, rather than emphasizing the content of the behaviors only. Furthermore, a definition of social skills needs to go beyond the initial interaction between males and females to include such factors as ways to meet people, formation of a peer group environment that would facilitate meeting members of the opposite sex, and ways of dealing with rejection and the more complex aspects of longer term intimate relationships. Nonetheless, the work of Sptizberg (1986; 1987), Spitzberg and Hurt (1987), and Duran (1983) may be helpful in identifying behavioral styles of competent and incompetent daters.

Dating Stages

An area needing further theoretical and empirical inquiry focuses on dating stages. To date, research has generally concentrated on the courtship process (i.e., casual dating, serious dating, engagement, marriage; Braiker & Kelley, 1979) and phases of interpersonal relationship development (Berger & Calabrese, 1975; Duck & Gilmour, 1981; Knapp, 1978). Specifically, Krain (1975) isolated three stages of dating: (a) casual (where each dated others, no one of whom was a preferred date); (b) serious (where only one dating partner is currently being dated and/or is at least a preferred date whether or not there is a formal going-steady status; and (c) marriage-bound (where there is an understanding that they will marry each other regardless of whether there is formal engagement). Greater theoretical attention needs to be placed on defining and describing the difference among casual dating, serious dating, going steady, and cohabitating relationships (Newcomb, 1981).

It would be ideal to conduct longitudinal studies on individuals dating for the first time who remain dating over time. The interpersonal communication process could be better understood using such couples for analysis. By taking a developmental approach, behavioral differences can be assessed throughout the life span of dating.

Theory Application

Future research also needs to emphasize the application of grounded theories to the study of dating. Recently, Fletcher, Fincham, Cramer, and Heron (1987) examined the role of attributions in the dating context. The authors concluded that attributional activity was more frequent within relationships when they were in the early stages, when the relationship was perceived as unstable and when important changes were taking place in the relationship.

Equity theory has also been applied to the dating context. Research by Hatfield, Walster, and Traupmann (1979) applied equity theory to dating couples' encounters and found that couples in equitable relationships had the most intensely sexual relationships. Most couples in equitable relationships were having sexual intercourse and most couples in inequitable relationships were not. Also, Walster, Walster, and Berscheid (1978) found that couples in equitable relationships had the most intensely sexual relations. In a similar study, Traupmann, Hatfield, and Wexler (1983) found that males and females who felt their relationships were equitable were more content and more satisfied with their sexual relations than those who felt inequitably treated.

Generalizability

Another area to be examined for future research is that of generalizability. Upon reviewing the dating literature, it seems necessary to isolate specific populations and generalize the results to only those populations. For instance, if an investigator is interested in assessing heterosocial competence among college students, then, the research should use college students and only genralize the results to a college population. However, if the population includes students who seek help from college counseling, then, these students should be investigated independently from those students who do not seek help. Research indicates the college students who seek personal-adjustment counseling differ significantly on factors that relate to treatment effectiveness from those who do not seek counseling (c.f., Galassi & Galassi, 1979).

Furthermore, individuals with different levels of datinag experiences need to be investigated. For instance, studies need to be conducted on beginning daters and people who differ in age, race, culture, educations, and social class (Dickinson, 1971, 1975).

Recent studies have examined dating after a divorce or after a termination of a relationship. Specifically, studies have assessed single-parents'
datiang behavior and intimacy patterns (e.g., Greenberg, 1979; Hunt,
1966; Hunt & Hunt, 1977; Rosenthal & Keshet, 1978; Staples, 1980).
In addition, recent research by Petronio and Endres (1985/86) suggests
that individuals who were single parents for 6 years or more, more
frequently went out with friends to restaurants than those single parents
who were divorced for a shorter time. Moreover, individuals who were
very recently single more frequently went on blind dates than did those
who had been single for a longer period of time. Findings also indicated
that the more recently a person is a single parent, the more strongly they
agree that those they date are on the make and that their dates are
superficial.

In another study by Petronio and Endres (1986), it was found that
"women without children in the home full-time find it easier to meet new
people than do men with or without full-time children" (p. 83–84). It
was also concluded that single fathers with or without full-time children
more frequently went out on blind dates than did single mothers.

By using diverse samples with varying levels of dating experiences,
advances can be made concerning the factors affecting dating behavior.
More so, such research would lend greater insights into the nature of
heterosocial competence.

Date Rape

One final area deserving future consideration is the relationship between
heterosocial competence and date rape. It may be that problems associated with the minimal dater are, in part, similar to the problems of those
who engage in date rape. Date rape on campus is an area of recent
examination. Perhaps 20% or more of college females have been victims
of rape or attempted rape (Kanin, 1971; Meyer, 1984).

Date rape appears to be a complex social problem that is poorly
understood. Researchers have attributed date rape to poor communication skills (Meyer, 1984), a lack of heterosexual skills and knowledge of
social skills (Abel, Blanchard, & Becker, 1978; Becker, Abel, Blanchard,
Murphy, & Coleman, 1978), inaccurate perceptions in cue reading (Lipton, McDonel, & McFall, 1987), and inaccurate attribution of blame for
date rape (Kanekau & Vaz, 1983; Richardson & Powell, 1982; Shotland
& Goodstein, 1983).

In a study examining the interpersonal behavior differences of females
experiencing date rape and those who have not, it was found that females
experiencing date rape reported being lonely and shy, unable to initiate
dates and introduce themselves to members of the opposite sex, and

generally were trusting of others (Prisbell & Stacy, 1987). The authors concluded that communication skills training programs need to be developed and implemented on college campuses. Thus, future research needs to explore those factors affecting one's behavior on dates which may contribute to date rape.

REFERENCES

Abel, G. G., Blanchard, E. B., & Becker, J. V. (1978). An integrated treatment program for rapists. In R. T. Rada (Ed.), *Clinical aspects of the rapist* (pp. 161–214). New York: Grune & Stratton.

Allen, B. P. (1976). Race and physical attractiveness as criteria for white subjects' dating choices. *Social Behavior and Personality, 4,* 289–296.

Arkowitz, H. (1977). Measurement and modification of minimal dating behavior. In M. Hersen (Ed.), *Progress in behavior modification* (Vol. 5, pp. 1–61). New York: Academic Press.

Arkowtiz, H., Hinton, R., Perl, J., & Himadi, W. (1978). Treatment strategies for dating anxiety in college men based on real-life practice. *The Counseling Psychologist, 7,* 41–46.

Arkowitz, H., Lichtenstein, E., McGovern, K., & Hines, P. (1975). The behavioral assessment of social competence in males. *Behavior Therapy, 6,* 3–13.

Barlow, D H., Abel, G. G., Blanchard, E. B., Bristow, A. R., & Young, L. D. (1977). A heterosocial skills behavior checklist for males. *Behavior Therapy, 2,* 229–239.

Bath, J. A. (1961). Problems of college students. *Journal of College Student Personnel, 3,* 33–36.

Becker, J. V., Abel, G. G., Blanchard, E. B., Murphy, W. D., & Coleman, E. (1978). Evaluating social skills of sexual aggressives. *Criminal Justice and Behavior, 5,* 357–368.

Berger, C. R., & Calabrese, R. J. (1975). Some explorations in initial interaction and beyond: Toward a developmental theory of interpersonal communication. *Human Communication Research, 1,* 99–112.

Berscheid, E., Dion, K., Walster, E., & Walster, G. W. (1971). Physical attractiveness and dating choice: A test of the matching hypotheses. *Journal of Experimental Social Psychology, 7,* 173–189.

Berscheid, E., & Walster, E. (1974). Physical attractiveness. In L. Berkowitz (Ed.), *Advances in experimental social psychology* (Vol. 7, pp. 157–215). New York: Academic Press.

Black, H. K. (1974). Physical attractiveness and similarity of attitude in interpersonal attraction. *Psychological Reports, 35,* 403–406.

Borkovec, T D., Stone, N. M., O'Brien, G. T., & Kaloupek, D. G. (1974). Evaluation of a clinically relevant target behavior for analog outcome research. *Behavior Therapy, 5,* 503–513.

Bowman, H. (1948). *Marriage for moderns.* New York: McGraw–Hill.

Braiker, H. B., & Kelley, H. H. (1979). Conflict in the development of close relationships. In R. L. Burgess & T. L. Huston (Eds.), *Social exchange in developing relationships* (pp. 135–186). New York: Academic Press.

Brennan, T., & Auslander, N. (1979). *Adolescent loneliness: An exploratory study of social and psychological pre-dispositions and theory.* Unpublished manuscript, Behavioral Research Institute, Boulder, CO.

Brislin, R. W., & Lewis, S. A. (1968). Dating and physical attractiveness: Replication. *Psychological Reports, 22,* 976.

Burgess, E., & Locke, H. (1945). *The family: From institution to companionship*. New York: American Book.

Byrne, D. (1961). The influence of propinquity and opportunities for interaction on classroom relationships. *Human Relations, 14*, 63–70.

Byrne, D., Ervin, C. R., & Lamberth, J. (1970). Continuity between the experimental study of attraction and real-life computer dating. *Journal of Personality and Social Psychology, 16*, 157–165.

Carducci, B. J., & Webber, A. W. (1979). Shyness as a determinant of interpersonal distance. *Psychological Reports, 44*, 1075–1078.

Cheek, J. M., & Busch, C. K. (1981). The influence of shyness on loneliness in a new situation. *Personality and Social Psychology Bulletin, 7*, 572–577.

Chess, S., Thomas, A., & Cameron, M. (1976). Sexual attitudes and behavior patterns in a middle-class adolescent population. *American Journal of Orthopsychiatry, 46*, 689–701.

Clarke, A. C. (1952). An examination of the operation of residual propinquity as a factor in mate selection. *American Sociological Review, 27*, 17–22.

Conger, J. C., & Conger, A. J. (1981). Components of heterosocial competence. In J. P. Curran & P. M. Monti (Eds.), *Social skills training: A practical handbook for assessment and treatment* (pp. 313–347). New York: Guilford Press.

Coombs, R. H., & Kenkel, W. F. (1966). Sex differences in dating aspirations and satisfaction with computer-selected partners. *Journal of Marriage and the Family, 28*, 62–66.

Critelli, J. W., & Waid, L. R. (1980). Physical attractiveness, romantic love, and equity restoration in dating relationships. *Journal of Personality Assessment, 44*, 624–629.

Crouse, B. B., & Mehrabian, A. (1977). Affiliation of opposite-sexed strangers. *Journal of Research in Personality, 11*, 38–47.

Curran, J. P. (1973). Correlates of physical attractiveness and interpersonal attraction in the dating situation. *Social Behavior and Personality, 1*, 153–157.

Curran, J. P., & Gilbert, F. S. (1975). A test of the relative effectiveness of a systematic desensitization program and an interpersonal skills training program with date anxious subjects. *Behavior Therapy, 6*, 510–521.

Curran, J. P., & Lippold, S. (1975). The effects of physical attraction and attitude similarity in dating dyads. *Journal of Personality, 43*, 528–539.

Curran, J. P., Little, L. M., & Gilbert, F. S. (1978). Reactivity of males of differing heterosexual social anxiety to female approach and non-approach cue conditions. *Behavior Therapy, 9*, 961.

Cutrona, C. (1982). Transition to college: Loneliness and the process of social adjustment. In L. A. Peplau & D. Perlamn (Eds.), *Loneliness: A sourcebook of current theory, research and therapy* (pp. 291–309). New York: Wiley.

Cutrona, C., & Peplau, L. A. (1979, April). *A longitudinal study of loneliness*. Paper presented at the annual meeting of the Western Psychological Association, San Diego.

Dickinson, G. E. (1975, August). Dating behavior of black and white adolescents before and after desegregation. *Journal of Marriage and the Family*, 602–608.

Dickinson, G. E. (1971). Dating patterns of black and white adolescents in a southern community. *Adolescence, 6*, 285–298.

Dodge, C. S., Heimberg, R. G., Hyman, D., & O/Brien, G. T. (1987). Daily heterosocial interactions of high and low socially anxious college students: A diary study. *Behavior Therapy, 18*, 90–96.

Duck, S., & Gilmour, R. (Eds.). (1981). *Personal relationship. 2: Developing personal relationships*. New York: Academic Press.

Duran, R. L. (1983). Communicative adaptability: A measure of social communicative competence. *Communcation Quarterly, 31*, 320–326.

Fischetti, M., Curran, J. P., & Wessberg, H. W. (1977). Sense of timing: A skill in heterosexual-socially anxious males. *Behavior Modification, 1,* 179–194.

Fletcher, G. J. O., Fincham, F. D., Cramer, L., & Heron, N. (1987). The role of attributions in the development of dating relationships. *Journal of Personality and Social Psychology, 53,* 481–489.

Galassi, J. P., & Galassi, M. D. (1979). Modifications of heterosocial skills deficits. In A. S. Bellack & M. Hersen (Eds.), *Research and practice in social skills training* (pp. 131–188). New York: Plenum.

Glasgow, R. E., & Arkowitz, H. (1975). The behavioral assessment of male and female social competence in dyadic heterosexual interactions. *Behavior Therapy, 6,* 488–498.

Green, S. K., Buchanan, D. R., & Heuer, S. K. (1984). Winners, losers, and choosers: A field investigation of dating initiation. *Personality and Social Psychology Bulletin, 4,* 502–522.

Greenberg, J. (1979). Single-parenting and intimacy: A comparison of mothers and fathers. *Alternative Lifestyles, 2,* 308–330.

Greenwald, D. P. (1978). Self-report assessment in high- and low-dating college women. *Behavior Therapy, 9,* 297–299.

Greenwald, D. P. (1977). The behavioral assessment of differences in social skill and social anxiety in female college students. *Behavior Therapy, 8,* 925–937.

Hagiwara, S. (1975). Visual versus verbal information in impression formation. *Journal of Personality and Social Psychology, 32,* 692–698.

Harrison, A. A., & Saeed, L. (1977). Let's make a deal: An analysis of revelations and stipulations in lonely hearts advertisements. *Journal of Personality and Social Psychology, 35,* 257–264.

Hatfield, E., Walster, G. W., & Traupmann, J. (1979). Equity and extramarital sex. In M. Cook & G. Wilson (Eds.), *Love and attraction: An international conference* (pp. 309–322). Oxford: Pergamon Press.

Heimberg, R. G., Harrison, D. F., Montgomery, D., Madsen, C. H., & Sherfey, J. A. (1980). Psychometric and behavioral analyses of a social anxiety inventory: The Situation Questionnaire. *Behavioral Assessment, 2,* 403–415.

Himadi, W. G., Arkowitz, H., Hinton, R., & Perl, J. (1980). Minimal dating and its relationship to other social problems and general adjustment. *Behavior Therapy, 11,* 345–352,

Hunt, M. (1966). *The world of the formerly married.* New York: McGraw–Hill.

Hunt, M., & Hunt, B. (1977). *The divorce experience.* New York: McGraw–Hill.

Huston, T. L. (1973). Ambiguity of acceptance, social desirability, and dating choice. *Journal of Experimental Social Psychology, 9,* 32–42.

Jones, W. H., & Carpenter, B. N. (1986). Shyness, social behavior, and relationships. In W. H. Jones, J. M. Cheek, & S. R. Briggs (Eds.), *Shyness: Perspectives on research and treatment* (pp. 227–238). New York: Plenum.

Jones, W. H., Cheek, J. M., & Briggs, S. R. (Eds.). (1986). *Shyness: Perspectives on research and treatment.* New York: Plenum.

Jones, W. H., Freeman, J. E., & Groswock, R. A. (1981). The persistence of loneliness: Self and other determinants. *Journal of Personality, 49,* 27–48.

Jones, W. H., Hansson, R. O., & Smith, T. G. (1980). *Loneliness and love: Implications for psychological and interpersonal functioning.* Unpublished manuscript, University of Tulsa.

Jones, W. H., & Russell, D. W. (1982). The social reticence scale: An objective instrument to measure shyness. *Journal of Personality Assessment, 46,* 629–631.

Kaats, G. R., & Davis, K. E. (1970). The dynamics of sexual behavior of college students. *Journal of Marriage and the Family, 32,* 390–399.

Kanekav, S., & Vaz, L. (1983). Determinants of perceived likelihood of rape and victims' fault. *Journal of Social Psychology, 1,* 147–148.

Kanin, E. J. (1971). Sexually aggressive college males. *Journal of College Student Personnel, 2,* 107–110.

Klaus, D., Herson M., & Bellack, A. S. (1977). Survey of dating habits of male and female college students: A necessary precursor to measurement and modification. *Journal of Clinical Psychology, 2,* 369–375.

Knapp, M. L. (1978). *Social intercourse: From greeting to goodbye.* Boston: Allyn & Bacon.

Krain, M. (1975, August). Communication among premarital couples at three stages of dating. *Journal of Marriage and the Family,* 609–618.

Kramer, R. M. (1978, April). *Some determinants of commitment levels in premarital relationships.* Paper presented at the annual meeting of the Rocky Mountain Psychological Association convention, Denver.

Lewinsohn, P. M. (1975). The behavioral study and treatment of depression. In M. Hersen, R. M. Eisler, & P. M. Miller (Eds.), *Progress in behavior modification* (Vol. 1, pp. 19–64). New York: Academic Press.

Lipton, D. N., McDonel, E. C., & McFall, R. M. (1987). Heterosocial perception in rapists. *Journal of Consulting and Clinical Psychology, 1,* 17–21.

Lipton, D. W., & Nelson, R. O. (1980). The contribution of initiation behaviors to dating frequency. *Behavior Therapy, 11,* 59–67.

Malatesta, V. J., & Adams, H. E. (1986). Assessment of sexual behavior. In A. R. Ciminero, K. S. Calhoun, & H. e. Adams (Eds.), *Handbook of behavioral assessment* (2nd ed., pp. 496–525). New York: Wiley.

Martinez-Diaz, J. A., & Edelstein, B. A. (1979). Multivariate effects of demand characteristics on the analogue assessment of heterosocial competence. *Journal of Applied Behavior Analysis, 12,* 1679–1689.

Martinson, W., & Zerface, J. (1970). Comparison of an individual counseling and a social program with non-daters. *Journal of Counseling Psychology, 17,* 36–40.

McCormack, S. H., & Kahn, A. (1980, May). *Behavioral characteristics of lonely and non-lonely college students.* Paper presented at the annual meeting of the Midwestern Psychological Association, St. Louis.

McCroskey, J. C., & Richmond, V. P. (1987). Willingness to communicate. In J. C. McCroskey & J. A. Daly (Eds.), *Personality and interpersonal communication* (pp. 129–156). Beverly Hills, CA: Sage Publications.

McCroskey, J. C., & Sheahan, M. E. (1978). Communication apprehension, social preference, and social behavior. *Communication Quarterly, 2,* 41–45.

Meyer, T. J. (1984, December). Date rape: A serious campus problem that few talk about. *Chronicle of Higher Education,* 12.

Morrison, R. L., & Bellack, A. S. (1981). The role of social perception in social skill. *Behavior Therapy, 12,* 69–79.

Muehlenhard, C. L., Koralewski, M. A., Andrews, S. L., & Burdick, C. A. (1986). Verbal and nonverbal cues that convey interest in dating: Two studies. *Behavior Therapy, 17,* 404–419.

Muehlenhard, C. L., & McFall, R. M. (1981). Dating initiation from a women's perspective. *Behavior Therapy, 12,* 682–691

Murstein, B. I. (1972). Physical attractiveness and marital choice. *Journal of Personality and Social Psychology, 22,* 8–12.

Murstein, B. I. (1976). *Who will marry whom? Theories and research in marital choice.* New York: Springer.

Newcomb, M. D. (1981). Heterosexual cohabitation relationships. In S. Duck & R. Gilmour (Eds.), *Personal relationships. vol. 1: Studying personal relationships* (pp. 131–164). New York: Academic Press.

Parks, M. R., Dindia, K., Adams, J., Berlin, E., & Larson, K. (1980). Communication apprehension and student dating patterns: A replication and extension. *Communication Quarterly, 2,* 3–9.

Pellegrini, R. J., Hicks, R. A., & Meyers-Winton, S. (1979). Situational affective arousal and heterosexual attraction. Some effects of success, failure, and physical attractiveness. *Psychological Record, 29,* 453–462.

Peplau, L. A., & Perlman, D. (Eds.). (1982). *Loneliness: A sourcebook of current theory, research and therapy.* New York: Wiley.

Perri, M. G. (1977). Behavior modification of heterosocial difficulties: A review of conceptual, treatment and assessment considerations. *JSAS Catalog of Selected Documents in Psychology, 7,* 75. (Ms. No. 15 30).

Petronio, S., & Endres, T. (1985/86). Dating and the single-parent: Communication in the social network. *Journal of Divorce, 2,* 83–105.

Petronio, S., & Endres, T. (1986). Dating issues: How single mothers and single fathers differ with full-time children in the household. *Journal of Divorce, 4,* 78–87.

Pilkonis, P. A., & Zimbardo, P. G. (1979). The personal and social dynamics of shyness. In C. E. Izard (Ed.), *Emotions in personality and psychopathology* (pp. 133–160). New York: Plenum.

Prisbell, M. (1982). Heterosocial communicative behavior and communication apprehension. *Communication Quarterly, 3,* 251–258.

Prisbell, M. (1983a, February). *The relationships among dating behavior, shyness, and loneliness among college students.* Paper presented at the annual meeting of the Western Speech Communication Association convention, Albuquerque, NM.

Prisbell, M. (1983b, April). *Dating: A question of social avoidance and distance.* Paper presented at the annual meeting of the Eastern Communication Association convention, Ocean City, MD.

Prisbell, M. (1986). The relationship between assertiveness and dating behavior among college students. *Communication Research Reports, 3,* 9–12.

Prisbell, M. (1987a). Factors affecting college students' perceptions of satisfaction in and frequency of dating. *Psychological Reports, 60,* 659–664.

Prisbell, M. (1987b). *Dating behavior as related to levels of loneliness.* Unpublished manuscript, Department of Communication, University of Nebraska at Omaha.

Prisbell, M., & Stacy, R. (1987). *Factors influencing dating initiation and dating satisfaction.* Unpublished manuscript, University of Nebraska at Omaha.

Reis, H. T., Nezlek, J., & Wheeler, L. (1980). Physical attractiveness in social interaction. *Journal of Personality and Social Psychology, 38,* 604–617.

Reis, H. T., Wheeler, L., Spiegel, N., Kernis, M. H., Nezlek, J., & Perri, M. (1982). Physical attractiveness in social interaction: vol. II. Why does appearance affect social experience? *Journal of Personality and social Psychology, 43,* 979–996.

Richardson, F. C., & Tasto, D. L. (1976). Development and factor analysis of a social anxiety inventory. *Behavior Therapy, 7,* 453–462.

Richardson, S., & Powell, J. L. (1982). Alcohol and rape: The effect of alcohol on attributions of blame for rape. *Personality and Social Psychology Bulletin, 3,* 468–476.

Richmond, V. P. (1984). Implications of quietness: Some facts and speculations. In J. A. Daly & J. C. McCroskey (Eds.), *Avoiding communication: Shyness, reticence, and communication apprehension* (pp. 145–155). Beverly Hills, CA: Sage Publications.

Rosenthal, K., & Keshet, H. (1978). The impact of childcare responsibilities on part-time or single-fathers: Changing patterns of work and intimacy. *Alternative Lifestyles, 1,* 465–491.

Rubenstein, C., & Shaver, P. (1982). The experience of loneliness. In L. A. Peplau & D. Perlman (Eds.), *Loneliness: A sourcebook of current theory, research and therapy* (pp. 206–223). New York: Wiley.

Rubin, Z. (1973). *Liking and loving: An invitation to social psychology.* New York: Holt, Rinehart, & Winston.

Russell, D. (1982). The measurement of loneliness. In L. A. Peplau & D. Perlman (Eds.) *Loneliness: A sourcebook of current theory, research and therapy* (pp. 81–104). New York: Wiley.

Russell, D., Peplau, L. A., Cutrona, C. (1980). The revised UCLA Loneliness Scale: Concurrent and discriminant validity evidence. *Journal of Personality and Social Psychology, 39,* 472–480.

Shaver, P., Furman, W., & Buhrmester, D. (1985). Transition to college: Network changes, social skills, and loneliness. In S. Duck & D. Perlman (Eds.), *Understanding personal relationships: An interdisciplinary approach* (pp. 193–219). Beverly Hills, CA: Sage Publications.

Shepherd, J. W., & Ellis, H. D. (1972). Physical attractiveness and selection of marriage partners. *Psychological Reports, 30,* 1004.

Shmurak, S. H. (1973). *A comparison of types of problems encountered by college students and psychiatric inpatients in social situations.* Unpublished manuscript, Indiana University.

Shotland, R. L., & Goodstein, L. (1983). Just because she doesn't want to doesn't mean it's rape: An experimentally based causal model of the perception of rape in a dating situation. *Social Psychology Quarterly, 3,* 220–232.

Spitzberg, B. H. (1987). Issues in the study of communicative competence. In B. Dervin & M. J. Voigt (Eds.), *Progress in communication sciences* (Vol. 8, pp. 1–46). Norwood, NJ: Ablex.

Spitzberg, B. H. (1986, November). *Validating a measure of interpersonal skills.* Paper presented at the annual meeting of the Speech Communication Association convention, Chicago.

Spitzberg, B. H., & Hurt, H. T. (1987). The measurement of interpersonal skills in instructional contexts. *Communication Education, 1,* 28–45.

Spreadbury, C. L., & Reeves, J. B. (1979). Physical attractiveness, dating behavior, and implications for women. *Personnel and Guidance Journal, 57,* 338–340.

Staples, R. (1980). Intimacy patterns among black, middle-class, single parents. *Alternative Lifestyles, 3,* 445–462.

Stroebe, W., Insko, C. A., Thompson, V. D., & Layton, B. D. (1971). Effects of physical attractiveness, attitude similarity, and sex on various aspects of interpersonal attraction. *Journal of Personality and Social Psychology, 18,* 79–91.

Teicher, J. D. (1972). The alienated, older, isolated male adolescent. *American Journal of Psychotherapy, 26,* 401–407.

Tesser, A., & Brodie, M. (1971). A not on the evaluation of a "computer date." *Psychonomic Sicence, 23,* 300.

Traupmann, J., Hatfield, E., & Wexler, P. (1983). Equity and sexual satisfaction in dating couples. *British Journal of Social Psychology, 22,* 33–40.

Twentyman, C. T., Boland, T., & McFall, R. M. (1981). Heterosocial avoidance in college males: Four studies. *Behavior Modifications, 5,* 523–552.

Twentyman, C. T., & McFall, R. M. (1975). Behavioral training of social skills in shy males. *Journal of Consulting and Clinical Psychology, 43,* 384–395.

Wallanger, J. L., Conger, A. J., Mariotto, M. J., Curran, J. P., & Farrell, A. D. (1980). Comparability of selection instruments in studies of heterosexual-social problem behaviors. *Behavior Therapy, 11,* 548–560.

Waller, W. (1937). The rating and dating complex. *American Sociological Review, 2,* 727–734.

Walster, E., Aronson, V., Abrahams, D., & Rottman, L. (1966). The importance of physical attractiveness in dating behavior. *Journal of Personality and Social Psychology, 4,* 508–516.

Walster, E., Walster, G. W., & Berscheid, E. (1978). *Equity: Theory and research*. Boston: Allyn & Bacon.

Walster, E., Walster, G. W., Piliavin, J., & Schmidt, L. (1973). "Playing hard to get": Understanding an elusive phenomenon. *Journal of Personality and Social Psychology, 26*, 113–121.

Watson, D., & Friend, R. (1969). Measurement of social-evaluative anxiety. *Journal of Consulting and Clinical Psychology, 33*, 448–467.

Wessberg, H. W., Mariotto, M. J., Conger, A. J., Farrell, A. D., & Conger, J. C. (1978). *The ecological validity of role plays in the assessment of hetero-sexual-social skill and anxiety*. Unpublished manuscript.

White, G. L. (1980). Physical attractiveness and courtship progress. *Journal of Personality and Social Psychology, 39*, 660–668.

Williams, C. L., & Ciminero, A. R. (1978). Development and validation of a heterosocial skills inventory: The survey of heterosexual interactions for females. *Journal of Consulting and Clinical Psychology, 6*, 1547–1548.

Winch, R. (1968). The functions of dating in middle-class America. In R. F. Winch & L. W. Goodman (Eds.), *Selected studies in marriage and the family* (pp. 505–507). New York: Holt, Rinehart, & Winston.

Woll, S., McMeen, R., & Bray, M. (1982, August). *Something in the way she smiles: Selection criteria in videodating*. Paper presented at the annual meeting of the American Psychological Association convention, Washington, DC.

Young, J. E. (1981). Cognitive therapy and loneliness. In G. Emery, S. D. Hollon, & R. C. Bedrosian (Eds.), *New directions in cognitive therapy: A casebook* (pp. 139–159). New York: Guilford Press.

10 Communication Between the Sexes: A Consideration of Sex Differences in Adult Communication

Sandra L. Ragan
University of Oklahoma

To write a chapter on sex differences[1] in adult communication is to assume a priori two basic tenets: (a) that sex is an independent variable meriting investigation and (b) that sex differences do, in fact, exist. In view of the abundant yet muddled literature in the area of human sex differences in communication, this chapter concentrates less on reviewing that literature for the reader than on attempting to elucidate the preceding assumptions and their implications for the conflicting, inconclusive findings generated by sex difference research. A new paradigm rooted in feminist theory and an ethnomethodological approach to the study of human behavior is proposed as a direction for further and perhaps more enlightening research in this area.

The communication discipline, along with its sister disciplines psychology and sociology, is rife with research exploring sex differences in adult communication behavior. Thorne, Kramarae, and Henley (1983), prominent researchers in sex differences in language and speech, reported that their 1983 bibliography includes over five times as many articles as it did in a similar 1975 listing. This trend continues in post-1983 research. In a more recent survey of literature, Foss and Foss (1988) surveyed

---

[1]The terms "sex" and "gender" have been used both differentially and interchangeably by researchers. Some have used "sex" to refer only to biological sex whereas "gender" has instead denoted sociological sex; others have used both terms synonymously. The fact remains, however, that most research in gender and communication has utilized biological sex of subject as an independent variable, not sociological sex. Thus, the distinction is an academic one in terms of how women's and men's behavioral differences are reported in the literature. In this chapter, the two terms are used interchangeably.

published articles concerning gender and communication in six communication journals for a 10-year period, 1977–1987. (Journals surveyed included five major research journals in the field—*The Quarterly Journal of Speech, Communication Monographs, Critical Studies in Mass Communication, Human Communication Research,* and the *Journal of Communication*—along with a journal devoted exclusively to gender and communication, *Women's Studies in Communication.*) The articles surveyed consist only of those in which sex or gender was the central focus of the study, rather than one of many variables investigated. In this respect, the total number of articles dealing with gender and communication reported by Foss and Foss—130—is a conservative manifestation of the widespread interest in research in communication and sex differences.

Given the abundance of literature in the area, what is it that we actually know about sex differences and human communication? Although we may be able to predict with confidence the occurrence of sex differences for a few specific communication behaviors in a few specific settings (e.g., Mulac, Lundell, & Bradac, 1986; Mulac, Weimann, Yoerks, Gibson, 1983 consistently report that females' use of adverbials to begin a sentence in a public speech may be seen as a potential linguistic marker of gender), we can make few claims about substantive, generalized sex differences in communication interaction across contexts.

One major problem in sorting out what we know about communicator differences with regard to sex is that sex role stereotypes have dramatically influenced our perception of sex differences. Most writers in the area agree that perceived differences, in accordance with masculine and feminine stereotypes for behavior, far outweigh actual differences confirmed by empirical studies (Pearson, 1985; Stewart, Cooper, & Friedley, 1986; Thorne et al., 1983). Further, any findings of differences—even those few that have been consistently replicated—have been colored inherently by the cultural verity that women and men are socialized from birth to behave differently, even if they are not genetically programmed to do so. Thus, our research findings are likely contaminated by our widely held stereotypes.

In addition to the dilemma of distinguishing real sex differences from sex-role stereotypes, our research in gender and communication obviously knows other problems. This is reflected even in the contradictory claims made by current researchers about what we know about gender and communication, as evidenced in the following:

1. The speech traits stereotypically associated with females are often posited as characteristics peculiar to them, and are often discussed as basic

identifying characteristics of the social group female. However, as several scholars have recently emphasized (e.g. Smith 1979), there is no evidence for categorical speech differences between men and women. (Kramarae, 1982, p. 85)

2. Men and persons of high status talk more than do women or low status persons. Men interrupt others more than women do, and women are the victims of more interruptions than are men. Men overlap women more than women overlap men. Women fall silent more often when they are interacting with men than do women or men in same-sex dyads, or than men do in mixed-sex dyads. The communicative patterns in this area imply that women are less competitive and aggressive in interactions; men appear to compete and win. Men talk, interrupt, and overlap more frequently, while women respond with silence. (Pearson, 1985, p. 199)

3. Although some authors have defined gender as the physiological sex of the communicator and others have operationalized gender as the scores on Sandra Bem's (1974) paper-and-pencil test of Sex Role Inventory, the inquiry has focused on the fundamental question, "Do males and females communicate differently?" After the accumulation of results from literally hundreds of studies, the answer to that question remains mired in confusing and often conflicting discussions. (Fisher, 1983, p. 225)

4. Situational and person variables notwithstanding, however, there appears to be a number of developing generalizations arising from the literature on sex differences in linguistic performance, all of which may be seen to originate in the expressive vs. instrumental dichotomy; that is, that ordinarily the female's stronger social-emotional orientation will be manifested in comparatively greater verbal supportiveness, empathy, expressed warmth, and conversational effort (Fishman, 1978) and relatively less active striving for conversational control. (McLaughlin, Cody, Kane, & Robey, 1981, p. 107)

5. Empirical evidence strongly suggests that some linguistic sex differences occur in at least some populations in some situations, but much more data are needed to specify the nature of differences and conditions under which they occur. . . . Although some studies have found substantial sex differences in specific linguistic variables, the research overall presents a confusing picture. . . . The result is a rich but disorderly data base including many seemingly conflicting findings. (Martin & Craig, 1983, p. 16–18)

These views reveal in part the inconsistency that marks current researchers' assessments of findings in gender and communication studies. This inconsistency might be interpreted also as representing the full continuum between the poles of tentativeness and certainty with which researchers characterize our knowledge of sex differences in language. Other than the fact that the empirical study of gender and communication is relatively new, having been inspired largely by the women's movement of the late 1960s, why are we so confused about what we know and do not know about women and men and their communication behavior?

Before attempting to answer this question in full, it might prove heuristic to digress a bit by tracing the research path of the investigation of one phenomenon in women's and men's interaction, verbal interruptions, in order to demonstrate in part why confusion reigns. The frequency of who interrupts whom and for what reason is commonly reported as a sex difference in interactive behavior, one that displays the familiar sex-role stereotypes of male-dominant/female-submissive. Recent textbooks in communication and gender, for example, reflect rare unanimity in their unqualified declaration that men interrupt women more than women interrupt men, and that these interruptions may well serve a dominance function that mirrors the relative power advantage men enjoy in the larger social sphere (Eakins & Eakins, 1978; Kramarae, 1981; Pearson, 1985; Borisoff & Merrill, 1985; Stewart et al., 1986).

The empirical literature on men's and women's use of interruptions, however, paints a far more equivocal picture. Although several studies have found asymmetry in the sexes' use of interruptions in the direction of boys interrupting girls and men interrupting women more than the reverse (Eakins & Eakins, 1978; Esposito, 1979; West & Zimmerman, 1983; Zimmerman, & West, 1975), other current research calls such findings into question. Kennedy and Camden (1983), for example, who videotaped 35 graduate students in six groups, did not find significant differences in men's and women's interruptions; nor did interruptions function as dominance behaviors in the transcripts they coded. Kennedy and Camden explained their discrepant findings in several ways: (a) the turn-taking constraints on conversation in group settings may have increased the social acceptability of interruptions, whereas previous research on interruptions focused only on couples in dyads; (b) past research that found sex differences in interruptions looked exclusively at frequency of interruptions rather than upon their functions in interaction; and (c) the subjects in this study were all graduate student peers—this may have had a strong interaction effect with dominance role behavior. In conclusion, Kennedy and Camden offered this caveat: "More research is needed that examines the function of communication between the sexes. It is perhaps not so important to know if there are, in fact, differences in the communication styles of women and men, but it does seem to be important to understand how these differences, if they do exist, affect relationships" (p. 58).

An even more recent study of women's and men's interruptive behaviors (Dindia, 1987) also suggests that men do not interrupt more than women and that women do not get interrupted more than men; more opposite-sex interruptions than same-sex interruptions were coded, regardless of sex of participant. Dindia audiotaped 60 undergraduates in dyadic interaction with partners with whom they were previously unacquainted; she then coded the transcribed conversations to isolate interruption sequences. Though this method appears very similar to the one used by Zimmerman and West (1975) and West and Zimmerman (1983), whose studies revealed male-dominant interruption patterns, Dindia explained her different results by citing a methodological innovation in statistical analysis employed in her experiment; that is, she isolated and tested the effects of sex of subject, sex of partner, and their interaction on the number of interruptions while controlling for between-partner correlation of number of interruptions. Previous studies that found sex differences in interruptions may have invalidly attributed to the effect of subject's sex rather than to an interaction effect, according to Dindia.

Thus, current empirical literature builds a shaky foundation for the assumption, commonly reported as displaying sex-role stereotypes in interaction, that interruptions function differentially for women and men.

How many more such reported sex differences in communicative behavior might be called into question? A look at 35 language variables which Mulac et al., (1986) have listed as potential discriminators of speaker gender in a public speaking context reveals that 28 of these have been shown to differentiate male and female language use. But for these 28 variables, empirical studies cited by Mulac et al. reveal the following:

1. For 9 of the variables, equivocal results obtained; that is, findings in the direction of one sex were contradicted by opposite findings in other studies
2. For 8 variables, sex differences were demonstrated by only one study each.
3. For 11 variables, sex differences were found. Yet for only 5 of these variables were findings replicated by more than two studies (i.e., vocalized pauses, tag questions, personal uncertainty verbs, intensive adverbs, and references to emotion).

Thus, generalizations about sex differences for particular communicative behaviors may rest on research findings that are both limited and equivocal. Besides being flawed by the inherent sex-role biases which color all our perceptions of men's and women's behaviors, such research is fraught with methodological problems as well, a factor alluded to by both Kennedy and Camden (1983) and Dindia (1987) in their explanations of why their research on interruptions produced inconsistent findings. Other prominent scholars in the area also cited methodological flaws. Thorne et al., (1983), for example, reported that the tendency of sex-differences research to study isolated communication variables rather than communicative behavior in context has produced results that are "not surprisingly, very complex and often contradictory" (p. 12). Such studies have shown very few expected sex differences. "The study of isolated variables almost invariably leads to further questions about the effects of setting, topic, roles, and other social factors that may interact with gender. It also raises questions about language function and use" (p. 13). Rather than treating gender as another independent variable, Thorne, Kramarae, and Henley suggested that researchers look at communication within contexts of actual use: "Complex descriptions of relationships among speakers—sensitive to gender in the context of setting, roles, and other social identities such as age, class, or ethnicity— yield more insight than an abstract search for isolated sex differences" (p. 16).

Fisher (1983) also discussed deficits in the literature on sex differences by citing confounding variables in research studies that lead to inconclusive findings. One source of confusion, he stated, is that perceptions of communication behavior are studied rather than direct observations of communication itself, a factor further complicated by our stereotypes of sex-role behaviors—"research that equivocates perceptions and behaviors, then, is as likely to discover differences among perceivers as among communicators" (p. 226). A second confounding variable is the sexual composition of groups studied; several researchers, including Knapp, Ellis, and Williams (1980) and Weitz (1976) have found that males and females communicate differently in same-sex and mixed-sex groups.

Yet a third variable, according to Fisher, is that researchers have focused on isolated actions of participants rather than on interaction in context, resulting in a "body of research [that] is nearly as varied as the number of different actions capable of being performed" and "is not without its share of confusion" (p. 226). There is empirical support for Fisher's complaints that sex difference research in communication needs to take into account situational or interactive variables: Mabry (1976) suggested that situational factors, for example, task ambiguity, contribute as much as sex of subject does to differences in communication behavior. LaFrance and Mayo (1979) concluded that although the sexes differed in nonverbal behaviors, "the interactional context affects what and how much gender-specific behavior is displayed" (p. 106). After finding in his own study that the competitive or cooperative orientations of interactants had a greater impact on their communication behavior than their sex did, Fisher concluded that further research in gender and communication differences "should take into account the interactional context and its potentially greater impact on communicative behaviors" (p. 237).

Even Mulac Lundell, & Bradac (1986) who have done programmatic work in sex differences in language use in public speaking situations assert that there is "a degree of 'fuzziness' of boundaries between male and female language use" (125). They further reported that a phenomenon they term "fluctuating overlap" suggests that "the language differentiating male from female communicators varies with time and place"; in other words, little replicability exists for features distinguishing male from female speakers. Mulac et al. explained the nature and amount of fluctuation in some of the same ways that Fisher (1983) did with references to culture, individual differences, and situational variables. Mulac, et al. further stated that the fluctuating overlap perspective suggests "weak" linguistic gender markers or "sex-preferential tendencies" with the possibility of "strong" or prototypical markers that are never or rarely shared. They provided the caveat that even those variables that have discriminated consistently across analyses (e.g., references to emotion and vocalized pauses) "are not rigidly associated with maleness or femaleness; they are only relatively strong in their connection with gender" (p. 125).

A report of the 1986 Conference on Gender and Communication Research corroborates many of the concerns just expressed. In this report, Wood and Phillips (1986) cited various speakers at the conference who critiqued research on gender differences: Dennis Gouran, for example, noted numerous design flaws that call into question the validity of many conclusions, including insufficient numbers of subjects to warrant generalizations, an overreliance on subjects' self-perceptions, and an inadequate assessment of directly observable communication behaviors. Constance Staley reiterated many of these concerns, adding further that research emphasizing sex differences may actually be perpetuating gender stereotypes. She aptly summarized several problems of sex-difference research in claiming that findings of differences are based on experimental studies using college subjects involved in artificial tasks who self-report perceptions rather than engage in actual behavir.

These flaws reported in the sex differences-in-communication literature possibly parallel those for social scientific research in general. Yet due to the further confounding effect of sex-role stereotypes that are inextricably linked to our findings of sex differences, such flaws may be even more insidious for this line of research. The validity of our findings is called into question not only in that we study student perceptions in laboratory contexts and then claim these perceptions are tantamount to sex differences in actual adult behaviors in natural interaction; but also in that our search for sex differences can only be conducted through the blinders of our stereotypical beliefs about appropriate gender behavior.

Given the substantive and repeated criticisms levelled at research in gender and communication, are current studies addressing the concerns raised? A review of recent research produces an equivocal answer. A perusal of articles dealing with gender issues published in *Communication Monographs* from 1981–1987, for example, reveals, almost without exception, a subject population of undergraduate students and a methodological reliance on experimental methods and statistical analyses of questionnaire data (e.g., Bradley, 1981; Cody & O'Hair, 1983; Miller, Reynolds, & Cambra, 1987; Montgomery & Norton, 1981; Petronio, Martin, & Littlefield, 1984; Warfel, 1984). (In one study from this sampling that also includes nonexperimental, nonquestionnaire data, Mulac et al. (1986) audiorecorded in-class speeches of undergraduate students and coded their transcripts of language differences in women and men.)

A look at articles published in *Human Communication Research* for the same period (1981–1987) appears to suggest a similar trend; most all studies dealing with communication and sex differences used undergraduate subjects in experimental settings (see, e.g., Bradley, 1987; Dindia, 1987; Fisher, 1983; McLaughlin et al., 1981; Mulac, Studley, Wiemann, & Bradac, 1987). Interestingly, however, all of the studies just cited made strides toward obtaining "natural" interaction between the sexes by asking subjects to engage in conversation with a partner who was a stranger, audio and/or videotaping their interactions, and then coding these interactions for sex differences. Thus, although these studies published in *HCR* used undergraduates in experimental settings, they also focused on communicators' interactive behaviors rather than on self-report, questionnaire data.

Reviewing the spring, 1987, issue of a third journal, *Women's Studies in Communication,* (a journal devoted exclusively to women, gender, and communication), also produces a mixed bag in terms of subject populations and research methods. Three of the four studies reported in that issue utilize undergraduate subjects (Johnson & Vinson, 1987; Owen, 1987; Weider-Hatfield, 1987); the fourth uses individuals employed at seven different organizations (Wheeless, Hudson, & Wheeless, 1987). Three of the studies (Weider-Hatfield; Johnson & Vinson; and Wheeless, et al.) also use questionnaire data, although the Johnson and Vinson study includes analysis of audiotaped role play as well. Owen's data are the diaries of students who recorded daily entries describing their dating relationships. In sum, most recent studies of gender and communication, both in this journal, and in others surveyed (including five national communication journals and the four regional ones) suggest that undergraduate students and questionnaire data are major sources of our knowledge about sex differences in human communication.

Of course, studies do exist that are methodological exemplars for the kind of research in gender and communication that feasibly produces more valid results. In addition to those studies already cited that have examined actual behaviors in interactive contexts rather than self-perceptions or isolated communication variables, there are others conducted in naturalistic settings that focus on the complex descriptions of relationships among speakers (e.g., Edelsky, 1981; Miller, 1985; Phillips, 1986). Still other researchers, though not conducting "field" studies per se, nevertheless have managed to closely approximate spontaneous social interaction in their research designs. Martin and Craig (1983), for example, looked at conversation in initial interaction for both same- and mixed-sex dyads. Their results do not support typical sex-role patterns of male/dominant, female/deferent but instead suggest that men and women differ in their communication behavior depending on the sex of their partner, particularly with female–female interaction. From their findings, Martin and Craig deduced that "there are not very large overall sex differences with respect to certain classes of communicative behavior in informal social interaction among middle class American college students" (p. 27). They suggested further that future research needs to look at the complexity of variables influencing communication in interaction, including the interactive effects of gender with topic and situation; in addition, subsequent research should examine the distinction between individual and dyadic variables in conversation as well as looking longitudinally at gender differences.

Still another researcher who has examined gender behavior in natural conversations has found few sex differences supporting cultural beliefs about how women and men talk. Shimanoff (1983, 1985) looked at the verbal expression of emotions in women and men in natural conversation, and in two separate studies has found few sex differences in the amount or quality of talk about emotions. In the first study, no sex differences emerged for 40 undergraduates who conversed in both same-sex and mixed-sex dyads. Shimanoff explained that her methodology might account for findings that are discrepant with both sex-role expectations and with previous studies—"one explanation is that the self-report, role-playing, and experimental data of previous studies merely reflect folklinguistics about how males and females talk or how they think they should talk, while the present study examined actual behaviors" (p. 177–178). In a 1985 study of married couples who tape-recorded their conversations, Shimanoff also found few differences in the actual emotional disclosures of husbands and wives. Although self-reports of these same subjects revealed that wives felt they disclosed more emotions and valued disclosure more than their husbands did, actual conversations did not bear this out. This discrepancy between perception and reality suggests further that we question stereotypical assumptions about women being more verbally expressive of emotion than men in everyday conversation.

It is simplistic and possibly invalid to assume, however, that more naturalistic studies will reveal fewer sex differences in women's and men's communication behavior than experimental studies, that sex differences have been found only when the research design is "flawed" by the use of undergraduate subjects or experimental methods or questionnaire data. We do not know enough about male and female communicative behavior, either from experimental *or* naturalistic studies, to make such claims. But it does appear reasonable that the more our research designs involve real people engaged in real behaviors in real settings, the more valid our results will be and the less contaminated by our expectations for women's and men's behavior.

Neither the criticisms of past research in gender and communication nor the prescription for a more naturalistic approach to studying the issues therein represent a radical approach to this area of communcation research. But there are several voices who are advocating a paradigm shift in the way that we view gender and, concomitantly, in the way that we conduct research on gender differences. These voices espouse a growing belief that our culture's conceptualization of gender and gender differences dramatically affects our research, and, in turn, partially accounts for its conflicting findings. The remainder of this chapter addresses that issue by posing current, and for some readers, radical perspectives for conducting future research in communication and gender.

Feminism has long been recognized as a primary motivator for the dramatic surge in the amount of literature on the effects of gender on human behavior. Thorne et al. (1983) remarked that the women's movement of the late 1960s spurred an unprecedented interest in investigating the relationships among women, men, and communication behavior. As several scholars acknowledge, however, the bulk of the research in gender and communication ironically has not been guided by a feminist perspective. Such a perspective, acording to Foss and Foss (1988) is one that sees gender as "a critical component of all dimensions of culture . . . it is not simply one of many variables that a researcher studies; instead, it is the major element studied" (p. 3–4). The feminist perspective challenges existing research perspectives both "by considering women's perceptions, meanings, and experiences as appropriate and important data for analysis" and by incorporating "the values and qualities that characterize women's experiences" (p. 5). Applied to communication research, this perspective involves "the asking of questions about the construction of our gender system through communication and about how gender informs communication" (p. 12). As Putnam (1982) noted, we should be as concerned in gender research with how communication behaviors determine gender as with how gender influences communication. Because a feminist perspective suggests a research paradigm inimical to the dominant research mode in its emphasis on "wholes rather than parts, process rather than structure, knowledge as a process of interconnection rather than hierarchy, approximate descriptions rather than absolute truth, and cooperation rather than competition" (p. 8), Foss and Foss claimed that feminist scholars may find it professionally pragmatic to conduct research studies within the mainstream research mode—studies that merely conceive of gender as another independent variable.

Recall that it is just this notion of gender as "another independent variable" that has produced research faulted by Thorne et al. (1983) and others as yielding conflicting, invalid findings. At this point in our search for an understanding of how one's biological sex and sociological gender affect one's communication behavior, it might be wise to heed not only the advice of those who advocate new research paradigms in exploring gender issues (e.g., Fisher, 1983; Foss & Foss, 1988; Shimanoff, 1983, 1985, 1987; Thorne et al. 1983; Wood & Phillips, 1986), but also of those who espouse a new approach altogether to our conceptualization of gender.

Such an approach has been articulated primarily by researchers in the ethnomethodological tradition who conceive of gender not as a fixed biological/sociological property but rather as a verb, as "work that we do to construct and maintain a particular gender system" (Rakow, 1986, p. 12). Rakow advocated: "In communication, gender research should mean being engaged in questions about the role of communication in the construction and accomplishment of a gender system" (p. 12). If we do not know what gender is but assume a priori that it is biological, static, dualistic, dimorphic, asymmetrical, mutually exclusive, polarized, and antagonistic, then our research necessarily is flawed and trivial, according to Rakow. She suggested that future gender research draw both from feminist theory and from the ethnomethodological approach to behavior. Although feminists and ethnomethodologists do not necessarily share a common ideological stance, they would both concur nonetheless that sex and gender are cultural, mutable categories of social organization.

Garfinkel's (1967) case study of Agnes, a transsexual raised as a boy who adopted a female identity at age 17 and later had a sex change operation, laid groundwork for current thinking of gender as cultural construction rather than as fixed characteristic. As West and Zimmerman (1987) asserted, the case of Agnes "demonstrates how gender is created through interaction and at the same time structures interaction" (p. 131). Following Garfinkel, ethnomethodologists Kessler and McKenna (1978) proposed that rather than being a collection of traits, behaviors, or even biological attributes, "femaleness" and "maleness" are instead cultural events; they are assigned by society in the "gender attribution process." Thus, the world of two biological genders that we live in may not be the only world. Explaining the vast growth in research on sex differences, Kessler and McKenna stated that if we believe there are two genders, we also confirm that belief in our research: "Our seeing of two genders leads to the "discovery" of biological, psychological, and social differences" (p. 168). For Garfinkel (1967), Kessler and McKenna (1978), Rakow (1986), and most recently, West and Zimmerman (1987), gender is a social accomplishment; it is work done by cultural members to convey not only what gender we should be assigned but also to assess and assign gender to others. As Rakow (1986) explained,

> Gender, in sum, is usefully conceptualized as a culturally constructed organization of biology and social life into particular ways of doing, thinking, and experiencing the world. Our particular gender system of two dimorphic and asymmetrical genders is one of only a variety of systems that could be structured. It is in communication that this gender system is accomplished . . . communication creates genders who create communication. (p. 23)

What then are the implications for research in gender and communication, if gender is reconceptualized as a cultural construction and not as a fixed entity? First of all, we would cease doing the kind of research for which gender (or more accurately, sex of subject) was another independent variable. We would stop making assumptions that men and women communicate differently only because their observable sex characteristics make them appear to us as dimorphic opposites; we might be more concerned instead with differences in socialization and other learning experiences. We would certainly be more concerned with relationships and interaction contexts than with isolated behaviors observed independently of social situations. We would engage in naturalistic research in order to directly observe communication behaviors rather than to gauge perceptions of sex role attributes. In this way, we might resist some of the stereotypes that have invaded so much of our past research in gender and communication, stereotypes that have inextricably linked our notions of what constitutes femininity and masculinity with what we expect to see, and thus do see in the behavior of female and male subjects. We would systematically study behavior in both professional and intimate relationships rather than being preoccupied with initial interaction of strangers. We would approach the study of gender in the same ways that gender is socially accomplished—through interaction over time; we would conceive of gender as a process requiring longitudinal inquiry and not merely the observation of college sophomores. Perhaps we might even learn to conceive of the "two" sexes with adjectives and attitudes that would replace biological, dualistic, mutually exclusive, polarized, and antagonistic. Until we can rid ourselves of some of the rigidly ingrained stereotypes that both have informed and invalidated our research in the area of gender and communication, we cannot hope to answer the question of how the two interact.

REFERENCES

Bem, S. L. (1975). The measurement of psychological androgyny. *Journal of Consulting and Clinical Psychology, 42*, 155–62.

Borisoff, D., & Merrill, L. (1985). *The power to communicate: Gender differences as barriers.* Prospect Heights, IL: Waveland Press.

Bradley, P. H. (1981). The folk-linguistics of women's speech: An empirical examination. *Communication Monographs, 48*, 173–90.

Bradley, P. H. (1987). Gender differences in persuasive communication and attribution of success and failure. *Human Communication Research, 13*, 372–85.

Cody, M. J., & O'Hair, H. D. (1983). Nonverbal communication and deception: Differences in deception cues due to gender and communicator dominance. *Communication Monographs, 50*, 175–92.

Dindia, K. (1987). The effects of sex of subject and sex of partner on interruptions. *Human Communication Research, 13*, 345–71.

Eakins, B. W., & Eakins, R. G. (1978). *Sex differences in human communication.* Boston, MA: Houghton Mifflin.

Edelsky, C. (1981). Who's got the floor? *Language in Society, 10*, 383–421.

Esposito, A. (1979). Sex differences in children's conversation. *Language and Speech, 22*, 213–220.

Fisher, B. A. (1983). Differential effects of sexual composition and interactional context on interaction patterns in dyads. *Human Communication Research, 9*, 225–38.

Fishman, P. M. (1978). Interaction: The work women do. *Social Problems, 25*, 397–406.

Foss, K. A., & Foss, S. K. (1988). Incorporating the feminist perspective in communication scholarship: A research commentary.

Garfinkel, H. (1967). *Studies in ethnomethodology.* Englewood Cliffs, NJ: Prentice-Hall.

Johnson, C., & Vinson, L. (1987). 'Damned if you do, damned if you don't': Status, powerful speech, and evaluations of female witnesses. *Women's Studies in Communication, 10*, 37–44.

Kennedy, C. W., & Camden, C. T. (1983). A new look at interruptions. *Western Journal of Speech Communication, 47*, 45–58.

Kessler, S. J., & McKenna, W.)1978). *Gender: An ethnomethodological approach.* New York: Wiley.

Knapp, M. L., Ellis, D. G., & Williams, B.A. (1980). Perceptions of communication behavior associated with relationship terms. *Communication Monographs, 47*, 262–278.

Kramarae, C. (1981). *Women and men speaking*. Rowley, MA: Newbury House.

Kramarae, C. (1982). Gender: How she speaks. In E. B. Ryan & H. Giles (Eds.), *Attitudes toward language variation: Social and applied contexts* (pp. 84–98). London: Edward Arnold.

LaFrance, M., & Mayo, C. (1979). A review of nonverbal behaviors of women and men. *Western Journal of Speech Communication, 43*, 96–107.

Mabry, E. (1976). *Female–male interaction in unstructured small group settings*. Paper presented to the annual meeting of the Speech Communication Association, San Francisco.

Martin, J. N., & Craig, R. T. (1983) Selected linguistic sex differences during initial social interactions of same-sex and mixed-sex student dyads. *Western Journal of Speech Communication, 47*, 16–28.

McLaughlin, M. L., Cody, M. J., Kane, M. L., & Robey, C. S. (1981). Sex differences in story receipt and story sequencing behaviors in dyadic conversations. *Human Communication Research, 7*, 99–116.

Miller, J. B. (1985). Patterns of control in same-sex conversations: Differences between women and men. *Women's Studies in Communication, 8, 2*, 62–69.

Miller, M. D., Reynolds, R. A., & Cambra, R. E. (1987). The influence of gender and culture on language intensity. *Communication Monographs, 54*, 101–12.

Montgomery, B. M., & Norton, R.W. (1981). Sex differences and similarities in communicator style. *Communication Monographs, 48*, 121–132.

Mulac, A., Lundell, T. L., & Bradac, J. J. (1986). Male/female language differences and attributional consequences in a public speaking situation: Toward an explanation of the gender-linked language effect. *Communication Monographs 53*, 115–129.

Mulac, A., Studley, L. B., Wiemann, J. W., & Bradac, J. J. (1987). Male/female gaze in same-sex and mixed-sex dyads: Gender-linked differences and mutual influence. *Human Communication Research, 13*, 323–43.

Mulac, A., Wiemann, J. M., Yoerks, S. W., & Gibson, T. W. (1983). *Male/female differences and their effects in like-sex and mixed-sex dyads: A test of interpersonal accommodation and the gender-linked language effect*. Paper presented at the Second International Conference, Social Psychology and Language, Bristol, England.

Owen, W. F. (1987). The verbal expression of love by women and men as acritical communication event in personal relationships. *Women's Studies in Communication, 10*, 15–24.

Pearson, J. C. (1985). *Gender and communication*: Dubuque, IA: William C. Brown.

Petronio, S., Martin, J., & Littlefield, R. (1984). Prerequisite conditions for self-disclosing: A gender issue. *Communication Monographs, 51*, 268–73.

Phillips, G. M. (1986). Men talking to men about their relationships. *American Behavioral Scientist, 29*, 321–41.

Putnam, L. L. (1982). In search of gender: A critique of communication and sex-roles research. *Women's Studies in Communication, 5, 1*, 1–9.

Rakow, L. R. (1986). Rethinking gender research in communication. *Journal of Communication, 36*, 11–26.

Shimanoff, S. B. (1983). The role of gender in linguistic references to emotive states. *Communication Quarterly, 31*, 174–79.

Shimanoff, S. B. (1985). Rules governing the verbal expression of emotions between married couples. *Western Journal of Speech Communication, 9*, 147–175.

Shimanoff, S. B. (1987). Types of emotional disclosures and request compliance between spouses. *Communication Monographs, 54*, 85–100.

Smith, P. M. (1979). Sex markers in speech. In K. R. Scherer & H. Giles (Eds.), *Social markers in speech* (pp. 109–46). Cambridge, MA: Cambridge University Press.

Stewart, L. P., Cooper, P. J., & Friedley, S. A. (1986). *Communication between the sexes: Sex differences and sex-role stereotypes.* Scottsdale, AZ: Gorsuch Scarisbrick.

Thorne, B., Kramarae, C., & Henley, N. (Eds.). (1983). *Language, gender and society.* Rowley, MA: Newbury House.

Warfel, K. A. (1984). Gender schemas and perceptions of speech style. *Communication Monographs, 51,* 253–267.

Weider-Hatfield, D. (1987). Differences in self-reported leadership behavior as a function of biological sex and psychological gender. *Women's Studies in Communication, 10,* 1–14.

Weitz, S. (1976). Sex differences in nonverbal communication. *Sex Roles, 2,* 175–183.

West, C., & Zimmerman, D. H. (1983). Small insults: A study of interruptions in cross-sex conversations between unacquainted persons. In B. Thorne, C. Kramarae, & N. Henley (Eds.), *Language, gender and society* (pp. 102–117). Rowley, MA: Newbury House.

West, C., & Zimmerman, D. H. (1987). Doing gender. *Gender and Society, 1,* 125–151.

Wheeless, V. E., Hudson, D. C., & Wheeless, L. R. (1987). A test of the expected use of influence strategies by male and female supervisors as related to job satisfaction and trust in supervisor. *Women's Studies in Communication, 10,* 25–36.

Wood, J. T., & Phillips, G. M. (1986). Report of the 1986 conference on gender and communication research. *Women's Studies in Communication 9,* 89–93.

Zimmerman, D. H., & West, C. (1975). Sex roles, interruptions, and silences in conversation. In B. Thorne & N. Henley (Eds.). *Language and sex: Difference and dominance* (pp. 105–129). Rowley, MA: Newbury House.

11 Social Communicative Competence in Adulthood

Robert L. Duran
University of Hartford

The impotance of research into communicative competence is underscored by federal and state initiatives designed to determine oral competencies for primary and secondary students (Backlund, Booth, Moore, Muller Parks, & Van Rheenen, 1982a). Further, legislators are turning to communication professionals for consultation on the establishment of basic communication competencies (Backlund, Brown, Gurry, & Jandt, 1982).

Currently 31 states have at least expressed an intention to develop assessment programs and curricula for speaking and listening skills at the primary and secondary levels (Backlund et al., 1982a). This interest is the result of legislation enacted in 1978. "Public Law 95-561 amended the Elementary and Secondary Education Acts of 1965 to include a definition of basic skills that includes reading, mathematics, written communication, and oral communication" (Backlund et al., 1982a, p. 126). In addition to interest at the primary and secondary levels, several colleges and universities across the country require an oral communication course as a general education requirement. Further, in response to the growing interest in oral communication standards and practices at all educational levels, the Speech Communication Association has established the Task Force on Assessment and Testing in 1981.

The rationale for the establishment of oral communicative competencies and the integration of curricula to improve oral skills is provided by estimates of communication problems in the population. Rubin (1982) examined each of the 19 competencies identified in the Communication Competency Assessment Instrument (CCAI) and reported that between

195

10% (understanding the difference between fact and opinion) and 49% (describing the point of view of someone who disagrees with him or her) of the participants had difficulties with the various competencies. The participants were college students, who would seem to represent the upper end of the population distribution with regard to communicative competence. Thus, the percentage of individuals experiencing communication difficulties would likely be greater.

The majority of research to date has been concerned with establishing conceptual and operational definitions of communicative competence. Spitzberg (1986a) observed that most competence researchers have utilized their own measures of communicative competence. As a result, most research efforts have been concerned with establishing the validity of one's own measure (the present author included) and not addressing other issues of communicative competence such as causes, effects, and treatments. Due to the paucity of research into the effects of communicative competence in adulthood, this review focuses on five areas: issues of communicative competence, conceptual approaches to the study of competence, measures of communicative competence, effects of competence, and directions for future research.

ISSUES OF COMMUNICATIVE COMPETENCE

Before reviewing various conceptualizations and operationalizations of communicative competence, it is necessary to discuss some issues concerning the nature of competence. These issues represent decision points for researchers interested in investigating the topic area. The way in which one resolves these issues has implications for the choice of conceptualization and measurement of communicative competence.

Although scholars differ on most of the issues, one point most scholars agree on directly or by implication is that communicative competence is comprised of three general components. McCroskey (1982) and others (Cegala, 1981; Duran & Kelly, 1984a; Rubin & Feezel, 1984; Spitzberg, 1981, 1983; Spitzberg & Cupach, 1984) have suggested communicative competence is comprised of three domains: cognitive, affective, and psycho-motor. Spitzberg (1983) discussed the three components of competence as being knowledge, motivation, and skill. The distinction between the two approaches is discussed later when dealing with the issue of contextually specific versus cross-contextual conceptualizations of competence. McCroskey (1982) explained that the cognitive domain "would include learning what are the available means, how they have been employed in various situations in the past, and being able to determine which ones have the highest probability of success in a given situation" (p. 5). According to McCroskey (1982) affective competence concerns an individual's attitudes and feelings toward the knowledge and behaviors of the cognitive and psycho-motor domains. The significance of the affective domain is in its mediation of the other two domains. For example, one may know "what to do" (cognitive competence) and not want to "do it" (affective competence). The psycho-motor domain of communicative competence is concerned with the skills necessary to produce perceptions of competence. Of the three domains of competence, the psycho-motor domain has received the most research interest. The acknowledgement of three general domains of communicative competence is necessary to explain an individual's performance in a specific context. It accounts for variations in performance across contexts, target persons, and topics of interaction. Variations in an individual's performance is the subject of the second and most controversial issue of communicative competence: state versus trait approaches to competence.

The terms *state* and *trait competence* are not accurate descriptors of the distinction between the two positions. Cupach and Spitzberg (1983) chose the terms *situational* and *dispositional*. Dispositional approaches to communicative competence attempt to explain behavioral tendencies that cut across several communication contexts. Typically, items that comprise dispositional instruments measure molar-level perceptions (Spitzberg, 1986a, 1986b, 1986c); for example, "I am verbally and nonverbally supportive of other people," and "People think I am witty" (Duran, 1983).

Situational approaches to communicative competence (Cupach & Spitzberg, 1981) reference a specific interaction or conversation (e.g., "I stumbled over words in this conversation," "In this conversation I was witty"). Cupach and Spitzberg (1983) stated "Situational measures assess a person's behavior in a given situation and are therefore event-focused" (p. 366). Situational measures of competence are well suited to molecular-level measurement, although this level of measurement is not a requisite of a situational approach. "Molecular impressions . . . are relatively discrete, focused, and low-level inferences. For example, judgment of an actor's eye contact, use of questions, turn-taking, etc., focus upon specific perceptual objects . . ." (Spitzberg, 1986c, p. 4). The choice of a dispositionally or situationally based approach to competence has implications for the types of questions one wants to investigate. Dispositionally based constructs enable one to investigate the process by which individuals perform competently across various contexts. The advantage of this approach is that it can lead to explanations of how people are able to be competent in a number of contexts which require different communication skills (Duran & Kelly, 1984a). This approach is limited in its diagnostic capabilities. Almost by definition dispositional approaches measure general molar impressions of communicative performance. Therefore, they lack the specificity of measurement necessary for remediation of skill deficits. The situationally based approaches, coupled with molecular-level perceptions provide information concerning specific behaviors. Researchers are able to explain an individual's performance in a specific encounter. Cupach and Spitzberg (1983) found that situationally based measures of competence were better predictors of situationally based outcome measures (feeling good, Prisbell, 1979; Prisbell & Andersen, 1980) than dispositional measures. "Multiple regression analysis revealed that dispositional predictors of state 'feeling good' were largely redundant with situational predictors and explained only about one-third as much variance" (Cupach & Spitzberg, 1983, p. 374). Further, molecular-level measurement assesses individuals' specific communicative behavior which leads to the gestalt, molar-level perceptions (Spitzberg & Cupach, 1985). As a result, molecular-level measures provide the diagnostic information necessary for the development of remediation programs. The disadvantage of the situational approach to communicative competence is that research results are tied to the specific stimulus situation assessed and, therefore, their generalizability is severely limited (Duran & Kelly, 1984a).

Both approaches to conceptualizing competence are warranted. One's choice of approach should be based upon the purpose of the investigation. If a researcher is interested in cross-contextual explanations and predictions of communicative competence then a dispositional approach is advised. If the phenomena of interest are tied to a specific context, target person, topic, and so forth, then a situationally based approach is appropriate.

A third issue dividing competence researchers is the locus of judgment of competent communication. Where do judgments of competence reside—in the individual, dyad, or third-party observers? Studies have indicated low to moderate correlations among these three perspectives. Research indicates that person A's communication satisfaction is more dependent upon A's perceptions of B's communicative competence than A's self-reported competence (Cupach & Spitzberg, 1981; Duran & Zakahi, 1987; Spitzberg, 1982). Further, Duran and Kelly (1984b) found that participants differing on self-reported social anxiety and competence were not differentially perceived in terms of their social skills by their interaction partners or third-party observers. Spitzberg and Cupach (1985) explained the divergence of perceptions, "these distortions in self- and other-observer perceptions could be due to attributional, physical, and information-processing characteristics" (p. 210). Attribution theory has posited that external factors (situational constraints) are used to explain self's performance whereas internal factors (personal disposi-tions) are used to explain one's partner's performance (Jones & Nisbett, 1971). "Physically, an actor's perceptual apparatus tends to be focused outward on the other rather than the self" (Spitzberg & Cupach, 1985, 210). "Information-processing characteristics" refers to the unique per-sonal information an individual possesses that might influence that per-son's self-perceived social performance.

The theoretical relevance of "locus of judgment" is the notion that different sources have different perceptions of the same communicative performance. This has implications for the choice of an approach to competence. A dispositional approach is best suited to self-reports of competence, whereas a situationally based approach is best measured by a combination of self and other reports of competence. Third-party observers might be most appropriate to report specific, concrete molecu-lar-level observations as demonstrated in a well-defined context.

The fourth issue concerns the meaning of the term *competence* and how it relates to or differs from effectiveness. McCroskey (1982) noted that conceptualizations stressing goal attainment as a requisite skill of a competent communicator (e.g., Wiemann, 1977) are serving to confuse and muddle the construct. "Clearly, competent communicators do not always accomplish their goals. Effectiveness as a definitional criterion of competence is not only excess baggage, it also will lead to inappropriate judgments of the competence of individuals" (McCroskey, 1982, p. 5). Spitzberg (1983), on the other hand, maintained that competence and effectiveness are both conceptually and empirically related. "The im-plication is that appropriate response usually is, to some degree, an effective response as well" (Spitzberg, 1983, p. 325).

The addition of effectiveness as a criterion for judgments of com-petence seems to add an unnecessary value judgment to an already complex construct. It presents difficulties when research becomes sophis-ticated enough to identify skills deficits and offer remediation. It is one issue to make a person competent and an entirely different issue to make a person effective. From a measurement perspective competence refers to the minimal skills necessary to produce perceptions of an adequate communicative performance (Duran & Elliot, 1984). Effectiveness would seem to presuppose competence and exceed those standards. Coupling effectiveness with competence would seem to provide ethical problems when applied to a remediation program. If an individual can-not interact with the minimal skills necessary to participate in an interac-tion, remediation would be appropriate and necessary. Whether a person is less effective than another requires a subjective judgment, raising ethical implications if one were to label another as incompetent because he or she is ineffective.

The final issue of communicative competence is the question of performance as a necessary criterion of the competence construct. McCroskey (1982) contended that performance and competence are two separate domains, that is, knowing what to do is different from doing it. He noted that some conceptualizations (e.g., Allen & Brown, 1976; Wiemann, 1977) define communication competence as the "ability to perform" or "demonstration of. . . . " McCroskey (1982) noted that a child may be able to point to a picture of an elephant, but when pointing to an elephant the child may be unable to identify what it is. Spitzberg (1983) contended that ultimately to determine a person's level of communicative competence, that person must demonstrate his or her abilities. As a result, performance and competence are de facto related. Of importance to scholars is that performance, competence, and affect are independently assessed when measuring one's communicative performance. This issue brings us back to the three domains of communicative competence: cognitive/knowledge, affective/motivation, and psychomotor/skills.

The purpose of this review of issues has been to present the decision points a researcher in the area of communicative competence must confront. Resolution of the various issues determines one's choice of conceptualization and operationalization. The following section reviews different approaches to the conceptualization of communicative competence.

CONCEPTUAL APPROACHES TO COMMUNICATIVE COMPETENCE

In the book, *Interpersonal Communication Competence* (Spitzberg & Cupach, 1984), various conceptualizations from different scholarly fields were reviewed identifying seven broad approaches to competence: fundamental competence, social competence, social skills, interpersonal competence, linguistic competence, communicative competence, and relational competence. For purposes of this discussion, "social skills" is subsumed within the social competence perspective due to the similarity of assumptions. Further, the authors note that these categories are not necessarily exhaustive nor mutually exclusive, rather they are general groupings by which conceptualizations of communicative competence can be organized.

Fundamental Competence

The most basic form of communicative competence is fundamental competence: "an individual's ability to adapt effectively to the surrounding environment over time" (Spitzberg & Cupach, 1984, p. 35). The critical feature of this definition is the focus upon adaptability, which is a universally accepted component of communicative competence (Brunner & Phelps, 1979; Duran & Kelly, 1984a; Foote & Cottrell, 1955; Hale & Delia, 1976; Hart & Burks, 1972). Because adaptability is universally accepted by scholars, fundamental competence is considered a starting point for more elaborate models of competence. Conceptualizations from this perspective of adaptability are concerned with the cognitive and perceptual processes involved with the ability to adapt one's communicative behaviors across contexts. Specifically, adaptability is accomplished by perceiving contextual parameters and enacting communication appropriate to the setting. As a result, researchers in this area are concerned with the psychological processes that facilitate cross-contextual performance. Concepts such as role taking, flexibility, behavioral repertoires, and style flexing aid in this process.

Spitzberg and Cupach (1984) summarized the fundamental competence approach "the sine qua non of fundamental competence is cross-situational adaptability . . . theories are concerned with the acquisition and development of adaptability and its cognitive precursors. The explanations for competence are generally cognitive and person-centered. Messages, per se, are not focal points for this literature" (p. 40). With regard to the issues discussed previously, fundamental competence is a dispositional approach best measured by molar-level perceptions.

Social Competence

Social competence models represent the second category of competence approaches. This approach has attempted to identify traits that enhance communicative performance, resulting in a number of different characteristics, related to competence (Spitzberg & Cupach, 1984, p. 43). Four characteristics are consistently identified: cognitive complexity, empathy, role taking, and interaction involvement.

Because communicative competence involves a cognitive component, one variable that would predict competence is cognitive complexity. A component of communicative competence is the ability to adapt to varying situations. As a result, an individual must be able to perceive contextual cues in various situations and adapt his or her behaviors and message strategies to that particular context. High-complexity individuals should be better able than low-complexity persons to perceive contextual parameters. By virtue of this ability, high-complexity individuals should be more adaptable and, hence, more communicatively competent than low-complexity individuals. Individuals differ in the number and content of constructs that are available to them for the analysis of a situation. Research has demonstrated that construct schemas are associated with listening skills, and message-making strategies (Delia & Crockett, 1973; Press, Crockett, & Delia, 1975). Further, cognitive complexity has been found to predict the ability to perceive others' motives and to adapt message strategies based upon those perceptions (Delia & Clark, 1977). Those who are relatively complex are more sensitive to inconsistencies between speakers' verbal and nonverbal channels than are less complex observers (Domangue, 1978).

Empathy and role taking are complementary skills. Spitzberg and Cupach (1984) noted, "role taking involves a mental and imaginative construction of another's role for purposes of managing interaction, whereas empathy is an emotional reaction to, or an affective experience of, another's emotional state" (p. 45). These two constructs operate in tandem to aid in the process of adaptation as discussed in the fundamental competence perspective. Empathy involves an affective response to the situation of another. This respone aids in the selection of role behaviors appropriate to the context. Role taking, in turn, may provide the framework from which to interpret another's affective state.

Role taking and empathy may contribute to the successful management of interactions. Interaction management is "concerned with the 'procedural' aspects that structure and maintain an interaction" (Wiemann, 1977, p. 199). Behaviors indicative of interaction management are eye contact, head nods, smooth interchange, topic control, and gesticulation. Basically, interaction management is concerned with the initiation, maintenance, and termination of conversations. Role taking and empathy may aid in the smooth management of interaction.

The distinction between fundamental competence and social competence deals with the degree of specificity of constructs that facilitate competent communication. Fundamental competence is concerned with general, cognitive abilities that enable individuals to adapt to changing social contexts. Social competence addresses the "specific abilities and behaviors that lead to particular successes" (Spitzberg & Cupach, 1984, p. 53).

Interpersonal Competence

In a general sense interpersonal competence is the strategic selection of communicative tacts that have the greatest likelihood of attaining the desired goal. This definition is the product of several conceptualizations. Interpersonal competence is concerned with one's ability to control and manipulate the social environment (Foote & Cottrell, 1955). This is accomplished by influencing the other's perceptions of the social context in such a manner as to facilitate self's goal attainment. Role taking, empathy, and interaction management are all critical to the ability to monitor and structure perceptions of a social interaction.

Other approaches view interpersonal competence as a problem-solving skill (Gotlib & Asarnow, 1980; Spivack, Platt, & Shure, 1976). Skills involved with interpersonal problem solving are: awareness of potential problems, generation of potential solutions, and ability to implement solutions (Spivack et al., 1976).

Consistent with the problem-solving orientation is Goffman's (1969) emphasis upon communication strategies. Strategic interaction necessitates that one can accurately perceive the other's perceptions of the evolving interaction and choose communication that accommodates the concerns and perceptions of the other. In short, it is the ability to project future "moves" on the part of the other and to have tacts appropriate and responsive to those moves. Spitzberg and Cupach (1984) summarized the interpersonal competence approach as "a strategic orientation to interaction, and this strategic orientation is very goal-oriented. Communication is seen as a means to the end of goal achievement, whether the goal is completely salient or only tacit" (p. 57).

Linguistic Competence

The fourth approach to the conceptualization of communicative competence reflects a message-centered approach. That is, competence is seen as a characteristic of the content and the structure of interaction, as opposed to a quality of the individual or dyad. Linguistic competence is concerned with the knowledge of the grammatical structure of messages. The principal proponent of linguistic competence is Chomsky (1965). Chomsky (1965) posited that generative grammar is an individual's innate knowledge of the rules underlying the production of messages. It consists of two components: surface structure and deep structure. Surface structure is one's ability to manipulate nouns, verbs, adjectives, adverbs, and so on, in different ways to create an infinite possibility of messages. Deep structure is not concerned with the syntactical construction of sentences, rather it is concerned with the semantic variations underlying messages. Chomsky (1965) maintained a distinction between competence and performance, the former being knowledge of language, the latter being the production of language.

Habermas (1970) proposed that competent interaction is not only the result of linguistic knowledge as articulated by Chomsky, but also knowledge of the implied role relations. Habermas (1970) introduced the concept of dialogue constitutive universals to explain an individual's knowledge of the pragmatic (Watzlawick, Beaven, & Jackson, 1967) implications of messages, specifically command-level awareness.

An integration of the two approaches to linguistic competence was provided by Jakobovitz (1970). He contended that there are three domains of meaning: linguistic, implicit, and implicative. Linguistic meaning is similar to Chomsky's notion of surface level knowledge—that is, knowledge of syntactical rules. Implicit meaning is awareness of the semantic variations of messages, similar to deep structure. Implicative meaning accommodates Habermas' acknowledgment of pragmatic implications, specifically, that messages mentally bind interactants in a role relationship.

Communicative Competence

The fifth approach is communicative competence. Spitzberg and Cupach (1984) defined this approach as "the ability to adapt messages appropriately to the interaction context" (p. 63). As they explained, one difference that differentiates linguistic from communicative competence is the former's exclusion of the production of messages as part of its constitutive definition. Performance is viewed as an integral part of competence, hence, communicative competence is not only knowing what to do but also doing it.

A second distinction between linguistic and communicative competence is that the latter, due to the inclusion of performance, is concerned with contextual appropriateness. That is, Chomsky (1965) assumed ideal communicators and was concerned with the generative rules underlying the production of ideal communication. Proponents of communicative competence consider that messages are contextually bound and, as such, are judged appropriate by the interactants in the context.

The ability to competently communicate in various contexts necessitates a repertoire of roles and social experiences. Spitzberg and Cupach (1984) explicated the relationship between appropriateness and role repertoires. "A person's knowledge is indicated by the range of his or her behavioral and contextual repertoire and accurate comprehension of the rules relating these behaviors and contexts" (p. 66).

Relational Competence

Relational competence is the final approach to the conceptualization of communicative competence. Relational competence grows out of the issue concerning effectiveness as a criterion for communicative competence. Effectiveness and appropriateness are viewed as necessary outcomes of a competent interaction. In this sense, relational competence and the social-skills model are similar. Unlike the social-skills approach, relational competence does not assume there are specific skills that are generally effective and appropriate to a specific context. Relational competence avoids norm-referenced (Duran & Elliot, 1984) skills, rather, judgments of competence are assumed only valid when made by the participants in the context. As a result, an effective interaction is one in which both interactants experience satisfaction.

Critical to the negotiation of a mutually satisfying interaction is concern for the other. "Other orientation" involves the skills of empathy, perceptiveness, and confirmation. It is the ability to perceive how the other is responding to the evolving social situation. Indicative of the relational competence approach is Wiemann's (1977) conceptualization of competence. He defined communicative competence as, "the ability of an interactant to choose among available communicative behaviors in order that he may successfully accomplish his own interpersonal goals during an encounter while maintaining the face and line of his fellow interactants within the constraints of the situation" (p. 198). Therefore, relational competence emphasizes the successful management of the dyadic relationship as the criterion for effectiveness.

One's choice of conceptual approach should be based on the nature of the research question posed, and one's resolution of the issues discussed earlier. Those subscribing to a dispositional approach should choose fundamental, social, interpersonal, or linguistic competence. These conceptual approaches assume competence to be cross-contextual, residing in the individual.

Those who wish to investigate situationally based judgments of competence should choose communication or relational competence. Both of these approaches base judgments of competence upon the individual's ability to perform appropriately within the social context, aware of dyadic expectations. These conceptual approaches can further be differentiated by the issues regarding competence versus effectiveness and competence versus performance. The relevance of these decision points are further evidenced when reviewing measures of communicative competence.

MEASURES OF COMMUNICATIVE COMPETENCE

As a result of extensive computer searches Spitzberg (1986a, 1986b) compiled a list of 1275 articles relevant to communication competence. These areticles yielded a list of 149 measures, which was subsequently reduced to 138 after peripherally related measures were eliminated.

These 138 measures were evaluated by using Cone's (1978) Behavioral Assessment Grid (BAG). The BAG classifies behavioral assessment approaches along three dimensions: content, method, and universes of generalization. Consistent with the dimensions of the BAG, Spitzberg developed 12 criteria by which to evaluate the 138 communicative competence measures (Spitzberg, 1986a, 1986b). Measures failing to meet any one of the 12 decision rules were excluded from review resulting in 12 measures.

These measures were divided into two categories, self- and other-reference instruments. Research concerning communicative competence has approached the construct from various loci of perceptions: self, other, and third-party observers/judges. Five measures were classified as self-reference instruments: Communicative Adaptability Scale (Duran, 1983), Interpersonal Communication Inventory (Bienvenu, 1971), Self-Efficacy Questionnaire for Social Skills (Moe & Zeiss, 1982), Self-Rated Competence Scale (Cupach & Spitzberg, 1981), and Social Performance Survey Schedule (Lowe & Cantela, 1978). Seven measures were classified as other-reference instruments: Behavioral Assessment of Communication Competency (Ruben, 1976), Communicative Competence Scale (Wiemann, 1977), Communicative Competency Assessment Instrument (Rubin, 1982), Conversational Skills Rating Scale (Spitzberg & Hurt, 1985), Rating of Alter-Competence (Cupach & Spitzberg, 1981), Simulated Social Interaction Test (Curran, 1982), and Social Interaction Test-Rating Scales (Trower, Bryant, & Argyle, 1978).

The Communicative Adaptability Scale (CAS, Duran, 1983) is operationalized by 6 dimensions: social confirmation, social composure, social experience, appropriate disclosure, articulation, and wit. The CAS consists of 30, 5-point Likert-type statements. The CAS's factor structure was originally validated on a student sample of 700 and an adult sample of 160 (Duran, 1983). The factor structure has remained consistent in over 9 studies published by the scale's author with adults and students for a total sample size of 4400 participants.

The Interpersonal Communication Inventory (ICI, Bienvenu, 1971) consists of 40 items measuring 12 dimensions: self-disclosure, awareness, evaluation and acceptance of feedback, self-expression, attention, clarity, avoidance, coping with feelings, dominance, perceived acceptance, and handling differences (Bienvenu & Stewart, 1976). Subsequent research using the ICI has failed to reproduce the 12-factor solution (Phelps & Snavely, 1980). Spitzberg (1986a) concluded that although the measure relates well with other trait measures of competence, its psychometric properties are too unstable to highly recommend the ICI.

Moe and Zeiss (1982) developed the Self-Efficacy Questionnaire for Social Skills (SEQSS). It is comprised of 12 situational descriptions which represent combinations of 3 situational characteristics: familiarity with conversant (stranger, acquaintance, friend), context (dyad, small group, public), and interest level of the conversation (interesting, dull). Further, participants rate their performance on 12 conversational skills (self-disclosure, humor, warmth, fluency, friendliness, assertiveness, positive outlook, confidence, social skills, attractiveness, trust, and clear communication). When completing the questionnaire, participants indicated for each situation, first, if they could perform the conversational skills and, second, with what degree of confidence. The SEQSS is an interesting measure because it provides an opportunity to measure participants communicative abilities across contexts.

The Self-Rated Competence Scale (SRC), developed by Cupach and Spitzberg (1981), was developed as a situational measure of competence. The item pool for the SRC was originally drawn from 18 measures related to communicative competence. Twenty-eight items were ultimately selected from a total pool of 300, measuring three dimensions: other orientation, conversational skills, and self-centered behavior (Cupach & Spitzberg, 1981). Spitzberg (1986a) reported the measure had been investigated in over 10 studies with about 3000 participants. As with the CAS, and the ICI, the SRC measures molar-level perceptions of communication performances. As a result, its utility as a diagnostic measure is limited to gestalt impressions of communicative abilities.

Lowe and Cantela (1978) initially developed the Social Performance Survey Schedule (SPSS) by having students list the social traits descriptive of their behavior and the behavior of others. The authors then generated behavioral statements indicative of those social traits. A total of 100 items were written resulting in 50 positive items (Part A) and 50 negative items (Part B). Spitzberg (1986a) noted that of the self-reference measures, the SPSS has received the most extensive investigation. Further, the SPSS is diagnostically valuable because the measure is comprised of molecular-level items.

The following instruments are other-reference instruments. "Other reference" refers to evaluations of one's partner. Often, studies utilize third-party ratings of self and other. These raters are referred to as judges. Some of the measures reviewed are adaptations of self-reference instruments.

The Behavioral Assessment of Communication Competency (BACC) was developed by Ruben (1976). The measure consists of seven dimensions: respect, empathy, role behavior, interaction management, interactive posture, orientation to knowledge, and tolerance for ambiguity. A singular Likert-type rating scale was constructed for each dimension. A brief paragraph defines each point on the Likert-type measure for each dimension. This instrument was originally constructed to measure intercultural adjustment. Spitzberg concludes that the BACC has adequate face validity but lacks an established or consistent psychometric history.

Wiemann (1977) developed the Communicative Competence Scale (CCS) which he based on Goffman's (1959, 1963, 1967) writings concerning the presentation of line and face-work. The CCS was originally conceived as five dimensions: empathy, affiliation/support, behavioral flexibility, social relaxation, and interaction management. However, subsequent factor analysis produced a one-factor solution. The measure is comprised of molar- as well as molecular-level items. The mixed content of the items limits the diagnostic capabilities of the measure.

The Communicative Competency Assessment Instrument (CCAI) was developed by Rubin (1982) to be used by third-party observers to assess individuals' communicative competence. Participants are required to give a 3-minute presentation, listen to a brief video-taped lecture, and respond to a number of directions and questions in an interpersonal context with an evaluator. An individual's communicative performance is evaluated on nineteen competencies: pronunciation, facial expression/tone of voice, articulation, persuasiveness, clarity of ideas, ability to express and defend viewpoint, recognize misunderstanding, distinguish fact from opinion, understand suggestions for improvement, identify instructions, summarize, introduce self to others, give accurate directions, describe another person's viewpoint, and describe differences of opinion. The validity of the CCAI is extensively reviewed (Rubin, 1982, 1985). The contextual domain used for the determination of the competencies is an academic environment which has not been demonstrated to generalize to interpersonal contexts. The predictive validity of the CCAI is still being assessed.

Spitzberg and Hurt (1985) developed the Conversational Skills Rating Scale (CSRS). The instrument was designed to be used as a self- and other-reference scale measuring both molar- and molecular-level perceptions of communicative competence in any interpersonal context. The measure was systematically developed beginning with open-ended interview questions to establish face validity and ending with empirical validation. The CSRS is a 30-item, 5-point Likert-type scale consisting of 25 molecular items and 5 molar items. The scale measures four dimensions: altercentrism, expressiveness, composure, and interaction management. The CSRS is a diagnostically valuable scale due to the specificity of skills inherent in molecular-level measurement.

The Rating of Alter-Competence (RAC), developed by Cupach and Spitzberg (1981), was designed in the same manner as the Self-Rated Competence Scale (SRC, Cupach & Spitzberg, 1981), measuring situationally specific competence as opposed to cross-contextual competence. Further, because a contextual measure of competence assumes that communicative competence is a product of the dyad, Cupach & Spitzberg (1981) found it necessary to develop a measure of a dyadic partner's communicative competence. The RAC is a 27-item, 5-point Likert-type scale comprised of two dimensions, other orientation and expressiveness. Spitzberg (1986b) noted that the RAC is "most useful when interest is in exploring the process of inferring others' overall competence in a given episode of interaction" (p. 24). This broad range utility is due to the molar-level of item specificity which operationalizes the RAC.

The Simulated Social Interaction Test (SSIT) consists of eight situations which are presented to participants orally or by means of a videotape. An interviewer provides the participant with a prompt and the participant's response is evaluated on two, 11-point, Likert-type items measuring anxiety and social skill. The eight interpersonal situations are disapproval, assertiveness, confrontation, interpersonal warmth, conflict with a relative, interpersonal loss, heterosexual contact, and receipt of compliments. Commenting upon the psychometric properties of the SSIT, Spitzberg (1986b) wrote "The SSIT is clearly the most comprehensively validated assessment procedure examined in this review. It has revealed very respectable content, construct, discriminant, and predictive validity. . . . If the SSIT has a weakness, it is that the information it provides is not diagnostically specific" (p. 28).

The final measure receiving a favorable recommendation from Spitzberg (1986b) is the Social Interaction Test-Rating Scales (SIT). The SIT (Trower et al., 1978) consists of a set of rating scales which measure social skills, both on a molecular- and molar-level. The molecular items measure vocal quality, nonverbal behaviors, and conversational skills. The molecular items are coded on a curvilinear scale such that "too much" or "too little" of a behavior is considered inappropriate. The molar-level items measure gestalt impressions of social skills. Spitzberg (1986b) noted that the validity of the scale has not been clearly established, however, its diagnostic utility seems promising given the molecular nature of the items.

One's choice of competence measure is basically dependent upon two issues: The first is whether the person is interested in measuring a participant's competence in a specific social context or interested in measuring an individual's cross-contextual competence. The measurements most appropriate for situational competence are SRC, CCAI, CSRS, RAC, and SIT. The appropriate instruments for dispositional competence are CAS, ICI, SEQSS, SPSS, BACC, CCS, and SSIT. The second issue concerns the level of specificity concerning perceptions of competence. Molar-level items measure generalized abilities and gestalt perceptions of competence. The molar-level of measurement is appropriate for studying the process of competent performances across contexts. Measures appropriate for molar-level observations are: CAS, ICI, SEQSS, SRC, BACC, CCS, RAC, and SSIT. Molecular-level perceptions identify and evaluate specific behaviors that lead to perceptions of competence. Molecular items are most valuable if a researcher is interested in diagnosis of communicative deficiencies leading to negative evaluations of one's competence. The scales providing molecular-level measurement are: CSRS, SPSS, CCAI, and SIT.

The following section reviews research results using various measures of communicative competence. The research is grouped into four categories: communicative competence and loneliness, communicative competence and shyness, communicative competence and attraction, and communicative competence and gender differences.

RESEARCH RESULTS

Communicative Competence and Loneliness

Surveying research into the relationship between competence and loneliness, a consistent pattern of communication skills deficiencies emerges. Lonely individuals engage in less intimate self-disclosure (Chelune, Sultan, & Williams, 1980; Solano, Batten, & Parrish, 1982) are more socially anxious (Bell & Daly, 1985; Spitzberg, 1980; Zakahi & Duran, 1985), report having fewer social experiences (Spitzberg & Hurt, 1985; Zakahi & Duran, 1982), and view themselves and their partners as less communicatively competent (Jones, 1982; Spitzberg & Canary, 1985; Zakahi & Duran, 1985). The significance of loneliness as a social problem is underscored by the fact that 15% of the population report being lonely (Rubinstein & Shaver, 1980). The consequences of loneliness include depression (Russell, Peplau, & Cutrona, 1980), hostility (Sermat, 1980), and, in extreme cases, suicide (Wenz, 1977). Loneliness has become a subject of interest to competence researchers because of the opportunity to remediate loneliness via skills training programs.

Exploring the etiology of loneliness, Zakahi and Duran (1982, 1985) investigated the relationships among communicative competence, communication apprehension, and loneliness. Initial results indicated that communication apprehension did not account for unique variance in loneliness when the effects of communicative competence (as measureed by the Communicative Adaptability Scale) were removed (Zakahi & Duran, 1982). A subsequent study was conducted due to refinements in the dimensional structures of both communication apprehension and communicative adaptability. Results indicated that social experience, social confirmation, and dyadic apprehension accounted for approximately 20% of the variance in loneliness. Essentially lonely individuals reported experiencing more dyadic apprehension, having fewer social experiences, and being less socially confirming than nonlonely individuals.

Complementing the research of Zakahi and Duran (1985), Bell and Daly (1985) investigated the relationship of loneliness to a host of personality variables, ranging from assertiveness to extraversion. Results indicated that lonely individuals reported being less socially composed, less conversationally responsive, less assertive, less disclosive, less friendly, less extraverted, and perceived themselves as less competent than nonlonely individuals. The authors stated "Loneliness may be more a function of people's patterns of communication behavior than of single dimensions of their communicator characteristics" (p. 137). They emphasized the need for a communication skills approach to the treatment of loneliness. Continuing his earlier work, Bell (1985) investigated differences in the conversational involvement of lonely and nonlonely individuals. From a total sample of 968 undergraduates, 120 individuals were selected to participate further in the study. Two groups were formed, 60 individuals indicated they were chronically lonely over a 2-year period, and 60 individuals were categorized as nonlonely. The two groups represented the top and bottom quartiles of the original sample. Participants were paired and rated as they engaged in a 10-minute "get acquainted" interaction. The data formed a 2 (lonely and nonlonely) × 2 (sex of participant) factorial design. The dependent variables were measures of behavioral involvement, cognitive involvement, perceived involvement, and perceptions of satisfaction and liking. Results indicate that lonely participants engaged in less talk, provided less vocal backchanneling, paid less attention to their partner, had lower recall of the interaction, were less satisfied, and perceived themselves as less conversationally involved than the nonlonely participants. Further, the lonely participants were perceived by their conversational partner as less likeable, less desirable as a friend and conversational partner, and perceived as not wanting a friend. Bell (1985) observed "that lonely people expect to be seen in a negative light. The results of this study are in line with these past findings. Lonely people believed their partners would report fewer desires for interaction, an expectation which proved correct" (p. 232). It appears that loneliness may be a function of a self-fulfilling prophecy, in which lonely individuals do not expect to be positively perceived and, as a result, communicate that expectation by being less other oriented and less attentive. This behavior is subsequently perceived and responded to negatively, ultimately confirming the lonely person's initial expectations.

How this self-fulfilling prophecy influences the acquisition of communication skills is clarified by Spitzberg and Hurt (1987). They measured loneliness at three times during a semester (weeks 3, 9, and 14). Measures of situationally based competence (Conversational Skills Rating Scale) and dispositional competence (Communicative Adaptability Scale) were administered to 160 participants. Participants were also paired and rated by observers as they interacted with one another. Lonely individuals perceived themselves and were perceived by coactors as less communicatively competent. Further, results indicated that the CAS was a better predictor than the CSRS across measures of loneliness. The largest contributor to loneliness from the CAS was social experience. Spitzberg and Hurt (1987) suggested that loneliness may be accompanied by an atrophy of communication skills. This explanation complements the explanation consistent with a self-fulfilling prophecy. A lack of social experience leads to less confidence and practice in social settings, thereby, lessening the opportunities for successful interactions.

Communicative Competence and Shyness

A similar pattern is observed with the relationship between communicative competence and social anxiety. The influence of social anxiety is underscored by the number of communicative competence constructs which include anxiety in their operationalizations (Argyle, 1969; Duran, 1983; Phelps & Snavely, 1980; Steffan, Greenwald, & Langmeyer, 1979; Wiemann, 1977). Some researchers have gone so far as to suggest social anxiety may be the inverse of communicative competence (Kelly, Chase, & Wiemann, 1979). This is not the position advanced by this review as will be articulated later in this discussion.

Investigating the relationships among communicative adaptability (Duran, 1983), communication apprehension (McCroskey, 1970) and self-esteem (Helmreich, Stapp, & Ervin, 1974), Duran (1983) found significant negative correlations between communication apprehension and communicative adaptability and self-esteem. Specifically, high apprehensives reported having fewer social experiences and less social composure than low apprehensives. A similar relationship was found using the shyness construct (Cheek & Buss, 1981). High shy participants perceived themselves as having more problems with articulation than did low shy participants (Duran & Kelly, in press).

In a study designed to further validate the factor structure of the Interaction Involvement Scale (Cegala, 1981), Cegala, Savage, Brunner, and Conrad (1982) correlated interaction involvement with several other constructs including extraversion, neuroticism, self-consciousness, communication apprehension, and communicative competence. Of particular interest to this review is the relationship of interaction involvement to the latter three variables. Significant positive correlations were obtained for the three IIS dimensions and communication competence (Wiemann, 1977). Significant negative correlations were observed between the three IIS dimensions (responsiveness, perceptiveness, and attentiveness) and self-consciousness and communication apprehension. Specifically, moderate negative correlations were found between the perceptiveness dimension of the IIS and communication apprehension in dyadic and group contexts. These results would suggest that the tense, shy, apprehensive individual may be unable to accurately perceive how the other is responding to him or her.

This finding is supported by research conducted by Duran and Kelly (1988a). Canonical correlation analysis produced a significant canonical root defined in set 1 by perceptiveness and defined in set 2 by social composure and social experience. One explanation for this result was that social anxiety may not only affect perceptions of performance, but also serve to inhibit the acquisition of social experiences. This cyclic relationship may serve to further reinforce negative perceptions of one's social performance, as well as to heighten anxiety when faced with novel social situations.

Studies examining self-perceptions of shy and not-shy individuals have found that shy participants report experiencing more tension and unpleasantness during interaction (Cheek & Buss, 1981; Clark & Arkowitz, 1975; Pilkonis, 1977) than not-shy people. Shy people have been found to perceive themselves as less socially skilled than their not-shy counterparts (Clark & Arkowitz, 1975). Further, when shy and not-shy participants were asked to assess how their communicative performance had been rated by their interaction partners, there was a significant difference between the two groups in their metaperceptions of communicative competence (Kelly & Duran, 1984). Specifically, shy participants underestimated the ratings they had received from their partners. A similar finding was obtained by Clark and Arkowitz (1975), who found that shy participants underestimated ratings of their social skills as compared to observers' evaluations.

As with loneliness, highly anxious individuals may perceive and demonstrate communicative skills deficiencies due to a self-fulfilling prophecy. When approaching a novel social situation, a shy individual experiences heightened anxiety, which leads to a negative expectation of communication performance. The shy person may visualize and predict an incompetent performance and then seek evidence of it in the form of dysfluencies, which, in turn, validate the original expectations. Ultimately, these negative expectations and the anxiety associated with social interaction may prohibit further social contact which leads to an erosion of social skills. Duran and Kelly (in press) stated, "this pattern of anxiety leading to hypercritical self-evaluations and lack of social experience appears to be self-reinforcing and cyclic" (p. 11).

It was mentioned earlier that anxiety may be the inverse of communicative competence. A more accurate description of the relationship between these constructs is that anxiety may interfere with the accurate perception of one's social performance. In extreme cases, anxiety may serve to inhibit a person's demonstration of competent communication by leading to the avoidance of social participation. In this case anxiety would influence the affective domain of communicative competence, such that, one may know what to do (cognitive competence), know how to do it (psycho-motor competence), but choose not to perform (affective competence).

Communicative Competence and Attraction

Another variable that may contribute to individuals' affective evaluations of their social performances is attraction. Several studies have investigated the relationship between communicative competence and attraction. In some studies attraction has been conceptualized, unidimensionally, as physical appearance (Chaiken, 1979; Goldman & Lewis, 1977; Reis, Nezleck & Wheeler, 1980). Other studies (Brandt, 1979; Duran & Kelly, 1988b; Zakahi & Duran, 1984) have employed a multidimensional measure of attraction which is comprised of three dimensions: task, social, and physical attraction (McCroskey & McCain, 1974). Most research investigating the relationship between competence and attraction has treated communicative competence as the dependent variable, tacitly assuming judgments of communicative performance are influenced by attractiveness. The direction of causality will be elaborated upon later in this discussion.

Goldman and Lewis (1977) investigated the influence of physical attractiveness upon social skills. They had participants engage in a telephone conversation in which their social skills were evaluated. The use of the telephone as the medium for communication controlled for the effects of physical appearance upon judgments of communicative performance. Independent judges rated the participants physical attractiveness. Results indicated a significant positive correlation between social skills and physical attractiveness. The authors noted, however, that there was only 8% shared variance.

Investigating the influence of physical attractiveness upon persuasiveness, Chaiken (1979) videotaped participants making a persuasive presentation. Observers rated the participants' physical attractiveness as well as a number of verbal and nonverbal characteristics of their presentation. Results indicated nonsignificant differences between attractive and unattractive speakers in terms of their vocal confidence, amount of gaze, and smiling.

Reis et al. (1980) investigated the number of social interactions in which attractive and unattractive individuals engage. The participants were required to keep a log of their interactions over a 10-day period. Additionally, photos of the participants were rated for attractiveness. Results indicated physically attractive males reported the highest frequency of interactions as compared to the other group. Further, physically attractive males reported more opposite-sex interactions than unattractive males. For both attractive males and females, they reported more social interactions than task-oriented interactions.

Zakahi and Duran (1984) investigated the relationship of communicative competence to physical attraction. The sample consisted of 214 dyads, instructed to meet on five occasions for a minimum of 30 minutes each. Participants completed self-reports and partner reports (perceptions of their dyadic partners) of attraction and communicative competence (as measured by the CAS). Physical attraction served as the independent variable and was classified via a median split procedure. Results indicated that physically attractive individuals were perceived as more competent than less attractive individuals. Further analysis treating attractiveness and competence as independent variables and alternating these variables as covariates, indicated that competence accounted for more variance in communication satisfaction (Hecht, 1978) than did attractiveness. Specifically, communicative adaptability accounted for 32% unique variance in communication satisfaction when physical attractiveness was the covariate. Physical attractiveness accounted for 5% unique variance when competence was the covariate. These results further substantiate the notion that physical attractiveness may be influential in initial interactions but its influence diminishes and is superceded by communicative abilities as social contact progresses.

The preceding four studies indicated that not only are attractive individuals perceived as more communicatively competent but also they may, in fact, be more communicatively skilled. Researchers explain the differences in skill level as due to greater opportunity for interaction afforded attractive individuals. More social experiences provide individuals with larger social repertoires and more frequent opportunities for practice and refinement of communicative skills.

Utilizing a multidimensional approach to attraction, Brandt (1979) investigated the relationship of task, social, and physical attraction to the dimensions of the communication style construct (Norton, 1978). Canonical correlation analysis was performed, producing two significant canonical roots. Root 1 was defined by social attraction, relaxed, animated, and open. Root 2 was defined by task attraction, language precision, and attentiveness.

Also utilizing McCroskey & McCain's (1974) measure of attraction, Duran and Kelly (1988b) investigated the influence of communicative competence upon task, social, and physical attraction. The prior studies treated competence as the dependent variable, tacitly assuming perceived attraction leads to perceptions of communicative competence. The question addressed in the Duran and Kelly study was: Are competent communicators perceived as more attractive? A pretest, posttest design was employed, in which the effects of pretests of task, social, and physical attraction were removed from post measures of the three attraction dimensions. Wiemann's (1977) communicative competence measure served as the independent variable. Students who did not know one another were paired (57 opposite-sex dyads) and asked to engage in a 10-minute "get acquainted" interaction. Prior to the interaction participants completed the pretests of attraction, and after the interaction they completed the competence measure and posttests of attraction. Results indicated that with the exception of physical attraction, communicative competence accounted for more variance than the covariate. Communicative competence accounted for 17% of the variance in the posttest of task attraction with the pretest of task attraction accounting for 11%. Similarly, communicative competence accounted for 16% of the variance in the posttest of social attraction with the pretest of social attraction accounting for 14% of the variance. Competence only accounted for 8% of the variance in the post measure of physical attractiveness, with the pretest of physical attractiveness accounting for 59% of variance in subsequent judgments of physical attractiveness. These results suggest that one's communicative competence can have an influence upon perceptions of attraction. The fact that competence accounted for 8% of the variance in physical attraction is encouraging. It would seem logical that physical attraction would have its largest impact upon perceptions during initial interactions and as social contact increased the influence of competence upon perceived attractiveness would also increase. Future research needs to address the influence of perceived communicative competence over the course of a relationship. Further, these results suggest that skills training may have an influence upon attraction.

Communicative Competence and Gender

The research concerning sex differences in communicative competence is somewhat disjointed and atheoretical. As with a number of studies that report sex differences, these differences were not the focal point of the study, but rather one of several variables investigated. The studies reported in this section have approached sex differences from a biological and psychological perspective. The former is referred to as sex differences, whereas the latter is referred to as gender differences.

In general, females are perceived as friendlier (Mehrabian, 1972), more sensitive to implied meanings (Henly, 1977; Pearson, 1985), animated (Mehrabian, 1972), disclosive (Cozby, 1973, Duran & Kelly, 1985; Jourard, 1971) and report having more social experiences (Duran & Kelly, 1985) than males.

One of the most comprehensive studies of sex differences in communicative performance was conducted by Montgomery and Norton (1981). They utilized the Communicator Style Measure (CSM), which consists of 10 dimensions: impression leaving, contentious, open, dramatic, dominant, precise, relaxed, friendly, attentive, and animated. Communicator image serves as the dependent variable for the construct. To assess the stability of the results, two samples were drawn: Sample 1, $n = 736$ (473 males and 263 females); Sample 2, $n = 382$ (238 males and 144 females). Both samples produced similar results with males more concerned with precision of language use, and females reporting being more animated when conversing. When placed in discriminant equations, precise and animated correctly classified between 61.5% to 66.3% of the participants. The researchers also investigated if different combinations of CSM dimensions differentially predicted an effective male and female communicator. Two CSM dimensions, dominant and impression learning, predicted an effective style (communicator image) for both sexes. The authors concluded that "males and females report more similarities than differences in communicator styles" (p. 131).

As part of a study to validate the Interaction Involvement Scale, Cegala et al. (1982) examined both sex and gender differences on a number of communication variables. A series of t tests were computed comparing males and females resulting in significant differences on perceptiveness, private self-consciousness, social anxiety, communication apprehension (meetings and public speaking), and Wiemann's (1977) dimensions of communicative competence (behavioral flexibility, interaction management, affiliation/support, empathy, and social relaxation). Cegala et al. (1982) reported that for males, perceptiveness appears to be related to empathy and private self-consciousness. In other words, perceptiveness for males seems to be related to self-awareness and perspective taking. For females, perceptiveness is related to public self-consciousness, supportiveness, and warmth. In addition to sex differences, Cegala et al. (1982) investigated gender differences (Bem, 1974). Results indicate that the androgynous group was significantly higher on perceptiveness than the masculine, feminine, and undifferentiated groups.

Eman Wheeless and Duran (1982) also investigated the relationship of gender to communicative competence. They utilized an early version of the CAS (referred to as the Social Management Scale) consisting of two dimensions: social experience (labeled *adaptability*) and social confirmation (labeled *rewarding impression*). Participants were 830 undergradualtes from a midwestern university. Participants completed the Bem Sex-Role Inventory (BSRI) and the Social Management Scale. Results indicate that androgynous individuals had the highest competence ratings overall, followed by feminine, masculine, and undifferentiated groups. Further, femininity, was the best predictor of rewarding impression, whereas masculinity was the best predictor of adaptability. Psychological gender orientation accounted for 36% of the variance in rewarding impression and 25% of the variance in adaptability.

The association of masculinity to a masculine gender orientation was supported by Reiser and Troost (1986). They studied the relationship of psychological gender orientation (BSRI) and communicative competence (Wiemann, 1977). Results indicate that masculinity for both males and females was significantly related to self-reported flexibility. Across the dimensions of competence (behavioral flexibility, affiliation/support, and empathy) feminine males were perceived as most competent, whereas androgynous males were perceived as least competent, and psychological gender orientation did not significantly differentiate females on the dimensions of competence. The authors noted that these results, specifically with regard to males, are counter to what theory would predict. It is maintained that these results may be supportive of a masculine model of gender-role identity in terms of communicative competence. That is, masculine traits are perceived as most socially competent.

Taken together, these studies present a mixed and confusing set of results. It appears that females report being and are perceived as warmer, friendlier, more immediate, disclosive, and socially experienced than males. Males, however, report being and are perceived as more adaptable, flexible, and precise than females. One immediate concern is that these results appear stereotypical and may be highly confounded with social desireability. It appears, however, that biological and psychological gender orientation do account for low to moderate amounts of variance in communicative competence. Specifically, femininity is associated with affiliative tendencies, whereas masculinity is associated with adaptability/flexibility.

DIRECTIONS FOR FUTURE RESEARCH

Future research should address the need for more diverse adult samples. This is particularly necessary for future work in the area of remediation and skills training. What is needed is normative data on various communicative competence measures, both dispositional (e.g., CAS, SEQSS, SSIT) and situational (e.g., SRC, CSRS, CCAI). Demographic data such as age, occupation, religion, educational experience, size of family, and birth order should be compiled as well. These data can provide valuable diagnostic information. A majority of the studies reviewed have utilized college samples which, when compared to the population as a whole, probably represent the upper third of the population. It could be argued that acceptance to college serves as a filter for competence. That is, some minimal level of competence is necessary for one to be successful in college. This minimal level is probably higher than the population mean. As a result, any normative standards from the college population would be unrealistically high for the general population. Therefore, future research should collect data on various competence measures from samples other than college students so that normative descriptive statistics can be generated.

A second area of future research concerns the experimental stimulus context used to stimulate interaction. Typically, to assess situational communicative competence, individuals are paired and asked to "get to know one another." Dispositional communicative competence is often assessed by molar-level statements regarding one's general impression of his or her communicative performance. These conditions require rather superficial commonplace interaction repertoires and, hence, may be testing a limited and narrow scope of communicative behaviors. Research needs to present individuals with novel contexts which challenge individuals' communicative abilities. Such contexts would test abilities to adapt to changing social contexts, manage novel interactions, maintain composure, and demonstrate concern for the other.

A third area of future research concerns cross-contextual assessment techniques. Most research designs have had participants interact in one social context with another individual and assess his or her communicative competence on the basis of that interaction. Future research needs to utilize measures and research designs that assess communicative performances across a number of social contexts. Viewing communicative competence as comprised of three general dimensions— cognitive, affective, and psycho-motor—it is necessary to utilize research designs that provide opportunities for individuals to demonstrate differing competencies in these domains. Different contexts provide lesser or greater demands of one's communicative abilities and individuals are likely to be competent in some contexts and not in others. If researchers are to gather normative data and develop skills programs to enhance communicative competence, it is necessary to assess participants' cross-contextual performances. Such investigations will also provide insight into cognitive competence by observing how individuals adapt their performance to the demands of different contexts.

Finally, future research should address the development and assessment of skills training programs. The ultimate value of research into communicative competence lies with the ability to remediate skills deficiencies with the purpose of improving the quantity and quality of an individual's interactions and relationships. For research in this area to be heuristically valuable, scholars must be able to assess and remediate communicative competence.

REFERENCES

Allen, R. R., & Brown, K. L. (1976). *Developing communication competence in children.* Skokie, IL: National Textbook.

Argyle, M. (1969). *Social interaction.* Chicago: Aldine Atherton.

Backlund, P., Booth, J., Moore, M., Muller Parks, A., & Van Rheenen, D. (1982a). A national survey of state practices in speaking and listening skill assessment. *Communication Education, 31,* 125–129.

Backlund, P. M., Brown, K. L., Gurry, J., & Jandt, F. (1982b). Recommendations for assessing speaking and listening skills. *Communication Education, 31,* 9–17.

Bell, R. A. (1985). Conversational involvement and loneliness. *Communication Monographs, 3,* 218–235.

Bell, R. A., & Daly, J. A. (1985). Some communicator correlates of loneliness. *The Southern Speech Communication Journal, 50,* 121–142.

Bem, S. L. (1974). The measurement of psychological androgyny. *Journal of Consulting and Clinical Psychology, 42,* 155–162.

Bienvenu, M. J., Sr. (1971). An interpersonal communication inventory. *Journal of Communication, 21,* 381–388.

Bienvenu, M. J., Sr., & Stewart, D. W. (1976). Dimensions of interpersonal communication. *Journal of Psychology, 93,* 105–111.

Brandt, D. R. (1979). On linking social performance with social competence: Some relation between communicative style and attributions of interpersonal attractiveness and effectiveness. *Human Communication Research, 5,* 223–237.

Brunner, C. C., & Phelps, L. A. (1979). *An examination of the relationship between interpersonal competence and androgyny.* Paper presented at the Communication Language and Gender Conference, Madison, WI.

Cegala, D. J. (1981). Interaction involvement: A cognitive dimension of communicative competence. *Communication Education, 30,* 109–121.

Cegala, D. J., Savage, G. T., Brunner, C. C., & Conrad, A. B. (1982). An elaboration of the meaning of interaction involvement: Toward the development of a theoretical concept. *Communication Monographs, 49,* 229–248.

Chaiken, S. (1979). Communicator physical attractiveness and persuasion. *Journal of Personality and Social Psychology, 37,* 1387–1397.

Cheek, J. M., & Buss, A. H. (1981). Shyness and sociability. *Journal of Personality and Social Psychology, 41,* 330–339.

Chelune, G. J., Sultan, F. E., & Williams, C. L. (1980). Loneliness, self-disclosure, and interpersonal effectiveness. *Journal of Counseling Psychology, 27,* 462–468.

Chomsky, N. (1965). *Aspects of the theory of syntax.* Cambridge, MA: MIT Press.

Clark, J. V., & Arkowitz, H. (1975). Social anxiety and self-evaluation of interpersonal performance. *Psychological Reports, 36,* 211–221.

Cone, J. D. (1978). The Behavioral Assessment Grid (BAG): A conceptual framework and a taxonomy. *Behavior Therapy, 9,* 882–888.

Cozby, P. (1973). Self-disclosure: A literature review. *Psychological Bulletin, 79,* 73–91.

Cupach, W. R., & Spitzberg, B. H. (1981). *Relational competence: Measurement and validation.* Paper presented to the annual meeting of the Western Speech Communication Association, San Jose, CA.

Cupach, W. R., & Spitzberg, B. H. (1983). Trait versus state: A comparison of dispositional and situational measures of interpersonal communication competence. *Western Journal of Speech Communication, 47,* 364–379.

Curran, J. P. (1982). A precedure for the assessment of social skills: The Simulated Social Interaction Test. In J. P. Curran & P. M. Monti (Eds.), *Social Skills Training* (pp. 348–398). New York: Guilford Press.

Delia, J. G., & Clark, R. A. (1977). Cognitive complexity, social perception, and the development of listener-adapted communication in six-, eight-, ten-, and twelve-year-old boys. *Communication Monographs, 44,* 326–345.

Delia, J. G., & Crockett, W. H. (1973). Social schemas, cognitive complexity, and the learning of social structures. *Journal of Personality, 41,* 413–429.

Domangue, B. B. (1978). Decoding effects of cognitive complexity, tolerance of ambiguity and verbal-nonverbal inconsistency. *Journal of Personality, 46,* 519–535.

Duran, R. L. (1983). Communicative adaptability: A measure of social communicative competence. *Communication Quarterly, 31,* 320–326.

Duran, R. L., & Elliot, S. M., (1984). *Determining who's competent and who's not: Establishing cut-off scores for measures of communication competency.* Paper presented to the International Communication Association Conference, San Francisco, CA.

Duran, R. L., & Kelly, L. (1984A). *Generalized communication competence: Most of the people some of the time.* Paper presented to the Eastern Communication Association Conference, Philadelphia, PA.

Duran, R. L., & Kelly, L. (1984b). *An investigation of the relationship of shyness to self-, partner-, observer-, and meta-perceptions of communication competence.* Paper presented to the Speech Communication Association Conference, Chicago, IL.

Duran, R. L., & Kelly, L. (1985). An investigation into the cognitive domain of communication competence. *Communication Research Reports, 2,* 112–119.

Duran, R. L., & Kelly, L. (1988a). An investigation into the cognitive domain of competence II: The relationship between communicative competence and interaction involvement. *Communication Research Reports, 2,* 91–96.

Duran, R. L., & Kelly, L. (1988b). The influence of communicative competence on perceived task, social, and physical attraction. *Communication Quarterly, 36,* 41–49.

Duran, R. L., & Kelly, L. (in press) The cycle of shyness: A study of self-perceptions of communication performance. *Communication Reports.*

Duran, R. L., & Zakahi, W. R. (1987). Communication performance and communication satisfaction: What do we teach our students? *Communication Education, 36,* 13–22.

Eman Wheeless, V., & Duran, R. L. (1982). Gender orientation as a correlate of communicative competence. *The Southern Speech Communication Journal, 48,* 51–64.

Foote, N. N., & Cottrell, L. S., Jr. (1955). *Identity and interpersonal competence.* Chicago: Univeristy of Chicago Press.

Goffman, E. (1959). *The presentation of self in everyday life.* Garden City, NY: Doubleday Anchor.

Goffman, E. (1963). *Behavior in public places.* New York: Free Press.

Goffman, E. (1967). *Interaction ritual.* Garden City, NY: Anchor.

Goffman, E. (1969). *Strategic interaction.* Philadelphia: University of Pennsylvania Press.

Goldman, W., & Lewis, P. (1977). Beautiful is good: Evidence that the physically attractive are more socially skillful. *Journal of Experimental Social Psychology, 13,* 125–130.

Gotlib, I. H., & Asarnow, R. F. (1980). Independence of interpersonal and impersonal problem-solving skills: Reply to Rohsenow. *Journal of Consulting and Clinical Psychology, 48,* 286–288.

Habermas, J. (1970). Toward a theory of communicative competence. In. H. P. Dreitzel (Ed.), *Recent Sociology* (No. 2, pp. 115–148). New York: Macmillan.

Hale, C. L., & Delia, J. G. (1976). Cognitive complexity and social perspective-taking. *Communication Monographs, 43,* 195–203.

Hart, R. P., & Burks, D. M. (1972). Rhetorical sensitivity and social interaction. *Speech Monographs, 39,* 75–91.

Hecht, M. L. (1978). The conceptualization and measurement of interpersonal communication satisfaction. *Human Communication Research, 4,* 253–264.

Helmreich, R. Stapp, J., & Ervin, C. (1974). The Texas Social Behavior Inventory (TSBI): An objective measure of self-esteem or social competence. *JSAS Catalog of Selected Documents in Psychology, 4,* 79.

Henley, N. (1977). *Body politics: Power, sex, and nonverbal communication.* Englewood Cliffs, NJ: Prentice-Hall.

Jakobovitz, L. A. (1970). Prolegomena to a theory of communicative competence. In R. C. Lugton (Ed.), *Language and the teacher: A series in applied linguistics: Vol. 6. English as a second language: Current issue.* Philadelphia: Center for Curriculum Development.

Jones, E. E., & Nisbett, R. E. (1971). *The actor and the observer: Divergent perceptions of the causes of behavior.* Morristown, VA: General Learning Corp.

Jones, W. (1982). Loneliness and social behavior. In L. A. Peplau & D. Perlman (Eds.), *Loneliness: A sourcebook on current theory, research, and therapy* (pp. 238–254). New York: Wiley-Interscience.

Jourard, S. (1971). *Self-disclosure: An experimental analysis of the transparent self.* New York: Wiley.

Kelly, C. W., Chase, L. J., & Wiemann, J. M. (1979). *Interpersonal competence: Conceptualization, measurement, and future considerations.* Paper presented at the Speech Communication Association Conference, San Antonio, TX.

Kelly, L., & Duran, R. L. (1984). *An investigation of the relationship of shyness to self-, partner-, observer-, and meta-perceptions of communication competence.* Paper presented to the Speech Communication Association Conference, Chicago, IL.

Lowe, M. R., & Cantela, J. R. (1978). A self-report measure of social skill. *Behavior Therapy, 9,* 535–544.

McCroskey, J. C. (1970). Measures of communication-bound anxiety. *Speech Monographs, 37,* 269–277.

McCroskey, J. C. (1982). Communication competence and performance: A research and pedagogical perspective. *Communication Education, 31,* 1–7.

McCroskey, J. C., & McCain, T. A. (1974). The measurement of interpersonal attraction. *Speech Monographs, 41,* 261–266.

Mehrabian, A. (1972). *Nonverbal communication.* Chicago: Adline–Atherton.

Moe, K. O., & Zeiss, A. M. (1982). Measureing self-efficacy expectations for social skills: A methodological inquiry. *Cognitive Therapy and Research 6,* 191–205.

Montgomery, J. M., & Norton, R. W. (1981). Sex differences and similarities in communicator style. *Communication Monographs, 48,* 121–132.

Norton, R. W. (1978). Foundation of a communication style construct. *Human Communication Research, 41,* 99–112.

Pearson, J. C. (1985). *Gender and communication.* Dubuque, IA: Wm. C. Brown.

Phelps, L. A., & Snavely, W. B. (1980). *Toward the measurement of interpersonal communication competence.* Paper presented at the Western Speech Communication Association Conference, Portland, OR.

Pilkonis, P. A. (1977). The behavioral consequences of shyness. *Journal of Personality, 45,* 596–611.

Press, A. N., Crockett, W. H., & Delia, J. G. (1975). Effects of cognitive complexity and perceiver's set upon organization of impressions. *Journal of Personality and Social Psychology, 31,* 865–872.

Prisbell, M. (1979). *Feeling good: Conceptualization and measurement.* Paper presented at the annual meeting of the Western Speech Communication Association, Los Angeles, CA.

Prisbell, M., & Anderson, J. F. (1980). The importance of perceived homophily, uncertainty level, feeling good, safety, and self-disclosure in interpersonal relationships. *Communication Quarterly, 3,* 22–33.

Reis, H. T., Nezlek, J., & Wheeler, L. (1980). Physical attractiveness in social interaction. *Journal of Personality and Social Psychology, 38,* 604–617.

Reiser, C., & Troost, M. K. (1986). Gender and gender-role identity influences upon self- and other-reports of communicative competence. *Sex Roles, 14,* 431–443.

Ruben, B. D. (1976). Assessing communication competency for intercultural adaptation. *Group and Organizational Studies, 1,* 334–354.

Rubenstein, C. M., & Shaver, P. (1980). Loneliness in two northeastern cities. In J. Hartog, J. R. Audy, & Y. A. Cohen (Eds.), *The anatomy of loneliness* (pp. 319–357). New York: International University Press.

Rubin, R. B. (1982). Assessing speaking and listening competence at the college level: The Communication Competency Assessment Instrument. *Communication Education, 31,* 19–32.

Rubin, R. B. (1985). The validity of the Communication Competency Assessment Instrument. *Communication Monographs, 52,* 173–185.

Rubin, R. B., & Feezel, J. D. (1984). *Elements of teacher communication competence: An examination of skills, knowledge, and motivation to communicate.* Paper presented at the Speech Communication Association Conference, Chicago, IL.

Russell, D., Peplau, L. A., & Cutrona, C. E. (1980). The revised UCLA loneliness scale: Concurrent and discriminant validity evidence. *Journal of Personality and Social Psychology, 39,* 472–480.

Sermat, V. (1980). Some situational and personality correlates of loneliness. In J. Hartog, J. R. Audy, & Y. A. Cohen (Eds.), *The anatomy of loneliness* (pp. 305–318). New York: International University Press.

Solano, C. H., Batten, P. G., & Parrish, E. A. (1982). Loneliness and patterns of self-disclosure. *Journal of Personality and Social Psychology, 43,* 524–531.

Spitzberg, B. H. (1980). *Loneliness and communication apprehension.* Paper presented at the Western Speech Communication Association Conference, San Jose, CA.

Spitzberg, B. H. (1981). *Competence in communicating: A taxonomy, review, critique, and predictive model.* Paper presented at the Speech Communication Association, Anaheim, CA.

Spitzberg, B. H. (1982). *Relational competence: An empirical test of a conceptual model.* Paper presented at the International Communication Association Convention, Boston, MA.

Spitzberg, B. H. (1983). Communication competence as knowledge, skill, and impression. *Communication Education, 32,* 323–329.

Spitzberg, B. H. (1986a). *A critical review of communicative competence measures I: Self-reference instruments.* Paper presented at the Speech Communication Association, Chicago, IL.

Spitzberg, B. H. (1986b). *A critical review of communicative competence measures II: Other-reference instruments.* Paper presented at the Speech Communication Association, Chicago, IL.

Spitzberg, B. H. (1986c). *Validating a measure of interpersonal skills.* Paper presented at the Speech Communication Association Conference, Chicago, IL.

Spitzberg, B. H., & Canary, D. J. (1985). Loneliness and relationally competent communication. *Journal of Social and Personal Relationships, 2,* 387–401.

Spitzberg, B. H., & Cupach, W. R. (1984). *Interpersonal communication competence.* Beverly Hills, CA: Sage Publications.

Spitzberg, B. H., & Cupach, W. R. (1985). Conversational skill and locus of perception. *Journal of Psychopathology and Behavioral Assessment, 7,* 207–220.

Spitzberg, B. H., & Hurt, H. T. (1985). *The measurement of interpersonal skills in instructional contexts.* Paper presented at the Speech Communication Association Conference, Denver, CO.

Spitzberg, B. H., & Hurt, H. T. (1987). The relationship of interpersonal competence and skills to reported loneliness across time. In M. Hojat & R. Crandell (Eds.), Loneliness: Theory, research, and applications. [Special Issue.]. *Journal of Social Behavior and Personality, 2,* 157–172.

Spivack, G., Platt, J. J., & Shure, M. B. (1976). *The problem-solving approach to adjustment.* San Francisco: Jossey–Bass.

Steffan, J. J., Greenwald, D. P., & Langmeyer, D. (1979). A factor analytic study of social competence in women. *Social Behavior and Personality, 7,* 17–27.

Trower, P., Bryant, B., & Argyle, M. (1978). *Social skills and mental health.* Philadelphia, PA: University of Pennsylvania Press.

Watzlawick, P., Beavin, J. H., & Jackson, D. D. (1967). *Pragmatics of human communication.* New York: W. W. Norton.

Wenz, F. V. (1977). Seasonal suicide attempts and forms of loneliness. *Psychological Reports, 40,* 807–810.

Wiemann, J. M. (1977). Explication and test of a model of communicative competence. *Human Communication Research, 3,* 195–213.

Zakahi, W. R., & Duran, R. L. (1982). All the lonely people: The relationship among loneliness, communicative competence, and communication anxiety. *Communication Quarterly, 30,* 203–209.

Zakahi, W. R., & Duran, R. L. (1984). Attraction, communicative competence, and communication satisfaction. *Communication Research Reports, 1,* 54–57.

Zakahi, W. R., & Duran, R. L. (1985). Loneliness, communicative competence, and communication apprehension: Extension and replication. *Communication Quarterly, 33,* 50–60.

12 *Marital Communication Across the Life Span*

Alan L. Sillars
William W. Wilmot
University of Montana

Most people included in studies of couple communication have been young (Zietlow, 1986), as were most researchers at the time they conducted these studies. This easily leads to a "young" model of couple communication; one which emphasizes the concerns, values, and developmental tasks of individuals in the period between mate selection and early parenthood. Given the volatility of this period, couple communication is, therefore, apt to appear as either an intense, intimate bonding experience or a struggle for relational survival. Intense bonding and relational crises appear at other stages of life as well, but often under different ground rules. For example, some elderly couples may seem emotionally dead for their "passively congenial" interaction style (Troll, 1982; Zietlow & Sillars, 1988), yet mutual dependence, sharing, stability, and marital satisfaction for this group tend to be high (Blieszner, 1988; Johnson, 1988, Troll, Miller, & Atchley, 1979).

A life-span perspective allows us to see communication patterns in context—as a consequence of the circumstances that particular individuals encounter. A life-span perspective reverses the direction of influence usually considered in marital communication literature. This literature emphasizes how communication could or should be altered to affect the state of the relationship (see Noller & Fitzpatrick, 1988; Sillars & Weisberg, 1987). In this chapter we are concerned with how events in the relationship shape communication, rather than how communication affects relationship adjustment. Obviously, these disparate perspectives need a fuller integration in future work but we first wish to explore fully the impact of life events on communication.

225

There is relatively little to go on in constructing a review of marital communication across the life-span. Although there are many studies of life-span development, few of these directly examine couple or family communication patterns. Therefore, our comments are necessarily speculative. Another limitation is that we cannot neatly distinguish cohort effects from life-span changes, because these are confounded in much of the relevant literature, as they are in our own lives. However, this limitation also turns out to be an advantage, because it forces us to take cohort effects seriously. Cohort effects are often as interesting as life stage events, because the values and beliefs of different cohorts also shape communication.

Generally, we can conceptualize three simultaneous influences on marital communication; those of (a) intrinsic developmental processes, (b) cohort, and (c) life stage. Intrinsic developmental processes include the development of shared meanings and modes of conduct over time. This factor is more linear than the other two. This is, over time relationships move in the direction of increasingly implicit, idiosyncratic, and efficient forms of communication (Bell, Buerkel-Rothfuss, & Gore, 1987; Cushman & Whiting, 1972; Hopper, Knapp, & Scott, 1981, Knapp, 1984). Sillars and Kalbflesch (in press) have suggested that an implicit–explicit, dimension underlies much of communication and is reflected in such areas as the development of unstated expectations and taken-for-granted meaning, use of a more efficient and context-dependent linguistic code, less self-conscious attention devoted to communication, indirectness, and more passive or internal strategies for responding to conflicts and problems. Highly implicit interactions are presumed to occur in relationships that are stable and homogeneous (i.e., where the individuals have extensive shared background experiences). Young couples tend toward the explicit end of this continuum, partly reflecting the relative newness and instability of this stage, but also reflecting expressive values and the greater heterogeneity of young couples due to the softening of traditional role expectations. An untested hypothesis that follows from the preceding line of reasoning is that explicit, verbal communication decreases, and implicit forms of communication increase over the marital career. Disruptions in this trend occur at transition points and crises, where families and couples temporarily lose their ability to function implicitly (Reiss, 1981). Reiss noted that families lose their repertoire of background assumptions and rituals during stressful and unfamiliar events and operate instead according to the setting of explicit rules, discussion of unclear events and explicit planning. During stable periods implicit understandings are reinitiated.

The remaining two factors, cohort effects and life-stage events, require less explanation. Cohort effects include some factors referred to previously, such as expressivity norms and marital ideologies identified with different age groups. Important life-stage events that affect couple communication include marriage, the birth of children, entry of children into school, exit of children from the home, and so forth. As previously suggested, implicit functioning should be disrupted at more stressful transition points.

Age and family life stage overlap. However, individuals may enter the family life cycle at different points and progress through it at different rates. Family life stages, such as those described by Duvall (1971), attribute great significance to developmental phases in child rearing. Because we also adopt this approach, some parts of our analysis are irrelevant to some types of people, for example, those who never marry, never have children, or do not live with their children. Despite the importance of these groups, they are outside of our purview.

OVERVIEW OF LIFE-STAGE RESEARCH

Although existing literature on marital communication across the life span is limited, it is still suggestive. Studies comparing marital communication in different life-stage groups are predominantly self-report studies of self-disclosure. This research indicates that reported self-disclosure declines with age. For example, Swensen, Eskew, and Kohlhepp (1981) found that elderly spouses reported less self-disclosure and had more unexpressed feelings with their mates than younger spouses. Self-disclosure was relatively stable for the first several life stages before decreasing in the "empty nest" period (i.e., following the departure of adult children) and retirement stages. The amount of unexpressed feelings steadily increased from the newlywed group through the retired group. Retired couples also reported the least expression of affection. A second cross-sectional study by Jourard (1971) also indicates that there was a decline in self-disclosure among older spouses. Jourard found that reported self-disclosure to opposite-sex friends and spouses increased up to age 40 and then declined. Despite important differences between Jourard's research and the Swenson et al. study (i.e., Jourard examined self-disclosure to opposite-sex friends in addition to spouses and did not include individuals over 56 in the sample), both studies indicate that there is a downward trend in self-disclosure during later years.

Although the preceding two studies do not indicate whether the decline in reported disclosure was attributable to developmental or cohort influences, a longitudinal study by Eskew (1978) found a decline in self-disclosure over a 2-year period which could not be attributed to cohort effects. The study examined six cohort groups between the ages of

47 and 75 and found that reported self-disclosure declined for all cohort groups studied. The self-disclosure scale used by Eskew was the same as that used by Swensen et al. (1981).

A study by Zietlow (1986) suggests that older couples are less disclosing then young couples about problem areas in marriage. Zietlow found a marginally significant decline in reported negative self-disclosure among married couples across five life-stage categories. The study also reveals nonsignificant decreases in the amount and intimacy of self-disclosure from early to later life stages.

We are aware of only a few observational studies of marital communication in diverse life-stage groups. Although these studies focus on problem solving and conflict, their implications are similar to the research on self-disclosure. In Illig's (1977) research, as in Zietlow's (1986) study, the elderly were less expressive of negative feelings than younger couples. Illig recorded the problem-solving discussions of 16 younger couples (with an average age of 24) and 16 retired couples (with an average age of 68). The elderly couples used fewer evaluation statements than young married couples, had fewer sequential evaluation–evaluation interacts, and were much less likely to disagree. Thus, as in the self-disclosure studies, the elderly were less expressive than younger couples.

Research by Zietlow and Sillars (1988) examined how younger and older couples communicated about areas of marital conflict. Comparisons were drawn between the conflict styles of 23 "young" couples (i.e., either newlyweds or couples with children at home), 24 middle-aged couples in the "launching" or "empty nest" phases (i.e., after the children had reached adulthood or left the home), and 26 retired, aging couples. Retired couples were the least analytic and most noncommital in their remarks. Generally, retired couples rated marital problems as nonsalient and their conversations were remarkably passive and congenial. Exceptions to this pattern were found among a small number of retired couples who behaved virtually the opposite, that is, they engaged in continual bickering throughout the discussions. Evidently, these were couples whose long-simmering conflicts had never been successfully addressed, their relationships possibly surviving due to economic necessity or cohort-related prohibitions against divorce. With these few exceptions, the conversations of retired couples were calm, fairly brief, characterized by pleasant digressions and reminiscing, and contained little or no acknowledgment of conflict in the marriage.

Young couples had a comparatively intense, engagement style of interaction, characterized by alternation between analytic, confrontive, and humorous remarks. Their interactions were much less static than the retired couples. That is, they frequently shifted styles of conflict, for example, by counter-balancing confrontive remarks with neutral or humorous statements. Young couples were far more likely to acknowl-edge conflict than retired couples. Indeed, young couples seemed well practiced at conflict and consequently did not invoke the extreme pat-terns of congeniality or bickering found among the older couples.

Although more difficult to characterize, the conversations of middle-aged couples were somewhat between the passivity of most retired couples and the intense style of young couples. Like the retired couples, middle-aged couples were also nonconflictive and noncommital in their discussions, but they became analytic when marital conflicts were salient. There was a matter-of-fact quality to these discussions. Although middle-aged couples were not as expressive as young couples, they discussed conflict areas directly, mostly speaking in neutral, objective language.

The preceding studies indicate declining expressivity and directness of marital communication over the stages of the family life cycle. The remainder of this chapter considers factors at each stage that may in-fluence and alter this trend. We have broken the life cycle into three rough categories: (a) young couples, referring to young, childless couples or parents of young (preteenage) children; (b) midlife couples, including parents of teenage children, "launching" and "empty nest" couples; and (c) retired and elderly couples. We also discuss one nonnormative stage of the family life cycle, that of divorce and remarriage. Divorce and remarriage have become so commonplace that these events deserve sepa-rate consideration. In addition, these topics help us to see how stressful transitions alter the general momentum toward more implicit forms of communication over time.

YOUNG COUPLES

Young couples are in exceedingly heterogeneous groups, because the designation applies to teenage marriages (usually associated with preg-nancy) as well as couples who delay childbearing until into their 30s or 40s. Both ends of this spectrum have become more typical in recent decades. From the 1950s to the 1970s both the number of adolescent pregnancies and the number of couples postponing childbirth increased, although the median age of mothers at first birth remained at about 22 years of age (Parke & Tinsley, 1984). Needless to say, teenage parents differ extensively from individuals who became parents in their late 20s, 30s, or beyond. Older parents are more likely to have completed their education, to be well established in their careers, and to be less stressed and more stable in a variety of respects. Young parents are more stressed for time as well as money, because family pressures conflict with career advancement. Not surprisingly, teenage marriages are two to three times as likely to result in separation and/or divorce than marriages that occur when the women is age 20 or older (Baldwin & Cain, 1980), and fathers who delay parenthood tend to be more involved in child care (Parke & Tinsley, 1984). Another difference between parents of young children who themselves are young versus couples who delay childbirth is that the two groups represent different cohorts. Parents who are now in their 30s and 40s may identify with the transcendentalism of the late 1960s and early 1970s, whereas individuals who came of age in the 1980s were reared under a more pragmatic culture, attuned to economic headlines and fears about "making it."

Despite their differences, there are other factors that unify the experiences of young couples and provide some coherence to the description of this phase of life. Early marriage and parenthood are usually tumultuous by comparison with later phases. Marriage and parenthood are cultural rites of passage into adulthood which bring about increased obligations to others, major new sources of stress as well as personal satisfaction, reorganization of friendship circles, and many other changes. The modal interaction style we have observed among young couples (i.e., contentious, analytic, and humorous) is a fitting adaptation to the rapid pulse of family life in the early stages.

Two factors during early marriage and parenthood combine to accentuate demands on communication. First, there are many issues to resolve during the initial integration of separate personalities and subsequent transformation from couple to family. Issues associated with family integration are made more urgent by the number of life transition points that often occur in close succession (e.g., finishing school, getting married, relocating, beginning careers, having the first child, placing children in school). Second, role expectations are more ambiguous and less consensual than in previous decades. Taken-for-granted role expectations enable individuals to form "silent arrangements" (Scanzoni & Szinovacz, 1980; Strauss, 1978), thereby limiting the number of issues that must be explicitly negotiated. Although traditional role expectations have not been abandoned, expectations for marriage are now more diverse than they were when older marriages were formed. Thus, young couples are faced with many pressing issues and have fewer a priori guidelines for resolving them than older cohorts. The relatively intense and expressive style of communication observed among young couples (Zietlow & Sillars, 1988) is to be expected under these conditions. In the remainder of this section we examine the preceding conditions affecting young couples more closely, concentrating first on social and cultural themes affecting young cohorts and then life-stage events in early marriage and parenthood.

Social and Cultural Themes Affecting Young Couples

The American concept of intimacy, which has undergone a slow evolution, has had a similar impact on marriages of the 1970s and 1980s. Most obviously, recent decades have seen much attention devoted to the role of women in society and to egalitarian values in marriage. In some measure this may be due to lower birthrates and dramatically increased employment rates of young mothers since the 1950s (Parke & Tinsley, 1984), which have increased autonomy and resources outside of the home for women. Increasing demands on fathers to share decision making, housework, and child care have not always succeeded in attracting male converts. For example, fathers do not appear to increase their share of the housework when mothers work outside the home, although they may increase their child contact some (Hoffman, 1984; Pleck, 1983). Still, egalitarian themes affect young couples even where the husband is reluctant to comply, because such themes undermine the certainty and authority of traditional role definitions. As intangible as it may appear, one of the greatest impacts of the movement toward equality in marriage is to increase role ambiguity and to multiply areas of potential conflict and negotiation.

A second cultural impact on young couples is the nearly religious significance attributed to communication in marriage and the strong stereotype of effective communication (Fitzpatrick & Badzinski, 1985). Since the 1950s, popular culture in the United States has shifted from a role-bound view of the ideal relationship, emphasizing descrete and tactful communication, to a process-oriented model anchored by such themes as openness, expressivity, honesty, and communication as "work" (Ellis, 1979; Katriel & Phillipsen, 1981; Kidd, 1975; Knapp, 1984). Thus, expressivity is generally valued more highly by young spouses than by those middle-aged and older (Dobson, 1983; Fengler, 1973; Thurnher, 1976). To be sure, not all young couples encorporate an expressive ideal in their actual communication (Sillars, Wilmot, & Hocker, in press), but it frequently remains a benchmark for evaluating the state of the relationship. Further, contemporary relationships are characterized by great diversity (Fitzpatrick, 1984), due partly to the mixing of cultural themes from past and present. For example, marriage may combine one spouse who believes in confronting disagreements with another spouse who finds such talk counter-productive, thereby resulting in an awkward asymmety (Sillars et al., in press). We assume that this type of confusion is probably most pervasive among young couples because the present trend is toward an increasingly pluralistic definition of marriage (Hareven, 1982).

Finally, young couples may carry a particularly high justificatory burden because of the increased acceptibility of divorce combined with higher standards for communication, affection, and companionship (Fitzpatrick & Badzinski, 1985). The result is that individuals may be more self-conscious and vigilant of the internal dynamics of the relationship than in long-established marriages.

Life Stage Events of Young Couples

The initial year or so of marriage is a period when the joint identity of the couple is solidified and innumerable areas of similarity and difference are located and confronted. Couples who cohabit prior to marriage may anticipate this adjustment process to some extent, although cohabiting individuals are not fully comparable to married couples, because marriage usually suggests much greater formal commitment. It is not certain what effect formal commitment has, however, it potentially speeds up the adjustment phase by reducing insecurities, allowing individuals to behave in a less guarded manner, and reducing tolerance for minor annoyances that might be ignored in the short run.

The initial adjustment phase is characterized by close monitoring of the relationship and more frequent and intense relationship communication than perhaps at any other period. The couple becomes preoccupied with the newness and awkwardness of the marriage. This self-preoccupation is also a cause and consequence of the fact that competing relationships receded in importance. Marriage initiates a decline in the amount of time spent with friends, which continues into middle-age (Blieszner, 1988; Larson & Bradney, 1988). Individual networks are renegotiated into a joint network that is more "couple-oriented" (Farrel & Rosenberg, 1977; Rands, 1988) and compartmentalized, associated with specific activities (Brown, 1981; Wilmot & Sillars, this volume).

The acclimation of spouses to one another is also a period when fantasy meets reality (Berscheid & Walster, 1974; Waller, 1938). Unrealistic expectations and benevolent misconceptions are diminished as individuals increasingly "act themselves." Romantic feelings may decline simply because the emotional intensity of the newlywed phase is too high to maintain (Berscheid & Walster, 1974); further, instrumental aspects of the living arrangement eventually acquire greater salience. Two impacts on communication are evident in these changes. First, as the emotional intensity and novelty of the relationship subsides and roles are established, taken-for-granted meaning begins to substitute for explicit communication about the relationship (Waller, 1938). Second, a greater proportion of communication is devoted to marital conflicts than gradually surface. These changes are supported by the research of Huston, McHale, and Crouter (1986) who studied 100 couples over the initial year of marriage. Over this period couples reported increased negativity, conflict, and ambivalence and decreased global satisfaction, satisfaction with the amount of interaction, physical intimacy, pleasurable activity, and love. The couples also reported at the end of 1 year that they spent less total time talking together and less time talking about the quality of the relationship, spent more of their time together on instrumental versus leisure activities, made less effort to change behavior to resolve problems, disclosed wants and concerns less to one another, and were less affectionate, approving, and disclosing. This dreary picture is somewhat misleading, because perceptions of the relationship were still on the positive side after 1 year, although less positive than initially. Thus, the relationships changed from an extremely high level of satisfaction and positive communication to a more realistic balance between the different elements in marriage.

Pregnancy and childbirth bring about another massive reorganization of the relationship. Parenting is a consuming experience, potentially the source of much joy but also stressful and restricting (Hoffman & Manis, 1978). The adjustment following childbirth is analogous to the adjustment period following marriage, there is a gradual decline from the emotional high experienced initially to a state more tempered by negative as well as positive feelings. Meyerowitz and Feldman (1966) observed a strong tendency for parents to agree that having a baby improved their relationship; however, only 65% said that things were going well 5 months after birth, whereas 85% said so immediately after delivery. Lips and Morrison (1986) interviewed first-time parents on three occasions during pregnancy and 1 month postpartum. The most frequently mentioned themes revealed an up-beat, family-centered mood during the period immediately surrounding pregnancy. Spontaneously mentioned themes included increased closeness with the spouse (mentioned by one parent or the other in 81% of couples), becoming a family rather than a couple (53%), the father's positive involvement in parenting (48%), and increased involvement with extended family (43%). It is interesting to compare these first impressions of parenting with enduring changes that occur.

The last theme, increased contact with kin, accurately describes a real change for most couples (Belsky & Rovine, 1984; Hoffman & Manis, 1978). The experience of pregnancy and childbirth may cause young couples to adopt a more empathic view of their own parents (Arbeit, 1975). However, increased contact and closeness with extended kin usually comes at the expense of contact with friends (McCannell, 1988; Richardson & Kagan, 1979; Stueve & Gerson, 1977). Young parents may find that they have less in common with childless couples, for example the schedules and activities of new parents become more child-centered and conversations may become one-sided monologues about the children (Bram, 1974). Social ties with other parents may increase (McCannell, 1988; Richardson, & Kagan, 1979), however, matching whole families in terms of their compatibilities is a complicated enterprise. Further, friendships between families are frequently disrupted by moves at this stage in life (Reisman, 1981). A couple may become insular as a result, with no close, nonkin friendships. These changes in the social network further reinforce a couple's inward turning and focusing upon themselves as a family unit. Further, demands for companionship in the marital dyad presumably increase as the social network contracts.

Another theme prominently mentioned in the Lips and Morrison (1986) study was the positive involvement of the father in parenthood. Ironically, the birth of the first child generally has a tradionalizing influence on marriage, prompting greater role specialization, male-dominated decision making, and a shift toward traditional ideology (Hoffman & Manis, 1978; Lamb, 1978; Meyerowitz & Feldman, 1966). In a cross-national survey of over 2000 husbands and wives, Hoffman and Manis (1978) found that fathers helped less with the housework after the birth of the first child and gave little assistance with child care. Other research indicates that fathers and mothers are equally affectionate with their babies but mothers are far more likely to take care of the infant (Parke & Sawin, 1976). The dependency of the infant combined with the strength of society's expectations about motherhood make it much more difficult for couples to maintain equivocal roles after childbirth (Lamb, 1978). Further, children promote pressure for role delegation because of increased need to economize on effort previously spent negotiating decisions and role obligations. "Enlightened" fathers may take on specific nontraditional roles, for example, by caring for older children when siblings are born (Lamb, 1978). In any event, there is likely to be some movement away from the degree of explicit communication and negotiation required by role sharing and greater implicit adjustment based on role delegation. It further stands to reason that this transition is a source of unhappiness for couples who were initially companionate and egalitarian (see Lamb, 1978; Lips & Morrison, 1986).

Finally, over 80% of the couples studied by Lips and Morrison spontaneously mentioned that increased closeness with the spouse had accompanied pregnancy and childbirth. The impact of children on marital satisfaction has attracted more comment and research then any single issue in the family life-span literature. Although a number of qualifications apply, the general picture constructed by this literature is that marital satisfaction declines with the birth of the first child and increases later in life after the children leave home (see Blieszner, 1988, Hicks & Platt, 1970; Rollins & Galligan, 1978; Spanier & Lewis, 1980; Troll et al., 1979). Of course, this effect is probably very different from couples who stumbled into parenting versus those who longed for children. Further, a decrease in marital satisfaction may be compensated by satisfactions received as a parent. Still, it should be obvious to any parent that children are a source of stress. Children demand time, energy, and attention, they complicate decision making, interrupt interactions between husband and wife, raise the emotional level of interactions, and increase geometrically the number of family issues and conflicts that arise. Issues involving day care, violin lessons, bed time, discipline, sugar cereal, television rules, and toy sharing are added to those that childless couples already face. New activities brought about by children (e.g., birthday parties, parent–teacher conferences, Campfire Girls, soccer tournaments, swimming lessons) increase the pace of family life and divert time and energy from couple-oriented activities. Couples with school-age children are particularly said to suffer from a "time-crunch" because the outside activities of children increasingly add to an already full agenda (Harry, 1976; Rollins & Galligan, 1978). Further, because children progress through developmental changes more rapidly than adults, they add instability to family relationships.

In sum, children add an element of chaos to couple interactions. The effects of couple communication are paradoxical. On the one hand, there are many issues and concerns to discuss. On the other hand, parents may be hard pressed to find sufficient time, energy, and privacy for adequate communication to occur. Instead, parental communication and decision making tends to embedded within other activities, such as meals, shopping trips, television shows, and trips to the laundromat (Sillars & Kalbflesch, in press; Weick, 1971). Couple communication in such a context is less carefully monitored or regulated and more frequently interrupted than when communication is isolated and managed as a separate event (Sillars & Kalbflesch, in press). Thus, children provide the impetus for much instrumental discussion of parenting issues, yet couple communication might be expected to decline through the early stages of child rearing because of constraints on time and energy. We assume that communication in companionate areas suffers the most, as a greater percentage of communication is devoted to decision making and conflict resolution. On the other hand, the parents' shared interest in the children's developmental progress can be a unifying theme and the subject of more "recreational" conversatiaons.

A composite picture of young couples is as follows. Young couples are more expressive, conflictive, and intense than older couples, by philosophy as well as circumstance. They are more likely to endorse expressivity and joint decision making and they are more pressed to confront conflicts and decisions surrounding early marriage and parenthood. However, the amount of explicit communication between spouses, particularly in companionate areas, probably declines through this period due to increased development of implicit expectations and the proliferation of competing demands and distractions of child rearing.

MIDLIFE COUPLES

Barring divorce, economic displacement or other unanticipated life-changing events, the middle years of the family life cycle are probably the most stable. Maturational changes in children from adolescence through young adulthood still add variety to family life, however, these changes happen less suddenly than the changes occuring in childbearing and early child-rearing years. In addition, the economic and career uncertainties that characterize earlier years are often resolved, and the adjustment between husband and wife is apt to be more complete. Of course, stability can also be experienced as stagnation, which partly accounts for the differing reactions people have to midlife. Midlife may be seen as the time when one has "arrived" (Reisman, 1981) due to increased influence, competence, material resources, and self-awareness. Others experience the proverbial midlife crisis, based on goals not achieved, opportunities missed, the loss of youth, and an increasing sense that life is finite (see Blieszner, 1988; Reisman, 1981).

Midlife may bring about the culmination of changes in marital communication that began early in the relationship. These changes involve increasing taken-for-granted assumptions and expectations, implicit adjustment to the spouse, and role segregation. During stable periods of midlife, implicit role expectations should increasingly substitute for explicit communication. It remains to be seen whether midlife couples actually talk less than young couples. They may in fact have more companionate interests to discuss, due to the reduced urgency of instrumental matters. However, a good bet is that midlife couples engage in less explicit metacommunication (i.e., talk about the marital relationship) than young couples. Close monitoring and explicit communication about a relationship declines during stable periods when concerns over relationship rules recede into the background (Watzlawick, Beavin, & Jackson, 1967). Explicit talk about the relationship may also be increasingly phrased in the past tense, reflecting a feeling that the marriage has graduated from the formative period and has leveled out from the extreme highs and lows experienced earlier.

Couples may become more interdependent during midlife in other subtle respects. A blurring of individual personalities and further consolidation of the identity of the couple may take place. Whereas young couples struggle to achieve a comfortable balance between individual autonomy and interdependence, midlife couples are more likely to have found equilibrium, with interdependence occuring in many ways that the couple cannot articulate. Blieszner (1988) reported that husbands and wives in middle age show greater psychological complementarity, using one another's characteristics to complete or balance individual traits. A possible example of this revealed in one study was that middle-aged men relied on their wives' support during stressful periods more than young men (Tamir, 1982).

Although stability is the modal characteristic of midlife marriage, there are, of course, changes and conflicts occuring in this period. Many people go through separation, divorce, and remarriage. We have devoted a separate section to these individuals, because their experience is often very different from first-married couples. Other disruptions include conflicts with adolescent children, changes in the husband–wife relationship as the children become more independent, and readjustment as the children leave home (i.e., the "empty nest" period).

Parental conflicts with teenage children are legend, although the militant independence of adolescents can be a mixed blessing. On the one hand, conflicts with teenagers may provoke husband–wife conflicts. In fact, one study found middle-aged women to be the most critical of their husbands, based on histories of conflict over and with teenage children. These women looked forward to the time when the children would leave so that the marriage might improve (Lowenthal, Thurnher, & Chiriboga, 1975). Parents also worry more about the safety and well-being of older children, and older children may especially interfere with privacy because of their awareness of sexual relations (Hoffman & Manis, 1978). On the other hand, a couple experiences more freedom and discretionary use of their time as the children get older. Marital relations may also become more salient as the role of caretaker diminishes. Hoffman & Manis (1978) found that the spousal relationship was more important to women after their children reached adolescence, suggesting a turning back toward the marriage after the distractions of early child rearing had eased. Thus, older children may both be a source of trouble and a stimulus for reconsolidating the parental coalition.

Another common change among midlife couples is that wives may become more assertive and more interested in career and personal fulfillment when released from the dependency of children (Baruch, Barnett, & Rivers, 1983; Blieszner, 1988; Rubin, 1979). This suggests a period of adjustment, characterized by renewed attention to and discussion of marital roles (see Blieszner, 1988). For some couples this phase is anticipated and welcomed. However, older cohorts may be caught off guard, due to cultural themes that prevailed in the United States from the late

1940s through the early 1960s. The prosperity of these times, in relation to the scarcity and insecurity of the war and depression years, encouraged a strong domestic ethos, in which the home was viewed as a sanctuary and the homemaker role was idealized (Elder, 1981). Marriage was seen as a full-time job, so women frequently gave up jobs at marriage or childbirth and did not return to the workforce (Elder, 1974). The husband's role as economic provider was similarly idealized. For individuals enculturated by these themes, the woman's reevaluation of her role may involve a shift in basic values and self-identity. This obviously has more severe repercussions for the marital relationship than say, when a women puts off law school simply to make some money or spend more time with the children when they are small.

The empty-nest phase generally appears to be a period when marital tensions ease and satisfactions increase (see Blieszner, 1988; Troll et al., 1979). Although the offspring may fret that their presence is dearly missed, this factor is compensated by increased freedom, privacy, time, and (sometimes) money. The companionship of children may be partly substituted by renewed frequency and intimacy of contacts with friends (Huston & Levinger, 1978; Larson & Bradney, 1988, Lowenthal et al., 1975). Close friendships are often a casualty of absorption into family activities during parenting stages (Blieszner, 1988; Huston & Levinger, 1978), with the number of friends reaching a low point when the children are teenagers, according to one study (Lowenthal et al., 1975). Although most people hold their adult children in deep regard, friends are usually less contentious, more similar, and better able to empathize with life-stage experiences.

Although the preceding changes suggest an optimistic view of the empty next stage, certainly the impact of this period depends on parental attachments. If the children are the focal point of the marriage and the main catalyst for fun, then maturation of the children will be experienced as a loss. Individuals who focus intensely on their role as parents are prone to midlife crises when the children leave (Bart, 1971). Presumably, the shock is greater if attachment to one's children is much stronger than attachment to one's spouse.

In summary, midlife is a stabilizing period for many couples; yet it still gives rise to changes, conflicts and occasionally, crises. In the research by Zietlow and Sillars (1988) that we commented on earlier, midlife couples confronted conflicts, yet their behavior suggested that substantial adjustments had been made and fundamental issues resolved. There was an "older but wiser" quality to the interactions of couples in the launching and empty-nest phases. These couples were brief but to the point and they discussed salient conflict issues directly, without the contentiousness and emotionality often demonstrated by young couples. The direct but subdued quality of these interactions suggests that adjustments in the relationship were still being made but fundamental issues concerning warmth, regard, dominance, trust, and so forth had been resolved or put aside. For many couples within the midlife period, disagreements appear not to threaten the most basic areas of convergence. Stark exceptions to this generalization are considered later when we examine the dissolution of marriages.

OLDER COUPLES

Due to increased life expectancies and reduced family sizes, the number of years couples are together after the children have left home has increased greatly (Hareven, 1982; Troll et al., 1979). The importance of the marital bond late in life is clear. Married individuals among the elderly have better health, higher morale, fewer insecurities, lower rates of institutionalization, greater social integration and they are far less likely to report being lonely (see Johnson, 1988; Simons, 1984).

Although the vitality of marriage is as important late in life as at any other point, marriage may service a different set of needs and values. Older couples tend to show a strong degree of commitment to the relationship, high interdependency, and high marital satisfaction (see Johnson, 1988; Troll et al., 1979), yet, marital relations within older couples are restrained and formal by comparison to young couples. Based on the studies reviewed earlier, older couples express less self-disclosure, affection, or criticism and their conversations are pleasant to a fault. Whereas young couples may devote considerable time and energy exploring feelings and talking about the relationship, older couples stress such topics of conversation as religion, home repairs, and health (Feldman, 1964; Rollins & Feldman, 1970; Troll et al., 1979). Of course, broad generalizations do not do justice to a large and heterogeneous group such as the elderly (Troll et al., 1979). Some older couples report being able to share any thought or feeling with one another (Foster, 1980). Others are conflict habituated (Zietlow & Sillars, 1988), remaining together in a sort of "armed truce" due to stigmas and prohibitions against divorce (Troll et al., 1979). Still, expressivity is discouraged by values held by many of the elderly, as well as developmental changes in relationships, for example, declining introspection about marital relations as adjustment becomes more complete, the rate of change slows and marital stress subsides.

The values that older couples apply to marriage are partly a function of the general cultural climate and partly attributable to unique experiences connected with later stages of life. We have already commented on the evolution of the American concept of intimacy from a role-bound perspective to a process-oriented model that idealizes open communication. Presumably this suggests that marriages in the 1930s began on different terms than recent marriages. Indeed, senior citizens recollecting their close relationships at an earlier age, reported less expression of feelings and confiding about problems than young adults reporting on current relationships (Rands & Levinger, 1979). Older couples are no doubt aware of how cultural perceptions of intimacy have changed during their lifetime (e.g., contrast *Family Ties* with *Leave It to Beaver*) but may still receive validation for the older model from within their own cohort. On the other hand, contemporary views of communication and intimacy have undoubtedly had some converts among the elderly, thereby contributing to the heterogeneity of this group.

Even aside from cohort-related values, older couples may adopt a different value perspective than young couples because of shifting needs and concerns later in life. Early marriage calls for flexibility, empathy, supportiveness, and problem-solving skill, because this is a period when many new roles and responsibilities are acquired, separate identities reconciled, and family policies established. Attraction and affection are extremely salient as well, because romantic love is the main reason people give for marrying. Late in marriage, attachment may substitute for attraction (Troll & Smith, 1976), and satisfaction may stem from a sense of "survivorship" and long-term sharing of experiences (Johnson, 1988). Thus, the relationship is evaluated based on what it has been through, not on what it has the potential to become. Presumably, spouses are more accepting of or resigned to the relationship as it stands and less optimistic about instituting fundamental change after many years. Stoic values, such as tolerance, forgiveness, and discretion are more congruent with this outlook than a process-oriented model that emphasizes negotiation, confrontation, and problem solving.

An additional consideration is that aging couples experience increasing vulnerability to social isolation and physical disability. Social networks may decline in old age due to decreased mobility, illness, and the death of friends (see Chown, 1981; Nussbaum, 1983). Spouses are increasingly reliant on one another for companionship in this situation. Eventually one spouse may become physically dependent on the other due to disability or illness. The values of older couples are responsive to these uncertainties and insecurities. For example, older couples tend to value emotional security, loyalty, obligation, and companionship over other important characteristics of marriage (Johnson, 1988; Parron, 1978; Reedy, 1977; Stinnet, Carter, & Montgomery, 1972). Whereas young couples may believe that it is better to separate than to remain in an unhappy relationship, elderly couples rarely divorce (Treas & Van

Hilst, 1976). Thus, concerns about communication and relationship enhancement tend to be superceded by norms of commitment and endurance among older couples.

The other factor affecting communication in older couples is reduced marital stress and conflict (Troll, 1982; Zietlow, 1986). Although some changes occuring late in life may be very stressful, they do not tend to produce the sort of divisive conflicts that are common early in marriage. Declining health or increasing social isolation, for example, may further cement the marital bond, as we have just noted. In part, the difference here is that stress and conflict earlier in marriage tend to center on relationship rules (e.g., parenting decisions, decision-making authority, individual autonomy), whereas stress late in life more typically stems from impersonal forces that are external to the relationship (e.g., ill health, bereavement, reduced mobility, the need to relocate). Another difference is that more roles are given up late in life than acquired, so marital relations face less competition.

Although retirement leads to redefinition of the marital relationship, this change is usually experienced positively. Relatively few adjustment problems are reported with retirement, except where individuals miss work or are financially strapped (McCubbin et al., 1980). Marital relations may improve with retirement because of reduced career stress and increased opportunity for shared leisure activities (Szinovacz, 1980). Retirement appears to trigger a softening of sex differences, with males becoming more reflective, dependent and affiliative and females becoming more assertive (Dobson, 1983; Gutmann, 1975). There is less normative pressure to do either masculine or feminine things subsequent to parenting and retirement (Dobson, 1983; Gutmann, 1975), so the sexes may become more similar and androgynous. This change probably increases reflection and communication about the relationship during adjustment to retirement, although the transition is rather benign, bringing about increased sharing, equality and companionship (Blieszner, 1988). Further, changes in sex-linked behavior can be subtle. In one study, retired husbands saw themselves as behaving in feminine ways, however, their wives apparently failed to notice any such behavior. Husbands' ratings of their own femininity decreased from the early stages of marriage up to retirement, at which point perceived femininity sharply increased. However, retired wives still saw their husbands in highly stereotyped, masculine terms (Sillars, in press; Zietlow, 1986).

The sheer amount of repetitiveness of interactions over many years, coupled with the relatively modest and benign changes occuring in older marriages, encourage more efficient, unconscious, and implicit forms of communication. For example, interactions may entail numerous traditions and rituals, agreements may be assumed and unspoken, a single gesture or a few words may convey complete ideas, and rich memories of shared experiences may be cued by a brief remark. Individuals may look inward to personal beliefs and recollections in order to understand the spouse's subjective experiences. Zietlow (1986) found that assumed similarity with the spouse was higher among older couples than among other life-stage groups, both in areas where actual similarity was high and in areas where it was not. At times, personal intuitions provide a valid substitute for explicit communication. Although Zietlow (1986) found older couples to be less expressive and disclosing than other life-stage couples, their understanding of one another was about the same (see also Sillars, in press). Thus, older couples may establish a communication system reminiscent of the "high context" transactions described by Hall (1977) and "pragmatic code" described by Ellis and Hamilton (1985). These concepts refer, in somewhat different ways, to transactions in which much of the information is in the receiver and context, and only minimal information explicitly coded within transmitted messages. Intimate couples generally behave more like high-context communication systems than strangers or acquaintances because of the opportunity for intense bonding and sharing of intimate experiences over time. However, implied meanings increasingly substitute for words where interactions are stable and repetitious and where background assumptions are closely in alignment (see Sillars & Kalbflesch, in press), conditions that particularly describe older couples.

DIVORCE, REDEFINITION, AND REMARRIAGE

In the final section, we consider how the momentum toward more implicit forms of communication across the family life span is dramatically altered by divorce and remarriage. The disorientation inevitably occuring with divorce is partly due to the inability of implicit assumptions and meanings derived from past interactions to clarify a relationship change of this magnitude. Similarly, the more self-conscious and explicit nature of communication in some second marriages reflects the fact that these relationships frequently experience a more complicated adjustment process than first marriages.

Divorce

Divorce has moved from an anomaly to a commonplace event. With young couples today there is a greater than 40% chance they will face divorce at some time (Norton & Glick, 1976). And, depending on such factors as economic conditions, the probability of divorce can reach over 50%, with better economic times accompanied by higher divorce rates.

Reaching a near normative status, however, does not mitigate the trauma associated with divorce—it still remains one of the most trying life transitions. Although all life transitions are important, the degree of stress on a married couple is related to whether they experience it as a "normal" transition or a crisis. The factors that distinguish between a transition and a crisis are (a) whether the transition is scheduled, (b) if the transition is controlled by individual choice, (c) if the transition is preceeded by a warning, (d) if the transition entails status gain rather than status loss, and (e) if there is a rite of passage associated with the transition (Hagestad & Smyer, 1982).

Divorce classifies as a crisis on all counts. First, divorce is usually unscheduled. Even though most couples are aware of the divorce rate, the statistical information does not help them prepare for a divorce in their own life. Often the person can neither predict the timing nor sequence of actions preceeding a divorce (Weiss, 1975). And, of course, a divorce is not controllable by one party. As Wilmot (1987) noted, most two-person systems are inherently prone to dissolution because it takes two to keep a system healthy and only one to destroy it. In almost all states in the United States, one partner can file for divorce and move the process forward, albeit sometimes slowly, with or without the consent of the other party. Divorce can be, therefore, an unwanted event thrust upon one.

Surprisingly, divorce also can come without much warning. As external observers, we can say that each partner "saw it coming," yet one of the most common features of unilaterally triggered divorce actions is that the spouse did not see it coming. Because most terminations are indirect and ambiguous on the part of the initiator (Baxter, 1984), the spouse misinterprets the communication. Imagine for a moment you are in a committed relationship. As the spouse slowly withdraws over time, works hard, and generally is in a "grumpy" period, most of us attribute such minor changes to alterations in the external world—needing extra money, the stress of child rearing, or other factors. However, a spouse can withdraw from the marriage using identical communication behavior. As Wilmot (1987) suggested, the two partners have "different relational frames" for interpreting the communication behavior. The initiator moving toward dissolution says, "I gave lots of hints about my dissatisfaction," whereas the spouse interprets the distancing in another light, namely "the normal ups and downs in marriage." These mismatched relational frames set the stage for one partner to be surprised with the announcement "I want a divorce."

Divorce also entails status loss, both individually and socially, with no rite of passage to accompany this loss. Frequently, divorcing spouses are not even present at the Court when their marriage is formally dissolved, choosing instead to have their attorneys appear. If the two people are present, the atmosphere has a surrealistic quality about it. One needs only to spend a morning during "time and motion" day in the local District Court to see the lack of social support for divorce. Couple after couple is processed through this crucial life crisis without support of friends, pledges of continued cooperation regarding rearing the children, or even coffee together to mark this important change. Whereas we honor the death of a person with funerals and memorial services, the demise of a relationship is usually ignored.

The divorce crisis has been accorded considerable attention in the literature with attendant foci on stress, adjustment difficulties, and other factors. But, the actual communication behavior during the divorcing process has received little actual study. There are a variety of theoretical perspectives on divorce (Duck, 1982), yet examination of the communication processes has been lacking. The following discussion, therefore, is often speculative and extrapolated from findings from other relationships, such as the dissolution of nonbonded romantic relationships.

One of the central communicative features of the divorcing process resides in the expressiveness and directness of communication—two themes, we highlighted previously. Whether the divorcing couple is young or middle-aged, they share for some period of time "memories, photo albums, home movies and material possessions" (Hagestad & Smyer, 1982, p. 168) that symbolize their shared life together. How they go about the process of uncoupling their intertwined lives can be seen as a function of the basic choices of expressiveness and directness.

We noted earlier that cohort effects on couples impact the types of communication they enact in their marriage. Such would also be expected to be the case in the dissolution process. One study examined the expression of conflict in couples and discovered that younger dissatisfied couples expressed their conflict in an "explosive" manner, whereas older dissatisfied couples more often used covert types of conflict (O'Brien, 1972). Only through detailed examination of divorces in each cohort category can we ascertain if these communicative patterns are followed during the relational demise.

Extant research on other dissolutions also highlights the direct/indirect continuum of communication events. Baxter's work found that dissolution tactics varied according to directness/indirectness and self/other orientation (Baxter, 1982, 1983). Further, the most common trajectory for dissolution of relationships was unilateral and indirect (Baxter, 1984). Such results seem consistent with our theoretical perspective on the divorcing process—that implicit, jointly understood communication process are more normative than previously thought.

The implicit, indirect nature of some marital communication patterns does, however, pose special difficulties during divorce. A married couple that operates from assumptive frames of understanding may find this approach failing them during the crisis of divorce. Whereas in the marriage meaning could be "taken for granted," during divorce the increase of stress and unclarity about the relationship produce substantial ambiguity. For example, during the dissolution process for both marriage and other romantic relationships there is considerable "relational oscillation" (Wilmot, 1987). Couples do not march step-by-step toward divorce, but rather, recycle between distance and closeness many times during the process. As a result, the divorcing couple has heightened need for explicit communication, yet they may have developed patterned responses of not being explicit. Divorce mediators, who work with couples to move them toward dissolution in a cooperative atmosphere, usually spend considerable time helping divorcing people to be explicit about their expectations of one another (Moore, 1986). The work of Baxter (1982, 1984), Wilmot, Carbaugh, and Baxter (1985), and Newman and Langer (1981) suggested that unilateral terminations make divorce adjustment more difficult, because other-directed blame in these situations makes direct discussion and negotiation between divorcing spouses exceedingly difficult to carry off. Stated another way, explicitness in the dissolution process aids in post dissolution adjustment as the formerly functional implicit patterns become counterproductive.

Redefinition and Remarriage

Once divorced, the couple has two major tasks, (a) redefining their relationship to the former spouse and (b) reestablishing new intimate relationships. Usually, these two tasks are intrinsically connected, and often the temporal ordering is altered. For example, one may become involved with another while still married, and the divorce occurs with the context of one or both spouses having other intimate partners. But regardless of the pathway, 80% of divorcing spouses remarry and these remarriages constitute over 30% of all marriages (Dean & Gurak, 1978). Although there is yet to be a comprehensive view of the Separation-Divorce-Remarriage process, general notions have been advanced (Rodgers, 1987) and some salient issues have emerged.

The redefinition of the spousal unit following divorce has not received enough attention, but one study is worthy of note. Ahrons and Wallisch (1987) studied the patterns of relationship of ex-spouses in their mid 30s who had been married, on the average, for 11 years. The redefined relationships were assessed 1 year and 3 years after divorce. One year after the divorce, only 25% of the ex-spouses interacted with each other at least once every few months on topics not related to the children. Only about 5% of the former spouses said they were very involved with their ex-spouse's life. After 3 years, their interaction continued to decrease, with only 9% having a high degree of interaction about events in the children's lives. Basically, "what interaction they do have is negative and their feelings toward each other are usually hostile. Some may be indifferent, but many still harbor the anger arising from the marriage and divorce" (Ahrons & Wallisch, 1987, p. 293).

Not only does communication with former spouses undergo serious decline, the world of the remarried is not a trouble-free existence either. The remarriage of former spouses causes emotional trauma, especially for ex-wives (Hetherington, Cox, & Cox, 1979), and the remarried face a higher risk of developing relationship stress (Cherlin, 1978). The most frequently cited sources of remarried difficulties are the children from the previous marriage (Messinger, 1976).

The central problem for remarried couples is trying to "blend" two diverse sets of implicit assumptions in an inherently different context. As Farrell and Markman (1986) stated, "having set the stage for a conflict avoidant relationship during mate selection, the remarried couple is then faced with having to work out the inevitable problems of domestic cohabitation in the absence of established mechanisms for negotiation" (p. 259). Implicit inexpressive communication, then, may work for a first married couple but its use becomes problematic as systemic complexities multiply.

It should come as no surprise, therefore, that remarried couples are more self-conscious, less spontaneous, and more apt to engage in explicit negotiation in comparison with intact married couples (Duberman, 1975; Kompara, 1980; Rosenbaum & Rosenbaum, 1978; Visher & Visher, 1978; Walker & Messinger, 1979; Weisberg, 1983). Several factors contribute. First, the reintegration of family units may provide an impetus for explicit rule setting and negotiation of family decisions. The obvious conflicts involving children in blended families are aggravated by the sudden formation of new parental and sibling bonds without the opportunity for gradual adjustment that exists in intact families (Duberman, 1975; Messinger, 1976). As a result, decision making tends to require much explicit attention and effort from remarried couples, because implicit forms of adjustment are often inapplicable or inadequate.

Second, remarried couples tend to be more heterogeneous in age, religion, and education (Dean & Gurak, 1978) and less traditional (Duberman, 1975; Messinger, Walker, & Freeman, 1978) than intact couples. Consequently, there is less foundation for spontaneous consensus and more need to explicitly communicate. Traditionalism may decline because of personal reorientations that individuals go through following divorce. Women tend to see themselves as more independent and desirous of an equalitarian relationship, whereas men see themselves as more nurturing following divorce (Messinger et al., 1978). Thus, roles are more achieved and less ascribed in remarried couples (Walker & Messinger, 1979).

Finally, the dramatic role transitions associated with divorce and remarriage create intense introspection about relationship processes. Weiss (1975) observed that divorced and separated spouses may be consumed by questions about "what went wrong." Their retrospective accounts seem partly motivated by a desire to construct predictability out of chaos and thereby avoid future mistakes (Weiss, 1975). The experrience of a previous divorce may create hypersensitivity to relational conflicts. For example, disagreements are more quickly seen as a prelude to divorce rather than simple bickering (Asmundson, 1981). In contrast, the experiences of intact couples are less tumultuous, more stable and more continuous, so monitoring of the relationship should subside with time.

CONCLUSION

With the "graying" of communication researchers, we are likely to see more interest in marital and family communication across the entire life span. Presently, most studies of marital communication are studies of young, intact couples. In this chapter we have considered how the normative experiences of young couples contrast with experiences during other periods of life. Communication may vary over the life span as a consequence of three factors: (a) intrinsic developmental processes, such as the evolution of more idiosyncratic and efficient forms of communication over time, (b) cohort-related experiences and values, and (c) life-stage events, such as parenting, retirement, and divorce. As a working hypothesis, we propose that explicit communication is emphasized during the initial adjustment to marriage but that explicit messages gradually give way to more implicit forms of interaction, for example, lower rates of expressivity, disclosure and monitoring of the relationship, an increasing store of taken-for-granted assumptions, traditions, and rituals, the use of the personal beliefs and intuitions to understand and predict the spouse, and more efficient, context-dependent messages. This momentum is periodically broken during transition phases, particularly stressful transitions which make implicit understandings at least temporarily obsolete. Thus, young couples appear to be the most intense and expressive group, elderly couples are the most passive and congenial, and middle-aged couples fall between the extremes. In the case of divorce and remarriage, new types of relationships are established. Couple communication is especially problematic in such relationships because implicit forms of adjustment are generally incapable of clarifying a relationship change of such magnitude.

REFERENCES

Ahrons, C. R., & Wallisch, L. S. (1987). The relatonship between former spouses. In D. Perman & S. Duck (Eds.), *Intimate Relationships: Development dynamics, deterioration* (pp. 269–296). Newbury Park, CA: Sage.

Arbeit, S.A. (1975). *A Study of women during their first pregnancy.* Unpublished doctoral dissertation, Yale University.

Asmundson, R. (1981). Blended families: One plus one equals more than two. In C. Getty & W. Humphreys (Eds.), *Understanding the family: Stress and change in american family life* (pp. 117–128). New York: Appleton–Century–Crofts.

Baldwin, W., & Cain, V. (1980). The children of teenage parents. *Family planning perspectives, 12,* 34–43.

Bart, P. B. (1971). Depression in middle-aged women. In V. Gornick & B. K. Moran (Eds.), *Women in sexist society.* New York: Basic Books.

Baruch, G., Barnett, R., & Rivers, C. (1983). *Lifeprints: New patterns of love and work for today's women.* New York: New American Library.

Baxter, L. A. (1982). Strategies for ending relationships: Two studies. *Western Journal of Speech Communication, 46,* 223–241.

Baxter, L. A. (1983). Relationship disengagement: An examination of the reversal hypothesis. *Western Journal of Speech Communication, 47,* 85–98.

Baxter, L. A. (1984). Trajectories of relationship disengagement. *Journal of Social and Personal Relationships, 1,* 29–48.

Bell, R. A., Buerkel-Rothfuss, N. L., & Gore, K. E. (1987). "Did you bring the yarmulke for the cabbage patch kid?": The idiomatic communication of young lovers. *Human Communication Research, 14,* 47–67.

Belsky, J., & Rovine, M. (1984). Social-network contact, family support, and the transition to parenthood. *Journal of Marriage and the Family, 46,* 455–463.

Berscheid, E., & Walster, E. (1974). A little bit about love. In T. L. Huston (Ed.), Foundations of interpersonal attraction. New York: Academic Press.

Blieszner, R. (1988). Individual development and intimate relationships in middle and late adulthood. In R. M. Milardo (Ed.), *Families and social networks* (pp. 147–167). Newbury Park, CA: Sage.

Bram, S. (1974). *To have or have not: A Comparison of parents, parents-to-be, and childless couples.* Unpublished doctoral dissertation, University of Michigan.

Brown, B. (1981). A life-span approach to friendship: Age-related dimensions of an ageless relationship. In H. Lopata & D. Maines (Eds.), *Research on the interweave of social roles: Vol. 2. Friendship* (pp. 23–50). Greenwich, CT: J.A.I. Press.

Cherlin, A. (1978). Remarriage as an incomplete institution. *American Journal of Sociology, 84,* 634–650.

Chown, S. M. (1981). Friendship in old age. In S. Duck & R. Gilmour (Eds.), *Personal relationships* (Vol. 2, pp. 231–246). New York: Academic Press.

Cushman, D., & Whiting, G. C. (1972). An approach to communication theory: Toward consensus on rules. *The Journal of Communication, 22,* 217–236.

Dean, G., & Gurak, D. (1978). Marital homogamy the second time around. *Journal of Marriage and the Family, 40,* 559–570.

Dobson, C. (1983). Sex-role and marital-role expectations. In T. H. Brubaker (Ed.), *Family relationships in later life* (pp. 109–126). Beverly Hills: Sage Publications.

Duberman, L. (1975). *The reconstituted family: A Study of married couples and their Children*. Chicago: Nelson–Hall.

Duck, S. W. (Ed.). (1982). *Personal relationships: Vol. 4. Dissolving personal Relationships*. London: Academic Press.

Duvall, E. M. (1971). *Family development*. Philadelphia: J.B. Lippincott.

Elder, G. H. (1974). *Children of the great depression*. Chicago: University of Chicago Press.

Elder, G. H. (1981). Social history and life experience. In D. H. Eichorn, J. A. Clausen, N. Haan, M. P. Honzik, & P. H. Mussen (Eds.), *Present and past in middle life* (pp. 3–312). New York: Academic Press.

Ellis, D. A. (1979). *Til Divorce Do Us Part: Communication descriptions and prescriptions in popular magazines, 1968–1978*. Unpublished masters thesis, Purdue University.

Ellis, D., & Hamilton, M. (1985). Syntactic and pragmatic code choice in interpersonal communication. *Communication Monographs, 52*, 264–278.

Eskew, R. W. (1978). *An Investigation of cohort Differences in the marriage relationships of older couples*. Unpublished doctoral dissertation, Purdue University.

Farrell, J., & Markman, H. J. (1986). Individual and interpersonal factors in the etiology of marital distress: The example of remarital couples. In R. Gilmour & S. Duck (Eds.), *The emerging field of personal relationships* (pp. 251–263). Hillsdale, NJ: Lawrence Erlbaum Associates.

Farrell, M. P., & Rosenberg, S. (1977). *Male friendship and the life cycle*. Paper presented at the American Sociological Association convention.

Feldman, H. (1964). Development of the husband–wife relationship. *Preliminary report, Cornell studies of marital development: Study in the transition to parenthood*. Cornell University.

Fengler, A. P. (1973). The effects of age and education on marital ideology. *Journal of Marriage and the Family, 35*, 264–271.

Fitzpatrick, M. A. (1984). A typological approach to marital interaction: Recent theory and research. In L. Berkowitz (Ed.), *Advances in experimental social psychology* (pp. 1–47). New York: Academic Press.

Fitzpatrick, M. A., & Badzinski, D. M. (1985). All in the family: Interpersonal communication in kin relationships. In M. L. Knapp & G. R. Miller (Eds.), *Handbook of interpersonal communication* (pp. 687–736). Beverly Hills: Sage.

Foster, B. G. (1980). *Self-disclosure and intimacy in long-term marriages: Case studies*. Unpublished doctoral dissertation. Kansas State University.

Gutmann, D. (1975). Parenthood: A key to the comparative study of the life cycle. In N. Datan & L. H. Ginsberg (Eds.), *Life-span developmental psychology: normative life crises* (pp. 167–184). New York: Academic Press.

Hagestad, G. O., & Smyer, M. A. (1982). Dissolving long-term relationships: Patterns of divorcing in middle age. In S. W. Duck (Ed.), *Personal relationships: Vol. 4. Dissolving personal relationships* (pp. 155–188). London: Academic Press.

Hall, E. T. (1977). *Beyond culture*. Garden City, NY: Anchor.

Hareven, T. K. (1982). American families in transition: Historical perspectives on change. In F. Walsh (Ed.), *Normal family processes*. New York: Guidion.

Harry, J. (1976). Evolving sources of happiness for men over the life cycle: A structural analysis. *Journal of Marriage and the Family, 38*, 289–296.

Hetherington, E. M., Cox, H., & Cox, R. (1979). Stress and coping in divorce: Focus on women. In J. Gullahorn (Ed.), *Psychology and women in transition* (pp. 95–128). New York: V. H. Winston & Sons.

Hicks, M. W., & Platt, M. (1970). Marital happiness and stability: A review of the research in the sixties. *Journal of marriage and the Family, 32*, 553–573.

Hoffman, L. W. (1984). Work, family and the socialization of the child. In R. D. Parke, R. Emde, H. McAdoo, & G. P. Sackett (Eds.), *Review of child development research* (Vol. 7). Chicago: University of Chicago Press.

Hoffman, L. W., & Manis, J. D. (1978). Influences of children on marital interaction and parental satisfactions and dissatisfactions. In R. M. Lerner & G. B. Spanier (Eds.), *Child influences on marital and family interaction* (pp. 165–213). New York: Academic Press.

Hopper, R., Knapp, M. L., & Scott, L. (1981). Couples' personal idioms: Exploring intimate talk. *Journal of Communication, 37*, 23–33.

Huston, T. L., & Levinger, G. (1978). Interpersnal attraction and relationships. In M. R. Rosesweig & L. W. Port (Eds.), *Annual review of psychology* Vol 29. Palo Alto, CA: Annual Review.

Huston, T. L., McHale, S. M., & Crouter, A. C. (1986). When the honeymoon's over: Changes in the marriage relationship over the first year. In R. Gilmour & S. Duck (Eds.), *The emerging field of personal relationships* (pp. 109–132). Hillsdale, NJ: Lawrence Erlbaum Associates.

Illig, D. P. (1977). *Distributional structure, sequential structure, multivariate information analysis, and models of communicative patterns of elderly and young, married and friendship dyads in problem-solving situations.* Unpublished doctoral dissertation. Pennsylvania State University.

Johnson, C. L. (1988). Relationships among family members and friends in later life. In R. M. Milardo (Ed.), *Families and social networks* (pp. 168–169). Newbury Park, CA: Sage.

Jourard, S. M. (1971). *Self-disclosure: An experimental Analysis of the transparent self.* New York: Wiley.

Katriel, T., & Phillipsen, G. (1981). "What we need is communication": "Communication" as a cultural category in some American speech. *Communication Monographs, 48*, 301–317.

Kidd, V. (1975). Happily ever after and other relationship styles: Advice on interpersonal relations in popular magazines, 1951–1973. *Quarterly Journal of Speech, 61*, 31–39.

Knapp, M. L. (1984). *Interpersonal communication and human relationships.* Boston: Allyn & Bacon.

Kompara, D. R. (1980), Difficulties in the socialization process of stepparenting. *Family Relations, 29*, 69–73.

Lamb, M. E. (1978). Influence of the child on marital quality and family interaction during the prenatal, perinatal, and infancy periods. In R. M. Lerner & G. B. Spanier (Eds.), *Child influences on marital and family interaction* (pp. 137–163). New York: Academic Press.

Larson, R. W., & Bradney, N. (1988). Precious moments with family members and friends. In R. M. Milardo (Ed.), *Families and social networks* (pp. 107–126). Newbury Park, CA: Sage.

Lips, H. M., & Morrison, A. (1986). Changes in the sense of family among couples having their first child. *Journal of Social and personal relationships, 3*, 393–400.

Lowenthal, M. F., Thurnher, M., & Chiriboga, D. (1975). *Four stages of life.* San Francisco: Jossey–Bass.

McCannell, K. (1988). Social networks and the transition to motherhood. In R. M. Milardo (Ed.), *Families and social networks* (pp. 83–106). Newbury Park, CA: Sage.

McCubbin, H. I., Joy, C. B., Cauble, A. E., Comeau, J. K., Patterson, J. M., & Needle, R. H. (1980). Family stress and coping: A decade review. *Journal of Marraige and the Family, 42*, 855–871.

Messinger, L. (1976). Remarriage between divorced people with children from previous marriages: A proposal for preparation for remarriage. *Journal, of Marriage and Family Counseling, 38*, 273–281.

Messinger, L., Walker, K. M., & Freeman, S. J. (1978). Preparation for remarriage following divorce: The use of group techniques. *American Journal of Orthopsychiatry, 48,* 263–272.

Meyerowitz, J., & Feldman, H. (1966). Transition to parenthood. *Psychiatric Research Reports, 20,* 78–84.

Moore, C. W. (1986). *The mediation process: Practical strategies for resolving conflict.* San Francisco, CA: Jossey–Bass.

Newman, H. M., & Langer, E. J. (1981). Post-divorce adaptation and the attribution of responsibility. *Sex Roles, 7,* 223–232.

Noller, P., & Fitzpatrick, M. A. (Eds.). (1988). *Perspectives on marital interaction.* Clevedon, England: Multilingual Matters Ltd.

Norton, A. J., & Glick, P. C. (1976). Marital instability: Past, present, and future. *Journal of Social Issues, 32,* 5–20.

Nussbaum, J. F. (1983). Relational closeness of elderly interaction: Implications for life satisfaction. *Western Journal of Speech Communication, 47,* 229–243.

O'Brien, J. E. (1972). *Interrelationship of conflict and satisfaction in unstable marriages: A methodological analysis.* Paper presented at the American Sociological Association convention, New Orleans.

Parke, R. D., & Sawin, D. B. (1976). The father's role in infancy" A re-evaluation. *The Family Coordinator, 25,* 365–371.

Parke, R. D., & Tinsley, B. R. (1984). Fatherhood: Historical and contemporary perspectives. In D. A. McCluskey & H. W. Reese (Eds.), *Life-span developmental psychology: Historical and generational effects* (pp. 203–248). New York: Academic Press.

Parron, E. (1978). *An exploratory study of intimacy in golden wedding couples.* Unpublished masters thesis, Rutgers University.

Pleck, J. H. (1983). Husbands' paid work and family roles: Current research issues. In H. Z. Lopata & J. H. Pleck (Eds.), *Research on the interweave of social roles, Vol. 3: Families and jobs* (pp. 251–333). Greenwich, CT: J.A.I. Press.

Rands, M. (1988). Precious moments with family members and friends. In R. M. Milardo (Ed.), *Families and social networks* (pp. 127–146). Newbury Park, CA: Sage.

Rands, M., & Levinger, G. (1979). Implicit theories of relationship: An intergenerational study. *Journal of Personality and Social Psychology, 37,* 645–661.

Reedy, M. N. (1977). *Age and sex differences in personal needs and the nature of love: A study of happily married young, middle-aged, and older adult couples.* Unpublished doctoral dissertation, University of Southern California, Los Angeles.

Reisman, J. M. (1981). Adult friendships. In S. Duck & R. Gilmour (Eds.), *Personal relationships* (Vol. 2, pp. 205–230). New York: Academic Press.

Reiss, D. (1981). *The family's construction of reality.* Cambridge, MA: Harvard University Press.

Richardson, M. S., & Kagan, L. (1979). *Social support and the transition to parenthood.* Paper presented at the American Psychological Association convention, New York.

Rodgers, R. H. (1987). Postmarital reorganization of family relationships. In D. Perlman & S. Duck (Eds.), *Intimate relationships: Development, dynamics, deterioration* (pp. 239–268). Beverly Hills, CA: Sage Publications.

Rollins, B., & Feldman, H. (1970). Marital satisfaction over the family life cycle. *Journal of Marriage and the Family, 32,* 20–28.

Rollins, B. C., & Galligan, R. (1978). The developing child and marital satisfaction of parents. In R. M. Lerner & G. B. Spanier (Eds.), *Child influences on marital and family interaction: A life-span perspective* (pp. 71–105). New York: Academic Press.

Rosenbaum, J., & Rosenbaum, V. (1978). *Stepparenting.* New York: E.P. Dutton.

Rubin, L. B. (1979). *Women of a certain age.* New York: Harper & Row.

Scanzoni, J., & Szinovacz, M. (1980). *Family decision-making: A developmental sex role model.* Beverly Hills: Sage Publications.

Sillars, A. L. (in press). Communication, uncertainty and understanding in marriage. In B. Dervin, L. Grossberg, B. O'Keefe, & E. Wartella (Eds.), *Rethinking communication: Vol. 2. Paradigm exemplars.* Newbury Park, CA: Sage.

Sillars, A. L., & Kalbflesch, P. J. (in press). Implicit and explicit decision making styles in couples. In D. Brinberg & J. Jaccard (Eds.), *Dyadic decision making.* New York: Springer–Verlag.

Sillars, A. L., & Weisberg, J. (1987). Conflict as a social skill. In M. E. Roloff & G. R. Miller (Eds.), *Interpersonal processes: New directions in communication research* (pp. 140–171). Newbury Park, CA: Sage.

Sillars, A. L., Wilmot, W. W., & Hocker, J. L. (in press). Communication strategies in conflict and mediation., In J. Wiemann & J. A. Daly (Eds.), *Communicating strategically: Strategies in interpersonal communication.* Hillsdale, NJ: Lawrence Erlbaum Associates.

Simons, R. L. (1984). Specificity and substitution in the social networks of the elderly. *Interpersonal Journal of Aging and Human Development, 18,* 121–139.

Spanier, G. B., & Lewis, R. A. (1980). Marital quality: A review of the seventies. *Journal of Marriage and the Family, 42,* 825–839.

Stinnet, N., Carter, L. M., & Montgomery, J. E. (1972). Older persons' perceptions of their marriages. *Journal of Marriage and the Family, 42,* 825–839.

Strauss, A. (1978). *Negotiations: Varieties, contexts, processes and social order.* San Francisco: Jossey-Bass.

Stueve, C. A., & Gerson, K. (1977). Personal relations across the life cycle. In C. Fischer (Ed.), *Networks and places: Social relations in the urban setting* (pp. 79–98). New York: Free Press.

Swenson, C. H., Eskew, R. W., & Kohlhepp, K. A. (1981). Stage of family life cycle, ego development, and the marriage relationship. *Journal of Marriage and the Family, 43,* 841–53.

Szinovacz, M. E. (1980). Female retirement: Effects on spousal roles and marital adjustment. *Journal of Family Issues, 1,* 423–440.

Tamir, L. M. (1982). *Men in their forties: The transition to middle age.* New York: Springer–Verlag.

Thurnher, M. 1976). Midlife marriage: Sex differences in evaluation and perspectives. *International Journal of Aging and Human Development, 7,* 129–135.

Treas, J., & Van Hilst, A. (1976). Marriage and remarriage rates among old Americans. *Gerontologist, 17,* 132–136.

Troll, J. (1982). *Continuations: Adult development and aging.* Monterey, CA: Brooks–Cole.

Troll, L. E., Miller, S. J., & Atchley, R. C. (1979). *Families in later life.* Belmont, CA: Wadsworth.

Troll, L., & Smith, J. (1976). Attachmenot through the life span: Some questions about dyadic relations in later life. *Human Development, 3,* 156–171.

Visher, E. B., & Visher, J. S. (1978). Common problems of stepparents and their spouses. *American Journal of Orthopsychiatry, 48,* 252–262.

Walker, K. N., & Messinger, L. (1979). Remarriage after divorce: Dissolution and reconstruction of family boundaries. *Journal of Family Process, 18,* 185–192.

Waller, W. (1938). *The family: A dynamic interpretation.* New York: Cordon.

Watzlawick, P., Beavin, J., & Jackson, D. D. (1967). *Pragmatics of human communication: A study of interactional patterns, pathologies and paradoxes.* New York: Norton.

Weick, K. E. (1971). Group processes, family processes, and problem solving. In J. Aldous, T. Condon, R. Hill, M. Straus & I. Tallman (Eds.), *Family problem solving: A symposium of theoretical, methodological and substantive concerns* (pp.3–54). Hinsdale, IL: Dryden Press.

Weisberg, J. (1983). *Communication in blended families.* Unpublished manuscript, Ohio State University.

Weiss, R. S. (1975). *Marital separation.* New York: Basic Books.

Wilmot, W. W. (1987). *Dyadic communication* (3rd ed.). New York: Random House.

Wilmot, W. W., Carbaugh, D. A., & Baxter, L. A. (1985). Communicative strategies used to terminate romantic relationships. *Western Journal of Speech Communication, 49,* 204–216.

Zietlow, P. H. (1986). *An analysis of the communication behaviors, understanding, self-disclosure, sex roles, and marital satisfaction of elderly couples and couples in earlier life stages.* Unpublished doctoral dissertation, Ohio State University.

Zietlow, P. H., & Sillars, A. L. (1988). Life stage differences in communication during marital conflicts. *Journal of Social and Personal Relationships, 5,* 223–245.

PART III

THE ELDERLY

13 The Grandparent–Grandchild Relationship

Valerie Cryer Downs, PhD
California State University, Long Beach

Research indicates that both grandparents and grandchildren derive varying degrees of satisfaction from interaction within this dyad. Some grandparents report a sense of continuity, and some grandchildren a sense of "self-identity," through grandparents' self-disclosure of oral history through narrative. Grandparents and grandchildren who have the opportunity for frequent interaction express feelings of closeness within the relationship. However, frustration and anger are often reported by both grandparents and grandchildren who do not have the opportunity for such interaction. Factors such as age of grandparents and grandchildren, gender, and kin position, appear to impact the opportunity for interaction, and perceived closeness within this unique relationship. The following review of literature is intended to further explicate what is currently known about grandparents and grandchildren.

GRANDPARENTS–GRANDCHILD RELATIONSHIPS

Introduction

In the presence of grandparent and grandchild, past and future merge into the present (Mead, 1972, p. 282).

Experience is shared through communication. This sharing of experiences has been described as the means by which individuals develop a sense of continuity and identity relating past events to present experience

257

(Mead, 1970, 1974). The family is the most ubiquitous context in which the sharing of experience takes place (Bochner, 1976).

The family can be described as a communicative system (Jackson, 1965). Individuals within the family system are interdependent in that the actions of one family member affect others within that system. The family system, however, consists not only of individuals within the traditional nuclear family group but extended family members, such as grandparents, as well (Beresford & Rivlin, 1969; Sussman, 1985). In fact, grandchildren perceive the role of grandparents as an integral part of the family system. For example, Kornhaber and Woodward (1981) described grandparents as family historians, mentors, wizards, nurturers, and role models for grandchildren. These roles are carried out by sharing stories of past experiences, for "in this way, a grandparent's stories become part of the child's own life story" (Kornhaber & Woodward, 1981, p. 168).

Unfortunately, families that function under what Kornhaber (1985) and Kornhaber and Woodward (1981) described as "the new social contract" often overlook the value of interaction between grandparents and grandchildren. Families are more mobile, and members of these families more independent than in the past (Beresford & Rivlin 1969). Not only do families move away from grandparents, but often grandparents move away from grandchildren as they themselves enter into retirement (Kornhaber & Woodward, 1981). Thus, there is potential for ambiguity or ambivalence associated with the grandparent role as it remains undefined within the particular family system (Wood, 1982). For example, one grandfather reported a great deal of frustration in knowing he had information and stories to share about the past, but infrequent visits with his grandchildren did not afford him the opportunity to do so:

> I get angry . . . or maybe it hurts. I can't give what I've got. I don't have the opportunity to pass it on, the funny stories. I'm not giving these youngsters what I should be passing on, what my grandfather passed on to me. I've still got it inside of me. What do I do with it when I'm gone? What will happen to the stories that he told me?" (Kornhaber & Woodward, 1981, p. 112).

Obviously, this type of communication holds a great deal of importance for some grandparents. Further, grandchildren who have the opportunity for frequent contact with grandparents report that stories of the past are a source of information or advice in dealing with their own life experiences. These stories provide a sense of continuity or identity with family history (Baranowski, 1982; Boyd, 1969; Kornhaber &

Woodward, 1981; Mead, 1970, 1974). Further, interaction affords both grandparents and grandchildren the opportunity to develop and maintain a meaningful relationship, for, in the words of Homans (1950), "the more frequently persons interact with one another, the greater in general is their affection for one another" (p. 242).

Titchener, D'Zmura, Golden, and Emerson (1963) suggested "we can see how certain necessities of the family's adaptation impair or enhance the development of identity through stages of maturation and how communicative and perceptual patterns impair or enhance the depth and clarity of the sense of identity" (p. 116). Further, Gilbert (1976) proposed that "identification and confirmation of self is one of the singularly most important functions of human communication, and that through it, family members are affirmed as 'human' and assigned status in social systems" (p. 225). Thus, interpersonal communication within the family context appears to be an integral component of family functioning and relational development.

Parent–child interaction within the family context, and specifically interaction within the mother–child dyad, is considered by many to be "the critical factor in the young (child's) organism's development" (Lewis, 1984, p. 1). However, Lewis (1984) suggested that other individuals, such as grandparents, contribute to the young child's learning and development. For example, Tinsley and Parke (1984) described grandparents' interaction with grandchildren as having both a direct and indirect influence on child development. Directly, grandparents can involve themselves through participation in recreation and child care. Indirectly, grandparents may provide a model of the aging process and the grandparental role. According to Perlmutter and Hall (1985) "the relationship a grandchild develops with a grandparent stretches far into the future, for it appears that the way the child experiences this relationship affects the way he or she relates to grandchildren half a century later" (p. 368).

Tinsley and Parke (1984) identify other reasons that demonstrate the need for research into the grandparent–grandchild relationship. In addition to evidence suggesting the influence of extended family members on child development, these researchers emphasize the need for life-span perspective of family functioning. In other words, "a life-span perspective alerts us to the changes that may ensue across adult development, which in turn, may alter the potential quality of the contribution that grandparents may make to the child's development" (Tinsley & Parke, 1984, p. 165). As the individuals within this relationship mature and/or change, the relationship also changes and develops. "Family members are continuously changing" and, in part, this change is in response to interaction with each other (Troll & Bengtson, 1979, p. 129). Thus, the interdependent nature of members within the family system is evidenced.

The Grandparent–Grandchild Dyad

The grandparent–grandchild relationship is characteristic of a communicative system, and thus, clearly exhibits potential for the analysis of interpersonal communication. For example, the grandparent–grandchild dyad is unique (Wilmot, 1979): It consists of individuals from two distinct generations of family lineage (Troll & Bengtson, 1979). Individuals within the relationship cannot be duplicated or replaced without the dyad being destroyed. In addition, the grandparent–grandchild dyad is an example of an ongoing interpersonal relationship often found within the family context (Jackson, 1965). Matthews and Sprey (1984) suggested that in order to fully understand grandparenthood, it must be investigated "within the structural context of extended family systems" (p. 46). Grandparents also represent significant others within the child's context of family relationships (Robins & Tomanec, 1962; Wilder, 1978). Consequently, grandparents are a valuable source of education and mediation in the life experiences of children (Leichter, 1979).

Interaction within the grandparent–grandchild relationship provides the opportunity for communicating ideas, information, and experiences that are available from no other source. Communication with significant others, and specifically grandparents, provides a context for the development of identity and self-confirmation as proposed by Ruesch (1951a); Ruesch and Bateson (1949); Titchener et al., (1963); and continuity for grandparents as described by Baranowski (1982); Cohler and Grunebaum (1981); Gilbert (1976); and Mead (1970, 1974).

In addition, the grandparent–grandchild relationship provides a viable example of the life-span perspective of family relationships (Tinsley & Parke, 1984). Statistics indicate that the life expectancy of women has increased almost 31 years (for men approximately 23 years) over the past two decades. Consequently, approximately 11% of men and women in the United States are 65 years or older, 70% of whom are grandparents (Ramirez Barranti, 1985). As a result, the chances of a child having at least two living grandparents is approximately 50%. Thus, both grandparents and grandchildren will have the experience of being grandparents and grandchildren for longer periods during their lifetimes (Tinsley & Parke, 1984; Von Hentig, 1945/1946).

Changing societal norms, mobility, economic status, and the middle generation have a definitive impact on the development and maintenance of the grandparent–grandchild relationship. According to Troll and Bengtson (1979):

"The generational process within the family simultaneously exerts an influence upon and is influenced by, the generational process in individual development throughout the course of life as well as by the succession of age cohorts in the larger society. Development of each individual in the family lineage as well as changes in the society to which the family belongs, are both intricately related to cross-generational relationships within the family" (p. 127).

The grandparent–grandchild relationship is not voluntary. The diversity of ages at which individuals become grandparents, in addition to the unacceptability of traditional "old age" behaviors associated with the grandparent role, have created the potential for a degree of ambiguity and ambivalence in becoming a grandparent (Wood, 1982). As a result, styles and roles of grandparenting manifested by older adults are a reflection of their age and desire to become involved in the grandparent role (Neugarten & Weinstein, 1964, 1968). Kahana and Coe (1969) described grandparenthood as an achieved rather than ascribed role because of the lack of prescription or definition of the role within our culture. However, Baranowski (1982), Kornhaber and Woodward (1981), and Mead (1974) place a great deal of importance on grandparent–grandchild interaction for the developing grandchild. They link emotional well-being, cultural and historical awareness, and the development of self-identity with intergenerational family relationships. Children lacking in this interaction, therefore, are perhaps deprived of the experience, nurturance, and support often associated with the grandparent–grandchild relationship.

Early investigations into the nature of the grandparent–grandchild dyad focused primarily on the enjoyable aspects of the relationship for grandparents. Specifically, grandparents reported a "pleasure without responsibility" orientation in their role as grandparent (Albrecht, 1954; Apple, 1956). In more recent investigations grandparents have been found, in some cases, to take a more participative approach to the upbringing of grandchildren especially in situations of divorce (Beal, 1979; Blau, 1984; Johnson, 1985; Wilson & DeShane, 1982), surrogate childcare (Updegraff, 1968), low socioeconomic status (Claven, 1978), or in Black communities (Hays & Mindel, 1973; Stack, 1974). According to Roebuck (1983), "contrary to the popular vision which sees grandparents playing a major role in past times and a decreasing role in the family of the present, grandma is much more of a living presence in the lives of her grandchildren now than she ever was in the past" (p. 257).

Ramirez Barranti (1985) suggested that "grandparents expand the age range and number of available adult role models for family members, providing children a resource beyond their parents with which to identify and to learn" (p. 350). For example, Kornhaber and Woodward (1981) concluded that grandparents provide children with a valuable role model for aging and grandparenting. However, Troll and Bengtson (1979) described a number of generational factors that may impact grandparents' roles in family functioning. Specifically, grandparents' attitudes toward their own life situations, their age cohort, and relations with their children largely determine the influence they have in their grandchildren's lives. Kornhaber (1985), and Kornhaber and Woodward (1981) described factors such as these as resulting from the "new social contract" implicit in family functioning. However, even in today's age of alleged family disintegration, grandparents remain a stabilizing force; they function as an "effective mechanism of group survival" (Von Hentig, 1945/1946, p. 392).

GRANDPARENTS AND GRANDCHILDREN

Grandparents

According to Hagestad (1985), "in a society where grandparents range in age from 30 to 110, and grandchildren range from newborns to retirees, we should not be surprised to find a wide variety of grandparenting styles" (p. 36). The onset of grandparenthood is not voluntary, and often parents are unprepared to accept a family position of grandparent that has been traditionally associated with old age even though many persons become grandparents when they are quite young (Johnson, 1983). Thus, the diversity of ages at which individuals become grandparents, in addition to the unacceptability of traditional old-age behaviors associated with the grandparental role, have created the potential for ambivalence associated with the role of grandparent (Johnson, 1983; Wood, 1982). Smith (1965), for example, emphasized that grandparenthood should not be equated with being "aged" as "grandparenthood often arrives at middle age" (p. 156).

Age, categorized by over 65 and under 65, is a strong predictor of the participation of grandparents in family life (Johnson, 1985). In a recent investigation, younger grandparents (45–65 years of age) consistently reported greater responsibility for discipline, child care, and offering advice than older grandparents (over 70) (Thomas, 1986). These feelings of responsibility were attributed to the recency with which younger grandparents had enacted the parental role in addition to the younger age of the parents and relative lack of experience in child care. Neugarten and Weinstein (1968), while evaluating the degree of comfort in and significance of the grandparental role, identified styles that characterize grandparenthood. Ironically, the most frequently reported styles were those of fun seeker (described as informal and playful) and distant figure (emerging on holidays and special occasions). The former was characterized by frequent and satisfying interaction, the latter by infrequent and somewhat symbolic interaction.

Within the same study, the significance and meaning of the grandparental role were also investigated. For some individuals, the significance of grandparenthood "constituted a source of biological renewal . . . and continuity" (Neugarten & Weinstein, 1968, p. 282). These grandparents expressed feelings of youthfulness and confidence that their lives would continue through their grandchildren. Others described their role as that of a resource person for financial assistance or "offering the benefit of the grandparent's unique life experience" (Neugarten & Weinstein, 1968, p. 283). In this way, grandparents reported that they contributed to the grandchild's welfare. In addition, some grandparents noted that their grandchildren were able to accomplish things that they were unable to accomplish in their own lifetimes.

Similar results were reported by Crawford (1981). In this investigation, grandparents reported a sense of biological renewal and continuation of the family through their relations with grandchildren. In addition, they acknowledged "emotional self-fulfillment and a chance of vicarious achievement" through interaction with grandchildren (Crawford, 1981, p. 501). On the other hand, Neugarten and Weinstein (1968) found that "27% of the grandmothers and 29% of the grandfathers reported feeling relatively remote from their grandchildren and acknowledged relatively little effect of grandparenthood in their own lives" (p. 283). This lack of effect is often attributed to strained relations with children (Neugarten & Weinstein, 1964, 1968).

Bengtson (1985) refers to diverse and symbolic aspects of grandparenting. Diversity describes the numerous and various social roles associated with grandparenthood (e.g., differences in age, sex, ethnic backgrounds). Symbolic aspects are those behaviors that grandparents seem to perform, primarily in relation to "being there" for other family members. For example, grandparents provide a buffer against fears of mortality felt by the parent generation. Upon the loss of grandparents, the second generation becomes the elder (and perhaps grandparents themselves), and are forced to face the characteristics associated with the onset of old age. A second aspect of "being there" is expressed by mere presence and the fact that parents still have their parents to turn to in time of stress or hardship (Bengtson, 1985; Hagestad, 1985). This aspect of "being there" can vary, however, according to the quality of the parent–child relationship prior to expressed need in relation to proximity, long-term commitment, and prior degree of intimacy (Johnson, 1983).

In the role of "family national guard," Bengtson (1985) described grandparents as having the capacity to provide their children with needed aid and care. This is a role that may be exchanged, however, as the resources and capabilities of grandparents become more limited. Morgan (1981) argued that aging is characterized by changing dependencies. Children are dependent upon parents, who as they age, depend upon their children. Ironically, at the same time elderly persons may be experiencing other losses (such as death of spouse or friends). They may also lose their independence and become more dependent upon their children. Although many elderly individuals prefer to remain independent, declining health can often change the status of dependency. Dependency on children is not a source of satisfaction for the elderly (Morgan, 1981).

According to Bengtson (1985), grandparents as elders can also be negotiators and transmitters of information, values, and attitudes. Bengtson and Kuypers (1971) described the need for transmission of similar values or beliefs as the generational stake. Younger individuals in their late teens or early 20s tend to emphasize differences between the generations rather than identifying similiarities. For example, Thompson, Clark, and Gunn (1985) found that parents perceive greater continuity (similarity) between generations than their children. However, the transmission of similar attitudes and values provides a degree of satisfaction for the older generation, much like the biological continuity described by Neugarten and Weinstein (1968).

Troll (1972) reported more similarity in values in relation to humanitarianism, moralism, and intellectualism between parent and child generations than among peers. These results indicate that transmission of values may be taking place. In addition, Troll (1971) found a moderate amount of similarity between grandparents and grandchildren in the areas of values and occupations. According to Troll (1971), "the possibility that the child models himself after grandparents as well as parents, or that at least patterns of behavior are transmitted by a modeling process from parent to child in succeeding generations, can lead logically to the possibility of continued modeling and socialization throughout adulthood" (p. 279).

Kivnick (1985) suggested that the meaning of grandparenting can be conceptualized along a set of dimensions. The dimensions identified by

Kivnick (1985) are descriptive of grandparents' conceptualization of the grandparental role. The dimensions are described as centrality, valued elder, immortality through clan, reinvolvement with personal past, and indulgence. Kivnick emphasized, however, that the meaning of grandparenthood is experienced individually; that is, with varying degrees on each dimension. The importance of each dimension for the individual may change as each individual ages. Johnson (1983) also emphasized the idiosyncratic nature of the grandparent experience, especially in relation to age.

The five styles of grandparenting described by Cherlin and Furstenberg (1985) are detached, passive, supportive, authoritative, and influential. In their investigation of a sample of grandparents with teenaged grandchildren aged 13–17, these researchers examined clusters of behaviors reported by grandparents as characteristic of their interaction with grandchildren. Although the sample was mostly female and somewhat older than average due to the older age of the grandchild, it was considered representative of that particular population. Subjects were requested to respond to questions regarding quantity of interaction with grandchildren (In the past 12 months, how often have you seen *the child?* In addition, questions regarding the quality or content of the interaction (Over the past 12 months, has *the child* asked you for your help with something?/Have you asked *the child* for help with something?) were asked. Questions regarding discipline and decision making were included.

Results of this investigation suggest the "detached" grandparent is older and emotionally distanced from the grandchild. The "passive" grandparent is described as minimally involved although able to interact frequently with the grandchild. An "influential" grandparent is frequently involved with the grandchild, often acting as surrogate parent. Those dimensions described as supportive or authoritative were most likely to be associated with grandfathers "reflecting typically male patterns of relating to family members" (Cherlin & Furstenberg, 1985, p. 105). The authors caution, however, that the sample contained a small number of grandfather respondents and may not be representative of all populations.

Robertson (1977) investigated types of grandparental roles internalized by grandmothers. Not surprisingly, as in other investigations, various grandparental types emerged reflecting the significance of the grandmother role for older women. Specifically, the grandmother types found were strongly related to individual life style, forms of activity between grandparent and grandchild, and the "enjoyable" nature of interaction with grandchildren. For example, grandmothers who infrequently interact with grandchildren were classified as "remote" in their role as grandparent. On the other hand, grandmothers who participated in frequent interaction were "apportioned" in their distribution of time spent with grandchildren. The types of grandmother roles that emerged were strongly related to educational level, marital status, employment status, and age of grandmother.

The Influence of Gender and Kin position

Research indicates there are differences between grandmothers and grandfathers and their perceptions of grandparenting. According to Nye and Berado (1981), these differences may be attributed to the fact that women undergo "anticipatory socialization" in preparation for the grandparental role (p. 328). In this way, grandmothers are more likely to develop a grandmother self-image prior to the birth of their grandchildren. The resulting satisfaction with the grandparental role is often affected. For example, in a recent investigation, grandmothers reported significantly higher satisfaction with grandparenting than grandfathers (Downs, 1988). However, grandfathers report significantly higher responsibility for child care and offering child-rearing advice than grandmothers (Thomas, 1986). Grandfathers often assume a "masculinized grandmother role involving such maternal tasks as feeding the grandchildren and babysitting for them" (Nye & Berardo, 981, p. 329). There are no significant differences between grandfathers and grandmothers, however, in relation to perceived responsibility for disciplining or helping grandchildren (Thomas, 1986).

Kivett (1985), while investigating relations between grandfathers and grandchildren, found that grandfathers most frequently interact with grandchildren who are closest geographically, and who are "the offspring of the adult child with whom there was also the most contact" (p. 567). Further, these grandfathers reported that grandchildren should assist grandparents financially; however, less than 20% of the grandfathers in this sample were receiving such assistance from grandchildren.

Research also indicates that grandfathers are relatively uninvolved in their role as grandparent (Hader, 1965; Hagestad, 1985; Neugarten & Weinstein, 1964). Hader (1965) suggested that perhaps one reason for the alleged lack of grandfather involvement may be the higher rate of male mortality. Perhaps for the grandfather, maintaining distance from grandchildren is essential for protecting the grandchild from experiencing the death of a significant other at a young age. Hagestad (1985) described this lack of involvement in terms of the "instrumental" versus "expressive" domains of interpersonal relationships. Whereas grandmothers tend to discuss subjects of emotional or relational content with their grandchildren, grandfathers often communicate in terms of practical aspects of the issues being discussed—often to the point of having certain issues identified as "subjects not to discuss with grandpa." Grandfathers also appear to be more involved with grandsons; grandmothers more involved with granddaughters (Hagestad, 1985).

Differences are also noted between maternal and paternal sets of grandparents and their relationships with grandchildren (Johnson, 1985). For example, Kahana and Kahana (1970) reported that grandchildren tend to favor maternal grandmothers because maternal grandmothers tend to indulge young children. Adult children also expressed feeling significantly closer emotionally to their maternal grandparents. Further, this emotional closeness was described as being even stronger toward the maternal grandmother than the paternal grandmother (Hoffman, 1979). Hartshorne and Manaster (1982) found that, among a high school student sample, visitations took place more frequently with maternal grandmothers than with paternal grandparents.

Crase and Hendrickson (1968) investigated preteen perceptions of maternal grandmothers and child-rearing practices. Results of this investigation indicated that preteen grandchildren perceive grandmothers as more permissive and "child-oriented" than their own mothers.

Although maternal grandmothers are more often integrated into family activity, the relationship with the grandchild remains primarily a symbolic one "depicted as old endeared family members who are central figures in family portraits" (Fischer, 1983, p. 67). Ambiguity associated with the grandparental role is further magnified by paternal grandparenthood (Fischer, 1983).

Matthews and Sprey (1985) concluded that grandchildrens' relationships with their grandparents must be considered as particularistic relationships rather than generalized cases. More specifically, grandchildren interviewed in this study suggested that "knowing" grandparents is not equivalent to "feeling close to" grandparents. This difference is largely determined by other relationships within the family context. For example, mothers' relationships with parents and in-laws, and fathers' relationships with parents and in-laws may impact the opportunity for grandparents and grandchildren to interact (Sprey & Matthews, 1982). Matthews and Sprey (1985) concluded that "close bonds between grandchildren and their paternal grandmothers are facilitated first, by the father's being perceived as close to his mother; second, by the mother's beingperceived as close to her mother-in-law" (p. 624). Further, "close bonds with the maternal grandmother are not dependent on these factors" (p. 624). This is perhaps due, once again, to the maternal kinkeeping function: Women are more likely to maintain family ties.

Difficulties within the grandparent–grandchild relationship often result from conflicts between intervening generations, in-law problems, and geographical separation resulting from family mobility (Albrecht,

1954). Robertson (1975) developed a theoretical perspective that further explicates the mediational function of parents in the grandparent–grandchild relationship. First, she suggested that when parents view grandparenthood as a meaningful role for their children, they encourage grandparent–grandchild interaction. If not, they are unlikely to encourage visitation or frequent interaction. Second, types of interaction are usually mediated by parents. For example, babysitting and home recreational activities may be allowed, but in moderation. Third, babysitting and home recreation are most frequently initiated by parents and grandchildren, other types of activities by grandparents.

Johnson (1985) described the role of grandparents in divorcing families. She suggested that grandparents are often the stabilizing force in children's lives when grandchildren are experiencing the divorce of their parents. According to Von Hentig (1945/1946) "grandparents, and especially grandmothers, reassume a sociological function the moment a gap has to be filled and missing members of the intermediary generation have to be replaced" (p. 389). The differences between maternal and paternal grandparents are also more defined depending upon the assigned custody of children after a divorce. Although maternal grandparents often continue interacting with grandchildren as before (via the kinkeeping function previously described) paternal grandparents must make special efforts to maintain contact with grandchildren. Johnson and Barer (1987) reported that paternal grandmotherhood remains an important role for grandmothers following a divorce because "a former daughter-in-law is no longer a son's wife, but she is still the mother of her grandchildren" (p. 334).

Differing perceptions of family obligations and rights in divorcing families, in addition to parents' desire for autonomy and independence, affect grandparents continued interaction with grandchildren after divorce (Johnson, 1985). In some cases, grandparents experience ambiguity in deciding upon the amount and type of assistance to be offered in situations of divorce (Johnson, 1983). Sometimes grandparents maintain a "hands-off" perspective regarding attention to grandchildren during their children's divorce. For example, Cherlin and Furstenberg (1986) concluded that grandparents are not frequently called upon for child care or assistance in divorcing families. As a result, some grandchildren do not have the stabilizing experience of grandparent–grandchild interaction during the divorce of their parents. Derdeyn (1985) described visits with grandparents as "a precious part of a child's experience" which should not be terminated following his or her parents' divorce (p. 285). On the contrary, "continuing contact between grandparents and grandchildren is an invaluable part of the course of family life," which often provides a positive influence in an otherwise negative family environment (Derdeyn, 1985, p. 285).

Many researchers encourage investigations into the cultural and social implications of the grandparent–grandchild relationship. For example, much of the research presented in this review focuses on grandparents within White, middle-class families. As Stack (1974) has demonstrated, however, Black families have a matriarchal focus and members usually remain in close geographical proximity. Thus, Black grandmothers frequently play a more integral role in family functions such as child care and discipline.

Clavan (1978) also concluded that among low socioeconomic groups, the maternal grandmother is more integrated into everyday family life. Maternal grandmothers in Black families often accept responsibility for care giving, especially in instances where mothers are employed. This is further illustrated by Stack (1974) in her work with kin networks in Black communities. Grandparents, and primarily the maternal grandmother, are integral in providing security and consistency in the lives of Black families. Hays and Mindel (1973) found that the extended kin networks (e.g., grandparents) are a more "salinet structure" for Black families than White families (P. 51). Thus, interaction within this network contributes to greater family cohesion and a more supportive family structure, that provides aid and comfort to family members when needed.

Grandchildren

Research investigating children's attitudes toward aging has produced conflicting results. For example, Bekker and Taylor (1966) suggested that children with grandparents and great-grandparents demonstrate less prejudice toward old age than children who have no living grandparents. These same results were found by Ivester and King (1977). The more favorable attitude toward the aged was also attributed to more awareness of the status of the elderly in our society (Ivester & King, 1977). In addition, Thomas and Yamomoto (1975) in their analysis of children's perceptions of older persons, found that children in 6th, 8th, 10th, and 12th grades demonstrated an absence of negative attitudes toward old age. Isaacs (1986) concluded that 4-year-old children demonstrate less age prejudice than their 6- and 8-year-old counterparts when describing the "life stories" of individuals of different ages pictured in photographs. Britton and Britton (1968) also found that young children were unable to differentiate age groups beyond the young-adult level.

In contrast, however, Burke (1982) found that children aged 4–7 years, who had limited contact with older adults, demonstrated stereotypical imagery of the elderly in addition to expressing concern over growing old themselves. Adolescents and middle-aged adults were found to reflect stereotypical attitudes with unknown, and nonstereotypical attitudes with known, older adults (Luszcz, 1985). Doka (1985/1986) found that programs of interaction for young and old people, although enhancing young people's perceptions of the elderly, failed to reduce stereotypical images of elderly persons. According to Troll (1971), however, frequent interaction with older persons tends to reduce age prejudice and stereotypical imagery of the elderly. For example, Hickey, Hickey, and Kalish (1968) concluded that interaction with older significant adults directly affects the development of perceptions of and attitudes toward the aged.

According to Kahana and Kahana (1970), children's perceptions of grandparents appear to vary with the age or developmental stage of the grandchild, and these perceptions serve as a basis for attitude and stereotype formation about adults and the aged. By investigating three age groups (4–5 years, 8–9 years, and 11–12 years), these researchers found that "children's views of grandparents parallelled developmental cognitive changes ranging from concrete perceptions of physical characteristics by the youngest children, through functional views of behaviors in the middle group, and finally to the emergence of an abstract interpersonal orientation among the oldest children" (Kahana & Kahana, 1970, p. 98). These results were equated with Piaget's (1954) views of learning. Whereas young children demonstrate less concrete thinking than children in middle age groups, children in middle and older age groups are more likely to approach formal operations in thinking. Thus, younger children more frequently describe their relationships with grandparents in terms of gift giving and play, whereas older children reflect upon the relational elements of their interaction with grandparents (Kahana & Kahana, 1970).

Robertson (1976) concluded that grandchildren (young adults aged 18–26) do not perceive their grandparents to be out of touch or old-fashioned. In addition, grandchildren in this study reported feeling a responsibility toward grandparents in relation to emotional support and providing help when needed. Subjects also indicated they felt that their grandparents were more like friends and had a great deal of influence in their lives. Although these grandchildren indicated they would appreciate frequent interaction with their grandparents, they concluded their grandparents would probably prefer interacting with their own friends and peers. In the Robertson study, interaction between grandparents and grandchildren was measured from a qualitative perspective (e.g., topics of discussion, evaluations of emotional closeness) rather than quantitative accounts of number of visits per designated time period.

In an investigation of college students' relationships with grandparents, Hartshorne and Manaster (1982) found that the grandparent–

grandchild relationship was considered important in the lives of these young adults. In addition, these subjects noted that, although geographical distance was a factor, they would prefer more frequent contact with grandparents. Cherlin and Furstenberg (1986) found that grandparents played an important role for grandchildren when they lived close by and were actively involved with the family on a day-to-day basis. These types of "valued grandparents" are also described as individuals with whom grandchildren enjoy interacting and learning, and who are usually accepting of change and adaptable to new situations (Boyd, 1969).

Family elders also represent wisdom and experience to younger generations (Aldous, 1965). Baranowski (1982), for example, concluded that grandparent–grandchild relationships were a source of important influence and learning for grandchildren. In an analysis of the grandparent–grandchild dyad, he found that grandparents provided a source of identity development, improved relationships with parents, and positive attitudes toward aging.

GRANDPARENTS AND GRANDCHILDREN: COMMUNICATION AND CONTINUITY BETWEEN GENERATIONS

Grandparents appear to adopt a variety of grandparenting styles, which are largely dependent upon their perception of the grandparental role and perhaps the age at which they become grandparents. In addition, differences have emerged regarding grandchildren and their relationships with grandmothers and grandfathers, and maternal and paternal grandparents. Because of the diversity of styles and perceptions of interaction with grandchildren, for some grandparents there is potential for ambiguity and ambivalence associated with the grandparental role (Wood, 1982). However, according to Hader (1965),

"it seems obvious that the grandparent can serve a modulating function of significance in view of both their presence and concern and real position of objectivity and experience. They can fulfill and be fulfilled. The goal of thoughtful involvement containing an appropriate degree of emotion by the elderly with their younger relatives should be studied and encouraged. Their potential for significant relating of a positive and cognitive type is illustrated by review of the literature as well as clinical example. It is important for us as researchers and interested professionals to be aware of these probabilities and to encourage some of the elderly to recognize their necessary roles" (p. 238).

Contrary to this ideology, however, Kornhaber (1985) described grandparents as having "turned their backs" on a whole generation. Grandparents no longer function within the traditional role described by our culture and the media. In many instances, grandparents are not 65 years of age or older as is expected in our culture. On the contrary, individuals who are grandparents range in age from their early 30s to 120. According to Wood and Robertson (1976) "grandparenthood has become a middle-age rather than old-age phenomenon" (p. 279).

Increased life expectancy (primarily for women) affords grandparents the opportunity to see grandchildren reach maturity, the birth of great-grandchildren, and sometimes great-great grandchildren (Troll, 1983). Grandparents often remain active in their own career and work roles or enjoy many years of retirement (Troll, 1985). For these individuals, grandparenting is described as a secondary activity (Aldous, 1985). Kornhaber and Woodward (1981) identified these grandparents as characteristic of family members who function under the "new social contract."

In an intensive investigation of more than 300 grandparent–grandchild dyads, Kornhaber and Woodward (1981) found effects of the "new social contract" on the relationship between grandparents and grandchildren. "Under the terms of the new social contract, no one is obliged to anyone else" (p. 97). Specifically, implicit rules regarding financial or emotional support, interaction, and family roles often prevent the development of emotional bonds characteristic of those within extended family relationships. Although grandparents often accept the role of distant relative (geographically and emotionally), they convey feeling of frustration with the lack of opportunity to interact with grandchildren. For example, this study found that grandparents demonstrated "feelings of regret . . . for the failure to pass on more of the family heritage to their grandchildren" (Kornhaber & Woodward, 1981, p. 75).

Grandchildren who reported infrequent visits with grandparents also expressed frustration and anger at being separated from them. Kornhaber and Woodward (1981) suggested that, as a result of infrequent interaction with grandparents, "these children possessed no knowledge of ancestry, no sense of bloodline . . . and no sense of the future as older people" (Kornhaber & Woodward, 1981, p. 42). On the other hand, grandparents and grandchildren who have the opportunity for frequent interaction disclosed considerable satisfaction and significance associated with the relationship. These feelings of satisfaction and significance are termed the *vital connection* between grandparents and grandchildren (Kornhaber & Woodward, 1981). The vital connection is a combination of factors including time and place, commitment to family, and altruism. Time and place refer to the opportunity to interact. Commitment to family refers to "a sense of family history and heritage and is rooted in the conviction that ties to family take emotional precedence over ties to society" (Kornhaber & Woodward, 1981, p. 70). For example, many of the grandparents in this investigation expressed a need to convey information about family history and past experience: as advice to grandchildren, as instilling a sense of identity through intergenerational continuity, and even feelings of "extinction" if the information was not conveyed (Kornhaber & Woodward, 1981).

Grandchildren also indicated a sense of "commitment t family" in learning family history from grandparents. Grandchildren who frequently interacted with grandparents reported that they enjoyed hearing stories about the grandchild's parents as children (Kornaber & Woodward, 1981). Updegraff (1968) found that "the grandmother seems to serve a somewhat modified role in the continuity of generations" by communicating family history or, more frequently, stories of mothers as children (p. 180). Some grandchildren reported that information shared by grandparents functions as advice or models for their behavior (Kornhaber & Woodward, 1981). For example, one 12-year-old grandchild was quoted as saying "Grandmother's easy to talk to about stuff in the past. She knows a lot about long-ago things that help me with the present" (Kornhaber & Woodward, 1981, p. 11).

The final factor characterizing the "vital connection" between generations is altruism, which refers to what Erikson (1959) called generativity or "a concern for establishing and guiding the next generation" (p. 67). Information shared through the "vital connection" appears integral not only to achieving feelings of continuity for grandparents, but social learning for the developing grandchild. Bengtson and Black (1973) concluded that through intergenerational continuity, older generations can adequately prepare younger generations for accepting adult social responsibilities. According to Bengtson and Black (1973), "the problem of generations . . . is to successfully transmit information that enables the young to function effectively in the increasingly complex social positions they encounter in adult life" (p. 208). Further, grandparents play an integral role in building "reasonable connections among our past, present, and future" (Bengtson, 1985, p. 24).

Mead (1974) described continuity as a vital connection between the past, present, and future which is provided, primarily, by interaction between generations. Within the family context, Hagestad (1985) referred to continuity as "a core of sameness transcending time and change" (p. 36). Mead (1974) emphasized that "the strength that comes from a sense of continuity with the past and hope for the future is sorely needed" (p. 248). However, the "absence of grandparents among the upwardly mobile, frequently moving, more prosperous working and middle classes was equally important as it contributed to a shallowness of family style" (Mead, 1974, p. 241). Families that function under the "new social contract," for example, may be lacking in the opportunity to interact and exchange information between generations.

Boyd (1969) described grandparenthood "as a social role that functions to coordinate the familial generations, to maintain family culture" (p. 90). Three factors were identified that influence the development of bonds between generations in the family (Boyd, 1969). First, proximity was reported by four generations of lower-, middle-, and upper-class families as integral to the development and maintenance of intergenerational bonds. Consequently, visitation was also considered important, and specifically, the grandparents' home was described as "an attractive center for family gatherings and vacations" (Boyd, 1969, p. 98). Finally, frequency of interaction between generations was reported as a factor that has the potential to both strengthen and weaken intergenerational bonds. Specifically, it strengthens when the opportunity for interaction was frequent; weakens when it was not. Overall, interaction with grandparents contributes to the strengthening of intergenerational bonds as "the grandparent can organize family functions around common interests and rituals that bring zest and meaning to life and bind the generations together into a closely knit whole" (Boyd, 1969, p. 99).

Grandparents play an integral role in family functioning as "they stimulate discussions of family history and relate interesting and timely anecdotes of bygone days" (Boyd, 1969, p. 98). Hagestad (1985) concluded that "through generational contacts, family members provide one another with bridges to historical times they themselves never knew or have trouble understanding" (p. 32). Mead (1974) described grandparents as maintaining a sense of historical continuity by providing a connection to the past and security about facing the future. Further, many grandparents have been witness to rapid change within our culture (Mead, 1970) and have the ability to make past events more "real" to grandchildren by recounting stories of their participation in those events (Mead, 1974). Thus, "in the presence of grandparent and grandchild, past and future merge into the present" (Mead, 1972, p. 282).

Frequency of intergenerational interaction is viewed by Bengtson, Cutler, Mangen, and Marshall (1985) as "associational solidarity" (p. 318). Specifically, associational solidarity combines aspects of both formal and informal interaction. Formal interaction is produced through occasions such as family reunions and ceremonies; informal interaction by brief visits or discussions. Both forms of interaction function to produce bonds between generations. In addition, associational solidarity is characterized by both direct (face-to-face) and indirect (telephone or mail) interaction. Whether interaction is formal or informal, direct or indirect, these researchers found that intergenerational interaction between grandparents and grandchildren was largely influenced or controlled by parents who function as a "bridge" between the two generations.

Hagestad (1985) noted that interaction between grandparents and grandchildren was also influenced by gender and kin position. Specifically, research indicates that

> the contrast between grandmothers and grandfathers fits Parson's and Bale's (1955) distinction between "instrumental" and 'emotional-expressive' leadership. The older men emphasized task-oriented involvement in spheres outside the family; the women were more likely to emphasize interpersonal dynamics and the quality of ties in the family. (Hagestad, 1985, p. 39)

Basically, this distinction is an indication that grandparents and grandchildren participate in same-sex, rather than cross-sex interaction patterns. Specifically, grandfathers interact more frequently with grandsons; grandmothers with granddaughters. Grandparent–grandchild interaction is also affected by kin position: maternal and paternal grandparenthood. As a result of the maternal kin-keeping function, much of the contact and interaction between generations is organized by women. According to Hagestad (1985), "women bring families together" (p. 41). Thus, more frequent interaction usually takes place between generations of maternal rather than paternal lineage.

CONCLUSION AND IMPLICATIONS

Obviously, interaction within the grandparent–grandchild dyad holds a great deal of value and importance for both grandparents and grandchildren. For grandparents, it provides the opportunity for continuity between generations; to see themselves carry on into the future. For grandchildren, interaction with grandparents provides access to the past and a sense of identity with family history. Given this link between interaction, continuity, and the development of self-identity, various implications for communication research are evident.

First, the grandparent–grandchild relationship must be identified as a viable context for the study of interpersonal communication. Ruesch and Bateson (1949) proposed, for example, that the structure of interpersonal relationships must be defined before communicative processes may be adequately investigated. These theorists suggested that exploring individual perceptions of, and views of, the relationship provides valuable insight into the meaning of the relationship for both participants. Further, information gained through mutual knowledge or agreement within a particular relationship promotes continuity, consistency, and relatedness between members of that system (Ruesch, 1951a). This "interrelatedness is understood best in terms of a system of communication" (p. 13).

Roles are viewed as facilitating the organization or structure of a particular social system. According to Ruesch (1951b), "awareness of a person's role in a social system enables others to guage correctly the meaning of his statements and actions" (p. 27). Thus, examination of the roles enacted within this relationship, as perceived by both grandparents and grandchildren, could provide valuable information regarding the structural nature of this relationship. For example, Neugarten and Weinstein (1964, 1968), and Cherlin and Furstenburg (1985) provided evidence that grandparents do perceive differing roles and responsibilities in their relationships with grandchildren. Further, the degree of significance of grandparenthood varies with respect to the grandparental role manifested by grandparents. Future research could attempt to identify the communicative nature of relational roles and perceived significance of the relationship reported by grandparents.

The opportunity for interaction, frequency of interaction, and factors inhibiting the opportunity for grandparents and grandchildren to interact also warrant investigation. Factors that appear to affect interaction within this intergenerational relationship parallel those comprising the "new social contract" explicated by Kornhaber and Woodward (1981). As previously mentioned, the "new social contract" often prevents the development of emotional bonds characteristic of those within extended family relationships. For example, grandparents' attitudes toward their own life situations, relations with their children, family mobility, in addition to grandparents' age and desire to become involved in the grandparental role, affect the opportunity for grandparents and grandchildren to interact.

Further, the family is comprised of ongoing dyadic relationships which characterize the developmental nature of interpersonal interaction. As individuals within the relationship change, the relationship also changes. Because grandparents and grandchildren function within their respective roles for longer periods during their lifetimes, there is ample opportunity for each individual to experience developmental and relational changes through communication within this unique relationship. Through the analysis of the structural aspects of this relationship as explicated by Ruesch and Bateson (1949), the grandparent–grandchild dyad can be established as a viable context for the study of interpersonal communication processes.

Kornhaber and Woodward (1981) provided numerous examples of both grandparents and grandchildren who reported a need to interact with each other. Those who had the opportunity for such interaction expressed a sense of satisfaction with the relationship. On the other hand, those grandparents and grandchildren who did not have the benefit of such interaction repeatedly disclosed frustration, and sometimes anger, at the consequences of infrequent interaction. Grandparents and grandchildren have the unique opportunity to exchange information and change and influence each other, and grandparents have the chance to develop a sense of continuity through interaction with grandchildren if other factors (both intrinsic and extrinsic to the relationship) do not inhibit that opportunity.

When grandparents and grandchildren do interact, one of the most frequently reported forms of interaction is grandparents' sharing of experiences, events or family history through stories (Kornhaber & Woodward, 1981). Although Webb (1985) explored specific topics of conversatin between grandparents and grandchildren, continued investigation into the meaning and importance of such interaction is needed. Further, the impact of perceived roles, opportunity for interaction, and other relational factors could be investigated with regard to the form and content of interaction that takes place within this unique relationship.

Overall, interaction with grandparents contributes to the strengthening of intergenerational bonds as "the grandparent can organize family functions around common interests and rituals that bring zest and meaning to life and bind the generations together into a closely knit whole" (Boyd, 1969, p. 99). Grandparents are integral to family functioning as "they stimulate discussions of family history and relate interesting and timely anecdotes of bygone days" (p. 98). Thus, in today's age of mobile families and independent family members, grandparents are a stabilizing force; the means by which grandchildren achieve a sense of family heritage and security about facing the future. Communication within this relationship could be the means by which that heritage is conveyed and a sense of security established. For grandparents, interaction with grandchildren affords them the opportunity to live through new experiences that they themselves could not otherwise experience. Further, they see themselves carry on through their grandchildren by providing a link between the past and the future: Communication could be the means by which this link is secured.

REFERENCES

Albrecht, R. (1954). The parental responsibilities of grandparents. *Marriage and Family Living, 16,* 201–204.

Aldous, J. (1965). The consequences of intergenerational continuity. *Journal of Marriage and the Family, 27,* 462–468.

Aldous, J. (1985). Parent-adult child relations as affected by the grandparent status. In V. L. Bengtson & J. F. Robertson (Eds.), *Grandparenthood* (pp. 117–132). Beverly Hills, CA: Sage Publications.

Apple, D. (1956). The social structure of grandparenthood. *American Anthropologist, 58,* 656–663.

Baranowski, M. D. (1982). Grandparent–adolescent relations: Beyond the nuclear family. *Adolescence, 17,* 375–384.

Beal, E. W. (1979). Children of divorce: A family systems perspective. *Journal of Social Issues, 35,* 140–154.

Bekker, L. D., & Taylor, C. (1966). Attitudes toward the aged in a multigenerational sample. *Journal of Gerontology, 21,* 115–118.

Bengtson, V. L. (1985). Diversity and symbolism in grandparental roles. In V. L. Bengtson & J. F. Robertson (Eds.), *Grandparenthood* (pp. 11–26). Beverly Hills, CA: Sage Publications.

Bengtson, V. L., & Black, K. D. (1973). Intergenerational relations and continuities in socialization. In P. B. Baltes & K. W. Schaie (Eds.) *Life-span developmental psychology: Personality and socialization* (pp. 207–234). New York, NY: Academic Press.

Bengtson, V. L., Cutler, N. E., Mangen, D. J., & Marshall, V. W. (1985). Generations, cohorts, and relations between age groups. In R. H. Binstock & E. Shanas (Eds.) *Handbook of aging and the social sciences* (pp. 304–338). New York, NY: Van Nostrand Reinhold.

Bengtson, V., & Kuypers, J. (1971). Generational differences and the developmental stake. *Aging and Human Development, 2,* 246–260.

Beresford, J. C., & Rivlin, A. M. (1969). The multigeneration family. In W. Donahue, J. L. Kornbluh, & L. Power (Eds.), *Living in the multigeneration family* (pp. 1–23). Ann Arbor, MI: Institute of Gerontology, University of Michigan.

Blau, T. H. (1984). An evaluative study of the role of the grandparent in the best interests of the child. *The American Journal of Family Therapy, 12,* 46–50.

Bochner, A. P. (1976). Conceptual frontiers in the study of communication in families: An introduction to the literature. *Human Communication Research, 2,* 381–397.

Boyd, R. (1969). The valued grandparent: A changing social role. In D. W. Donahue, J. L. Kornbluh, & L. Powers (Eds.), *Living in a miltigenerational family* (pp. 90–106). Ann Arbor, MI: Institute of Gerontology, University of Michigan.

Britton, J. O., & Britton, J. H. (1968, September). *Age discrimination of children and adults through projective pictures.* Paper presented at the annual meeting of the American Psychology Association, San Francisco, CA.

Burke, J. L. (1982). Young children's attitudes and perceptions of older adults. *International Journal of Aging and Human Development, 14,* 205–222.

Cherlin, A., & Furstenberg, F. F. (1985). Styles and strategies of grandparenting. In V. L. Bengtson & J. F. Robertson (Eds.), *Grandparenthood* (pp. 97–116). Beverly Hills, CA: Sage Publications.

Cherlin, A., & Furstenberg, F. F. (1986). *The new american grandparent: A place in the family, a life apart.* New York, NY: Basic Books.

Clavan, S. (1978). The impact of social class and social trends on the role of grandparent. *The Family Coordinator, 27,* 351–358.

Cohler, B. J., & Grunebaum, H. U. (1981). *Mothers, grandmothers, and daughters: Personality and childcare in three-generation families.* New York: NY: Wiley.

Crase, D. R., & Hendrickson, N. (1968). Maternal grandmothers and mothers as perceived by pre-teen children. *Journal of Home Economics, 60,* 181–185.

Crawford, M. (1981). Not disengaged: Grandparents in literature and reality, an empirical study in role satisfaction. *Sociological Review, 29,* 499–519.

Derdeyn, A. P. (1985). Grandparent visitation rights: Rendering family dissension more pronounced. *American Journal of Orthopsychiatry, 55,* 277–287.

Doka, K. J. (1985/1986). Adolescent attitudes and beliefs toward aging and the elderly. *International Journal of Aging and Human Development, 22,* 173–188.

Downs, V. C. (1988). *The grandparent–grandchild relationship: Communication and continuity between generations.* Unpublished doctoral dissertation, University of Oklahoma.

Erikson, E. H. (1959). Identity and the life cycle: Selected papers. *Psychological Issues, 1,* 18–164.

Fischer, L. R. (1983). Transition to grandmotherhood. *International Journal of Aging and Human Development, 16,* 67–78.

Gilbert, S. J. (1976). Empirical and theoretical extensions of self-disclosure. In G. R. Miller (Ed.), *Explorations in interpersonal communication* (pp. 197–216). Beverly Hills, CA: Sage Publications.

Hader, M. (1965). The importance of grandparents in family life. *Family Process, 4,* 228–240.

Hagestad, G. O. (1985). Continuity and connectedness. In V. L. Bengtson & J. F. Robertson (Eds.), *Grandparenthood* (pp. 31–48). Beverly Hills, CA: Sage Publications.

Hartshorne, T. S., & Manaster, G. J. (1982). The relationship with grandparents: Contact, importance and role conception. *International Journal of Aging and Human Development, 15,* 233–255.

Hays, W. C., & Mindel, C. H. (1973). Extended kinship relations in black and white families. *Journal of Marriage and the Family, 35,* 51–56.

Hickey, T., Hickey, L., & Kalish, R. A. (1968). Children's perceptions of the elderly. *Journal of Genetic Psychology, 112,* 227–235.

Hoffman, E. (1979). Young adult's relations with their grandparents: An exploratory study. *International Journal of Aging and Human Development, 10,* 299–309.

Homans, G. C. (1950). *The human group.* New York, NY: Harcourt, Brace, & World, Inc.

Isaacs, L. W. (1986). The development of childrens' prejudice against the aged. *International Journal of Aging and Human Development, 23,* 175–194.

Ivester, C., & King, K. (1977). Attitudes of adolescents toward the aged. *The Gerontologist, 17,* 85–89.

Jackson, D. D. (1965). The study of the family. *Family Process, 4,* 1–20.

Johnson, C. L. (1983). A cultural analysis of the grandmother. *Research on Aging, 5,* 546–568.

Johnson, C. L. (1985). Grandparenting options in divorcing families: An anthropological perspective. In V. L. Bengtson & J. F. Robertson (Eds.), *Grandparenthood* (pp. 81–96). Beverly Hills, CA: Sage Publications.

Johnson, C. l., & Barer, B. M. (1987). Marital instability and the changing kinship networks of grandparents. *The Gerontologist, 27,* 330-335.

Kahana, B., & Kahana, E. (1970). Grandparenthood from the perspective of the developing grandchild. *Developmental Psychology, 3,* 98–105.

Kahana, E., & Coe, R. M. (1969). *Perceptions of grandparenthood by community and institutionalized aged.* Proceedings of the 77th Annual Convention of the American Psychiatric Association, 735–736.

Kivett, V. R. (1985). Grandfathers and grandchildren: Patterns of association, helping, and psychological closeness. *Family Relations, 34,* 565–571.

Kivnick, H. Q. (1985). Grandparenthood and mental health: Meaning, behavior, and satisfaction. In V. L. Bengtson & J. F. Robertson (Eds.), *Grandparenthood* (pp. 151–158) Beverly Hills, CA: Sage Publications.

Kornhaber, A. (1985). Grandparenthood and the 'new social contract'. In V. L. Bengtson &

J. F. Robertson (Eds.), *Grandparenthood* (pp. 159–172). Beverly Hills, CA: Sage Publications

Kornhaber, A., & Woodward, K. L. (1981). *Grandparents/grandchildren: The vital connection.* Garden City, NY: Anchor Press/Doubleday.

Leichter, H. J. (1979). Families and communities as educators: Some concepts of relationship. In H. J. Leichter (Ed.), *Families and communities as educators* (pp. 3–94). New York: Teachers College Press.

Lewis, M. (1984). Social influences on development: An overview. In M. Lewis (Ed.), *Beyond the dyad,* (pp. 1–13). New York: Plenum

Luszcz, M. A. (1985). Characterizing adolescents, middle-aged, and elderly adults: Putting the elderly into perspective. *International Journal of Aging and Human Development, 22,* 105–122.

Matthews, S. H., & Sprey, J. (1984). The impact of divorce on grandparenthood: An exploratory study. *The Gerontologist, 24,* 41–47.

Matthews, S. H., & Sprey, J. (1985). Adolescents' relationships with grandparents: An empirical contribution to conceptual clarification. *Journal of Gerontology, 40,* 621–626.

Mead, M. (1970). *Culture and commitment: A study of the generation gap.* Garden City, NY: Natural History Press, Doubleday.

Mead, M. (1972). *Blackberry winter.* New York: William Morrow.

Mead, M. (1974). Grandparents as educators. *Teachers College Record, 76,* 240–249.

Morgan, L. A. (1981). Aging in a family context. In R. H. Davis (Ed.), *Aging: Prospects and issues.* Los Angeles, CA: USC Press.

Neugarten, B. L., & Weinstein, K. K. (1964). The changing american grandparent. *Journal of Marriage and the Family, 26,* 199–204.

Neugarten, B. L., & Weinstein, K. K. (1968). The changing american grandparent. In B. L. Neugarten (Ed.), *Middle age and aging* (pp. 280–285). Chicago, IL: University of Chicago Press.

Nye, I. F., & Berardo, F. M. (1981). The role of grandparenthood. In L. D. Steinberg (Ed.), *The life cycle: Readings in human development* (pp. 325–330). New York: Columbia University Press.

Perlmutter, M., & Hall, E. (1985). *Adult development and aging.* New York: Wiley.

Piaget, J. (1954). *The construction of reality in the child.* New York: Basic Books.

Ramirez Barranti, C. C. (1985). The grandparent/grandchild relationship: Family resource in a era of voluntary bonds. *Family Relations, 34,* 343–352.

Robertson, J. F. (1975). Interaction in 3-generation families, parents as mediators: Toward a theoretical perspective. *International Journal of Aging and Human Development, 6,* 103–110.

Robertson, J. F. (1976). Significance of grandparents: Perceptions of young adult grandchildren. *The Gerontologist, 16,* 137–140.

Robertson, J. F. (1977). Grandmotherhood: A study of role conceptions. *Journal of Marriage and Family, 39,* 165–174.

Robins, L. N., & Tomanec, M. (1962). Closeness to blood relatives outside the immediate family. *Journal of Marriage and Family Living, 24,* 340–346.

Roebuck, J. (1983). Grandma as revolutionary: Elderly women and some modern patterns of social change. *International Journal of Aging and Human Development, 17,* 249–266.

Ruesch, J. (1951a). Values, communication and culture: An introduction. In J. Ruesch & G. Bateson (Eds.), *Communication: The social matrix of psychiatry* (pp. 3–20). New York: W.W. Norton.

Ruesch, J. (1951b). Communication and human relations: An interdisciplinary approach. In J. Ruesch & G. Bateson (Eds., *Communication: The social matrix of psychiatry* (pp. 21–49). New York: W. W. Norton.

Ruesch, J., & Bateson, G. (1949). Structure and process in social relations. *Psychiatry, 12,* 105–124.

Smith, H. E. (1965). Family interaction patterns of the aged: A review. In A. M. Rose and W. A. Peterson (Eds.), *Older people and their social world* (pp. 143–161). Philadelphia: F. A. Davis Co.

Sprey, J., & Matthews, S. H. (1982). Contemporary grandparenthood: A systemic transition. *The Annals, 464,* 91–103.

Stack, C. B. (1974). Sex roles and survival strategies in an urban black community. In M. Z. Rosaldo & L. Lamphere (Eds.), *Women, culture, and society* (pp. 113–128). Stanford, CA: Stanford University Press.

Sussman, M. B. (1985). The family life of old people. In R. H. Binstock & E. Shanas (Eds.), *Handbook of aging and the social sciences.* New York: Van Nostrand Reinhold.

Thomas, E. C., & Yamamoto, K. (1975). Attitudes toward age: An exploration in school age children. *International Journal of Aging and Human Development, 6,* 117–130.

Thomas, J. L. (1986). Age and sex differences in perceptions of grandparenting. *Journal of Gerontology, 41,* 417–423.

Thompson, L., Clark, K., & Gunn, W. (1985). Developmental stage and perceptions of intergenerational continuity. *Journal of Marriage and the Family, 47,* 913–920.

Tinsley, B. R., & Parke, R. D. (1984). Grandparents as support and socialization agents. In M. Lewis (Ed.), *Beyond the dyad,* (pp. 161–194). New York: Plenum.

Titchener, J. L., D'Zmura, T., Golden, M., & Emerson, R. (1963). Family transaction and derivation of individuality. *Family Process, 2,* 95–120.

Troll, L. E. (1971). The family of later life: A decade review. *Journal of Marriage and the Family, 33,* 263–290.

Troll, L. E. (1972). Is parent–child conflict what we mean by the generation gap? *The Family Coordinator, 21,* 247–349.

Troll, L. E. (1983). Grandparents: The family watchdogs. In T. Brubaker (Ed.), *Family relationships in later life* (pp. 63–74). Beverly Hills, CA: Sage Publications.

Troll, L. E. (1985). The contingencies of grandparenting. In V. L. Bengtson & J. F. Robertson (Eds.), *Grandparenthood* (pp. 135–150). Beverly Hills, CA: Sage Publications.

Troll, L., & Bengtson, V. (1979). Generations in the family. In W. R. Burr, R. Hill, R. I. Nye, & I. L. Reiss (Eds.), *Contemporary theories about the family* (Vol. 1, pp. 127–161). New York: The Free Press.

Updegraff, S. G. (1968). Changing role of the grandmother. *Journal of Home Economics, 60,* 177–180.

Von Hentig, H. (1945/1946). The sociological function of the grandmother. *Social Forces, 24,* 389–392.

Webb, L. (1985). Common topics of conversation between young adults and their grandparents. *Communication Research Reports, 2,* 156–163.

Wilder, C. (1978). From the interactional view: A conversation with Paul Watzlawick. *Journal of Communication, 28,* 35–46.

Wilmot, W. W. (1979). *Dyadic communication.* Reading, MA: Addison-Wesley.

Wilson, K. B. & Deshane, M. R. (1982). The legal rights of grandparents: A preliminary discussion. *The Gerontologist, 22,* 67–71.

Wood, V. (1982, Winter). Grandparenthood: An ambiguous role. Generations: *Journal of the Western Gerontological Society,* 18–24.

Wood, V., & Robertson, J. F. (1976). The significance of grandparenthood. In J. F. Gubrium (Ed.), *Time, roles, and self in old age* (pp. 278–304). New York: Human Sciences Press.

14 Relationships with Siblings in Later Life

Victor G. Cicirelli
Purdue University

Jon F. Nussbaum
University of Oklahoma

INTRODUCTION

The relationship with a sibling is among the earliest relationships experienced by an individual in our society, beginning with the first awareness of the sibling in infancy and extending until the end of life. Most children have at least one sibling and the relationships persist until old age. From 75% to 93% of people over age 65 have at least one living sibling (Cicirelli, 1980; Clark & Anderson, 1967; Harris and Associates, Inc., 1975; Shanas et al, 1968), and for most the relationships with siblings remain meaningful in the later years (Allan, 1977; Cicirelli, 1980, 1982; Ross & Milgram, 1982; Troll, 1971).

NATURE OF THE SIBLING RELATIONSHIP

Before proceeding to examine sibling relationships in later life, however, it is important to consider just what is meant by a sibling relationship. On the purely formal level, the sibling relationship is the state of being connected by consanguinity, that is, having both biological parents in common. This formal biological definition is of little value in understanding the sociopsychological nature of sibling relationships. For these purposes, we regard sibling relationships as the total of the interactions (actions, verbal, and nonverbal communication) of two or more individuals who share common biological parents, as well as their knowledge, perceptions attitudes, beliefs, and feelings regarding each other, from the time when one sibling first became aware of the other. (See Cicirelli, 1985, for a more extended discussion of the definition of sibling relationships). Closer examination of the definition reveals that the sibling relationship includes both overt actions and interactions between a sibling pair as well as the covert subjective cognitive and affective components of the relationship.

The relationship between siblings has many characteristics that distinguish it from other human relationships. First, the siblings share a common biological heritage, having 33% to 66% of their genes in common (Scarr & Gracek, 1982). Second, the sibling relationship is an ascribed relationship which exists by virtue of their common parentage; thus siblings have a commitment to maintain the relationship throughout their lives. It is rare for siblings to break off the relationships or to completely lose touch (Cicirelli, 1980). Third, the relationship has a longer course than any other relationship in most cases. It extends from the birth of the younger child until the death of one of the siblings. Indeed the cognitive and emotional aspects of the sibling relationship may begin for the older child in the months when the impending birth of a sibling is expected (Nadelman & Begun, 1982). Fourth, the sibling relationship is probably more egalitarian than most other relationships (Sutton-Smith & Rosenberg, 1970). Finally, the long shared history of intimate family experiences distinguish the sibling relationship from nonfamily relationships. In the early years, siblings may eat, sleep, bathe, dress, work, and play together. In these years, patterns of intimate communication develop between siblings as they talk about common family experiences. As they continue into adult life, this foundation of common meanings and experiential referents is taken for granted.

The Family as a System

Although a given relationship between siblings involves two individuals, the relationship does not occur in isolation but within the larger context of the family system and the society where it takes place.

The family system consists of three major subsystems: the parent–parent (or spousal) subsystem, the parent–child subsystem, and the child–child (or sibling) subsystem. According to family systems theory, what happens within any subsystem affects and is affected by events within other subsystems. For example, the relationship between two siblings is influenced by each child's relationship with the parents. Thus, if a parent especially favors one child and has a particularly close relationship, the result may be rivalry between the siblings. Or, on the other hand, conflict between the siblings can lead to conflict in the spousal subsystem if each parent takes a different approach to the problem between the siblings.

Within the family system, coalitions of more or less stable composition (e.g., between two or more siblings or between a child and parent) may be formed for the purpose of exercising power or based on mutual interests or temperament (Bank & Kahn, 1975, 1982; Minuchin, 1974; Schvaneveldt & Ihinger, 1979). Within the sibling subsystem, such alliances may consist of dyads, triads, or larger groups, depending on family size, age, sex, mutual interests, and so on.

Of the three major family subsystems, the sibling subsystem is usually the most enduring, with some sibling dyads continuing to exist for 80 or 90 years. Over the lengthy period of time marking a sibling relationship, the family system undergoes numerous changes. Thus far, we have talked about the nuclear family system of childhood. The family system over the life span may be looked upon as composed of various overlapping nuclear family systems. For example, an individual may take the role of the child in the nuclear family system of childhood, but assume the role of parent in the nuclear family of procreation which that individual heads as a middle-aged adult. As the individual grows older, the family system and the individual's roles in the system both change. Roles go from child to spouse and parent, and then to grandparent or even great-grandparent. With the passage of time and changes in the family system, certain earlier roles are given up, for instance, grandchild and then child. The family of origin gradually erodes over time as members die and only fragments of the system remain, as in a sibling dyad. The parts remain after the whole is gone, but the whole endures in the parts as memories and symbolic representations within the individuals remaining (Cicirelli, 1985, 1988).

The sibling subsystem is most interdependent with the other subsystems of the family early in life, but becomes relatively more autonomous as the family grows older. This makes it more possible to study siblings independently of the larger family in the latter part of life.

Changes in the Sibling Relationship Over Time

The relationship between any two individuals is said to follow a developmental course or career with an initiation phase, a maintenance phase, and a decline and dissolution phase. Changes in the relationship are attributed to major life events, environmental and social changes, and so on (Ginsburg, 1986). In the case of sibling relationships, the relationship begins in early childhood as basic attachments develop. Then the relationship enters a lengthy maintenance phase which extends over the major portion of the life span. The intensity of the relationship fluctuates as one sibling or another experiences a major life event or environmental change (e.g., school, puberty, leaving home, marriage, parenthood, widowhood, retirement, and so on). Siblings interact with greater intensity at certain periods; some may not meet or communicate directly for an extended interval, although other family members may provide the linkage of communication. Intentional dissolution of the sibling relationship is rare, taking place only when one sibling or the other has committed some relatively serious transgression of the other's trust or expectations. For most sibling pairs, the relationship either ends abruptly with the death of one sibling or gradually dissolves with other declining functions near the end of life.

Developmental Tasks

The notion of sibling developmental tasks is useful in describing changes in the sibling relationship over the life span. By developmental tasks, we mean certain social behaviors which are to be accomplished by most, if not all, siblings in our culture over the course of the life span (Cicirelli, 1980; Goetting, 1986). Goetting has outlined developmental tasks of siblings in three major life stages, based on her review of sibling research findings. In the first stage, childhood and adolescence, siblings provide companionship and social support to each other. Older siblings are expected to undertake delegated caregiving responsibilities for their younger siblings. Also, siblings are expected to provide a variety of direct services for each other, including the formation of sibling coalitions for dealing with parents, providing needed resources to one another, physical protection, teaching of skills, and so on. In the second stage, early and middle adulthood, siblings still provide companionship and emotional support to each other. They may provide aid and direct services, such as help during illness, babysitting, money lending, and sharing of other resources. Also, siblings in middle adulthood cooperate in the care of elderly parents in their declining years and finally act together to dismantle the parental home and divide the estate after the parents' death. In the third life stage identified by Goetting, old age, siblings continue to provide companionship and emotional support; the intensity of the relationship may increase due to the need to compensate for losses of other family members and friends. Siblings provide shared reminiscence and perceptual validation for each other, clarifying events and relationships that occurred earlier in life and placing them in mature perspective. In old age, siblings work to resolve any sibling conflicts and rivalries that have persisted from earlier years. Finally, siblings continue to provide aid and direct services to each other when the situation demands it.

Siblings can also aid each other in facing common problems of aging and their own mortality (Cicirelli, 1980).

Although some of the developmental tasks previously listed are characteristic of a particular life stage, others (e.g., companionship and emotional support, and aid and direct services) seem to be tasks that extend over the entire life span. It should be remembered that there has been no research directed to establish the existence of these developmental tasks as behaviors that are generally expected in our culture. Thus, the preceding listing is best interpreted as a summary of frequently observed sibling behaviors at certain stages of life rather than as expected behaviors.

Sibling Contact in Later Life

Findings on the extent of contact between siblings in later years have been reviewed elsewhere (Cicirelli, 1980, 1985; Goetting, 1986; Scott, 1983; Troll, 1971) and is not presented in detail here. In spite of the fact that interaction between siblings becomes volitional in their adult years and may be limited by geographic proximity, costs, and availability of transportation, health, and various competing activities and obligations, siblings do continue to maintain contact in the latter part of life. Approximately half of all people over age 65 see a sibling at least once a week, although percentages of older people reporting weekly contact with siblings ranged from 17% to 69% in various studies (Allan, 1977; Cicirelli, 1980, 1982; Leigh, 1982; Rosenberg & Anspach, 1973; Scott, 1983; Shanas, 1973). Percentages reporting sibling visits at least monthly were still higher, ranging up to 93% for younger adults residing in the same city (Adams, 1968). At the other end of the scale, only 3% of the elderly had no contact with a sibling in at least 2 years (Cicirelli, 1979). Frequencies of telephoning are highly correlated with face-to-face visiting; it appears that telephoning supplements visiting behavior rather than substituting for it (Cicirelli, 1980; Scott, 1983). Writing is infrequent for most siblings. According to Scott (1983), two-thirds of elderly siblings never wrote and only a fifth wrote as often as monthly. In sum, the available evidence indicates siblings visit and see each other in old age, although the amount of contact appears to decrease somewhat with age.

Sibling Attachment and Closeness of Feeling

Most siblings feel some degree of affectional closeness for one another throughout their lives. In a study of sibling relationships of elderly individuals over age 60 (Cicirelli, 1979), 53% reported feeling "extremely close" to the sibling with whom they had the most contact, whereas another 30% reported feeling "close." Only 6% did not feel close at all. Other studies have also reported similar feelings of closeness between elderly siblings (Allan, 1977; Cumming & Schneider, 1961; Ross & Milgram, 1982). Both men and women reported feeling closer to female siblings and to their middle-born siblings. Also, sibling closeness tended to be greater in working-class families than in middle-class families, whereas Johnson (1982) found stronger bonds between siblings in Italian-American than in non-Italian Protestant families. It appears that differing cultural expectations associated with ethnic groups and socio-economic status level may both contribute to differences in the closeness of the sibling relationship. It may be that economically hard times as well as ethnic identification may lead to a stronger sibling bond. Siblings also reported considerable value consensus in the latter part of life (Cicirelli, 1979; Ross & Milgram, 1982; Suggs & Kivett, 1983).

The relationship between elderly siblings is generally a compatible one (Cicirelli, 1985), with 88% reporting that they get along well with their siblings, 74% reporting that they gain considerable or very great satisfaction from the sibling relationship, and 68% feeling able to discuss intimate topics with the sibling. Although most elderly siblings feel close and have a compatible relationship, a smaller proportion is able to share intimate details of their lives and disclose feelings and personal problems. Such relationships may seem superficial, but it must be remembered that few other relationships are conducted at a more intimate level (Duck & Miell, 1986).

A recent study by Gold (1986) developed a typology of relationships between elderly siblings, based on patterns of psychological involvement, closeness of feelings, contact, and exchanges of support between siblings. The five types of sibling relationships identified were: intimate (14%), congenial (30%), loyal (34%), apathetic (11%), and hostile (11%). Although the percentage of sibling relationships that may be characterized as intimate is small, the great majority of sibling relationships (the 78% consisting of the congenial, loyal, and the intimate relationships) enjoy moderate to strong psychological involvement and emotional support between the siblings involved.

In attempting to explain the persistence of the sibling bond into old age, we have looked to attachment theory (Ainsworth, 1972; Bowlby, 1979, 1980). The major points of this reasoning are outlined here; the interested reader is referred to Cicirelli (1983, 1985) for a fuller discussion. Briefly, attachment refers to an emotional or affectional bond between two people, it is essentially identified with, having love for, and the desire to be with the other person, and represents an internal state within the individual. In infancy and early childhood, attachment is inferred from the child's behavior as it seeks to maintain proximity, contact, or communication with the parent. Somewhat later in time, a protective aspect of attachment develops in which the child takes measures to prevent the loss of the valued object. This protective behavior is distinct from attachment behavior and complementary to it in that it is concerned with preserving or restoring the threatened existence of the attached figure rather than merely restoring proximity. Examples of protective behavior are caring for the attached figure in time of illness, alerting the person to danger, and so on. According to Bowlby, attachment does not end in childhood or early adolescence, but endures throughout life. At later ages, the attachment behaviors are manifested in a stage-appropriate way through periodic communication, visiting, and responses to reunions, whereas protective behavior is shown in helping and care-giving behavior that attempts to maintain the survival of the attached figure and preserve the emotional bond.

There is evidence for attachment to siblings in childhood (Bank & Kahn, 1982; Dunn & Kendrick, 1982; Stewart, 1983), and the phenomenon has been extended logically to adulthood and old age. Troll and Smith (1976) studied attachment between various family members in adulthood, finding that scores on a measure of attachment were higher for parents than for siblings, but were higher for siblings than for other kin. Troll and Smith regard attachment to siblings as a bond that is able to override separation and distance, even persisting after the death of the attached figure. Bank and Kahn (1982) cited numerous examples of strong sibling bonds throughout adulthood. Our own work with elderly subjects indicates that ties to deceased siblings remain as strong as to those who are still living.

To explain the maintenance of the sibling bond over the extended separations in space and time that occur in adulthood, we have argued that the propensity for closeness and contact with the attached figure (the sibling) continues throughout life but is satisfied on a symbolic level (Cicirelli, 1983). Identification is the mechanism by which symbols are used to establish closeness and contact on a psychological level, and is an essential ingredient of the affective bond. Through the process of identification, the individual can feel close to the sibling by calling forth the symbolic representation of the sibling and experiencing a sense of closeness thereby. The symbolic contact can be supplemented from time to time with visits and other communications. The role of symbolic processes in the development and maintenance of the attachment bond to siblings has been observed by other researchers (Bank & Kahn, 1982; Dunn, 1984; Ross & Milgram, 1982). Feelings of closeness to siblings are seen as originating in childhood, involving a symbolic representation of the child's place in the family; memories of early closeness and internalized shared values, goals, and interests maintain the bond in spite of the separation in adulthood.

Sibling Rivalry in Later Life

Sibling rivalry is an aspect of the sibling relationship that is considered important by psychotherapists and developmental psychologists during the childhood years. It has often been assumed that childhood rivalries dissipate when siblings reach adulthood, although notable examples to the contrary abound, from the Biblical rivalry of Cain and Abel to the present day. Feelings of sibling rivalry also persist into adulthood and old age, when they may be expressed in more subtle forms, such as using the sibling as a standard of comparison (Troll, 1975). Sibling rivalry may also be reactivated in certain critical situations in adult life, such as care of a parent or division of an estate (Berezin, 1977; Laverty, 1962). In our own work (Cicirelli, 1985), we found that elderly siblings reported a low incidence of rivalrous behavior. Only 10% reported arguments, 6% reported bossing or other attempts at sibling domination, 8% reported feelings of competition with the sibling, and only a few incidents of jealousy, hostility, snobbishness, and so on. About a third of the elderly respondents felt that conflicts with the sibling would increase if they were to live together again. When sibling rivalry was compared for various cross sectional age groups, rivalry was found to decline with age (Cicirelli, 1982).

Other studies using more clinical methods of investigation have reported rivalry to be more prevalent in later life. Gold (1986) found resentment of the sibling on the basis of her extended interview techniques to be moderate to strong among the hostile, apathetic, and loyal types (a total of 56%), although moderate envy was reported only for the hostile type (11%). Ross and Milgram (1982) used clinical group interviews to uncover sibling rivalry in adulthood and old age, arguing that many people find it difficult or shameful to admit to feelings of sibling rivalry in adulthood. They found that 71% of the siblings they interviewed admitted to rivalrous feelings with a sibling at some point in their lives, most frequently arising in childhood or in adolescence. Some 26% reported that they had overcome earlier feelings of sibling rivalry, but 45% still reported feeling some rivalry in their adult years. Ross and Milgram found that the maintenance of rivalry in adulthood appeared to depend on continued parental favoritism, competitive behaviors between siblings, feeling excluded from family interactions (coalitions between other siblings), persistence of assigned roles and labels, and never discussing the feelings wth the sibling involved in order to improve the relationship. Yet, by late adulthood and old age the renewal and repair of sibling relationships takes on considerable importance to many people (Gold, 1986; Ross & Milgram, 1982); when the reasons for the rivalry are reevaluated from the mature perspective of late adulthood, the rivalry may well disappear or diminish in intensity. Bedford (1986), using an adaptation of the Thematic Apperception Test to measure rivalry, found that older adults revealed as many themes of sibling rivalry in their responses as did younger adults, and that women expressed more conflict in the relationship with siblings than did men. She concluded that the projective methodology was tapping feelings not typically reported.

Present research has not settled the question of just how extensive sibling rivalry is in later years. In general, however, the evidence indicates that siblings value their relationship highly in the later years and seem to have developed ways of interaction that avoid conflict and overt rivalry.

Ambivalent Relationships

Unless rivalry is extreme, sibling rivalry is not inconsistent with feelings of closeness. Troll, Miller, and Atchley (1978) theorized that there is a basic love–hate ambivalence in human relationships, with positive and negative feelings varying with the ebb and flow of the relationship. Ambivalent sibling relationships have been noted in childhood as well as in adulthood (Dunn & Kendrick, 1982; Nadelman & Begun, 1982). One possible interpretation of ambivalence is that there is a dialectic between the two in sibling relationships, which leads to individual growth and growth in the relationship (Cicirelli, 1982). Excessive closeness can interfere with the development of an individual identity whereas excessive rivalry can be totally destructive, but some rivalry may be an incentive to growth, whereas the closeness provides the support within which growth can take place. Another interpretation of ambivalence is that closeness and rivalry are situation specific, with closeness appearing in some situations and rivalry in others.

FUNCTIONS OF THE SIBLING RELATIONSHIP IN LATER LIFE

Sibling relationships have a variety of funtions in the lives of older people, some of which are reviewed here.

Companionship and Psychological Support

Exchange of psychological support and providing companionship probably constitute the most important functions of sibling relationship in old age. The fact that most older siblings maintain contact has already been noted. Scott (1983) examined activities reported by siblings and other kin. Visits, reunions, and happy family occasions were the most frequent sibling activities reported, followed by various types of recreational activities (home, commercial, and outdoor), and by shopping, church, and miscellaneous other activities. When proximity was controlled, frequency of these sibling activities compared quite favorably with similar activities with children. Various authors have found that most sibling relationships in old age are companionate in nature (Adams, 1968; Cicirelli, 1982, 1985; Johnson, 1982; Troll et al., 1978).

Siblings also exchange confidences, offer advice, share common interests, and provide psychological support for one another. Although we found that 78% of adult siblings reported a high degree of compatibility with their siblings and only 4% got along poorly (Cicirelli, 1982), relatively fewer felt that they could discuss topics of an intimate nature with their siblings and only 8% frequently talked over important decisions with siblings. Compatibility with siblings was even higher in old age; 88% felt high compatibility, 66% felt they could discuss intimate topics with the sibling and 16% talked over important decisions. They communicated most often in regard to family matters, but shared views on many other topics as well.

Whether the sibling relationship leads to a more positive adjustment and greater life satisfaction in old age is open to question, with both positive and negative evidence in the literature. Cumming and Henry (1961) found that elderly with living siblings had higher morale than those who did not. Ross and Milgram (1982) concluded that the sibling relationship was of great value to the elderly; in addition, we found that elderly with more frequent interaction with siblings maintained a greater sense of control in life (Cicirelli, 1977, 1980). Those men with sisters had a greater sense of emotional security, whereas women with sisters were stimulated and challenged in their social roles. In contrast, a large-sample study of elderly that controlled for a number of possible confounding variables failed to find a significant relationship between frequency of sibling interaction and morale (Lee & Ihinger-Tallman, 1980). More recent studies have qualified this finding, however. McGhee (1985) confirmed the findings of Lee and Ihinger-Tallman with regard to the effect of frequency of sibling interaction on life satisfaction, but found that the mere availability of a sister was a significant predictor of life satisfaction in women and approached statistical significance among men. McGhee's results suggest that any positive effects of a relationship with siblings on morale and adjustment derives from the simple existence of the relationship and not from the frequency with which the siblings interact. O'Bryant (1986) examined sibling support and older widows' well-being and found that interaction with married sisters predicted higher positive affect among older widows. The relationship was more complex than it appeared on the surface, however, for widows who received support from sisters when nearby adult children did not provide support perceived the sibling support negatively.

Relationships with sisters appear to be particularly important in old age, whether it is a sister–sister or a brother–sister bond. One could attribute this to women's greater interest in initiating family relationships; however, Gold (1986) found that brothers initiated sibling contacts with sisters about as often as sisters contacted brothers. What seems more likely is that women's emotional expressiveness and their traditional roles as nurturers account for the importance of relationships with sisters.

Reminiscence

Because siblings share a long and unique history, reminiscing about earlier times together is an activity in which siblings engage at many points in the life span, although it seems to become more valuable in old age. Reminiscence in itself is simply thinking or talking about the past. In old age, reminiscence becomes part of the life review process (Butler, 1963), in which past experiences are analyzed, evaluated, and reintegrated in relation to present events, values, and attitudes. Prompted by the realization of biological decline in later years, the life review allows the individual to resolve old conflicts and to achieve integrity in the latter portion of life. Butler's hypothesis that spontaneous reminiscence in the life review led to better adjustment in old age has been supported by a number of studies, at least among those who engaged in reminiscence because they valued the activity (Coleman, 1986; Molinari & Reichlin, 1985; Osgood, 1985). There is little research of reminiscence of experiences with siblings. We found (Cicirelli, 1982) that older people discussed old times more frequently with their siblings than with their adult children. The fewer the remaining siblings in the family, the greater the extent of the reminiscing. This indicates that siblings do play an important role in reminiscing. As the remaining members of their families of origin, siblings can use reminiscences of old times together and clarify events and relationships that took place in earlier years and to place them in mature perspective. Ross and Milgram (1982) observed that sharing recollections of childhood experiences appeared to be a source of comfort and pride for the elderly, evoking the warmth of early family life and contributing to a sense of integrity that life had been lived in harmony with the family. Gold's (1986) elderly subjects reported that reminiscing about sibling relationships during the course of the interview helped them to put their current relationships with siblings into a meaningful context, helped them to understand present events, and helped them to appreciate the significance of sibling relationships in their lives. Sibling reminiscence may prove to be a valuable tool in therapeutic situations as well (Cicirelli, 1988).

Sibling Helping Behavior

Another major aspect of the sibling relationship in old age is the help that siblings can provide for each other. In middle age, siblings are seen as a source of aid in time of crisis (Troll, 1975), caring for children and sharing household responsibilities. For most, however, mutual aid is relatively infrequent (Adams, 1968). Among the elderly, siblings sometimes provide a great deal of help. After the death of the mother, a daughter may take on the mother's role in looking after others in the family. Similarly, after the death of a spouse, a brother or sister may assume many of the deceased spouse's duties for a sibling (Townsend, 1957). Such role substitution may help to explain the growth in closeness between cross-sex siblings that has been observed later in life.

In our own study (Cicirelli, 1979), we found relatively few elderly who depended on siblings as a primary source of support. Most help in families is exchanged in a vertical direction, with children (after the spouse) viewed as the primary source of support in old age. If the need for help becomes too great for the spouse or children to handle or if the normal scheme of family obligations is disturbed, siblings then tend to step in to give help. Indeed, some 60% of the elderly we interviewed (Cicirelli, 1979) regarded their siblings as a source of support to be called on in a crisis, although only 7% (or fewer, depending on the type of help involved) regarded a sibling as a primary source of help. Surprisingly, sibling help became more important among the oldest age groups. This was also noted by Hoyt and Babchuk (1983). If occasional and supplementary help had been considered in the study, the contribution of siblings would surely have been much greater. Scott (1983) noted that siblings gave relatively little assistance in old age compared to that given by children, although the amount of help was relatively greater when sibling proximity was controlled in the analysis. Help was greater when a brother or sister fell ill, needed transportation, or needed to make household repairs. Similar results were obtained by O'Bryant (1986) in her study of elderly widows. In all these studies, the elderly regarded the psychological support from siblings as highly important. They seemed to gain a great sense of support from knowing that siblings were ready to give aid in time of trouble, although their help might be called for only on rare occasions (Allan, 1977; Cicirelli, 1979, Cumming & Schneider, 1961).

Siblings' general readiness to give help was illustrated in our recent study of hospitalized elderly (Cicirelli, in press). About half the elderly patients wanted psychological support from their siblings, which they received in the form of visits and telephone calls. Only about 20% reported receiving any kind of tangible sibling help while in the hospital, and only about 6% wanted or expected instrumental help from siblings once they had returned home.

Three conclusions can be drawn from the literature on sibling helping in old age: Siblings play a greater role in giving psychological support than in instrumental help, siblings play a complementary role to spouse and adult children in giving help (although such supplementary help may be crucial in helping the elderly to maintain their independence), and help is greater in time of illness or other crisis situations.

IMPLICATIONS FOR THE STUDY OF COMMUNICATION

The article thus far has reviewed our knowledge, based upon existing literature, of the sibling relationship in later life. The great majority of this literature which frames our knowledge has been authored by social scientists who name psychology or sociology as their "home" discipline. Although one would expect psychologists and sociologists to actively research the sibling relationship across the life span, one would not expect the researchers who reside in the field of communication to totally ignore the sibling relationship. This neglect of the sibling relationship by communication scholars is even more startling when one considers that numerous interpersonal communication researchers specialize in the study of relationships. The final section of this article discusses the implications of the present state of knowledge concerning sibling relationships in later life for communication researchers with suggestions for future directions of research.

Perhaps the most significant implications of the literature addressing the sibling relationship for communication scholars are those derived from findings that document the importance of sibling interaction in later life. We know from the literature that siblings continue to interact throughout the life span and that this interaction serves different functions during different developmental life phases. Our knowledge of sibling interaction, though, only scratches the surface. Although we know that siblings continue to interact throughout life and have uncovered several functions of this interaction, the process of the interaction itself has yet to be studied. Communication scholars who pride themselves in the study of interaction process can fill the missing informational gap between interaction and function. For instance, we do not have a clear understanding of the messages shared by siblings in later life or how these messages have changed over the lifetime, which may reflect the changing functions of the relationship. We do not know how individuals couched within a family context have maintained their relationship through communication for as many as nine decades. Finally, we do not know the pragmatic role that sibling communication plays in serving the functions of companionship, reminiscence, and helping behavior. Communication scholars need to investigate those communicative acts within the sibling relationship that signal companionship, reminiscence, and helping behavior.

Moving beyond the purely descriptive information, which can flow from studying the communication shared by siblings, is the role communication plays in defining the sibling relationship itself. Sibling research has shown that brothers and sisters feel close to one another throughout their lives. Yet, the sister relationship seems to be particularly important in old age for both brothers and sisters. The nature of a relationship with a sister in later life must in some way be qualitatively different than a relationship with a brother. Though explanations for the importance of the sister relationship have been posited, no definitive research has been undertaken to outline the core differences between a relationship with a brother than with a sister in later life. Perhaps, one key difference is the messages shared by elderly individuals with their sisters.

The importance of maintaining close family relationships throughout life is well documented. Receiving most of the attention from social researchers has been the spouse relationship in later life and the adult-child/elderly-parent relationship. The nature of the lifelong close sibling relationship and the possible effects of this relationship have not received much attention. Communication researchers can add to the growing body of literature exploring successful aging by uncovering the unique qualities of the close sibling relationship in later life and link these qualities to psycho-social well-being and adjustment to old age.

An additional implication of the literature addressing the sibling relationship in later life for communication scholars is the reliance upon attachment theory as the explanation of continued closeness between siblings throughout life. Attachment is maintained by symbolic processes which include communication. Many communication scholars consider the communicative act between individuals to be essentially a symbolic exchange of information. Sibling researchers point to this exchange as serving the function to maintain the relationship for long periods. Communication scholars may be able to further clarify the essential symbolic nature of sibling communication and point more specifically at how the communicative act aids to maintain high levels of attachment throughout life.

The researchers who are currently investigating the sibling relationship throughout the life span have essentially used traditional survey methods to describe siblings. Although these research methods are quite appropriate for the questions that have been generated, they do not reflect those methods recently utilized to describe relationships within the communication discipline. Thus, a final suggestion for those who are interested in describing sibling relationships throughout life is to utilize multiple methods that include various conversation analytic techniques. Conversation analysis is a systematic, structural analysis of naturalistic occuring conversation with the purpose of uncovering patterns of message exchange that can be linked to such relational variables as closeness and dominance. This type of new analytic method could provide valuable information that could help to bring into better focus the nature of the sibling relationship in later life.

REFERENCES

Adams, B. N. (1968). *Kinship in an urban setting*. Chicago: Markham.

Ainsworth, M. D. (1972). Attachment and dependency: A comparison. In J. L. Gerwirtz (Ed.), *Attachment and dependency* (pp. 97–137). New York: Wiley.

Allan, G. (1977). Sibling solidarity. *Journal of Marriage and the Family, 39,* 177–184.

Bank, S. P., & Kahn, M. D. (1975). Sisterhood–brotherhood is powerful: Sibling subsystems and family therapy. *Family Process, 14,* 331–337.

Bank, S. P., & Kahn, M. D. (1982). *The sibling bond*. New York: Basic Books.

Bedford, V. H. (1986, November). *A comparison of thematic apperceptions of sibling affiliation, conflict, and separation at two periods of adulthood*. Paper presented at the 39th Annual Scientific Meeting of the Gerontological Society, Chicago.

Berezin, M. A. (1977). Partial grief for the aged and their families. In E. Pattison (Ed.), *The experience of dying* (pp. 279–286). Englewood Cliffs, NJ: Prentice-Hall.

Bowlby, J. (1979). *The making and breaking of affectional bonds*. London: Tavistock.

Bowlby, J. (1980). *Attachment and loss: Vol. III. Loss, stress, and depression*. New York: Basic Books.

Butler, R. N. (1963). The life review: An interpretation of reminiscence in the aged. *Psychiatry, 26,* 65–76.

Cicirelli, V. G. (1988). Interpersonal relationships among elderly siblings: Implications for clinical practice. In M. Kahn & K. G. Lewis (Eds.), *Siblings in therapy* (pp. 435–456). New York: W.W. Norton.

Cicirelli, V. G. (in press). Family support in relation to health problems of the elderly. In T. H. Brubaker (Ed.), *Family relationships in later life* (2nd ed.). Newbury Park, CA: Sage.

Cicirelli, V. G. (1977). Relationship of siblings to the elderly person's feelings and concerns. *Journal of Gerontology, 32,* 317–322.

Cicirelli, V. G. (1979, May). *Social services for elderly in relation to the kin network* (Report). Washington, DC: NRTA-AARP Andrus Foundation.

Cicirelli, V. G. (1980). Sibling influence in adulthood: A life span perspective. In L. W. Poon (Ed.), *Aging in the 1980s* (pp. 455–462). Washington, DC: American Psychological Association.

Cicirelli, V. G. (1982). Sibling influence throughout the lifespan. In M. E. Lamb & B. Sutton-Smith (Eds.), *Sibling relationships: Their nature and significance across the lifespan* (pp. 267–284). Hillsdale, NJ: Lawrence Erlbaum Associates.

Cicirelli, V. G. (1983). Adult children's attachment and helping behavior to elderly parents: A path model. *Journal of Marriage and the Family, 45,* 815–825.

Cicirelli, V. G. (1985). Sibling relationships throughout the life cycle. In L. L'Abate (Ed.), *The handbook of family psychology and therapy* (Vol. 1, pp. 177–214). Homewood, IL: Dorsey Press.

Clark, M., & Anderson, B. (1967). *Culture and aging: An anthropological study of older Americans.* Springfield, IL: C.C. Thomas.

Coleman, P. (1986). Issues in the therapeutic use of reminiscence with elderly people. In I. Hanley & M. Gilhooly (Eds.), *Psychological therapies for the elderly* (pp. 41–64). London: Croom Helm.

Cumming, E., & Henry, W. (1961). *Growing old.* New York: Basic Books.

Cumming, E., & Schneider, D. (1961). Sibling solidarity: A property of American kinship. *American Anthropologist, 63,* 498–507.

Duck, S., & Miell, D. (1986). Charting the development of personal relationships. In R. Gilmour & S. Duck (Eds.), *The emerging field of personal relationships* (pp. 133–143). Hillsdale, NJ: Lawrence Erlbaum Associates.

Dunn, J. (1984). Sibling studies and the developmental impact of critical incidents. In P. B. Baltes & O. G. Brim, Jr. (Eds.), *Life-span development and behavior* (Vol. 6, pp. 335–353). Orlando, FL: Academic Press.

Dunn, J., & Kendrick, C. (1982). *Siblings: Love, envy, and understanding.* Cambridge, MA: Harvard University Press.

Ginsburg, G. P. (1986). The structural analysis of primary relationships. In R. Gilmour & S. Duck (Eds.), *The emerging field of personal relationships* (pp. 41–62). Hillsdale, NJ: Lawrence Erlbaum Associates.

Goetting, A. (1986). The developmental tasks of siblingship over the life cycle. *Journal of Marriage and the Family, 48,* 703–714.

Gold, D. T. (1986). *Sibling relationships in retrospect: A study of reminiscence in old age.* Doctoral dissertation, Northwestern University, Evanston, IL.

Harris, L., and Associates Inc. (1975). *The myths and realities of aging in America.* Washington, DC: National Council on Aging.

Hoyt, D. R., & Babchuk, N. (1983). Adult kinship networks: The selective formation of intimate ties with kin. *Social Forces, 62,* 84–101.

Johnson, C. L. (1982). Sibling solidarity: Its origin and functioning in Italian-American families. *Journal of Marriage and the Family, 44,* 155–167.

Laverty, R. (1962, January). Reactivation of sibling rivalry in older people. *Social Work* (pp. 23–30).

Lee, G. R., & Ihinger-Tallman, M. (1980). Sibling interactions and morale. *Research on Aging, 2,* 367–391.

Leigh, G. K. (1982). Kinship interaction over the family life span. *Journal of Marriage and the Family, 44,* 197–208.

McGhee, J. L. (1985). The effects of siblings on the life satisfaction of the rural elderly. *Journal of Marriage and the Family, 47,* 85–91.

Minuchin, S. (1974). *Families and family therapy.* Cambridge, MA: Harvard University Press.

Molinari, V., & Reichlin, R. E. (1985). Life review reminiscence in the elderly: A review of the literature. *International Journal of Aging and Human Development, 20* (2), 81–92.

Nadelman, L., & Begun, A. (1982). The effect of the newborn on the older sibling: Mother' questionnaires. In M. E. Lamb & B. Sutton-Smith (Eds.), *Sibling relationships: Their nature and significance across the lifespan* (pp. 13–37). Hillsdale, NJ: Lawrence Erlbaum Associates.

O'Bryant, S. L. (1986, November). *Sibling support and older widows' well-being.* Paper presented at the 39th Annual Scientific Meeting of the Gerontological Society, Chicago.

Osgood, N. J. (1985). *Suicide in the elderly: A practitioner's guide to diagnosis and mental health intervention.* Rockville, MD: Aspen.

Rosenberg, G. S., & Anspach, D. F. (1973). Sibling solidarity in the working class. *Journal of Marriage and the Family, 35,* 108–113.

Ross, H. G., & Milgram, J. I. (1982). Important variables in adult sibling relationships: A qualitative study. In M. E. Lamb & B. Sutton-Smith (Eds.), *Sibling relationships: Their nature and significance across the lifespan* (pp. 225–249). Hillsdale, NJ: Lawrence Erlbaum Associates.

Scarr, S., & Gracek, S. (1982). Similarities and differences among siblings. In M. E. Lamb & B. Sutton-Smith (Eds.), *Sibling relationships: Their nature and significance across the lifespan* (pp. 357–381). Hillsdale, NJ: Lawrence Erlbaum Associates.

Schvaneveldt, J. D., & Ihinger, M. (1979). Sibling relationships in the family. In W. R. Burr, Hill, R., Nye, R. I., & Reiss, I. L. (Eds.), *Contemporary theories about the family: Vol. I. Research-based theories* (pp. 453–467). New York: Free Press.

Scott, J. P. (1983). Siblings and other kin. In T. H. Brubaker (Ed.), *Family relationships in later life* (pp. 47–62). Beverly Hills, CA: Sage Publications.

Shanas, E. (1973). Family-kin networks and aging in cross-cultural perspective. *Journal of Marriage and the Family, 35,* 505–511.

Shanas, E., Townsend, P., Wedderburn, D., Fries, H., Milhoi, D. & Stehouver, J. (1968). *Older people in three industrial societies.* New York: Atherton.

Stewart, R. B. (1983). Sibling attachment relationships: Child–infant interaction in the strange situation. *Developmental Psychology, 19,* 192–199.

Suggs, P. K., & Kivett, V. R. (1983, November). *Rural/urban elderly and siblings: Their value consensus.* Paper presented at the 36th Annual Scientific Meeting of the Gerontological Society, San Francisco.

Sutton-Smith, B., & Rosenberg, B.C. (1970). *The sibling.* New York: Holt, Rinehart, & Winston.

Townsend, P. (1957). *The family life of old people: An inquiry in East London.* Glencoe, IL: Free Press.

Troll, L. E. (1971). The family of later life: A decade review. *Journal of Marriage and the Family, 33,* 263–290.

Troll, L. E. (1975). *Early and middle adulthood.* Monterey, CA: Brooks/Cole.

Troll, L. E., Miller, S., & Atchley, R. (1978). *Families of later life.* Belmont, CA: Wadsworth.

Troll, L., & Smith, J. (1976). Attachment through the life span: Some questions about dyadic bonds among adults. *Human Development. 19.* 156–170.

15 The Influence of Age Difference in Marriage on Longevity

Laurel Klinger-Vartabedian
Wichita State University

Lauren Wispe
University of Oklahoma

INTRODUCTION

The extent to which internal and external perceptions of marital roles exert influence on the morbidity and mortality of individuals is largely unexplored. However, previous research findings have concluded that generally persons who are married are healthier and live longer than nonmarried persons (Gove, 1972; Kitagawa & Hauser, 1973; Verbrugee, 1979). Of particular interest are those variables within marriage that contribute to the statistical benefits granted through matrimony. Findings regarding the influence of age-disparate marriages on longevity suggest intriguing differences in mortality for men and women based upon their spouse's age. Our own work has not directly addressed the nature of marital interaction that contributes to these findings but instead has proven that a persistent relationship between spouse age difference in marriage and longevity does exist. However, previous studies in the areas of longevity research and marital interaction provide a backdrop for understanding and exploring the influence of social and interpersonal dynamics on the human life span. First, an overview is presented which outlines both the mythological and empirical elements of longevity study. Second, age difference in marriage is discussed with regard to demographic trends, interpersonal considerations, marital roles, and longevity factors. Finally, possible explanations for the interplay in marriage between presumably social inputs, such as spouse age, and physiological outcomes, namely, increased or decreased life expectancy, are discussed.

LONGEVITY LITERATURE

From ancient times to the present, the search for prolongation of life and restoration of youth has been continuous. Although efforts to understand factors contributing to longevity have taken a more empirical approach in the last century, the underlying motivation for such research has probably altered little since ancient times. Old age and its accompanying physical changes have been dreaded in many cultures, but particularly in western civilizations. In part, old age has been feared because it has been viewed as a time of obsolescence and a prelude to death.

The quest for longevity can be found in historical literature and can be divided into three main themes; (a) the antediluvian theme, which suggests people lived longer in the past, (b) the rejuvenation theme, which promises the possibility of restoration of youth, and (c) the hyperborean theme, which assumes that societies or cultures blessed with long life exist (Birren & Clayton, 1975). It could be argued that the hyperborean theme continues to propel research and certainly is evident in popular writing. This theme implies genetic proclivity or a social or physical environment conducive to long life (See Benet, 1976; Halsell, 1976; Leaf, 1973). Reports persist that some regions in the world including Soviet Armenia, Vilcabamba Ecuador, and the land of Hunza in the Pakistani part of Kashmir have persons with life spans as great as 170 years. Leaf (1973) who led expeditions to these three areas declared that all three cultures had four common features: strong family ties; strenuous daily exercise; nutritious, well-balanced diets; and an active sex life into advanced old age. However, lack of systematic record keeping and age exaggeration may account for reports of increased longevity (Mazess & Forman, 1979). Schmeck (1981) reported that a Japanese man who lived to be 114 years old was the greatest authenticated case of human longevity. Generally, researchers do agree that there is a limit of 110–120 years in the human life span, but there is less agreement as to what factors influence the wide variation in human mortality. The following discussion provides an overview of genetic, biological, and gender-related determinates of longevity, whereas the subsequent discussion explores possible interpersonal and social factors.

Biology as Destiny

The statement that "the best way to assure oneself of long life is to choose long-lifed parents" is humorous but nevertheless, the best predictor of longevity. Different biological theories suggest that progressive damage to DNA, predetermined life spans built into cells, or perhaps hormonal control explain variations in life spans. Regardless of the underlying causes it is evident that gender is a strong predictor of longevity. There appears to be a biological bais, corroborated through animal and human studies, which suggests that the female is genetically superior to the male in terms of longevity (Palmore & Jeffers, 1971). Genetically based secondary sex characteristics which produce differences in behavior, rate of metabolism and body structure were believed to extend female life span although certainly arguments for vast social differences deserve consideration as well. In 1982 life expectancy at birth in the United States was 70.8 years for White males and 65.4 for non-White males. White females had an average life span of 78.5 years while non-White females had a life expectancy of 74.1 years. The differential which favors females has fluctuated between 7.5 and 7.8 years since 1968 (Met Life Insurance Co., 1983). In the previous century women had a higher mortality rate than men due to lower level of health care and complications related to pregnancy. However, since 1900 women have enjoyed increasingly lower mortality rates than men (Kitagawa & Hauser, 1973).

The Biological/Sociological Link

The relationship between verbal and nonverbal communication and physiology has been explored in work on interpersonal synchrony (Davis, 1973), though more recently researchers (Levenson and Gottman, 1983; Gottman & Levenson, 1985) have linked physiological reactions in marital interaction and satisfaction. Zajonc, Addmann, Murphy, & Niedenthal (1987) reinforced the notion that married people grow to look alike over time and additionally found that those who grew more alike in appearance had happier marriages. He proposed, in a controversial theory, that not only do emotions influence facial expressions but that facial expressions help produce emotions and moods. Reactions to others result in facial mimickry and this physically empathic response may in turn produce shared emotions. Biochemical or physiological changes resulting from social influences may in fact undergird the "biology as destiny" approach to longevity study.

One area in which this is apparent is in the relationship between sexual functioning and longevity. Palmore (1985) reported that continuing sexual relations were a significant predictor of longevity for men, whereas past enjoyment of sexual relations was a predictor for women. The extent to which original vitality may result in continued sex drive and longevity rather than sex drive resulting in increased vitality, presumably through hormone production, is unknown. Certainly, there is a long tradition of literature and folklore associated with older men and continued virility related to having a younger spouse or mistress. (Notably, there is no equivalent literature or mythology available chronicling benefits for the older woman and the younger male). As an elixir to King David in his old age, his servants urged that he be brought the fairest virgin in Israel. In both ancient India and China, sexual organs of wild animals were ingested in order to improve vigor and offset the decline of age, and within the past century transplants of monkey glands and injections of testicular materials from animals were performed in Europe and America (Puner, 1974). Rosenfeld (1976) pointed out that Sophocles produced both literature and progeny late in life, while history documents that Rabbi Joseph Caro (1488–1575) had a son in his 70th year when he married for the second time, and upon marrying a third time had another son at age 83.

The fact that these events were considered worthy enough to be recorded may suggest that the social statements made by these happenings, rather than the biological factors are most relevant. Palmore (1985) further suggested that quantity of sexual functioning seemed important to males, whereas quality of past relationships was the key for women. Interestingly, sexual functioning's link to longevity reflects a stereotypical view of gender differences and sexual mores in society at large. Perhaps the larger issue is the view of oneself as vital, and sexual functioning provides one measure that differs by gender and surely differs from individual to individual as well. Or possibly what begins as a social statement of physical prowess and vitality is somehow translated into a physical outcome.

Interpersonal and Social Factors

Although acknowledging the central importance of genetic and physical factors numerous researchers have stressed the importance of social influences on longevity. Factors such as social status, income, education, the self-system, happiness, secondary group activity, and usefulness all have an impact on successful aging. Interpersonal relationships, both quantitative and qualitative, play an important role because age often brings increased isolation and lowered levels of communication with others (Hess, 1974). The beneficial relationship between social support and general health (Berkman, 1983), mental health (Harel & Deimling, 1984), stress and well-being (Krause, 1986), and mortality (Blazer, 1982) has been demonstrated. Marriage is a fundamental role relationship which provides continuity and companionship for individual partners.

Persons who are married have a greater life expectancy at all ages except females 20–24. Verbrugee (1979) in a discussion of marital status and mortality identified three popular explanations for lower mortality rates among married persons. Selection theory suggests that only the healthier and more desirable marry, whereas the less healthy or less desirable are screened out. A second explanation is that married persons are happier and less stressed than nonmarried persons and as a consequence engage in less risk taking, which would result in illness or injury. The third belief is that married persons have more social support for their health problems, thereby reducing the severity of illness leading to mortality. Although women do not appear to be as sensitive to the advantages of marital status as do men, the following figures illustrate the benefits derived from marriage. Puner (1974) found that mortality rates were 29% higher for single men than for married men, 42% higher for widowed men, and 54% higher for divorced men. The death rate was 15% higher for single women, 26% higher for widows, and 43% higher for divorced women.

Marriage Roles

Communication with others is central to the formation and maintenance of social roles. Tamir (1979) noted that communication with others anchors individuals within the society. It is the medium through which we structure our view of the world and our view of self. Woelfel (1976, p. 70) pronounced that, "removal from the information stream may well lead to important declines in the health of the aging population and perhaps shorten life spans to an unknown extent." Additionally, clear and direct relationships among social support factors, physical health, mental health, life satisfaction and self-esteem in the elderly have been identified (Holahan & Holahan, 1987; Revicki & Mitchell, 1986). As a consequence of these findings concerning aging in general, along with studies dealing directly with longevity, the idea that social roles influence physical well-being has been well documented. Less understood are the specific ways in which this interface occurs. Communication may be viewed as what the marital role communicates to society at large and how the couple interacts with others, or communication might be viewed as the exchange that occurs between partners in the relationship.

AGE DIFFERENCES IN MARRIAGE

Age differences between spouses and the special social and interpersonal circumstances created by virtue of one partner being a different age from the other partner are the primary focus of this investigation. First, a brief review of a few demographic studies that have bearing on the social relationship between marital trends and marital status is undertaken.

Subsequently attention is given to the interpersonal consequences of age homophily and heterophily in marriage. Finally, the few articles that combine age difference in marriage with mortality are discussed along with own research in the area.

Demographic Trends

In our society husbands are traditionally older than their wives. A cross-national survey, (Casterline, Williams, & McDonald, 1986) found that marriages in which the wife was older were avoided in most cultures. Additionally it was concluded that age-difference distributions in marriage could be interpreted in terms of (a) kinship structure and (b) status of women. As age at marriage increases for men, spouse age differences increase. Goldman and Lord (1983) offered two explanations for the disproportionate number of older male–younger female marriages in the United States. First, supply dictates that there are more single women than single men at all marriageable ages. Second, these unions occur because of "societal norms and preferences through which men have frequently sought the beauty and vigor of younger women and have obtained it by economic dominance of the relationship" (p. 191). Current data suggest that although the traditional older male marriage predominates, a slight shift is occurring in marriage patterns in the United States. In 1983, in 6.2% of all marriages the bride was 5 years older than the groom. This represented a 67% increase since 1970 (NCHS, unpublished tables, 1970a, 1983). Bride-older marriages have become more frequent since 1970, but it should be noted that grooms 6+ years older have increased by 4.6%, whereas brides 6+ years older have increased by 1.9%. Correspondingly, grooms 10+ years older increased 2.4%, whereas during that time period brides 10+ years older increased only .6% (See Table 15.1). These recent statistics reflect an increase in marriages in which the wife is *slightly* older. In marriages with large age differences the older male–younger female pattern is overwhelmingly dominant and increasing at a faster rate than wife-older unions as illustrated in Table 15.1.

Demographic data on age differences in marriage must be interpreted cautiously because average age differences may not clearly represent the trends that are occuring at the extremes. Demographic data reflect normative trends in marital selection. Alterations in these patterns may reflect alterations in underlying role expectations and are therefore important social components of longevity study. An interesting example of this is provided by Presser (1975) who wrote "if female aspirations for achievement outside the home have changed, even smaller age differences

Table 15.1
Variations of Age Differences in Marriage (1970, 1983)

	All Marriages (%)	Bride Younger (%)	Bride Same Age (%)	Bride Older (%)	Groom 6+ Years older (%)	Bride 6+ Years Older (%)	Groom 10+ Years Older (%)	Bride 10+ Years Older (%)
1970	1,674,104 (100)	1,194,671 (71)	216,051 (13)	263,382 (16)	300,219 (17.9)	47,223 (2.8)	123,988 (7.4)	17,332 (1)
1983	1,890,791 (100)	1,285,018 (68)	202,617 (11)	403,156 (21)	425,576 (22.5)	88,656 (4.7)	184,413 (9.8)	30,527 (1.6)
Percent Change	—	−3%	−2%	+5%	+4.6%	+1.9%	+2.4%	+.6%

Note. Derived from NCHS unpublished tables 1970, 1983.

between spouses and an increasing proportion of women marrying youn-ger men may follow" (p. 192). Her interpretation of the impact of female social roles clearly reflects changing marital patterns from 1970 to 1983.

To better understand the extent to which so called "May-December" marriages occur, it should be noted that approximately 8% of all couples enter into marriages that have age differences of more than 10 years. Persons who have been married more than once are more likely to be in age-heterogamous marriages, whereas remarried men marrying never-married women have the largest average age differences, (Vera, Berardo, & Berardo, 1985). In addition, age differences increase as husband's age at marriage increases, whereas the age difference remains relatively con-stant for women.

Interpersonal Factors in Marriage

As previously mentioned, it has been suggested that one explanation for lower mortality rates in married persons is that they are happier and less stressed than nonmarried persons. It seems logical then to explore the dynamics of marriages with large age differentials to determine whether they enjoy the same degree of happiness and success as marriages with smaller age differentials. Udry (1971) and Atkinson and Glass (1985) both reported that the relative age of spouses was not a significant factor in marital happiness or success. However, Wilson (1982) reported that in primary marriages, divorce occurred more frequently for wives whose husbands were younger than average. Bumpass and Sweet (1972) found that among women who married very young, marital instability de-creased with greater age differences between them and their husbands until the age difference became "large enough to be socially significant" (p. 762). Marriages with extremely large age differences and marriages in which the wife was older than the husband were subject to higher rates of divorce. Three main factors were associated with these findings: (a) consensus in values decreases as age differences increase; (b) the power structure of the family may be jeopardized, especially when the wife is older, and (c) persons who marry with great age disparity may have personal characteristics that lower their probability of marital success.

Two studies have examined the effect of age differentials on the power structure of the marital dyad. Blood and Wolfe (1962) reported that when husbands were 10 or more years older than their wives they were more influential than when age differences were reduced. With large age differences, the older spouse in the marriage tended to be more dominant and powerful. Presser (1975) suggested that women married to older men "may feel less assertive (and their husbands more powerful) because of the discrepancy in age and achievement" (p. 197). However, at the time when the marriage occurs the younger woman–older man relationship may be beneficial for both parties if they are seeking power or status from marriage. Seidenberg (1972) contended that by marrying an older man, a woman can achieve economic and social rewards without years of struggle. Sontag (1972) noted that when older men marry extremely young women as in the cases of Pablo Casals, Charles Chaplin, William O. Douglas, Strom Thurmond, or Fred Astaire, people view such a marriage as unusual but plausible. She stated, "for a man a late marriage is always good public relations. It adds to the impression that despite his advanced age, he is still to be reckoned with." She suggested that such a marriage makes a statement about a man's power, his ability to possess, and his continued worth to society, whereas for the older woman such a marriage is often greeted with dismay by society and is an infrequent occurrence.

Marital Roles Across Time

It should be noted that these studies did not look at subjects across time and it is quite possible that an older spouse would have more power than a younger spouse until physical decline begins, at which point roles might be reversed. Also, because age-disparate marriages might contain one partner who is "old" and one who is "middle-aged," differences in marital perception across the age span are also an important consideration. Two primary themes of relational love have been identified in a plethora of literature. Love appears to have a natural progression across the life span toward deeper levels of intimacy from passion to a more serene and tender love. Secondly, sociologists suggest that there are two basic marital types: (a) the traditional relationships in which normative rules are sex differentiated along traditional lines in terms of roles and domination and, (b) companionship relationships that center around communicative or affective aspects of the union (Reedy, Birren, & Schaie, 1981). Similarities far outnumbered differences across life-span development and among generations. Notably though, they found that young adult lovers had higher ratings for communication and both middle-aged and younger couples valued sexual intimacy, whereas older couples rated affection and loyalty as relatively more important. They suggested, "whereas communication may be more critical to a sense of attachment, bonding and behavioral control in young relationships, the bonding force in long-standing relationships may come more from the history of the relationship itself" (Reedy et al., 1981, p. 62). Margolin and White (1987) reported that physical attractiveness played a greater role in husbands' assessments of sexual interest, happiness, and faithfulness. They suggested that the demand for physical attractiveness in women is not lessened by age or by marital duration suggesting that a double standard of aging exists in which men at all ages attach more importance to female attractiveness than females do to male appearance. Finally, it is noteworthy that Albrecht, Bahr, & Chadwick (1979) found few changes from the traditional patterns of family and gender-related roles when comparing young, middle-aged, and older couples. Surprisingly, far more similarities than differences occurred across the different age groups. A more current assessment of trends would be desirable but generally it appears that many of the outward societal trends have yet to have an impact on deeply held beliefs about marital roles and male/female status.

Longevity Factors

In the current literature there are only five studies that directly address the influence of age differences between spouses on longevity. They are (a) Rose's (1964) study of Spanish American War veterans; (b) Rose and Bell's (1971) research on longevity in which they explored the effect of a younger wife along with 68 other variables; (c) an English population study, which explored age difference and mortality in marriage (Fox, Bulusu, & Kinlen, 1979); (d) Foster, Klinger-Vartabedian, and Wispe's (1984) study on male longevity; and (e) Klinger-Vartabedian and Wispe's (in press) research on female longevity and age difference in marriage.

Rose (1964) used subjects who comprised a long-lived sample (ages 72–92). The subjects differed from the general population in regard to marital status since 92% of the sample were married, compared to 58% of all males 75 years and over in the general population at that time. Rose (1964) concluded that these subjects married at a later age than the average population and as a result had younger-than-average wives. Marrying a younger wife was presumed to be conducive to longevity because she was less likely to be lost by death and the benefits of her care would to continuous. Marrying younger spouses enabled the men to maintain a spouse into old age, thereby affording unbroken nurturing or caretaking it was determined. Matter (1979) found that individuals who were married longer and younger had greater life expectancies. This finding lends credence to the caretaking hypothesis but Matter's conclusions about early marriage contradict the sample characteristics in Rose's study of long-lived veterans who married at a later age.

Rose and Bell (1971) using a sample of 500 White males, again found that having a younger wife was a good predictor of longevity, presumably because of the continuous care she provided. They also found that the health variable was made more important by being married to a younger wife. They suggested that perhaps a younger wife takes better care of her husband but also makes special demands that require a better health level from her husband. Another related explanation is that the man makes extra demands on himself when married to a younger wife, which in turn, enhance health and longevity.

A third demographic study, conducted in England found that age combinations in which the husband was either the same age or older than his wife were associated with lower morbidity than were other combinations (Fox et al, 1979). Additionally, having a husband slightly younger was also conducive to longevity for women. However, men married to older or extremely younger women were subject to higher mortality, whereas women married to much younger or somewhat older men were also generally subject to greater mortality. The authors state that adherence to the social norm of males being older than females, on the average, reduced mortality for both men and women. Noting the high mortality rate of men who marry women more than 20 years of age younger than themselves, they suggest that the death rates are at the level expected only for sick people. They deduced that there may be a tendency toward the sick and lonely marrying young "nurses," or for the young marrying in the anticipation of inheriting wealth. Although these explanations can only be considered speculation, the mortality rates in marriages with large age differences were found to be substantially higher than in similar age marriages.

The two remaining studies include demographic investigations undertaken by Foster et al. (1984) and Klinger-Vartabedian and Wispe' (in press). These studies used data from the U.S. Census (1972) and the National Mortality Followback Survey (1970) to determine standard mortality ratios for men and women married to spouses younger, older, and the same age. Foster et al. (1984) found that men married to younger women tended to live longer, and they agreed with the findings that mortality rates were higher with marriages to older women. It should be noted that the English data allowed greater examination of extreme age differences so the finding (Fox et al., 1979) that men married to significantly younger women died sooner than expected does not necessarily contradict the U.S. findings. Klinger-Vartabedian and Wispe determined that the same relationship found with men was repeated with women. Women married to husbands 1–14 years younger lived longer than expected, whereas women married to husbands 1–14 years older experienced higher mortality rates than would be expected (See Fig. 15.1).

These findings were explained in terms of premarital selections factors and/or as a function of the biological, social, or psychological elements of

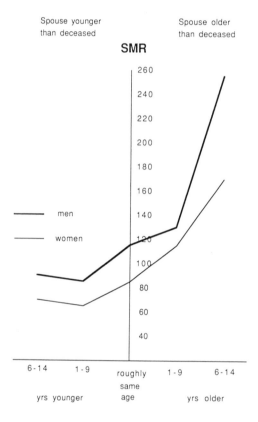

MALE AND FEMALE MORTALITY
BASED ON SPOUSE AGE DIFFERENCE

FIGURE 15.1.   SMR's base rate = 100. Numbers above 100 mean more deaths occurred than expected, whereas numbers below 100 mean fewer occurred.

marital interaction. Selection may dictate that the older person who attracts a younger person was healthier or more vital than his or her peers and would have lived longer regardless of their spouse's age. Inversely, the selection theory suggests that for some reason the younger person also has characteristics that predispose them to higher mortality. The second explanation is that interrelationship with a younger spouse somehow enlivens an older person biologically, psychologically, or socially, whereas the opposite effects occurs for the younger spouse. Observation of the combined data showed an intriguing age-based effect. On the average, older spouses lived longer than expected and younger spouses died sooner than expected. Thus, it would appear that an intimate partnership with another may create a "mortality mean." It is as if the older person is granted a portion of the younger spouse's life span, while the younger person forfeits those years. For the most part, deviations from this pattern occurred when marriage age difference became extreme and no longer conformed to socially sanctioned patterns. The primary exception would be women married to spouses up to 14 years younger. A comparison of the U.S. male and female data is presented in Table 15.2.

DISCUSSION

Limitations of Data

Lack of appropriate marriage data has been an impediment in studying age differences in marriage (Mensch, 1986; Vera et al., 1985). Longevity research in this area is hampered because it is difficult to find matching mortality data necessary to make comparisons between living and deceased populations. Difficulties in studying marital partners are exacerbated because fewer women marry younger men, and more women outlive their husbands. Because combined mortality and marriage data is difficult to find it is obvious that it is impossible to find data containing more specialized information , such as number of marriages, duration of marriage, and interpersonal factors. Recognizing these limitations, the primary significance of investigations into age-difference in marriage and longevity lies in the discovery that spouse age differences do contribute to mortality differences.

Table 15.2
Adjusted Standard Mortality Ratios Combined for Younger and Older Spouses

Age at Death	Wives 1–24 Yrs. Younger	Wives 4 yrs Younger to 14 Yrs. Older	Husbands 1–14 Yrs. Younger	Husbands 4 Yrs. Younger to 14 Yrs. Older
50–54	85	247	86	112
55–59	94	192	67	125
60–64	82	139	54	116
65–69	113	145	62	124
70–74	71	163	58	133
75–79	95	97	—	—
Deceased all ages	90	164	65	122

Normative Issues

There is supporting evidence that age-appropriate marital roles and the accompanying normative issues may have an impact on longevity. Certainly in 1970 the socially acceptable marriage of an older man and younger woman resulted in lower mortality. The opposite situation, that of an older woman and younger man, resulted in extremely high mortality for the male. Although the effects were not as pronounced, marriage to an older husband resulted in higher mortality overall for women, whereas a younger husband was beneficial for longevity. Data that explored the younger husband union beyond 14 years difference was too limited to report conclusively but suggestive results indicated that mortality rates for women climb dramatically (and in a parallel fashion to Fox et al., 1979) when husbands are substantially younger.

Marriage to a younger spouse, within a socially prescribed range may be particularly socially rewarding. A relationship with an even slightly younger spouse may promote a positive self-concept, while enabling the older spouse to maintain a positive and perhaps envied role in society. The older spouse may become more vital in his or her own view, and thus, a positive spiral of social and personal reinforcement is created. On the other hand, a society that tends to categorize women as growing "old" before their male counterparts (Neugarten, Moore, & Lowe, 1968) is unlikely to offer as much positive reinforcement for the older woman–younger man relationship, particularly in the case of extreme age differences. Supporting this idea and the double standard, which rules marital selection, are the combined U.S. and English findings that a younger wife is beneficial to a man until age difference reaches 25+ years, while a younger husband is beneficial up to approximately 10–14 years.

Marital roles are obviously defined not only from the outside by society, but from within by the marital partners. Interestingly, with the exception of Gove (1972) longevity research has largely ignored intrapersonal or interpersonal elements in role relationships as they pertain to physical outcomes. The extent to which nontraditional roles can disrupt a marriage has been explored in terms of the power structure. Berko, Wolvin, and Wolvin (1980) noted that traditional roles to some extent offered a sanctuary from stress. They reported that when traditional roles in marriages are questioned, "this stress increases the need for good communication patterns in order to allow a couple to cope with conflicts about who is responsible for what role and about how to deal with the need for changes and adjustment to those changes" (p. 6). Therefore, the possibility is raised that traditional role relationships avoid some stress-producing situations that nontraditional relationships engender.

Secular Change

Palmore and Jeffers (1971) noted that one of the primary difficulties in longevity study is accounting for secular changes. Secular changes refer to changes in society and in the behavior patterns of persons studied. Presumably, subjects born in the same year will live under similar environmental and societal conditions. Current literature suggests that marital partners are more alike than different across age spans. Seidenberg (1972) pointed out that there are strong social norms that govern acceptable marriage patterns. He noted that "it is an accepted universal custom, an almost inalienable right no matter what social strata are involved, that older men have free and uninhibited access to younger women. It is the exception in courting, mating, and marriage that the woman is older" (p. 9). Although it would seem likely that a decade and one-half later these words would ring false, the previously mentioned demographic trends, along with basic issues such as male/female attractiveness show only the beginnings of change.

Future Directions

The use of cross cultural data might be another approach that could be taken to further examine the hypothesis and help corroborate the "social norms" and "interpersonal" explanations that have been advanced. A comparison of societies with different traditional age patterns might reveal different longevity patterns, thus supporting the notion that social influences are operative. It is possible that the minor differences between the English and U.S. data reflect cultural differences.

Communication research in the area of age difference warrants further examination. Numerous interpersonal and intrapersonal variables could be examined. Additionally, because the relevance of age difference in marriage may change over the duration of the marriage, studies that combine both developmental and interactive approaches might be useful tools for examining age differences in marriage and its consequences. Currently, we can prove only that a relationship exists between age difference in marriage and longevity. The way in which age similarities and differences between partners operate to influence longevity is a relationship that must be investigated further.

CONCLUSIONS

If in fact longevity differences related to spouse age differences are linked to social, psychological and/or interpersonal causation, it seems an unfortunate statement of social values. If the "mortality mean" is socially induced, it is a reinforcement of stereotypical views regarding age. It becomes a fulfillment of the "rejuvenation theme" in which the younger partner provides the magic elixir simply by being young. Additionally, the wide range in which a younger wife provides benefit to an older husband in the English data and the particularly deleterious effects of having an older wife as shown in both English and U.S. data sets suggest little progress in terms of greater equality between the sexes.

The past two decades seem to be a time of great social change in regard to our understanding of gender and aging in our society. However, our perceptions of secular change often greatly exceed the actual change of deeply held norms. Future mortality trends may show whether awareness of agism and sexism have been internalized and translated into greater equality between men and women in all ages in marital selection. In a more egalitarian society, assuming a social explanation, age differences in marriage should not effect longevity.

Finally, because the truth is often found between the extremes, the longevity effect may be a combination of social and biological explanations. Zajonc et al. (1987) speculated that marital partners grow to look alike through the delicate dance of social response and physiological reaction. Likewise, the causal factors of age difference in marriage and longevity may be equally intertwined. If our own age is factored against the age of our spouse, resulting in a longer or shorter life span, the implications are unsettling and intriguing.

ACKNOWLEDGMENT

The authors wish to thank Cheryl Olson for her assistance with this manuscript.

REFERENCES

Albrecht, S. L., Bahr, H., & Chadwick, B. A. (1979). Changing family and sex roles: An assessment of age differences. *Journal of Marriage and the Family, 41,* 41–50.

Atkinson, M., & Glass, B. (1985). Marital age heterogamy and homogamy 1900 to 1980. *Journal of Marriage and the Family, 47,* 685–691.

Benet, S. (1976). *How to live to be 100: The life-style of people of the caucus.* New York: Dial Press.

Berkman, L. F. (1983). The assessment of social networks and social support in the elderly. *Journal of the American Geriatrics Society, 31*(12), 743–749.

Berko, R., Wolvin, A., Wolvin, D. (1980). *Communicating: A social and career focus.* Boston: Houghton Mifflin.

Birren, J., & Clayton, V. (1975). History of gerontology. In D. Woodruff & J. Birren (Eds.), *Aging: Scientific perspectives and social issues.* New York: Van Nostrand.

Blazer, D. (1982). Social support and mortality in an elderly community population. *American Journal of Epidemiology, 115,* 684–694.

Blood, R., & Wolfe, D. (1962). *Husband and wives: The dynamics of married living*. New York: Basic Books.

Bumpass, L., & Sweet, J. (1972). Differentials in marital stability. *American Sociological Review, 37*, 754–766.

Casterline, J.B., Williams, L., & McDonald P. (1986). The age difference between spouses: Variations among developing countries. *Population Studies, 40*, 353–374.

Davis, F. (1973). *Inside intuition: What we know about nonverbal communication*. New York: McGraw-Hill.

Foster, D., Klinger-Vartabedian, L., & Wispe, L. (1984). Male longevity and age differences between spouses. *Journal of Gerontology, 30*, 117–120.

Fox, J., Bulusu, L., & Kinlen, L. (1979). Mortality and age differences in marriage. *Journal of Biosocial Science, 11*, 117–131.

Goldman, N., & Lord, G. (1983). Sex differences in life cycle measures in widowhood. *Demography, 20*, 177–195.

Gottman, J., & Levenson, R. (1985). Physiological and affective predictors of change in relationship satisfaction. *Journal of Personality and Social Psychology, 49*, 177–195.

Gove, W. (1972). Sex, marital status, and mortality. *American Journal of Sociology, 79*(1), 45–67.

Halsell, G. (1976). *Los viejos: Secrets of long life from the sacred valley*. Emmaus, PA: Rodale Press.

Harel, Z., & Deimling, G. (1984). Social resources and mental health: An empirical refinement. *Journal of Gerontology, 39*, 747–752.

Hess, B. (1974). Stereotypes of the aged. *Journal of Communication, 24*, 76–85.

Holahan, C. K., & Holahan, C. J. (1987). Self-efficacy, social support, and depression in aging: A longitudinal analysis. *Journal of Gerontology, 42*(1), 65–68.

Kitagawa, E., & Hauser, P. (1973). *Differential mortality in the United States: A study of socioeconomic epidemiology*. Cambridge, MA: Harvard University Press.

Klinger-Vartabedian, L. & Wispe, L. Age Difference in Marriage and Female Longevity. *Journal of Marriage and the Family* (in press)

Krause, N. (1986). Social support, stress, and well-being among older adults. *Journal of Gerontology, 41*(4), 512–519.

Leaf, A. (1973). Everyday is a gift when you are over 100. *National Geographic, 143*, 93–119.

Levenson, R., Gottman, J. (1983). Marital interaction: Physiological linkage and affective exchange. *Journal of Personality and Social Psychology, 45*, 587–597.

Margolin, L., & White, L. (1987). The continuing role of physical attractiveness in marriage. *Journal of Marriage and the Family, 49*, 21–27.

Matter, D. (1979). Biographical factors associated with longevity in male Kansas pioneers. *Psychological Reports, 45*, 843–852.

Mazess, R., & Forman, S. (1979). Longevity and age exaggeration in Vilcabamba Ecuador. *Journal of Gerontology, 34*(1), 94–98.

Mensch, B. (1986). Age differences between spouses in first marriages. *Social Biology, 33*, 229–240.

Metropolitan Life Insurance Company (1983). Life expectancy in the United States. *Statistical Bulletin 64*, 12–16.

Neugarten, B., Moore, J., & Lowe, J. (1968). Age norms, age constraints and adult socialization. In B. Neugarten (Ed.), *Middle age and aging*. Chicago, IL: University of Chicago Press.

Palmore, E. (1985). Predictors of longevity differences. In E. Palmore, E. Busse, G. Maddox, G. Nowlin & I. Siegler (Eds.), *Normal Aging III* (pp 29–36). Durham, N.C.: Duke Univ. Press.

Palmore, E., & Jeffers, F. (1971). *Prediction of life span*. Lexington, MA: Heath Lexington Books.

Presser, H. (1975). Age differences between spouses: Trends, Patterns and social implications. *American Behvioral Scientist, 19,* 190–205.

Puner, M. (1974). *The good long life: What we know about growing old.* New York: Universe Books.

Reedy, M. N., Birren, J. E., & Schaie, K. W. (1981). Age and sex difference in satisfying love relationships across the adult life span. *Human Development, 24,* 52–66.

Revicki, D., & Mitchell, J. (1986). Social support factor structure in the elderly. *Research on Aging, 8*(2), 232–247.

Rose, C. (1964). Social factors in longevity. *Gerontologist, 4,* 27–37.

Rose, C., & Bell, B. (1971). *Predicting longevity.* Lexington, MA: Heath.

Rosenfeld, A. (1976). *Prolongevity.* New York: Knopf.

Schmeck, H. (1981, May 3). Extending the life span may be just impossible. *New York Times,* p. E7.

Seidenberg, R. (1972). Older women and younger men. *Sexual Behavior, 4,* 9–17.

Sontag, S. (1972, September 23). The double standard of aging. *Saturday Review,* pp. 29–38.

Tamir, L. (1979). *Communication and the aging process.* New York: Pergamon Press.

U.S. Bureau of the Census (1972). *1970 census of the population, subject reports, marital status* (Publication No. PC-2-4C). Washington, DC: U.S. Government Printing Office.

U. S. National Center for Health Statistics (1970a). [Marriage statistics]. Unpublished tables.

U.S. National Center for Health Statistics (1970b). *National Mortality Followback Survey, 1966–68.* Tape documentaion package. (NTIS No. PB80-117146). Springfield, VA: National Technical Information Service, U.S. Department of Commerce.

U.S. National Center for Health Statistics (1983). [Marriage statistics]. Unpublished tables.

Udry, J. (1971). *The social context of marriage* (2nd ed.). New York: Lippincott.

Vera, H., Berardo, D., & Berardo, F. (1985). Age heterogamy in marriage. *Journal of Marriage and the Family, 47,* 523–565.

Verbrugee, L. (1979). Marital status and health. *Journal of Marriage and the Family, 41,* 267–85.

Wilson, B. (1982, April). *Age differences between spouses and marital instability.* Paper presented at the meeting of Population Association of America, San Diego, CA.

Woelfel, J. (1976). Communication across age levels. In H. J. Oyer & E. J. Oyer, (Eds.), *Aging and communication* (pp. 63–73). Baltimore: University Park Press.

Zajonc, R. B., Addmann, P. K., Murphy, S. T., & Niedenthal, P. M. (1987). Convergence in the physical appearance of spouses. *Motivation and Emotion, II, 4,* 335–346.

16 Mass Media and the Elderly: A Uses and Dependency Interpretation

James D. Robinson
University of Dayton

In attempting to understand the media use of the elderly, it is important to do more than list the number of hours per day the average individual watches television or list the 10 most popular magazines for people 65 years of age or older. Although it is important to know how much time is spent with the various media and the content preferences of the elderly, it is also important to organize such information into a theoretical scheme. By imposing a theoretical scheme on the information, the data can be more easily understood and additional insight can be gained.

The chapter is organized into three sections. The first section discusses the elderlys' use of television, radio, newspapers, magazines, books, and films. The second section addresses the way the elderly are commonly portrayed in the various mass media, the content preferences of the elderly, and the treatment of the issues facing the elderly in the mass media. The final section of this chapter attempts to interpret the research findings presented in the first two sections of this chapter from the Uses and Dependency Perspective proposed by Rubin and Windahl (1986). This theoretical position is a hybrid or integration of the Uses and Gratifications Perspective and the Media Dependency Model.

MEDIA USE OF THE ELDERLY

Research into media usage suggests that the elderly spend nearly 50% of their day with the various mass media. Research suggests television viewing is the most frequently reported daily leisure activity for elderly

319

Americans (DeGrazia, 1961; Kubey, 1980; Market Opinion Research, 1975; Schramm, 1969). Although estimates vary, it is safe to say that the elderly watch between 5 and 6 hours of television a day (Bower, 1973; Danowski, 1975; Korzenny & Neuendorf, 1980; TV Dimensions '86, 1986). In fact, the elderly watch more television than any other age cohort including children (Bower, 1973; TV Dimensions '86, 1986).

Television consumption across the life span can be best described as being curvilinear. Young children watch a great deal of television and their viewing drops off somewhat during adolescence. Viewing increases again through adulthood and into old age (Bogart, 1972; Bower, 1973; Chaffee & Wilson, 1975; Harris & Associates, 1975; Hoar, 1961; Steiner, 1963; TV Dimensions '86, 1986). Nielsen ratings indicate that men 50 years of age and older watch about 1 hour more television a day than men between the ages of 25 and 49. Women over the age of 50 watch about 3 hours a week more than men of the same age. It is interesting to note that living conditions do not seem to impact television viewing. People living in nursing homes, retirement communities, and in private dwellings all watch about the same amount of television.

When the elderly watch television, they prefer to watch informative programs such as the news, documentaries, talk shows, and public affairs programming (Bower, 1973; Davis, 1971; Korzenny & Neuendorf, 1980; Meyersohn, 1961; Rubin & Rubin, 1981, 1982; Steiner, 1963, Wenner, 1976). Not surprisingly, the elderly also enjoy game shows, travelogues, and family dramas. Elderly men enjoy sports programming and elderly women report preferring soap operas (Barton, 1977; Bower, 1973; Danowski, 1975; Davis, 1971; 1980; Rubin & Rubin, 1981, 1982; TV Dimensions '86, 1986; Young, 1979).

The Elderly and Radio Use

As a rule people listen to the radio less as they grow older. The average adult listens to the radio between 2 and 3 hours a day, whereas older adults listen to the radio about 1 hour a day (Chaffee & Wilson, 1975; Harris & Associates, TV Dimensions '86, 1986; Young, 1979). When they listen to the radio the elderly prefer talk radio (Turow, 1974), news, local affairs, and weather (Comstock, Chaffee, Katzman, McCombs, & Roberts, 1978; Young, 1979).

Recently, however, Davis and Davis (1985) found that the elderly have begun spending more time listening to the radio. They suggest changes in programming (e.g., big band music and talk radio) and programming that is more consistent with the needs of the elderly are the primary reasons for this increase in radio usage.

The Elderly and Newspaper Use

In general, the amount of time spent reading decreases with age (Gordon, Gaitz, & Scott, 1976; Harris & Associates, 1975; McEnvoy & Vincent, 1980). Danowski (1975) found that the average elderly adult spends about 80 minutes a day reading books, magazines, and newspapers. Approximately 30 minutes is spent reading magazines, 45 minutes is spent reading newspapers, and the few remaining minutes are spent reading books. Danowski's daily reading estimates are fairly consistent with research by Beyer and Woods (1963) and TV Dimensions '86 (1986).

Newspaper readership, generally, increases across the life span (American Newspaper Publishers Association [ANPA], 1973; Burgoon & Burgoon, 1980; Chaffee & Wilson, 1975). The estimates that 67% of the people between 18 and 34 years of age read a newspaper daily, whereas 83% of the people between 35 and 64 typically read a newspaper. Eighty-four percent of those people 65 years of age or older read a daily newspaper. Newpaper readership increases until about the age of 70 and then drops off "precipitously" (Chaffee & Wilson, 1975; Doolittle, 1979). This drop off in newspaper readership has been attributed to presbyopia–vision deficits associated with aging.

Much like their television and radio program preferences, the elderly prefer informative newspaper articles over entertainment. Public affairs, news, political articles, letters to the editor, crime stories, obituaries, and health articles are commonly read (ANPA, 1973; Chaffee & Wilson, 1975). Because older women significantly outnumber men, research suggesting the elderly do not read the sports section must be taken with a grain of salt.

The Elderly and Magazine Use

Magazine readership declines with age (ANPA, 1973; Harris & Associates, 1975; TV Dimensions '86, 1986) and drops off dramatically at the age of 70 (Chaffee & Wilson, 1975). As you recall, Danowski (1975) reported that the elderly spend about 30 minutes a day reading magazines. This estimate is somewhat higher than other estimates of magazine readership. Recent marketing research indicates that the elderly spend just over 16 minutes a day reading magazines (TV Dimensions '86, 1986).

In an excellent piece of research, Frank and Greenberg (1980) found that the elderly read very few magazines when compared to the total adult population. In fact only very alienated adults read fewer magazines than the elderly. When the elderly read magazines they prefer *Reader's Digest, TV Guide, Better Homes and Gardens, Good Housekeeping, Family Circle, McCalls, Ladies Home Journal, Women's Day, Home and Garden,* and *National Geographic.* Again, this list of the top 10 magazines reflects the fact that women live longer than men.

Marketing research suggests that magazine readers are generally affluent and well educated. Barton and Schreiber (1978) contended that the more educated individual is less likely to rely on television and radio for news and more likely to use newspapers and magazines for information. This conclusion is consistent with other research findings (e.g., Doolittle, 1979; Hwang, 1972).

The Elderly and Book Use

The average elderly adult only spends about 5 minutes a day reading a book (Danowski, 1975) and is much less likely to read a book than younger adults (McEnvoy & Vincent, 1980). In fact, McEnvoy and Vincent (1980) found that people 65 years of age and older accounted for 25% of all the nonreaders, even though that group only respresents 13% of the population. Elderly individuals living alone tend to read more books than elderly people living with a spouse, and reading books was unrelated to other media usage (Kent & Rush, 1976; McEnvoy & Vincent, 1980). It appears that books may be used to escape "reality" or learn about one's self, but are not typically used to fulfill social and interpersonal needs. McEnvoy and Vincent (1980) also found, contrary to popular belief, that the cost of reading material did not preclude the elderly from reading. They did, however, tend to buy paperback books.

The Elderly and Film Usage

Not surprisingly, film consumption declines with age (Meyersohn, 1961). In fact, Market Opinion Research (1975) found that only 4% of the elderly people they surveyed felt movies were an important leisure activity. In contrast, 67% reported that television was important, 45% said visiting friends was important, and 39% said reading was important. Consistent with other content preferences, the elderly prefer informational films over comedy and horror-mystery films (Handel, 1950). With the advent of videotape rentals, the film consumption of the elderly may have changed. Research in this area is needed.

MEDIA CONTENT AND PORTRAYALS OF THE ELDERLY

A great deal of research has been conducted that examines the way the elderly have been portrayed in the mass media. Researchers have looked at the way the elderly are portrayed in jokes, advertisements, cartoons, birthday cards, game shows, soap operas, popular magazine articles, adult, adolescent and children's literature, advice columns, poetry, newspaper articles, and photographs. In general, media portrayals of the elderly are stereotypical, resulting in the creation and perpetuation of myths.

An interesting argument about the relationship between media portrayals and social status was articulated by Hacker (1951). Hacker suggested that groups and individuals of low social status receive less frequent and less favorable treatment in the mass media than groups and individuals of high social status. This thesis has received a great deal of support.

In addition, scholars have also argued that the media helps to shape common perceptions of groups and individuals within a society. Gerbner and his colleagues suggest that unrealistic portrayals of the elderly may serve to create unrealistic perceptions and expectations about aging and the elderly among media audiences. It appears that the process of cultivating unrealistic attitudes may be more complex than was once thought. Factors such as the relative availability of additional and contrary information, direct experience, and education, in part, influence the impact of mediated messages.

Television Content and Portrayals of the Elderly

A great deal of research has demonstrated that the elderly are grossly underrepresented on television (Arnoff, 1974; Danowski, 1975; Gerbner, Gross, Signorelli, & Morgan, 1980; Levinson, 1973; Mertz, 1970; Northcott, 1975; Petersen, 1973). Estimates vary, but most studies indicate that the elderly represent less than 5% of the characters found on television. Gerbner and his colleagues (1980) suggested that the elderly represent about 2.5% of the characters on all television programming. Arnoff (1974) and Northcott (1975) found prime time figures for elderly characters to be just under 5% and 1.5%, respectively.

Elderly women are even more grossly underrepresented on television than elderly men. Although elderly women greatly outnumber elderly men in the population (e.g., widowhood is 36% at the age of 65),

Petersen (1973) observed that an elderly man can be found on television about every 20 minutes. Elderly women appear about once every 4 hours, making the ratio about 11 to 1. More recently Gerbner et al. (1980) reported that the ratio of elderly men to women television characters is closer to 3 to 1. Danowski (1975) reported that the elderly are also unlikely to be contestants on game shows or members of the studio audience.

Underrepresentation, however, is not the only criticism that can be made about the portrayal of the elderly on television. Elderly characters are also stereotypically depicted. Research suggests that the elderly are portrayed as being reliant on younger adults (Northcott, 1975), unlikely to be romantically involved, and often depicted as being emotionally stunted or emotionally shallow (Harris & Feinberg, 1977). In addition, the elderly are often portrayed as being sick, frail, unhappy, and un-attractive (Arnoff, 1974; Carmichael, 1976; Gerbner et al., 1980; Harris & Associates, 1975; Harris & Feinberg, 1977). Arnoff (1974) also found that the elderly are often cast as evil characters, and seldom the hero.

Obviously, every character portrayed as being over 65 years of age are not cast negatively. Research by Harris and Feinberg (1977) suggests that elderly men are most favorably and commonly found on talk shows, comedies, public affairs, and informational programming. Elderly women are most favorably depicted on soap operas. On the soaps they are depicted as being more potent, influential, and central to the story than on other programming (Barton, 1977; Downing, 1974; Ramsdell, 1973). In addition, on the soaps elderly women are depicted as being less reliant on younger adults than they are portrayed on other kinds of programming.

Newspaper Content and Portrayals of the Elderly

Despite the considerable time and importance the elderly place on a daily newspaper, very little research has examined newspaper portrayals of the elderly. The few attempts that have been made to document newspaper portrayals of the elderly indicate that newspaper treatments of the elderly are also problematic.

Broussard, Blackmon, Blackwell, Smith, and Hunt (1980) examined 10 daily metropolitan newspapers and concluded that the amount of space allocated to stories about the elderly was disproportionate to the number of elderly people in the population. Research by Evans and Evans (in Peterson & Karnes, 1976) suggests that in the five metropolitan dailies they examined, the amount of space devoted to articles about the elderly did not significantly increase between 1965 and 1975. In a similar study, MacDonald (1973) analyzed one midwestern newspaper and found that the number of stories about the elderly had increased between 1963 and 1973. Further research is needed to see if this trend exists in newspapers in general.

Although MacDonald (1973) found that the number of stories about the elderly had increased, many of the articles treated the elderly in a condescending manner. In addition, the elderly were portrayed stereotypically, the articles were not balanced, and most of the information in the articles was not balanced.

More recently Buchholz and Bynum (1982) examined the *New York Times* and the *Daily Oklahoman* and found the treatment of the elderly to be balanced. In addition, over 40% of the articles depicted the elderly as being active. All of the news is not so good, however. Buchholz and Bynum (1982) also reported that 97% of the articles were obituaries, retirement notices, anniversaries, public policy pieces, and stories about fraud and the elderly. Less than 3% of the stories were about issues facing the elderly. In light of the fact that 25% of the "stories" were obituaries, it is no wonder Buchholz and Bynum concluded, "The surest way for the aged to get into the news columns was to die" (p. 86). In light of the importance the elderly place on the newspaper for accurate information, these findings are particularly disturbing.

Magazine Content and Portrayals of the Elderly

Nussbaum and Robinson (1986) examined the way the elderly are portrayed in popular magazines and found that between 1970 and 1979 portrayals of the elderly did not improve. Much the same as Carmichael (1976) found in examining television portrayals of the elderly, Nussbaum and Robinson (1986) found that 50% of the articles depicted the elderly as being bitchy, slow, sad, senile, stubborn, and lonely.

The elderly were not, however, portrayed as being completely helpless, nor were all of the articles negative portrayals. Nearly 35% of the articles described the elderly as being wise, loving, talkative, cheerful, trustworthy, and kind. Unfortunately, there were other problems with many of the articles.

Sixty percent of the stories offered medical solutions to the problems facing the elderly and very few of the articles acknowledged the importance of social support in the health and life quality of the elderly. The family of the elderly individual were not often acknowledged as a primary helping agent in the lives of the elderly. This is in clear contradiction to the research into the social support network of the elderly that suggests much of the social support the elderly receive comes from the family (c.f. Cicirelli, 1979).

Research into the advertisements of popular magazines has yielded similar results. Gantz, Gartenberg, and Rainbow (1980) found the elderly to be poorly represented in magazine advertisements. They reported that less than 6% of the advertisements contained an elderly model and only 3% of the models shown were elderly.

A more recent investigation examined the advertisements in magazines that are commonly read by elderly readers and magazines written specifically for an elderly readership. The results indicated that over 75% of advertisements in magazines written for an elderly readership (*Fifty Plus, Modern Maturity, Retirement Life,* and *Retirement Living*) contained an elderly model and over 70% of all the models were over 65 years of age. These advertisements portrayed the elderly as being active and vigorous people. In contrast, *Reader's Digest, TV Guide, Better Homes and Gardens,* and *McCalls* are the magazines most commonly read by the elderly and the results were quite different. Only 4% of the models were elderly and only 8% of the advertisements contained one or more older model.

Although a great deal of effort has been expended examining media portrayals of the elderly, much less emphasis has been placed on examining the kind of information and advice offered audience members about the process of aging. The inaccuracies in information and advice offered may well be a more significant problem than unrealistic fictional portrayals of the elderly. More research into the impact of inaccurate information needs to be done.

THE USES AND DEPENDENCY MODEL

In their Uses and Dependency Model, Rubin and Windahl (1986) integrated the Uses and Gratifications Perspective with the Media Dependency Model. This hybrid model is an attempt at rectifying the conceptual shortcomings of previous media use and effects theories by recognizing that large-scale social/structural institutions, social relations, and the individual characteristics of audience members influence media use and the effects of that use. In addition, the theory provides a more developmentally oriented perspective to understanding the elderlys' use of the media.

To call the uses and gratifications perspective a single theory is somewhat misleading because there have been several different variations of the theory proposed. Although this state of conceptual ambiguity has resulted in a great deal of comment and criticism, the different variations share common assumptions about the nature of media use and users. Those common assumptions are central to the uses and dependency model.

The uses and dependency model assumes that media usage is goal oriented and purposeful. That is to say that people use the mass media for good reason—to fulfill their needs. Scholars have argued for years about the nature of needs, but essentially a need is an internal state or feeling that motivates people to behave in such a way as to alleviate that need or discomfort. Thus, the decision to listen to a Neil Young album or watch a St. Louis Cardinal game on television is motivated by the needs of the audience member. Audience needs motivate the choice of media and influence the content selection of an audience member.

The uses and dependency model also assumes that audience members actively shape the messages they receive and that audience involvement and participation in the communication process is the key determinant of media effects. Rubin and Windahl (1986) went so far as to suggest that messages do not influence audience members unless that individual has "some use for a medium or its messages" (p. 36). From this perspective, people not only choose to expose themselves to messages that they think will help them fulfill their needs, but they also shape or alter the messages they receive in the attempt to fulfill their needs. Thus, the same message may serve different needs for different audience members. In fact, the same message may fulfill different needs for the same individual at different times.

The uses and dependency model also assumes that mass media usage is only one way that people go about satisfying needs. When people find themselves lonely they may call a friend on the phone or they may try to loose themselves in a book. Still others may use drugs/alcohol, sleep, take up a new hobby, or bury themselves in their work to meet their needs. Media use is just one functional alternative to face-to-face interaction.

In summary, the assumptions of the uses and dependency model described are those that are commonly held by uses and gratifications theorists. The uses and dependency model assumes that people use the media to fulfill their needs, the needs people have guide their media usage behavior and in part determine the effect of the mass media. Of course the mass media is only one way that people go about fulfilling their needs.

Rubin and Windhal (1986) proposed the integration of the uses and gratifications perspective with the dependency model because they recognize that factors other than the individual needs of audience members shape media usage and effects. Some of these factors have been identified by Ball-Rokeach and DeFleur (1976) in their writings about media dependency. They wrote:

This general societal system sets important limitations and boundaries on the media system and has considerable impact on its characteristics, information-delivery functions, and operating procedures. The societal system also has enormous impact upon persons; it gives rise to mechanisms that inhibit arbitrary media influence, such as individual differences, membership in social categories, and participation in social relations. The societal system also operates to create needs within persons that facilitate media alteration effects, namely the needs to understand, act in, and escape in fantasy from one's world. Finally, the interdependencies of the society's social systems and its media shape how people can and do develop dependencies on the media to satisy needs, thereby setting the media effects process into motion. (p. 25)

In this extract, Ball-Rokeach and DeFleur have suggested that the structure of social institutions, the social network of audience members, economic, and political conditions also influence media use and effects. In addition, they suggested that the structure of society and the needs of audience members also shape media content and the mass media industry. In short, you cannot understand media use and effects unless you understand the tripartite relationship between society, audience, and the mass media industry. Mass media usage and effects cannot be understood in isolation.

The concept media dependency is most easily understood in terms of information availability. An individual having only one source of information about a topic is highly dependent on that source for the information. From the uses and dependency perspective, then, media content is most likely to influence an audience member when he or she is reliant or dependent on that source for information. Any factor, then, that results in increased reliance on a source for information increases the likelihood of an audience member being influenced by the media.

Ball-Rokeach and DeFleur (1976) identified several social conditions that result in audience dependency on the mass media. They suggested that people become reliant or dependent on the mass media when other functional alternatives become unavailable or less useful. For example, Gerson (1966) found that when Black school children were bussed to a predominantely White school, they reported using television to "learn how to act" because other agencies of socialization were unavailable or less useful.

Ball-Rokeach and DeFleur (1976) also pointed out that media dependence occurs in times of social conflict and change. The dramatic demographic changes occurring today in the United States could precipitate media dependence. Further, Ball-Rokeach and DeFleur suggested that the likelihood of media dependence increases as complexity and specialization within a society increases. Because specialization results in less common experiences among members of society, people become more reliant on the mass media for that common experience and insight into nonmembership groups.

Ball-Rokeach and DeFleur also argued that audience members and the social structure influence the media industry (which is also part of the social structure). The economic goals of the mass media industry should reflect the needs of audience members and social conditions. We would expect, then, that the mass media would change in response to the changes in the demographics of the United States. Evidence supporting that expectation is plentiful. The increases in big band sounds on the radio, the increase in the number of elderly models in advertisements geared toward the elderly reader, and the increase in special interest magazines geared toward an elderly readership discussed earlier in this chapter are three examples of the industry's response to changing demographics and audience needs.

A Summary of the Uses and Dependency Model

As Rubin and Windahl (1986) suggested the assumptions of media dependency fit nicely with the assumptions of the uses and gratifications perspective. The uses and gratifications perspective suggests that audience needs guide media usage and the dependency model provides insight into the origins of those needs. In addition, the dependency model identifies some of the barriers difficulties an audience member faces in their attempt to meet their needs.

The dependency model also points out some of the conditions under which the media is likely to influence audience members. Further, the model also points out conditions under which the media industry is likely to be responsive to audience needs. Finally, the dependency model reminds us that cultural, economic, judicial, and political factors play an important role in understanding media usage and effects. Media usage cannot be understood in isolation from these other important factors. This new theory recognizes, for example, that our interpersonal relationships affect our media usage and our media usage affects our interpersonal behavior and relationships. This new theory also provides insight into the media usage patterns of the elderly.

A Uses and Dependency Interpretation of the Elderly's Media Usage

Although previous research has identified several typologies of the uses and gratifications people derive from the mass media, Bleise (1982) recently interviewed 214 elderly adults to find out what they gained from the mass media. Quite similar to other uses and gratifications typologies, Bleise found the elderly using the media for 10 reasons: They are:

1. To supplement or substitute for face-to-face conversations and relationships.
2. To gather topics of conversation for future interpersonal interactions.
3. To learn about groups and subgroups in society that they have little information or exposure and learn what "society" thinks of those groups.
4. To learn what is considered to be appropriate behaviors in various situations (including age-appropriate behavior).
5. For intellectual stimulation and activity.
6. For self-improvement (e.g., exercise programs and for learning a new language).
7. As a less costly substitute for other activities.
8. For networking and mutual support.
9. For entertainment and passing the time.
10. For "company" and safety. (p. 575)

What can we conclude about the elderly and their media usage? It is safe to say that the elderly spend a great deal of time with the mass media and the majority of that time is spent watching television. Television usage is high with young children, decreases during adolescence and increases through adulthood and old age. From the uses and dependency perspective we would expect that those changes in behavior are the result of changes in the functional alternatives for need fulfillment. During childhood, as in old age, the number of sources for need fulfillment decrease.

A reduction in the number of friends or the availability of those friends should change the media use patterns of the elderly. As Bleise (1982) pointed out the telephone is often used to substitute for face-to-face interaction and this appears to be the result of diminished mobility. In the case people having lost many or all of their friends, it seems likely that media use may be substituted for interaction. This seems to be the case with reading books. McEnvoy and Vincent (1980) and Kent and Rush (1976) found that elderly people living alone read more than elderly people living with others. Interestingly enough, reading books was also found to be unrelated to other media usage.

Changes in sensory, cognitive, and communicative skills may also lead to an increased reliance on the mass media for need fulfillment. Decreased visual acuity seems likely to lead to decreases in time spent reading and in some cases an increase in television usage. Because of the redundancy in the audio and visual channels of television, sensory decline seems likely to have less impact on television usage.

In addition, the hearing loss associated with aging (presbycusis) is compounded under conditions of anxiety and the fear of being evaluated (Corso, 1977; Jarvik & Cohen, 1973). Because television characters cannot evaluate audience members, audience members may actually hear television programming better than they hear people talk face-to-face. This is particularly true because the volume of the television can be increased without fear of embarrassment.

Hearing deficits seem likely to reduce radio usage. Announcers speaking at a fast rate, distortion, reverberation, static, and a lack of visual cues (e.g., lip reading) may make radio programming difficult to understand. It also seems likely that people having difficulty hearing may not spend much time listening to music—particularly if the music available is not familiar. More research into the elderlys' use of music is needed.

Interestingly enough, Oyer and Paolucci (1970) found that elderly people suffering from presbycusis have more stress and tension in their marriages than elderly couples without hearing problems. Thus, hearing difficulties make conversation more difficult and may contribute to a reduction in the satisfaction derived from interpersonal interaction. Such conditions make the elderly ripe for reliance on television. In some cases the elderly may actually create parasocial relationships with media characters as a substitute for face-to-face interaction. Decreases in mobility and the death of friends may also contribute to media dependence and the creation of parasocial relationships. More research in this area is needed, although several studies have demonstrated such parasocial activity occurs when other functional alternatives are unavailable (Bierg & Dimmick, 1979; Cassata, 1967; Graney, 1975; Graney & Graney, 1974; Turow, 1974; Wenner, 1976).

It also seems likely that the combination of decreased mobility, sensory, cognitive, and communicative skill decline and often a reduction in the number of relational partners will, result in the elderly becoming more dependent on the mass media for information about the world around them. Because the elderly tend to prefer content that is informational in nature, it seems unlikely that the elderly are intentionally disengaging from society. Rather, the evidence seems to suggest the elderly are employing the mass media to remain in "touch." The media can generate topics for future conversation, provide common experiences for viewers, and in some cases replace actual face-to-face interaction. Substituting the media for actual interpersonal interaction seems to be guided by desperation rather than preference.

Although the media industry may try to change to meet the needs of audience members, all audience members are not created equally. Contrary to popular opinion, the mass media industry is not in business to manufacture programming or content. The mass media industry creates audiences and sells those audiences to advertisers. Large audiences are important, but as we have seen with the advent of special interest magazines, the right audience is more important than a large audience for many advertisers. Is there any other explanation for televising golf? The ratings are low, but the people who watch are wealthy, making them more desirable to many advertisers.

Although the media industry may be interested in the elderly because of the large number of people 65 years of age and older, do not expect to see dramatic changes in programming until there is more incentive to do so. The amount of disposable income an audience has is often more important than the number of people watching a particular show.

It is not hard to imagine why researchers are concerned when the media provides inaccurate information about aging and the elderly. Inaccurate information would seem unlikely to lead to good decisions. However the problem is deeper than it may initially appear and may be described as the agenda-setting hypothesis. Topics or issues in the media may gain a great deal more importance in the minds of audience members than they actually deserve because the issue is legitimized by being in the media. If people think that the solution for the problems facing the elderly can best be solved using medicine (as many magazine and newspaper articles suggest), then little research and emphasis will be placed on the importance of social support to the life quality and longevity of the elderly.

This phenomenon is called "agenda setting" and refers to the media setting the agenda of audience members. As Shaw and McCombs (1977) suggested "the mass media may not be successful at telling us what to think , but they are stunningly successful at telling us what to think about (p. 5). If the media is telling us to think about the wrong issues—well the implications are obvious.

The fact that the media portrays the elderly in a stereotypical fashion, however, is also problematic. There is clear evidence that people hold negative attitudes toward the elderly and aging (Bennett & Eckman, 1973; Botwinick, 1984; Kastenbaum, 1964; Palmore, 1982), and there is clear evidence that media portrayals are stereotypical. The link between acquiring the stereotypical attitudes from the mass media, though less clear cut, certainly seems reasonable.

Gerbner and his colleagues may have found the link between portrayal and attitude creation. Gerbner suggested that television viewers can and do cultivate perceptions of the world based on the way things are portrayed on television. In a recent investigation Gerbner et al., (1980) found that heavy television viewers think there are fewer elderly people in the world because they are so infrequently seen on television. Further, heavy viewers reported feeling that older people are less bright, more closed minded, less alert, and less productive than light or occasional viewers.

Other researchers have argued that Gerbner's work is flawed. Many of the criticisms, interestingly enough, indicate that cultivation occurs when audience members are dependent on the media (Comstock et al., 1978; Passuth & Cook, 1985; Robinson, 1972).

Research by Langer and associates has demonstrated that holding stereotypical attitudes has far greater effect than has previously been thought. Langer and Abelson (1974) found that people labeled as being "mental patients" are evaluated very differently than people labeled as being "job applicants." After watching a videotaped interview, subjects were asked to evaluate the behavior of the actor as being pathological or normal. When the subjects believed they were watching a "mental patient" they were confident his behavior was pathological. However, when the same videotaped interview was shown to subjects believing the actor to be a "job applicant," they found his behavior to be well adjusted.

In a more recent investigation, Langer and Benvento (1978) found that those labels actually influence the behavior of the stigmatized individual. Asked to perform a simple task, the people labeled "boss" performed about twice as well on the task as the people labeled "assistant." In fact, the assistants performed significantly worse than they had on the same task before they were stigmatized or labeled "assistants."

In a similar investigation, Langer (1983) asked people to watch a videotape and evaluate the behavior of the actor. In one condition the elderly actor pretended to forget something, and in the other condition a younger actor pretended to forget some detail. Langer found that adults over the age of 25 were much more likely to evaluate an elderly actor as being senile than they were to evaluate a younger actor as being senile. Further, Langer found that elderly people evaluate other elderly people more positively than do younger adults. However, those same older adults also feel that negative traits commonly associated with growing old (e.g., forgetfulness, being ill, mentally incompetent, or being physically incapable of performing a task) are evaluated as being much more negative than younger adults' evaluation those characteristics.

The implications of this research are clear. Stereotypical portrayals can contribute to stereotypical attitudes. Particularly when the stereotypes are commonly accepted and common in the mass media and when other sources of information about the stigmatized group are unavailable. Langer points out that such attitudes result in less favorable evaluations of the self, inhibits performance of tasks, and decreases perceptions of environmental control. Stereotypical portrayals can contribute to a reduction in life quality for young and old people alike. In fact, holding ageist attitudes may well lead young people to be less inclined to prepare for old age and retirement.

Much research into the elderly's use of the mass media is needed. The research, however, must examine many factors discussed within this chapter. Media usage is just one type of behavior and cannot be understood in isolation from other social behavior and institutions. Further, media usage patterns occur throughout the life span. Future research should look at how media usage and other social behavior change across the life span. Then, and only, then will we be able to begin to understand the real role the mass media plays in our lives.

REFERENCES

American Newspaper Publishers Association News Research Bulletin (1973, April 26). News and editorial content and readership of the daily newspaper. *American Newspaper Publishers Association,* Washington, DC.

Arnoff, C. (1974). Old age in prime time. *Journal of Communication, 24,* 86–87.

Ball-Rokeach, S., & DeFleur, M. (1976). A dependency model of mass-media effects. *Communication Research, 3,* 3–21.

Barton, R. (1977). Soap operas provide meaningful communication for the elderly. *Feedback, 19,* 5–8.

Barton, R., & Schreiber, L. (1978). Media and Aging: A critical review of an expanding field of communication research. *Central States Speech Journal, 29,* 173–186.

Bennett, R., & Eckman, J. (1973). Attitudes toward aging. In C. Eisdorfer & P. Lawton (Eds.), *The psychology of adult development and aging.* Washington, DC: The American Psychological Association.

Bierg, J., & Dimmick, J. (1979). The late night radio talk show as interpersonal communication. *Journal Quarterly, 56,* 92–96.

Binstock, R. (1983). The aged as scapegoat. *The Gerontologist, 23,* 136–143.

Bleise, N. (1982). Media in the rocking chair: Media uses and functions among the elderly. In G. Gumpert & R. Cathcart (Eds.), *Intermedia: Interpersonal communication in a Media World.* (3rd ed.). New York: Oxford Press.

Bogart, L. (1972). Negro and white media exposure: New evidence. *Journalism Quarterly, 49,* 15–21.

Botwinick, J. (1984). *Aging and Behavior* (3rd ed.). New York: Springer.

Bower, R. (1973). *Television and the Public.* New York: Holt Rinehart, & Winston.

Buchholz, M., & Bynum, J. (1982). Newspaper presentation of America's aged: A content analysis of image and role. *The Gerongologist, 22,* 83–88.

Burgoon, J., & Burgoon, M. (1980). Predictors of newspaper readership. *Journalisn Quarterly, 54*(4), 589–596.

Carmichael, C. (1976). Communication and gerontology. Interfacing disciplines. *Journal of Western Speech Communication Association, 40,* 121–129.

Cassata, M. (1967). *A study of the mass communications behavior of 177 members of the Age Center of New England.* Unpublished Doctoral Dissertation. Bloomington, Indiana: University of Indiana.

Cassata, M. (1985). *Television looks at aging.* New York: Television Information Office.

Chaffee, S., & Wilson, D. (1975). *Adult life cycle changes in mass media usage.* Paper presented at the annual meeting of the Association for Education in Journalism, Ottawa, Canada.

Cicirelli, V. (1979, May 31). *Social services for the elderly in relation to kin network,* Report to the NRTA-AARP, Andrus Foundation.

Comstock, G., Chaffee, S., Katzman, N., McCombs, M., & Roberts, D. (1978). *Television and human behavior.* New York: Columbia University Press.

Corso, J. (1977). Sensory process and age effects in normal adults *Journal of Gerontology,* 26, 90–105.

Danowski, J. (1975). *Information aging: Interpersonal and mass communication patterns at a retirement community.* Paper presented at the meetings of the Gerontological Society, Louisville.

Davis, R. (1971). Television and the older adult. *Journal of Broadcasting, 15,* 153–159.

Davis, R. (1980). *Television and the aging audience.* Los Angeles, CA: University of Southern California Press.

Davis, R., & Davis, J. (1985). *TV's image of the elderly: A practical guide for change.* Lexington, MA: Lexington Books

DeGrazia, S. (1961). The uses of time. In R. Kleemier (Ed.), *Aging and leisure.* New York: Oxford University Press.

Doolittle, J. (1979). News media use by older adults. *Journalism Quarterly, 56*(2), 311–345.

Downing, M. (1974). Heroine of the daytime serial. *Journal of Communication, 24,* 130–137.

Frank, R., & Greenberg, M. (1980). *The public's use of television.* Beverly Hills: Sage Publications.

Gaitz, C., & Scott, J. (1975). Analysis of letters to "Dear Abby" concerning old age. *The Gerontologist, 15,* 47–50.

Gantz, W., Gartenberg, H., & Rainbow, C. (1980). Approaching invisibility: The portrayal of elderly in magazine advertisements. *Journal of Communication, 30,* 56–60.

Gerbner, G., Gross, L., Signorelli, N., & Morgan, M. (1980). Aging with television: Images on television drama and conceptions of social reality. *Journal of Communication, 30*(1), 37–47.

Gerson, W. (1966). Mass media socialization behavior: Negro-white differences. *Social Forces, 45,* 40–50.

Gordon, C., Gaitz, C., & Scott, J. (1976). Leisure and lives: personal expressivity across the lifespan. In R. Binstock & E. Shannas (Eds.), *Handbook of aging and the social sciences* (pp. 310–341). Van Nostrand Reinhold, New York.

Graney, M. (1974). Media use as a substitute activity in old age. *Journal of Gerontology, 29,* 322–324.

Graney, M. (1975). Communication uses and the social activity constant. *Communication Research, 2,* 347–366.

Graney, M., & Graney, E. (1974). Communication activity substitution in aging. *Journal of Communication, 24,* 88–96.

Hacker, H. (1951). Women as a minority group. *Social Forces, 30,* 39–44.

Handel, L. (1950). *Hollywood looks at its' audience.* Urbana, IL: University of Illinois Press.

Harris, L., & Associates, Inc. (1975). *The myth and reality of aging in America*. Washington, DC: The National Council on Aging.

Harris, A., & Feinberg, J. (1977). Television and aging: Is what you see what you get? *The Gerontologist, 17*, 464–468.

Hoar, J. (1961). A study of free time activities of 200 aged persons. *Sociology and Social Work, 45*, 157–163.

Hwang, J. (1972). *Information seeking and opinion leadership among older Americans*. Unpublished Doctoral Dissertation, University of Oregon, Eugene, OR.

Jarvik, C., & Cohen, D. (1973). A biobehavioral approach to intellectual change with aging. In C. Eisdorfen & M. Canton (Eds.), *The psychology of the lifespan* (pp. 288–326). Washington, DC: American Psychological Association.

Kastenbaum, R. (1964). *New thoughts on old age*. New York: Springer.

Kent, K., & Rush, R. (1976). How communication behavior of older persons affects their public affairs knowledge. *Journalism Quarterly, 53*(1), 40–46.

Korzenny, F., & Neuendorf, K. (1980). Television viewing and the self concept of the elderly. *Journal of Communication, 30*, 71–80.

Kubey, R. (1980). Television and aging: Past, present and future. *The Gerontologist, 20*, 16–35.

Langer, E. (1983). *The psychology of control*. Beverly Hills: Sage Publications.

Langer, E., & Abelson, R. (1974). A patient by any other name . . .: Clinician group differences in labeling bias. *Journal of Consulting and Clinical Psychology, 42*, 4–9.

Langer, E. & Benevento, A. (1978). Self-induced dependence. *Journal of Personality and Social Psychology, 36*, 886–893.

Levinson, R. (1973). From Olive Oyle to Sweet Polly Purebred: Sex role stereotypes and televised cartoons. *Journal of Popular Culture, 9*, 561–572.

MacDonald, R. (1973, November). *Content analysis of perceptions of aging as represented by the new media*. Paper presented at the meetings of the Gerontological Society, Miami Beach.

Market Opinion Research (1975). In H. Oyer & E. Oyer (Eds.) *Aging and Communication* (pp. 99–108). Baltimore, MD: University Park Press, 99–118.

McEnvoy, G., & Vincent, C. (1980). Who reads and why? *Journal of Communication, 30*(1), 134–140.

Mertz, R. (1970). *Analysis of the portrayal of older Americans in commercial television programming*. Paper presented at the annual meetings of the International Communication Association, Chicago, IL.

Meyersohn, R. (1961). A critical examination of commercial entertainment. In R. Keemeir (Ed.), *Aging and Leisure*. New York: Oxford University Press.

Northcott, H. (1975). Too young, too old—age in the world of television. *The Gerontologist, 15*, 184–186.

Nussbaum, J., & Robinson, J. (1986). Attitudes toward aging. *Communication Research Reports, 1*, 21–27.

Robinson, J. (1972). Toward defining the function of television. In E. Rubinstein, G. Comstock, & J. Murray (Eds.), *Television and Social behavior: Vol. 4. Television in day-to-day patterns of use*, 199–228.

Oyer, E., & Paolucci, B. (1970). Homemaker's hearing losses and family integration. *Journal of Home Economics, 62*, 257–262.

Palmore, E. (1982). Attitudes toward the aged: What we know and need to know. *Research on Aging, 4*, 333–348.

Passuth, P., & Cook, F. (1985). Effects of television viewing on knowledge and attitudes about older adults: A critical reexamination. *The Gerontologist, 25*(1), 69–77.

Peterson, D., & Karnes, E. (1976). Older people in adolescent literature. *The Gerontologist, 16,* 225–231.

Petersen, M. (1973). The visibility and image of old people on television. *Journalism Quarterly, 50,* 569–573.

Ramsdell, M. (1973). The trauma of TV's troubled soap families. *Family Coordinator, 22,* 299–304.

Robinson, J. (1972). Toward defining the functions of television. In E. Rubinstein, G. Comstock, & J. Murray (Eds.), *Television and social behavior:* Vol. 4. *Television in day-to-day patterns of use* (pp.   –) Washington: U.S. Government Printing Office.

Rubin, A., & Rubin, R. (1981). Age, context, and television use. *Journal of Broadcasting, 25,* 1–13.

Rubin, A., & Rubin, R. (1982). Older person's TV viewing patterns and motivations. *Communication Research, 9,* 287–313.

Rubin, A. & Windahl, S. (1986). The uses and dependency model of mass communication. *Critical Studies in Mass Communication, 3*(2), 184–199.

Schramm, W. (1969). Aging and mass communication. In M. Riley, J. Riley & M. Johnson, (Eds.), *Aging and Society:* Vol. 2. *Aging and the professions* (pp.   –). New York: Russell Sage Foundation.

Shaw, D., & McCombs, M. (1977). *The emergence of American political issues.* St. Paul, MN: West.

Steiner, G. (1963). *The people look at television.* New York: Knopf.

Turow, J. (1974). Talk show radio as interpersonal communication. *Journal of Broadcasting, 18,* 171–179.

TV Dimensions (1986). Time Buying Services, Inc. New York.

Wenner, L. (1976). Functional analysis of TV viewing for older adults. *Journal of Broadcasting, 20,* 77–88.

Young, T. (1979). Use of the media by older adults. *American Behavioral Scientist, 23,* 119–136.

17 Communication and Dying: The End of the Life-Span

Teresa L. Thompson
University of Dayton

This book has discussed various aspects of communication throughout the life span of an individual. This chapter focuses on what happens at the end of that life span and the communication accompanying those events. Although the study of communication surrounding death and dying is a relatively new area, there is already much that can be learned from an examination of the available literature. Several of the more commonly studied areas related to death and dying are *not* the focus of our discussion, because they are not primarily communicative issues. Such topics include death fear and death anxiety and the causes of death. Nor do we spend much time discussing social distance toward the dying, except as it is manifested in communicative behavior. We also limit our discussion of bereavement, except to mention the few studies that have focused on communication toward the bereaved.

Instead, our discussion focuses on the following issues: (a) should the dying be told? (b) communication of the dying, (c) coping with dying especially as it is affected by interpersonal communication; (d) talking about dying; (e) helping dying children communicate about death; (f) families of the dying; and (g) communication between dying patients, their families, and care providers. We begin with a few introductory comments about death and dying.

INTRODUCTION

The fact that death and dying have been the subject of little investigation is exemplified by Patterson's (1981) comment that 90% of the books on

339

aging published between 1956 and 1976 devoted less than 5% of their space to the topic. Indeed, 65% of those books devoted less than 1% of their space to the issue. It was only during the late 1960s and 1970s that we began to see *any* research on the topic. Since this time, our conceptualization of death has changed somewhat. For instance, McKenzie (1980) differentiated between death as an *event* and dying as a *process*. Our concern in this essay is communication during the process of dying. Earlier, Kalish (1976) drew a distinction between death as an *organizer of time* (i.e., the end of the life span) and death as *loss* or *punishment*. These are obviously very different views.

There is little doubt that the dying are avoided and stigmatized by their status (Epley & McCaghy, 1977/78), especially by those who perceive themselves as similar to the dying person (Smith, Lingle, & Brock, 1978/79) and those who see the dying person as less attractive and in more pain (Sherman, Smith, & Cooper, 1982). This avoidance is evidenced in the notion of social death (Kallish, 1976), in which the dying person is treated as dead before the event actually occurs. Kalish also pointed out that anticipatory grieving by family members may bring about social death. Sudnow (1967) observed social death occuring among both family members and hospital staff. In his ethnographic study, instances were reported of autopsy prints being filled out and bodies wrapped prior to death. One woman, after hearing that her husband was dying, immediately went home and gave away his clothes. Imagine his surprise when he recovered and went home to empty drawers and closets.

Our concern about avoidance of the dying has intensified in light of the current AIDS crisis. Although we typically think of dying as a biological process, the work of Lopez and Getzel (1984) highlights the role that communication plays in the death of AIDS patients. That communication may even be a causal agent is demonstrated by Holt's (1969) analysis of "death by suggestion," in which communication actually brings about death. Of more common concern, however, is interpersonal communication surrounding a person who is dying of biological causes. One of the central issues related to this is the question: Should the dying person be told that he or she is dying?

DEATH TELLING

Although Todd and Still (1984) found that most physicians preferred not to give explicit information or prognoses even to patients who may realize that they are dying, most health-care providers are now more open about such communication. In 1966, Verwoerdt provided physicians with an entire list of questions to facilitate their decision about whether the patient should be told about impending death, but Carey and Posavac (1978/79) described "a shift toward more openness with terminal patients on the part of physicians over the last decade" (p. 67). Studies of various health-care providers over the years have substantiated this finding (Channon & Ballinger, 1984; Eggerman & Dustin, 1985/86; Kram & Caldwell, 1969). Taking a somewhat more sophisticated perspective, Hicks and Daniels (1968) concluded that, "it did not matter so much exactly what, when or how a patient was 'told' about his disease and prognosis, as much as whether the involved physician made himself readily available to the patient in an ongoing and meaningful interpersonal way to respond to the patient's fluctuating day-to-day psychological needs" (p. 47).

Even when patients initiate the topic of their own deaths, many physicians do not openly discuss the issue. Kastenbaum (1967a) found that, in this situation, 17.6% of the physicians discussed the issue, 13.1% reassured the patient, 19.1% denied it, 26.1% were fatalistic, and 24.1% changed the subject.

A related issue focuses on telling the family of the dying patient about the prognosis. Verwoerdt (1966) advocated telling the strongest family member first, and warned that the guilt felt by family members may make it difficult for them to make reasoned decisions. Koocher (1986) discussed the balance between the advantages and hazards of anticipatory grief brought about by telling the family members of impending death.

When family members are told about a terminal prognosis and the patient is *not* informed a potential double-binding situation develops. Drawing parallels to the schizophrenogenic double bind, Erickson and Hyerstay (1974) observed that "significant others emit incongruent verbal and nonverbal messages as they attempt to conceal the patient's impending death" (p. 287). The patient may fear being labeled as paranoid if he or she responds to these cues, and insensitive if he or she does not respond to them. Erickson and Hyerstay concluded by suggesting that efforts to conceal the truth are harmful and should be avoided. Similarly, Schulz and Aderman's (1980) review of the research indicates that awareness of impending death does lead to depression, but patients still need and want to know about their prognoses.

The classic work of Glaser and Strauss (1966, 1977) has delineated for us four "awareness contexts" for the dying person: (a) closed, characterized by no knowledge of impending death; (b) suspicion; (c) mutual pretense, in which both the dying person and staff and significant others pretend that the person will live; and (d) open, which occurs when death is acknowledged by all. Glaser and Strauss observed that a wall of sorts still exists in the open awareness context. Bryant (1986) discussed similar awareness contexts and pointed out that it is the fear of death that prevents conversation about it in the mutual pretense context. McKenzie (1980) summarized the rules governing mutual pretense: (a) avoid dangerous topics; (b) pretend that the dying will share in the future; (c) engage in small talk; (d) ignore the topic of death; and (e) keep the situation normal.

Such a lack of communication about death is common even between married couples (Doshan, 1985; Hinton, 1981). Hinton found that only 35% of couples had openly shared their awareness that one of them could be dying. In another 34% of the couples one of the spouses had expressed their awareness, but the other had denied it. Interestingly, "there was freer communication about dying if the spouse considered the marital relationship had been 'average' or 'poor' rather than 'very good'" (p. 337). Doshan's (1985) results are similar; he also indicated that the individuals who did communicate about impending death believed that the experience had been beneficial to themselves and their spouses. Such communication also lead to better adjustment in widows and widowers after the death had occured.

COMMUNICATION OF THE DYING

Because communication is a dyadic process, we must look at the communication of both members of the dyad while still using the dyad itself as the unit of analysis. We know from past research that the pain typically accompanying terminal illness affects communication (Shanis, 1985). When an individual is in pain, that is all he or she can think about. Message sending becomes more difficult. Changes in verbalizations have also been noted with impending death, including decreased organization in communication (Lieberman, 1968) and more expressions of hopelessness (Verwoerdt & Elmore, 1967). These changes occur even when the patient has not been told that he or she is dying.

Other changes in communication include an increased emphasis on verbalizations about concerns for the family (Kastenbaum & Aisenberg, 1972) and the sending of contradictory messages (Baider, 1977). Baider argued that these contradictory messages occur because "The patient's acts of reference do not evoke in others the experience he is trying to convey. Not only is his process of dying an experience that is unique to him, the patient, but also, in his own ambivalence of 'Why me?' he sends contradictory messages: of anger, fear and guilt" (p. 24). At this stage, it is not unusual for patients to express a wish for death. One patient who survived such an experience wrote, "Thank God that those who were

continually with me *knew that I truly wanted to live* despite my ambivalence" (Jaffe, 1977, p. 330, emphasis original).

Two studies have also reported nonverbal changes with impending
death. Again, these changes occur whether or not the patient knows that
he or she is dying. Beigler (1957) described such changes as sunken eyes,
an expression of terror and a black cast to the eyes as "an aid in the
prognostication of impending death" (p. 171). More recently, Antonoff
and Spilka (1984) observed a patterning of facial expressions in early,
middle, and later stages of illness. In particular, facial expressions indicating fear and sadness, as operationalized by Ekman, Friesen, and
Tomkin's (1971) Facial Affect Scoring Technique, changed in a patterned
manner throughout the stages.

How a patient communicates is also related to the health care he or
she will receive. Belsky (1984) cited evidence indicating that more aggressive patients live longer. Arguing that being sick does not, in and of itself,
lead to acquiring access to life-sustaining medical services, Watson
(1976/77) found that patients must express aspirations to get well and be
willing to seek help and cooperate with those who are technically competent. Patients who did not do this were relegated to a near-death status
and were less likely to receive medical care.

In potential contradiction to this point, Noyes and Clancy (1977)
described a societal confusion between the sick and dying roles. Although
the sick role encourages dependency, the dying role requires independence and withdrawal from society. However, people who express
a *wish* to die, unless they are really suffering or are severely disabled, will
be held responsible for their deaths. They advocate a reestablishment of
the dying role as a legitimate one. It would appear, however, that the
dying role would lead to behavior that would make patients less likely to
receive medical care, according to Watson's findings.

Two other special problems have been described in the literature on
dying individuals. Silverberg (1985) articulated some issues that are
particularly relevant to terminally ill male patients or males involved
with a family member who is terminally ill. He argued that traditional
sex roles for men lead to a fear of loss of control, preoccupation with
achievement and success, and constrained emotionality. All of these
make dealing with and communicating about death more difficult for
men than it is for women.

A second problem that has been discussed in the literature is the
loneliness of the dying patient (Dubrey & Terrill, 1975). This is even a
problem for dying children (Krulick, 1978). This loneliness is caused by
avoidance of both the patient *and* the issue of dying during communication (Gluck, 1977). Thus, loneliness is *caused by* the communication that
occurs, and is *reflected in* how terminal patients communicate. Lonely

terminal individuals communicate about maintaining hope, religious faith, and their increasing dependency on others (Dubrey & Terrill, 1975). Coping with this loneliness is one aspect of the more general issue of coping with dying.

COPING WITH DYING

Many different types of coping strategies have been identified in the literature on death and dying. Four "preterminal orientations" have been described: acceptance, apathy, apprehension, and anticipation (Weisman & Kastenbaum, 1968; Troll, 1982). Weisman and Kastenbaum also identified two more general types of dying individuals: (a) those who are withdrawn and inactive, yet aware and accepting of imminent death; and (b) those who are aware of the prospect of death, yet who remain actively involved in life. Similarly, McKenzie (1980) discussed different coping strategies. Some dying people may be reluctant to take on new commitments or projects and may want to spend their remaining time in meaningful ways. Others will withdraw. Some will become depressed and anxious. Just as we all live differently, we all die differently.

Many readers are no doubt familiar with the oft-discussed *stages* of dying, especially as expressed in the work of Kubler-Ross (1969). These stages include: (a) denial and isolation; (b) anger; (c) bargaining; (d) depression; and (e) acceptance. Although Kubler-Ross argued that the stages may be nonsequential and repetitive, others have tried to apply them more literally. In an examination of the research, Schulz and Aderman (1974) concluded that there is little support for Kubler-Ross' stages and that there is not any definite order to the dying process. The only exception to this is some consensus that depression does occur before death. Findings such as this have caused Pattison (1978) to offer more general phases of dying: (a) acute (during the initial crisis); (b) chronic living-dying (as fears are worked through); and (c) terminal (characterized by withdrawal and little hope).

Arguments have been offered against the rigid application of any stage theory of dying, based on the fear that we might rush a person from one stage to another or treat behavior as "merely a stage." This may negate the validity of the patient's experiences and be disconfirming. Further, legitimate complaints may be passed off as simply being signs of the anger phase (Belsky, 1984).

Other research has indicated that having some control over how death is handled makes it easier to cope with impending terminality (Marshall, 1979). Marshall contrasted two residential facilities, one in which dying was organized *for* the patients and one in which it was organized *by* the patients. Death was handled much less morbidly in the second than in the first, indicating that control may have positive effects.

Interpersonal relationships are also an important determinant of coping with dying (Carey, 1974; Gluck, 1977). Relationships that allow for communication about death and provide emotional support without denial are more helpful (Gluck, 1977). This is true of relationships with health care providers as well as family and friends (Arnstein, 1974).

Denial of impending death is a common coping mechanism (Feifel & Branscomb, 1973; Kalish, 1976; Magni, 1972). Denial is not all bad, despite the fact that it is usually regarded as dysfunctional in the thanatological literature. Bellin (1981/82) has argued that denial may help preserve relationships threatened by the knowledge of terminal illness and may serve to "forestall social withdrawal by the patient and his/her social circle, as well as promoting role enactments necessary to medical treatment" (p. 25). This argument would indicate that awareness should not be forced on the person for whom denial is serving such functions.

Denial, however, also has negative effects. It may block physician–patient communication or lead to delays in receiving health care (Verwoerdt, 1966). Fortunately, most patients would rather talk about dying than deny it.

TALKING ABOUT DYING

That most terminally ill individuals, given an opportunity, will talk about their illness and impending death has been well substantiated (Doshan, 1985; Simmons & Given, 1980). One study found that, although nurses claimed that their patients did not want to talk about death, 47 out of 51 of the patients *did* talk about the topic within 10–15 minutes of interaction time (Simmons & Given, 1972). Simmons and Given's observation also indicated that most patients immediately attempted to talk about their death after learning of the diagnosis.

The positive effects of such communication have also been documented. Not only does such communication help the dying person face his or her fatal illness (Gluck, 1977), but it also alleviates tension and eases depression (Saul & Saul, 1973). Dying patients who are not allowed to talk about their deaths develop a reputation among health-care providers for "acting-out" (Chandler, 1965).

Inherent in some of the observations just mentioned is the finding that health-care providers and others attempt to avoid talking with a patient about death (Simmons & Given, 1972). Gluck (1977) examined the reasons for this avoidance, and found that they include fear of emotional involvement (leading to little contact), feeling at a loss about what to say, lack of knowledge about what the patient has been told, feeling that terminal patients are "failures," preoccupation with equipment and technical skills, fear of the patient's anger, or fear that the patient will cry. Weinstein (1977) also found a trend toward a relationship between death anxiety and conversational avoidance of death.

Others have offered suggestions for talking about dying. The suggestions offered by Simmons and Given (1972) include the following:

1. Listen more than you talk;
2. Don't give "stock" answers or lie;
3. Don't pretend that everything will be all right or talk about the future as if the dying person will be there;
4. Don't give the patient more detail than he or she wants;
5. Listen to the dying person's life review;
6. Don't discourage hopes, but don't provide false hope;
7. Don't be condescending, disapproving, or depressed—provide approval; and
8. Don't try to win control struggles—terminal patients have very little control over most aspects of their lives.

Many of these suggestions are consistent with the suggestions offered by Miller and Knapp (1986), who also reminded us that there is really nothing "right" or appropriate to say to someone who is dying. Communication will not change the reality they are confronting. Miller and Knapp advocated a reflexive approach to communication with someone facing fatality.

Two other findings related to talking about death should also be mentioned in passing, although their focus is much different than the other research that has been reviewed. Cowgell (1977) found that suicide threats increased the likelihood that people receiving them would talk about death and dying. And Bryant (1986) has described the euphemisms used in "funeralese" to talk about death without really talking about it, such as "the loved one," "resting quietly in the slumber room," "travel," "departure," and "passed away" (p. 228).

The question of talking about death becomes particularly problematic when the person who is dying is a child. This is the issue to which we now turn.

DYING CHILDREN

Although parents are typically reluctant to communicate with terminally ill children about impending death (Issner, 1973), research has indicated that such communication is necessary (Issner, 1973; Karon & Vernick,

1968; Krulick, 1978). Bryant (1986) has described the difficult situation in which lack of communication about impending death places a child. He found that parents and staff try to help the child to deny death by employing fairy tales, using euphemisms, and being overly nice. The child notices that adults are behaving differently and builds up his or her fears about death. These fears are internalized, because the child does not want to burden parents or the staff. The child tries to cope with the fear of death all by him- or herself.

The data suggest that coping occurs much more effectively when accompanied by open communication. For instance, childhood cancer survivors with whom adults have openly communicated about possible death grow up to be better adjusted than those who did not participate in such communication (Koocher, 1986).

Because communication about a child's impending death is not easy, some researchers have examined methods of facilitating this process. Husband and Broaddhus (1984) suggested the use of children's books and stories as therapeutic metaphors. They found that this provided "an indirect, nonthreatening form of communication that can lead to a more direct sharing of feelings" (p. 17). Adams-Greenly (1984) offered seven principles of intervention to help a dying child communicate about serious illness and death: (a) ascertain the child's perceptions; (b) understand the child's symbolic language; (c) clarify reality—dispel fantasy; (d) enlist parental support; (e) encourage the expression of feelings; (f) promote self-esteem through mastery; and (g) make no assumptions. Also focusing on a symbolic level, Spinetta, Rigler, and Karon (1974) suggested the use of interpersonal distance measures with three-dimensional figures to assess a dying child's sense of isolation.

It is perhaps indicative of how uncomfortable the notion of children dying makes us as researchers that more work has focused on helping children adjust to the death of others than on helping children cope with their own impending deaths. Several studies have examined the impact of sibling death on surviving children (McCown & Pratt, 1985; Mufson, 1985; Pollock, 1986) and have concluded that verbal communication about the issue is necessary to facilitate coping and decrease negative social behaviors and psychological problems (Leon, 1986). The same is true in regard to informing children about a parent's terminal illness (Rosenheim & Reicher, 1985).

Family support also helps a child's adjustment to the death of a significant other (Weber & Fournier, 1985). Additionally, Weber and Fournier concluded that "highly cohesive families were less likely to allow children to participate (in decision making) and had less understanding about death, while families with balanced cohesion levels reported joint parent–child decision making. . . . Findings indicate that children may understand more about death than parents can accept" (p.

43). Two other studies have indicated that peer support and communication help children cope with the death of a significant other (Heller & Schneider, 1977/78; Lister & Ward, 1985). Peer support is also helpful for other family members. One study, for instance, found that families who receive support are able to adjust even to the death of a child with spina bifida without relational or mental health problems (Dorner & Atwell, 1985).

FAMILIES OF THE DYING

Communication Themes

Quite a bit of research has focused on families of the dying. Perhaps the most interesting of this work is that which has examined the *communication themes* apparent in these families. Based on a participant observation study, Cawley (1984, 1985) identified four overlapping and interweaving themes:

1. Changing relationships, especially focusing on changing roles and new levels of dependence/independence and helping;
2. Experiencing uncertainty about the disease and its physical effects, the impending death, how to deal with each other, one's own feelings, abilities to provide care and comfort, the appropriateness of various institutions, and "why" this is happening. Efforts were made to ease this uncertainty through communicating about it and attempting to
3. Make sense of the experience. Interesting, family members appeared to do this by expressing their *own* preferences for how they would want to be treated in this situation; and
4. Making decisions, which focused on "weighing the cost benefits *to themselves* of meeting the person's wishes as to how, when and where he/she would live until death . . . only minimal consideration was given to the dying person's wishes and little effort was made to elicit them" (Cawley, 1985, p. 25, emphasis original).

Some of these themes, especially the notion of changing relationships, have been echoed in the work of other researchers (Gluck, 1977; Koocher, 1986; Paterson, 1985). Paterson described in some detail the changes that occur after the impending death has been diagnosed and the individual begins to attempt to resume his or her former life, if only for a short while. Paterson observed other family members adopt a protective role in an effort to stop this behavior. "No period during the illness was as conflict-ridden as this one . . . or brought as much emotional hurt or so disturbed family solidarity" (p. 256). The families coped with this conflict through disengagement, reorganization, or coercion.

The notion of conflict was also inherent in the work of Krant and Johnston (1978). They found that communications within the family of a dying individual were typically discordant and guarded.

One of Cawley's themes, previously discussed, includes mention of the role of helping in these families. Gray-Snelgrove (1982) also observed that care giving is an important part of the reconciliation of relationships in terminal families.

Greaves (1983) also described some themes emerging in the families of dying individuals. These focused on: (a) lack of communication, although all family members had things they wanted to say; (b) desire to resolve interpersonal conflicts, but fear of causing more conflict or being blamed for waiting until the person was dying to do it; and (c) the dialectic between wanting to be remembered positively by the family and feelings of rage, injustice, impotence, dependency, and alienation.

Another such juxtaposition has been noted in the work of Bergen (1980). She observed that "families of cancer patients appear to communicate more positively during the advancing stage while previous research indicated that patients are most positive during the initial stage of illness" (p. 3624-A).

Characteristics of Communication

As has been mentioned several times, communication in a family changes when one member of the family is dying. Balder (1977) found that topics in such families are selected for their explicit, nonthreatening meaning. New information is not discussed. "Communication then becomes a meaningless process of exchanged verbal messages with a predictable form and content and a stereotyped mode of blocking the entrance of any new internal or external information" (Balder, 1977, p. 25). Violating this process leads to disqualification or disconfirmation.

The characteristics of the communication of such families have also been related to medical outcomes. For instance, Weisman and Warden (1975) found that those who lived longer than expected tended to maintain good, responsive relationship with others, especially in the terminal phase of their disease. Morgenson (1973) also concluded that human interactions slow the death process. More specifically, Reiss, Gonzalez, and Kramer (1986) determined that there is a correlation between delayed closure in family problem solving and a lack of medical complications. They also found a relationship between family coordination, accomplishment, and integration and early death.

The Reiss et al. (1986) article, subtitled "On the weakness of strong bonds," concludes with one another interesting finding about the families of dying individuals. It was proposed that strong families demonstrated a paradoxical vulnerability, which leads them to exclude the ill member as a last effort to cope. Further, the patients used medical compliance to demonstrate acceptance of this exclusion.

McCubbin, et al. (1983) found a positive relationship between family interaction patterns and the health of a child with cystic fibrosis. Similarly, death due to childhood asthma has been correlated with unsupportive families (Fritz, Rubinstein, & Lewiston, 1987).

Families and Health-Care Providers

In a rather paternalistic discussion of interacting with the families of dying individuals, Verwoerdt (1966) offered numerous suggestions for fellow health-care providers. These include such things as advising the family about the frequency and duration of visits, helping them make decisions, shielding the patient from family members who upset him or her, side-stepping attacks, and so forth. That few care providers spend much time worrying about interacting with family members is perhaps indicated by some of the empirical reports of provider–family interaction.

For instance, family members are critical of the way information is communicated to them, but they still rely on the physician's interpretation to form their own opinions (Krant & Johnston, 1978). Gold's (1984) observations indicate similar dissatisfaction. These families found care providers inconsiderate and insensitive. They felt that the hospital staff was cold, inhibited, arrogant, and flip. Bad news was frequently delivered over the phone or with no warning. Some physicians were supportive at the beginning, but distanced themselves as the patient worsened. Service people were unpleasant, although nurses were better as sources of support. Richter (1984) also found that nurses are in a unique position to help the spouses of dying patients.

One study reported poor communication between physicians and family members even about do-not-resuscitate (DNR) orders. Seventy-eight percent of those decisions to code a patient DNR were made without consulting the patient or the family.

Sudnow's (1967) observational study of dying in a hospital may be the most interesting yet undertaken. Within that treatise, he described examples of physicians predicting a patient's impending death to the family *after* the death had already occurred. The physician could then return 20 minutes later and announce the actual death. Additionally, he found that family interest in the patient could determine whether or not tests and treatment would be conducted. Sudnow also provided a detailed analysis of the communication patterns accompanying death announcements.

After the Death

Because our focus in this chapter is on communication during the process of dying, we do not spend much time describing what happens after the death of a patient. But a few studies focusing on this issue are interesting enough to warrant mention. Several authors have suggested that experiencing the death of others improves adjustment to one's own impending death (Carey, 1974; Patterson, 1981), but only if one has observed that death is accepted by those around one (Marshall, 1975).

It has also been pointed out that relationships do not end with death (Unruh, 1983). We continue our attachments to others and "consult" with them about decisions. Building on the notion of relational continuation or conclusion, Fieweger (1980; Fieweger & Smilowitz, 1984) found that over one-half of respondents reported that they had an unfinished relationship with the person who had died. They wanted to say additional things to the person or do additional things for them.

Most of the research on bereavement has focused on coping mechanisms and internal psychological processes, but two studies have examined communication toward the bereaved. Davidowitz and Myrick (1984) looked at "helping" statements given to the bereaved. They found that advice was given about 47% of the time, but was only helpful 3% of the time. Reassurance was the second most popular message, but it, too, was viewed as helpful only 3% of the time. Overall, 89% of the messages were viewed as unhelpful. Communication with the survivors of a suicide victim is even more constraining and difficult than is communication with the survivors of those who died by accident or natural causes (Calhoun, Abernathy, & Selby, 1986).

CARE PROVIDERS AND THE TERMINALLY ILL

The tendency of health-care providers to avoid communication with the dying and about death has been mentioned earlier in this essay (cf. Redding, 1980). Other evidence of this tendency can be found in the fact that physicians who have first agreed to participate in research later refuse to participate when they discover that the research is about dying (Caldwell & Mishara, 1972). Doctors in this study claimed that they would be less effective if they thought about death too much. Such attitudes are reinforced by the "detached concern" that is taught in

medical schools (Schulz & Aderman, 1980). Even mental health professionals, who should be better trained at dealing with the dying, tend to
avoid them (Belsky, 1984; Kastenbaum & Aisenberg, 1972). Avoidance
seems to be associated with the fear of not knowing what to say (Field &
Howells, 1986). Other evidence indicates that this avoidance is related to
a perceived need to remain within the traditional doctor–patient
framework, which would be threatened by the physicians' acknowledgment of helplessness (Todd & Still, 1984).

In a study focusing specifically on nurses, Hurley (1975) provided
some more specific conclusions about avoidance. She indicated that
avoidance occurred only when the nurse was disturbed about the
patient's impending death or pain, when the patient lingered, or when the
patient had perceived high social-loss value. Avoidance is also manifested
in the tendency of care providers to place those who are dying farthest
from the nurses' station (Watson, 1973) and to take longer to respond to
them (LeShan, Bowers, & Jackson, 1969).

During a participant observation study of interaction between staff
and patients, Buckingham, Lack, and Mount (1976) found little interaction, little eye contact, and no signs of closeness. Patients were referred to
by the name of their disease and the negative aspects of their conditions
were accentuated. Nonverbal behaviors were also discussed by Rodabough and Rodabough (1981), who suggested that a " 'stage' in the
dying process may simply be a response to the nonverbally communicated expectations of interactors with dying persons" (p. 257).

The language used about the dying was also mentioned in Sudnow's
(1967) classic treatise. He described staff members saying such things as
"She'll probably terminate this week," in front of the patient and expect-
ing the patient not to understand the message. Other analyses of verbal
interaction have categorized nurses' communication with dying patients
as reassurance, denial, or changing the subject 80% of the time (Kastenbaum, 1967b). Less than 20% of the nurses actually discussed the
patients' thoughts and feelings with them. Similarly, Duff and Hollingshead (1968) found that evasions were used by staff dealing with dying
cancer patients 86% of the time. Koenig (1980) provided a particularly
good discussion of how such communication can be handled more effectively, as he reminded us that the *experience* of being cared for is more
important than the words that are used. In a more complex discussion,
Wood (1975) discussed the creative tension that must be maintained
between the fact that the patient is now alive and the fact that he or she
will soon die.

Finally, some research has examined death announcements. Glaser
and Strauss (1968a, 1968b) noted that proclamations of the death prediction are the physician's responsibility, that such announcements tend

to become more explicit and precise as death approaches, and that the staff is visibly upset when the trajectory is miscalculated. Once the death has occurred, five different strategies are used for announcing the death (Clark & LaBeff, 1982): (a) direct delivery; (b) oblique delivery, which tries to forewarn the receiver; (c) elaborate delivery, which provides the entire sequence of events; (d) nonverbal delivery; and (e) conditional delivery, in which the sender waits for the receiver to provide appropriate cues. The type of delivery to be used depends on the circumstances surrounding death, the relationship of the receiver to the dead person, and so on. The need for education for people who will be delivering such messages has been stressed (Clark & LaBeff, 1982; Hall, 1982).

CONCLUSIONS

It is perhaps surprising that there exists as much research, mentioned in this essay, on the topic of communicating with the terminally ill. Although the topic is extremely important, it is also rather uncomfortable and depressing. It is a credit to the social scientists and medical personnel who have done this research that so much does exist. But many questions still remain unanswered, perhaps because they are particularly uncomfortable or difficult to study. Most of the research that we have reviewed indicates a lack of communication with dying individuals, although some communication does occur. We need more research on the content of such conversations. Similarly, some of the more provocative research mentioned herein indicates a relationship between a dying person's communication or his or her family's communication and medical outcomes. This should surely be investigated in more detail.

Much of the research that is available is attitudinal rather than behavioral. One must ask which is more important for a dying person: the attitudes of others toward him or her or how he or she is treated by others? It would not be surprising if behaviors were perceived as more important than attitudes. Because behaviors are not always indicative of attitudes, it would seem that communicative behaviors rather than attitudes should be the focus of future research.

Many of the studies cited herein, particularly those found in the medical literature, report conclusions based upon very small samples. Some of these articles report case studies: others with two, three, or four subjects are not unusual. We have tried to rely on reports with such limited generalizability very little. Nonetheless, future researchers should be aware of this limitation in past research. Researchers, of course, are only able to examine the subjects who are available. This is not an independent variable that can ethically be manipulated for experimental study.

The reader will note that many of the studies mentioned herein present the same conclusions over and over again: "we need more communication; we need more open communication," and so on. In addition, too much of this research has been based on a rather simplistic conceptualization and operationalization of communication. It has simply looked at the absence or presence of communication or defined communication as open or closed. Communication theory now provides us with much more sophisticated and appropriate models that should be applied to this setting. Of particular interest might be the relational control literature or the research on confirmation versus disconfirmation. We must look at the *characteristics* of this communication rather than at its absence or presence, because communication is always present in a dyad.

In addition, little of this research has taken a life-span developmental perspective. Although there have been suggestions that the treatment of the dying changes with the increasing age of the terminally ill person, this has yet to be systematically examined in any way. Numerous opportunities are thus available for future researchers. In this future research, it is important that we move away from the sometimes inherent assumption that the loss of a younger person is more serious than the loss of an older person.

ACKNOWLEDGMENTS

The author would like to thank Brenda Cooper for helpful assistance during the preparation of this manuscript.

REFERENCES

Adams-Greenly, M. (1984). Helping children communicate about serious illness and death. *Journal of Psychosocial Oncology, 2,* 61–72.

Antonoff, S. R., & Spilka, B. (1984). Patterning of facial expressions among terminal cancer patients. *Omega: Journal of Death and Dying, 15,* 101–108.

Arnstein, R. L. (1974). The threat of death as a factor in psychological reaction to illness. *Journal of the American College Health Association, 23,* 154–156.

Baider, L. (1977). The silent message: Communication in a family with a dying patient. *Journal of Marriage and Family Counseling, 3* (3), 23–28.

Beigler, J. S. (1957). Anxiety as an aid in the prognostication of impending death. *Archives of Neurology and Psychiatry, 77,* 171–177.

Beilin, R. (1981/82). Social functions of denial of death. *Omega: Journal of Death and Dying, 12,* 25–35.

Belsky, J. (1984). *The psychology of aging.* Monterey, CA: Brooks/Cole.

Bergen, C. E. (1980). Perceptions of the stages of cancer: Students versus nursing personnel. *Dissertation Abstracts International, 40(7-A)*, 3624.

Bryant, D. D. (1986). The doctor and death. *Journal of the National Medical Association, 78*, 227–235.

Buckingham, R., Lack, S., & Mount, B. (1976). Living with the dying: Use of the technique of participant observation. *Canadian Medical Association Journal, 115*, 1211–1212.

Caldwell, D., & Mishara, B. L. (1972). Research and attitudes of medical doctors toward the dying patient. *Omega: Journal of Death and Dying, 3*, 341–346.

Calhoun, L. G., Abernathy, C. B., & Selby, J. W. (1986). The rules of bereavement: Are suicidal deaths different? *Journal of Community Psychology, 14*, 213–218.

Carey, R. G. (1974). Emotional adjustment in terminal patients: A quantitative approach. *Journal of Counseling Psychology, 21*, 433–439.

Carey, R. G., & Posavac, E. J. (1978/79). Attitudes of physicians on disclosing information to and maintaining life for terminal patients. *Omega: Journal of Death and Dying, 9*, 67–77.

Cawley, M. A. (1984). *Weaving the shroud: Participant observations of communication themes in families facing death.* Unpublished doctoral dissertation, University of Washington.

Cawley, M. A. (1985). *Weaving the shroud: Participant observations of communication themes in families facing death.* Paper presented at the Annual Convention of the Speech Communication Association, Denver.

Chandler, K. A. (1965). Three processes of dying and their behavioral effects. *Journal of Consulting Psychology, 29*, 296–301.

Channon, L. D., & Ballinger, S. E. (1984). Death and the preclinical medical student: Vol. 11. Attitudes toward telling the terminal patient the prognosis. *Death Education, 8*, 399–404.

Clark, R. E., & LaBeff, E. E. (1982). Death telling: Managing the delivery of bad news. *Journal of Health and Social Behavior, 23*, 366–380.

Cowgell, V. G. (1977). Interpersonal effects of a suicidal communication. *Journal of Consulting and Clinical Psychology, 45*, 592–599.

Davidowitz, M., & Myrick, R. D. (1984). Responding to the bereaved: An analysis of "helping" statements. *Death Education, 8*, 1–10.

Dorner, S., & Atwell, J. D. (1985). Family adjustment to the early loss of a baby born with spina bifida. *Developmental Medicine and Child Neurology, 27*, 461–466.

Doshan, T. (1985). *Communication about dying between terminally ill people and their spouses.* Unpublished doctoral dissertation, University of Iowa.

Dubrey, R. J., & Terrill, L. A. (1975). The loneliness of the dying person: An exploratory study. *Omega: Journal of Death and Dying, 6*, 357–371.

Duff, R. S., & Hollingshead, A. B. (1968). *Sickness and society.* New York: Harper & Row.

Eggerman, S., & Dustin, D. (1985–86). Death orientation and communication with the terminally ill. *Omega: Journal of Death and Dying, 16*, 255–256.

Ekman, P., Friesen, W. V., & Tomkins, S. S. (1971). Facial affect scoring technique (FAST): A first validity study. *Semiotica, 3*, 37–58.

Epley, R. J., & McCaghy, C. H. (1977/78). The stigma of dying: Attitudes toward the terminally ill. *Omega: Journal of Death and Dying, 8*, 379–393.

Erickson, R. D., & Hyerstay, B. J. (1974). The dying patient and the double-bind hypothesis. *Omega: Journal of Death and Dying, 5*, 287–298.

Feifel, H., & Branscomb, A. B. (1973). Who's afraid of death? *Journal of Abnormal Psychology, 81*, 282–288.

Field, D., & Howells, K. (1986). Medical students' self-reported worries about aspects of death and dying. *Death Studies, 10*, 147–154.

Fieweger, M. (1980). *Self-reported strategies in relational conclusion: How do we say goodbye to dying persons.* Paper presented at the Annual Convention of the Eastern Communication Association, Ocean City, MD.

Fieweger, M., & Smilowitz, M. (1984). Relational conclusion through interaction with the dying. *Omega: Journal of Death and Dying, 15,* 161–172.

Fritz, G. K., Rubinstein, S., & Lewiston, N. J. (1987). Psychological factors in fatal childhood asthma. *American Journal of Orthopsychiatry, 57,* 253–257.

Glaser, B. G., & Strauss, A. L. (1966). *Awareness of dying.* Chicago: Aldine.

Glaser, B. G., & Strauss, A. L. (1977). The ritual drama of mutual pretense. In S. H. Zarit (Ed.), *Readings in aging and death: Contemporary perspectives* (pp. 271–276). New York: Harper & Row.

Glaser, B. G., & Strauss, A. L. (1968a). Temporal aspects of dying as a nonscheduled status passage. In B. Neugarten (Ed.), *Middle age and aging* (pp. 520–530). Chicago: University of Chicago Press.

Glaser, B. G., & Strauss, A. L. (1968b). *A time for dying.* Chicago: Aldine.

Gluck, M. (1977). Overcoming stresses in communication with the fatally ill. *Military Medicine, 142,* 926–928.

Gold, M. (1984). When someone dies in the hospital. *Aging,* No. 345, 18–22.

Gray-Snelgrove, R. H. (1982). *The experience of giving care to a parent dying of cancer: Meanings identified through the process of shared reflection.* Unpublished doctoral dissertation, University of Toronto.

Greaves, C. C. (1983). Death in the family: A multifamily therapy approach. *International Journal of Family Psychiatry, 4,* 247–261.

Hall, M. N. (1982). Law enforcement officers and death notification: A plea for relevant education. *Journal of Police Science and Administration, 10,* 189–193.

Heller, D. B., & Schneider, C. D. (1977/78). Interpersonal methods for coping with stress: Helping families of dying children. *Omega: Journal of Death and Dying, 8,* 319–331.

Hicks, W., & Daniels, R. S. (1968). The dying patient, his physician, and the psychiatric consultant. *Psychosomatics, 9,* 47–52.

Hinton, J. M. (1981). Sharing or withholding awareness of dying between husband and wife. *Journal of Psychosomatic Research, 25,* 337–343.

Holt, W. C. (1969). Death by suggestion. *Canadian Psychiatric Association Journal, 14,* 81–82.

Hurley, B. A. (1975). Problems of interaction between nurses and dying patients. *Dissertation Abstracts International, 36(6-B),* 3123.

Husband, E., & Broadhus, D. A. (1984). Children's books and stories as therapeutic metaphors: An intervention with seriously ill children. *Paedovita, 1,* 17–21.

Issner, N. (1973). Can the child be distracted from his disease? *Journal of School Health, 43,* 468–471.

Jaffe, L. (1977). Letter to seminar students in "Methods of Intervention with the dying." *Death Education, 1,* 325–337.

Kalish, R. A. (1976). Death and dying in a social context. In R. H. Binstock & E. Shanas (Eds.), *Handbook of aging and the social sciences* (pp. 483–507). New York: Van Nostrand Reinhold.

Karon, M., & Vernick, J. (1968). An approach to the emotional support of fatally ill children. *Clinical Pediatrics, 7* (5).

Kastenbaum, R. (1967a). Multiple perspectives on a geriatric "Death Valley." *Community Mental Health Journal, 3,* 21–29.

Kastenbaum, R. (1967b). The mental life of dying patients. *Gerontologist, 7,* 97–100.

Kastenbaum, R., & Aisenberg, R. (1972). *The psychology of death,* New York: Springer.

Koenig, R. (1980). Dying vs. well-being. *Perspectives on death and dying, 2,* 9–22.

Koocher, G. P. (1986). Coping with a death from cancer. *Journal of Consulting and Clinical Psychology, 54,* 623–631.

Kram, C., & Caldwell, J. M. (1969). The dying patient. *Psychosomatics, 10,* 293–295.

Krant, M. J., & Johnston, L. (1978). Family members' perceptions of communications in late stage cancer. *International Journal of Psychiatry in Medicine, 8,* 203–216.

Krulick, T. (1978). *Loneliness in school age children with chronic life threatening illness.* Unpublished doctoral dissertation, University of California-San Francisco.

Kubler-Ross, E. (1969). *On death and dying.* New York: Macmillan.

Leon, I. G. (1986). The invisible loss: The impact of perinatal death on siblings. *Journal of Psychosomatic Obstetrics and Gynaecology, 5,* 1–14.

LeShan, L., Bowers, M., & Jackson, E. (1969). *Counseling the dying.* New York: Nelson & Sons.

Lieberman, M. A. (1968). Psychological correlates of impending death: Some preliminary observations. In B. Neugarten (Ed.), *Middle age and aging.* (pp. 509–519). Chicago: University of Chicago Press.

Lister, L., & Ward, D. (1985). Youth hospice training. *Death Studies. 9,* 353–363.

Lopez, D. J., & Getzel, G. S. (1984). Helping gay AIDS patients in crisis. *Social Casework, 65,* 387–394.

Magni, K. G. (1972). The fear of death. In A. Godin (Ed.), *Death and presence* (pp. 125–138). Brussels: Lumen Vitae Press.

Marshall, V. W. (1975). Socialization for impending death in a retirement village. *American Journal of Sociology, 80,* 1124–1144.

Marshall, V. W. (1979). Organizational features of terminal status passage in residential facilities for the aged. In J. Hendricks & C. D. Hendricks (Eds.), *Dimensions of aging* (pp. 117–130). Cambridge, MA: Winthrop.

McCown, D., & Pratt, C. (1985). Impact of sibling death on children's behavior. *Death Studies, 9,* 323–335.

McCubbin, H. I., McCubbin, M. A., Patterson, J. M., Cauble, A. E., Wilson, L. R., & Warwick, W. (1983). CHIP: Coping health inventory for parents: An assessment of parental coping patterns in the care of the chronically ill. *Journal of Marriage and the Family, 43,* 359–370.

McKenzie, S. C. (1980). *Aging and old age.* Glenview, IL: Scott, Foresman.

Miller, V. D., & Knapp, M. L. (1986). The *post nuntio* dilemma: Approaches to communicating with the dying. In M. McLaughling (Ed.), *Communication Yearbook 9* (pp. 723–738). Beverly Hills: Sage.

Morgenson, D. F. (1973). Death and interpersonal failure. *Canada's Mental Health, 21* (3–4), 10–12.

Mufson, T. (1985). Issues surrounding sibling death during adolescence. *Child and Adolescent Social Work Journal, 2,* 204–218.

Noyes, R., & Clancy, J. (1977). The dying role: Its relevance to improved patient care. *Psychiatry, 40,* 41–47.

Paterson, G. W. (1985). Pastoral care of the coronary patient and family. *Journal of Pastoral Care, 39,* 249–261.

Patterson, S. L. (1981). On death and dying. In F. J. Berghorn & D. E. Schafer (Eds.), *The dynamics of aging* (pp. 83–99). Boulder, CO: Westview Press.

Pattison, M. E. (1978). The living-dying process. In C. A. Garfield (Ed.), *Psychosocial care of the dying patient* (pp. 145–153). New York: McGraw–Hill.

Pollock, G. H. (1986). Childhood sibling loss: A family tragedy. *Annual of Psychoanalysis, 14,* 5–34.

Redding, R. (1980). Doctors, dyscommunication, and death. *Death Education, 3,* 371–385.

Reiss, D., Gonzalez, S., & Kramer, N. (1986). Family process, chronic illness, and death: On the weakness of strong bonds. *Archives of General Psychiatry, 43,* 795–804.

Richter, J. M. (1984). Crisis of mate loss in the elderly. *Advances in Nursing Science, 6* (4), 45–54.

Rodabough, T., & Rodabough, C. (1981). Nurses and the dying: Symbolic interaction as a precipitator of dying "stages." *Qualitative Sociology, 4,* 257–278.

Rosenheim, E., & Reicher, R. (1985). Informing children about a parent's terminal illness. *Journal of Child Psychology, 26,* 995–998.

Saul, S. R. & Saul, S. (1973). Old people talk about death. *Omega: Journal of Death and Dying, 4,* 27–35.

Schulz, R., & Aderman, D. (1974). Clinical research and the stages of dying. *Omega: Journal of Death and Dying, 5,* 137–143.

Schulz, R., & Aderman, D. (1980). How the medical staff copes with dying patients: A critical review. *Perspectives on death and dying, 2.* 143–144.

Shanis, H. S. (1985). Hospice: Interdependence of the dying with their community. In W. A. Peterson & J. Quadagno (Eds.), *Social bonds in later life* (pp. 369–387). Beverly Hills: Sage.

Sherman, M. F., Smith, R. J., & Cooper, R. (1982). Reactions toward the dying: The effects of a patient's illness and respondents' beliefs in a just world. *Omega: Journal of Death and Dying, 13,* 173–189.

Silverberg, R. A. (1985). Men confronting death: Management versus self determination. *Clinical Social Work Journal, 13,* 157–169.

Simmons, S., & Given, B. (1972). Nursing care of the terminal patient. *Omega: Journal of Death and Dying, 3,* 217–225.

Simmons, S., & Given, B. (1980). Nursing care of the terminal patient. *Perspectives on death and dying, 2,* 115–123.

Smith, R. J., Lingle, J. H., & Brock, T. C. (1978/79). Reactions to death as a function of perceived similarity to the deceased. *Omega: Journal of Death and Dying, 9,* 125–138.

Spinetta, J. J., Rigler, D., & Karon, M. (1974). Personal space as a measure of a dying child's sense of isolation. *Journal of Consulting and Clinical Psychology, 42,* 751–756.

Sudnow, D. (1967). *Passing on.* Englewood Cliffs, NJ: Prentice–Hall.

Todd, C., & Still, A. W. (1984). Communication between general practitioners and patients dying at home. *Social Science and Medicine, 18,* 667–672.

Troll, L. E. (1982). *Continuations: Adult development and aging.* Monterey: Brooks, Cole.

Unruh, D. R. (1983). Death and personal history: Strategies of identity preservation. *Social Problems, 39,* 340–351.

Verwoerdt, A. (1966). *Communication with the fatally ill.* Springfield, IL: Thomas.

Verwoerdt, A., & Elmore, J. L. (1967). Psychological reactions in fatal illness. Vol. 1. The prospect of impending death. *Journal of the American Geriatric Society, 15,* 9.

Watson, W. H. (1973, May 13–15. *The social organization of aging and dying: An exploratory study of some institutional factors.* Paper presented at the Invitational Conference on Environmental Research and Aging. Sponsored by Washington University and St. Louis University, St. Louis, MO.

Watson, W. H. (1976/77). The aging sick and the near dead: A study of some distinguishing characteristics and social effects. *Omega: Journal of Death and Dying, 7,* 115–123.

Weber, J. A., & Fournier, D. G. (1985). Family support and a child's adjustment to death. *Family Relations: Journal of Applied Family and Child Studies, 34,* 43–49.

Weinstein, M. H. (1977). *The effects of facilitativeness, age differential, and death anxiety of counseling students on conversational avoidance—death and general.* Unpublished doctoral dissertation, University of Miami.

Weisman, A. D., & Kastenbaum, R. (1968). *The psychological autopsy: A study of the terminal phase of life.* Community Mental Health Monograph #4. New York: Behavioral publications.

Weisman, A. D., & Warden, J. W. (1975). Psychosocial analysis of cancer deaths. *Omega: Journal of Death and Dying, 6,* 61–75.

Wood, B. G. (1975). Interpersonal aspects in the care of terminally ill patients. *American Journal of Psychoanalysis, 35,* 47–53.

AUTHOR INDEX

SUBJECT INDEX